D0154188

OMNIVM
LVX
CIVIVM
MDCCCLII
MDCCC
LXXVIII
BOSTON
PUBLIC
LIBRARY

Essays on
THE NOBILITY OF MEDIEVAL SCOTLAND

Essays on THE NOBILITY OF MEDIEVAL SCOTLAND

Edited by
K. J. STRINGER
University of Lancaster

JOHN DONALD PUBLISHERS LTD
EDINBURGH

ISBN 0 85976 113 4

Exclusive distribution in the United States of America and Canada by Humanities Press Inc., Atlantic Highlands, NJ07716, USA.

Phototypesetting by H.M. Repros, Glasgow
and printed in Great Britain by Bell & Bain Ltd., Glasgow.

CONTRIBUTORS

Geoffrey Barrow: Sir William Fraser Professor of Scottish History and Palaeography, University of Edinburgh

Barbara E. Crawford: Lecturer in Medieval History, University of St Andrews

Alexander Grant: Lecturer in Medieval History, University of Lancaster

Norman Macdougall: Lecturer in Scottish History, University of St Andrews

Ann Royan: Research Student in Scottish History, University of Edinburgh

Grant G. Simpson: Senior Lecturer in Scottish History, University of Aberdeen

Geoffrey Stell: Investigator, the Royal Commission on the Ancient and Historical Monuments of Scotland

Keith Stringer: Lecturer in Medieval History, University of Lancaster

Bruce Webster: Senior Lecturer in Medieval History, University of Kent at Canterbury

Jenny Wormald: Lecturer in Scottish History, University of Glasgow

Alan Young: Senior Lecturer in History, College of Ripon and York St John, York

ILLUSTRATIONS

Plates (between pp. 200 and 201)

Figures

Tables

ABBREVIATIONS

The abbreviation of Scottish works has been facilitated by the guidelines set out in *List of Abbreviated Titles of the Printed Sources of Scottish History to 1560,* published as a supplement to the *Scottish Historical Review,* October 1963. Minor conventional abbreviations are not noted.

Aberdeen Reg.	*Registrum Episcopatus Aberdonensis* (Spalding and Maitland Clubs, 1845)
Anderson, *Early Sources*	*Early Sources of Scottish History 500 to 1286,* ed. A.O. Anderson (Edinburgh, 1922)
Anderson, *Scottish Annals*	*Scottish Annals from English Chroniclers 500 to 1286,* ed. A.O. Anderson (London, 1908)
APS	*The Acts of the Parliaments of Scotland,* ed. T. Thomson and C. Innes (Record Commission, 1814–75)
Arbroath Liber	*Liber S. Thome de Aberbrothoc* (Bannatyne Club, 1848–56)
Barrow, *Bruce*	G.W.S. Barrow, *Robert Bruce and the Community of the Realm of Scotland,* 2nd edn. (Edinburgh, 1976, reprinted 1982)
Barrow, *Era*	G.W.S. Barrow, *The Anglo-Norman Era in Scottish History* (Oxford, 1980)
Barrow, *Kingdom*	G.W.S. Barrow, *The Kingdom of the Scots* (London, 1973)
BL	British Library, London
Bodl.	Bodleian Library, Oxford
Book of Seals	*Sir Christopher Hatton's Book of Seals,* ed. L.C. Loyd and D.M. Stenton (Oxford, 1950)
Brackley Deeds	W.D. Macray, *Collection of Brackley Deeds at Magdalen College, Oxford,* ed. R. Ussher (Buckingham, 1910) [Reprinted from articles in the *Buckinghamshire Advertiser* in an edition of six copies, of which one is in the BL, press-mark 9905.h.22.]
CChR	*Calendar of the Charter Rolls preserved in the PRO* (London, 1903–27)
CClR	*Calendar of the Close Rolls preserved in the PRO* (London, 1892– ; in progress)
CDS	*Calendar of Documents relating to Scotland,* ed. J. Bain (Edinburgh, 1881–8)
Chron. Bower	Walter Bower, *Joannis de Fordun Scotichronicon cum Supplementis et Continuatione,* ed. W. Goodall (Edinburgh, 1759)
Chron. Fordun	John of Fordun, *Chronica Gentis Scotorum,* ed. W.F. Skene (Edinburgh, 1871–2)
Chron. Lanercost	*Chronicon de Lanercost* (Maitland Club, 1839)
Chron. Melrose	*The Chronicle of Melrose,* ed. A.O. Anderson *et al* (London, 1936)
CIPM	*Calendar of Inquisitions Post Mortem . . . preserved in the PRO* (London, 1904– ; in progress)
ClR	*Close Rolls of the Reign of Henry III preserved in the PRO* (London, 1902–38)
Coldstream Chartulary	*Chartulary of the Cistercian Priory of Coldstream* (Grampian Club, 1879)

Comp. Pge.	*The Complete Peerage* by G.E. C[okayne], revised by V. Gibbs *et al* (London, 1910–59)
Coupar Angus Chrs.	*Charters of the Abbey of Coupar Angus,* ed. D.E. Easson (SHS, 1947)
Cowan (Easson), *Religious Houses*	D.E. Easson, *Medieval Religious Houses: Scotland,* 2nd edn. by I.B. Cowan (London, 1976)
CPatR	*Calendar of the Patent Rolls preserved in the PRO* (London, 1891– ; in progress)
CPL	*Calendar of Entries in the Papal Registers relating to Great Britain and Ireland. Papal Letters* (London, 1893– ; in progress)
CurRR	*Curia Regis Rolls . . . preserved in the PRO* (London, 1922– ; in progress)
Dryb. Lib.	*Liber S. Marie de Dryburgh* (Bannatyne Club, 1847)
Duncan, *Scotland*	A.A.M. Duncan, *Scotland: The Making of the Kingdom* (Edinburgh, 1975)
Dunfermline Reg.	*Registrum de Dunfermelyn* (Bannatyne Club, 1842)
EHR	*The English Historical Review*
ER	*The Exchequer Rolls of Scotland,* ed. J. Stuart *et al* (Edinburgh, 1878–1908)
EYC	*Early Yorkshire Charters,* vols. i–iii (1914–16), ed. W. Farrer; vols. iv–xii, ed. C.T. Clay (Yorkshire Archaeol. Soc., Record Ser., Extra Ser., 1935–65)
Fees	*The Book of Fees commonly called Testa de Nevill* (London, 1920–31)
Foedera	*Foedera, Conventiones, Litterae,* etc., ed. T. Rymer (Record Commission, 1816–69)
Gilbertine Chrs.	*Transcripts of Charters relating to the Gilbertine Houses of Sixle, Ormsby, Catley, Bullington, and Alvingham,* ed. F.M. Stenton (Lincoln Record Soc., 1922)
Glasgow Reg.	*Registrum Episcopatus Glasguensis* (Bannatyne and Maitland Clubs, 1843)
HMC	Royal Commission on Historical Manuscripts. 1st to 9th Reports cited by number; others by name of owner or collection
Holm Cultram Reg.	*The Register and Records of Holm Cultram,* ed. F. Grainger and W.G. Collingwood (Cumberland and Westmorland Antiquarian and Archaeol. Soc., Record Ser., 1929)
Holyrood Liber	*Liber Cartarum Sancte Crucis* (Bannatyne Club, 1840)
Inchaffray Chrs.	*Charters, Bulls and other Documents relating to the Abbey of Inchaffray,* ed. J. Dowden *et al* (SHS, 1908)
Kelso Liber	*Liber S. Marie de Calchou* (Bannatyne Club, 1846)
Lawrie, *Charters*	*Early Scottish Charters prior to 1153,* ed. A.C. Lawrie (Glasgow, 1905)
Lind. Cart.	*Chartulary of the Abbey of Lindores,* ed. J. Dowden (SHS, 1903)
Loyd, *Origins*	L.C. Loyd, *The Origins of some Anglo-Norman Families,* ed. C.T. Clay and D.C. Douglas (Harleian Soc., 1951)
Macdougall, *James III*	N. Macdougall, *James III: A Political Study* (Edinburgh, 1982)
Melrose Liber	*Liber Sancte Marie de Melros* (Bannatyne Club, 1837)
Moray Reg.	*Registrum Episcopatus Moraviensis* (Bannatyne Club, 1837)
Nichols, *Leicester*	J. Nichols, *The History and Antiquities of the County of Leicester* (London, 1795–1815)

NLS	National Library of Scotland, Edinburgh
Northumberland Hist.	*A History of Northumberland.* Issued under the direction of the Northumberland County History Committee (Newcastle upon Tyne, 1893–1940)
Paisley Reg.	*Registrum Monasterii de Passelet* (Maitland Club, 1832; New Club, 1877)
Palgrave, *Docs. Hist. Scot.*	*Documents and Records illustrating the History of Scotland,* ed. F. Palgrave (London, 1837)
Paris, *Chron. Maj.*	Matthew Paris, *Chronica Majora,* ed. H.R. Luard (Rolls Ser., 1872–83)
PRO	Public Record Office, London
PSAS	*Proceedings of the Society of Antiquaries of Scotland*
RCAHMS	Royal Commission on the Ancient and Historical Monuments of Scotland
RMS	*Registrum Magni Sigilli Regum Scotorum,* ed. J.M. Thomson *et al* (Edinburgh, 1882–1912)
Rot. Scot.	*Rotuli Scotiae in Turri Londinensi . . . asservati,* ed. D. Macpherson *et al* (Record Commission, 1814–19)
RRS	*Regesta Regum Scottorum,* ed. G.W.S. Barrow *et al,* i (1153–65), 1960; ii (1165–1214), 1971; vi (1329–71), 1982
St Andrews Liber	*Liber Cartarum Prioratus Sancti Andree in Scotia* (Bannatyne Club, 1841)
St Bees Reg.	*The Register of the Priory of St Bees,* ed. J. Wilson (Surtees Soc., 1915)
Scone Liber	*Liber Ecclesie de Scon* (Bannatyne and Maitland Clubs, 1843)
Scots Pge.	*The Scots Peerage,* ed. J. Balfour Paul (Edinburgh, 1904–14)
SHR	*The Scottish Historical Review*
SHS	Scottish History Society
Simpson, 'RQ'	G.G. Simpson, 'An Anglo-Scottish Baron of the thirteenth century: The acts of Roger de Quincy, earl of Winchester and Constable of Scotland' (unpublished Edinburgh University Ph.D. thesis, 1965)
SRO	Scottish Record Office, Edinburgh
Stevenson, *Documents*	*Documents Illustrative of the History of Scotland, 1286–1306,* ed. J. Stevenson (Edinburgh, 1870)
Stones and Simpson, *Great Cause*	*Edward I and the Throne of Scotland, 1290–1296: An Edition of the Record Sources for the Great Cause,* ed. E.L.G. Stones and G.G.Simpson (Oxford, 1978)
Stones, *Relations*	*Anglo-Scottish Relations, 1174–1328: Some Selected Documents,* ed. E.L.G. Stones (Oxford, 1970 reprint)
Stringer, *Earl David*	K.J. Stringer, *Earl David of Huntingdon, 1152–1219: A Study in Anglo-Scottish History* (Edinburgh, 1985)
TCWAAS	*Transactions of the Cumberland and Westmorland Antiquarian and Archaeological Society*
TDGAS	*Transactions of the Dumfriesshire and Galloway Natural History and Antiquarian Society*
TGAS	*Transactions of the Glasgow Archaeological Society*
Theiner, *Monumenta*	*Vetera Monumenta Hibernorum et Scotorum Historiam Illustrantia,* ed. A. Theiner (Rome, 1864)
VCH	*Victoria History of the Counties of England*

Watt, *Dictionary*	D.E.R. Watt, *A Biographical Dictionary of Scottish Graduates to A.D. 1410* (Oxford, 1977)
Watt, *Fasti*	D.E.R. Watt, *Fasti Ecclesiae Scoticanae Medii Aevi ad annum 1638,* 2nd draft (St Andrews, 1969)
Wigtownshire Chrs.	*Wigtownshire Charters,* ed. R.C. Reid (SHS, 1960)

CONTENTS

INTRODUCTION

The origins of this book may be traced to the inaugural meeting of the Scottish Baronial Research Group held under the auspices of Dr Grant Simpson in the Clerk Register's Room, HM General Register House, Edinburgh, on 9 March 1969. At that time a small body of established scholars and young research students, then representing the Universities of Cambridge, Edinburgh, Glasgow, Newcastle upon Tyne, Oxford and St Andrews, were brought together by a common interest in the nobility of medieval Scotland and by a desire to pool knowledge through the reading of discussion papers or more informal exchanges. It was felt that the men and families whose territorial power and local leadership made them a cardinal force in medieval Scottish society had been very much neglected by other historians. Most of all, the nobles appeared to have suffered as, to borrow the words of K.B. McFarlane, 'the victims of a strong prejudice in favour of the Crown'.[1] Thus there was an unwillingness to discuss individual barons save from the viewpoint of the king, and there was a marked tendency to malign the nobility for a chronic turbulence and a natural antagonism towards the monarchy. The Group was founded partly in reaction to these trends, in the belief that studies of the nobility from within its own milieu would contribute usefully to a fuller understanding of Scotland's medieval past. It has continued to meet on a yearly basis, and new members have occasionally been added to the existing nucleus. Nevertheless, the present-day followers of the Scottish baronage scarcely form a large company. In 1985, as in 1969, the fact is that despite its seminal importance the medieval Scottish nobility has yet to attract the same degree of attention by historians as its counterpart in England. What has changed in the intervening years is that scholars have increasingly begun to grapple with the problems, to suggest possible answers, and to identify lines of fruitful further inquiry. It is therefore timely that this volume should appear, to indicate what has been done and also to point to what can and should be done.

Thirteen essays by eleven different authors have been selected to illuminate the nobility's main activities, preoccupations and aspirations. There are certain obvious relationships between chapters. These concern, among other issues, the strong influence of Anglo-Norman England upon earlier medieval Scotland, patterns of land accumulation by the aristocracy, noble residences, the legal and administrative aspects of baronial lordship, clientage networks, and dealings between the magnates and the Church. Several essays drive home the importance of recognising that, prior to the wars of independence, the nobility in Scotland was closely bound by ties of kinship and property with the nobility in England; and others serve to emphasise the inherent worthlessness of any interpretation which subscribes to, in Sir Frank Stenton's phrase, 'the myth of a perpetual opposition between the baronage and the Crown'.[2] But the principal purpose of this book lies not so much in the interconnected discussion of historical themes, which given the current state of knowledge would without doubt be premature, as in the illustration of the main possibilities, and limitations, of the available sources: most notably, charters, chronicles, genealogical material, and the archaeological heritage. Each chapter is thus a study in its own right, designed to show how much can be gleaned through detailed analysis of, say, an individual magnate or a particular noble family, or through adventurous inquiry on a broader scale. The one approach is, of course, indispensable to the other. Taken together, they bring us closer towards a true 'History' of the nobility of medieval Scotland, a work to which members of the Baronial Research Group wish to contribute in their future researches and, if opportunity allows, through a further collaborative venture.

A number of the following chapters began life in the form of articles in journals, and one chapter was originally published in a book which is now out of print. All these contributions have been revised for publication here, and in most cases the modifications are substantial, not least because authors have been able to take advantage of a less restricted format in order to introduce fresh evidence and elaborate their arguments. We are extremely grateful for the alacrity with which the editors and publishers concerned have given the necessary permission to reprint material, and we thank them for it. Chapter 1 first appeared in *Château Gaillard: études de castellologie médiévale,* v (1972); Chapter 2 in *Northern Scotland,* ii (1974–7); Chapter 6 in *The Scottish Historical Review,* lvii (1978); Chapter 9 in *Prospect* (quarterly newspaper of the Royal Incorporation of Architects in Scotland), xiv (1982); Chapter 12 in *The Innes Review,* xxiii (1972); and Chapter 13 in *The Scottish Nation,* ed. G. Menzies (BBC Publications, 1972). In Chapter 3, free use is made of two previously published articles: 'Dryburgh abbey and Bozeat, Northants: a sidelight on early Anglo-Scottish estate management', *The Innes Review,* xxiv (1973), and 'The early lords of Lauderdale and St Andrew's priory at Northampton', *History of the Berwickshire Naturalists' Club,* xl (1974). Likewise, the joint authors of Chapter 8, which results from their independent researches, wish it to be known that material has been drawn from the article 'James the Stewart of Scotland', which one of them published in *The Stewarts,* xii, no. 2 (1965).

It is, finally, a most pleasant duty to express our collective thanks to John Tuckwell of John Donald Publishers Ltd, who has taken an enthusiastic interest in this project from the beginning and has helped to speed its conclusion.

Keith Stringer, 1985

1. K.B. McFarlane, *The Nobility of Later Medieval England* (Oxford, 1973), p.3.
2. F.M. Stenton, 'The changing feudalism of the Middle Ages', reprinted in *Preparatory to Anglo-Saxon England: Being the Collected Papers of Frank Merry Stenton,* ed. D.M. Stenton (Oxford, 1970), p. 206.

1

CHARTER EVIDENCE AND THE DISTRIBUTION OF MOTTES IN SCOTLAND

Grant G. Simpson and Bruce Webster

Our intention in this essay is to bring together evidence mainly from twelfth- and thirteenth-century Scottish charters and the archaeological evidence for the distribution of mottes in Scotland, and to discuss some of the implications which follow from this.

Until the twelfth century Scotland was on the fringes of European civilisation and there was hardly any trace of the type of central government which already existed, for instance, in England or Germany. There were kings of the Scots; but their authority was more akin to the sway of a 'high king' over a series of tribes. In the later eleventh and the twelfth centuries, however, a line of kings who had very close connexions with England, especially David I (1124–53), began to establish centralised authority of a more developed kind.[1] The way in which they did this was very much determined by geography. Scotland is divided by mountains into a series of coastal regions and river valleys; and the direct power of the kings was for long limited to the east-central and south-eastern regions, to Angus, Fife, Lothian and the Tweed valley. They managed during the twelfth century to extend their direct authority to the north of the ridge of mountains called the Mounth into the lands along the Moray Firth; but in the centre and in the south-west, from Atholl down to Annandale, Nithsdale and Galloway, they had to rely on various forms of more or less indirect rule. Across the Great Glen, the highlands and islands of the western seaboard remained remote from them. Royal authority just extended into Ross and there were occasional expeditions further north, but most of the far west was Celtic in culture and at this period was under the authority, direct or indirect, of the kings of Norway. There are some early castles in this western seaboard region, but they are a separate and interesting problem.[2] There are hardly any mottes in the area and we have therefore not considered it in this chapter.

In the twelfth century the kings were trying to bring the government of Scotland into line with what was then normal practice in more developed states; but Scotland was a small country, and in scale at least the closest parallels for her institutions are to be found not in the large states of England, France or Germany, but in some of the great fiefs of France, such as Normandy or Flanders. In this process the monarchs from David I onwards encouraged the settlement of barons from England and even some directly from France and Flanders.[3] Most of these settlers were established in small fiefs of one knight's feu or thereabouts, but in the areas which the king could not rule directly some great feudal estates were created. The best-known early ones are those of the Stewarts in Renfrewshire and Ayrshire, the

Morvilles in Lauderdale and the Bruces in Annandale. Thus feudal land tenure was introduced; and at the same period other institutions appear: a structure of local government based on royal officials called sheriffs, the burgh as a legal concept, and a reformed ecclesiastical system which involved territorial bishoprics and regular monastic houses. Features such as feudal holdings, burghs and monasteries can be easily plotted on maps (Figs. 1–3), and these maps reveal the geographical pattern of such developments.[4] As one might expect, they are concentrated particularly in the areas where royal control was at its greatest.

So far we have said nothing of the castle; and the main problem we want to discuss is how the castle fits into these processes. In Normandy, Flanders and England the castle was at the very centre of feudalisation and the development of governmental organisation. Where does it come in Scotland? It was certainly an alien import introduced by the same foreign settlers who were involved in every other aspect of the twelfth-century revolution.[5] It has long been known that in addition to surviving stone castles Scotland has a good collection of mottes. Until 1972 the only published distribution map of these was that based on the pioneer researches made over eighty years ago by Dr David Christison.[6] His distribution was almost entirely concentrated in the south-west and was nearly blank for the rest of the country. But many mottes have been identified since 1898, and around 250 are now known: the more certain of these are shown in Fig. 4, and a provisional list appears in Appendix I, below.[7] This distribution shows a fair spread of mottes in Fife, Angus, the north-east and Moray, though there are hardly any in Lothian; but the thickest concentrations are still in Menteith, the Clyde valley and above all in Ayrshire and the lands bordering on the Solway Firth. The whole distribution is still heavy in the south-west.

This distribution is obviously different from that of the other phenomena which we have plotted; it is also very different from that of castles recorded either in charters or in chronicles. To plot the latter distribution effectively, it has been necessary to include references down to the end of the reign of Alexander II in 1249. The mention of castles in the sources is very much a matter of chance, and only by going to 1249 can one reveal a number of castles which certainly existed many decades before they are referred to in writing. The distribution of castles is shown at Fig. 5 and they are listed in Appendix II. If we compare the two maps (Figs. 4 and 5) the contrast is obvious, but in a sense it is also unreal. The distribution of documentary references, like the other documentary distributions which it resembles, reflects very closely the spread of the available documents. Most of the evidence is in the form of written titles to land, and the use of such titles is itself part of the twelfth-century revolution in government. This map is plotting on the whole not so much the distribution of castles *per se* as the castles which occurred within the area of a more developed centralised government.

There is however obviously a special problem in Lothian. There are documentary records of castles at Edinburgh, Eldbotle and Dirleton,[8] and a few more occur not long after 1249; but there is only one reasonably certain motte in the area, at Castle Hill, North Berwick. At Dirleton there still exists a fine thirteenth-century castle, but the documents also refer to a *vetus castellum cum fossis suis* at Eldbotle, which is

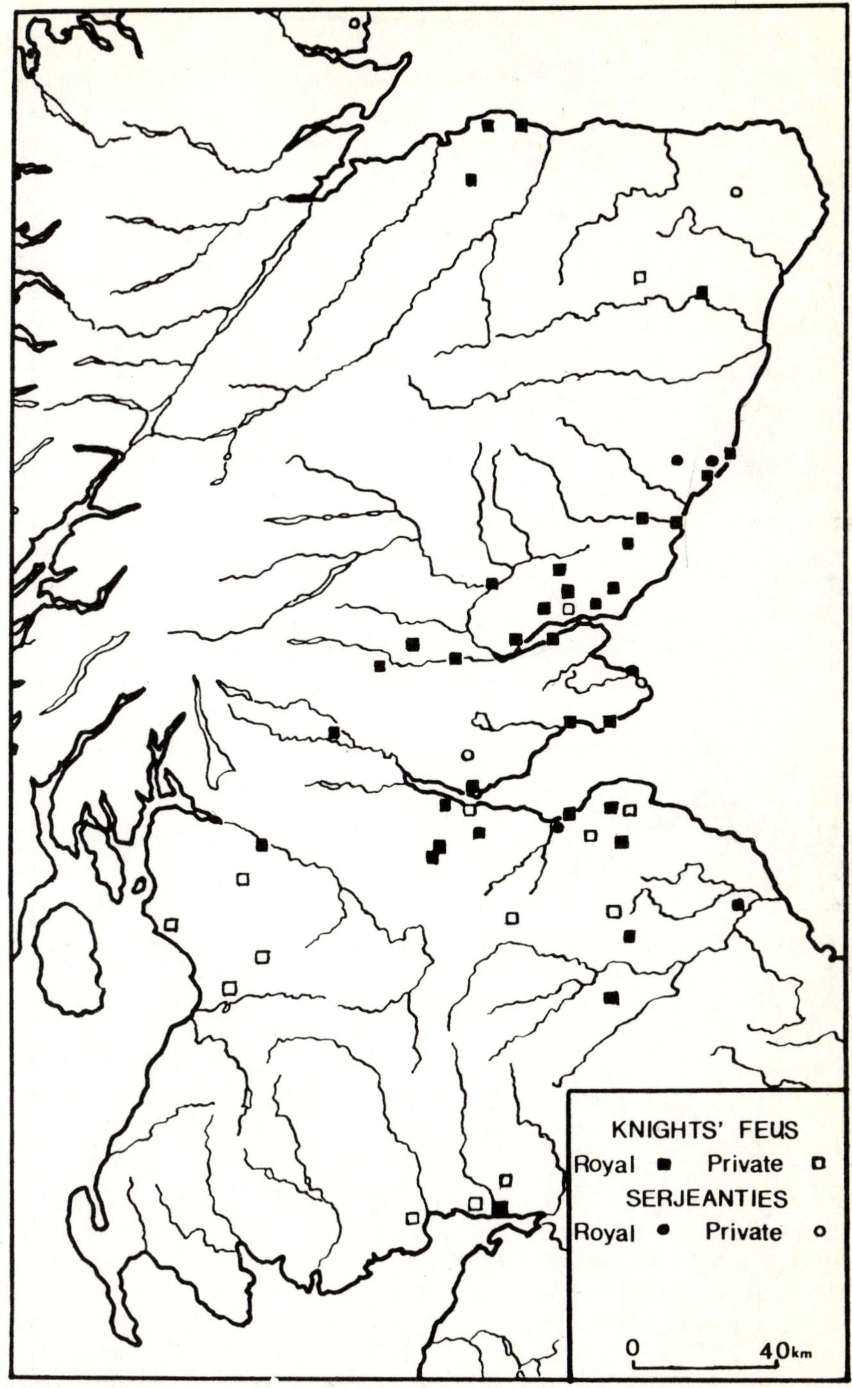

Fig. 1. Distribution of feudal holdings recorded by 1214.

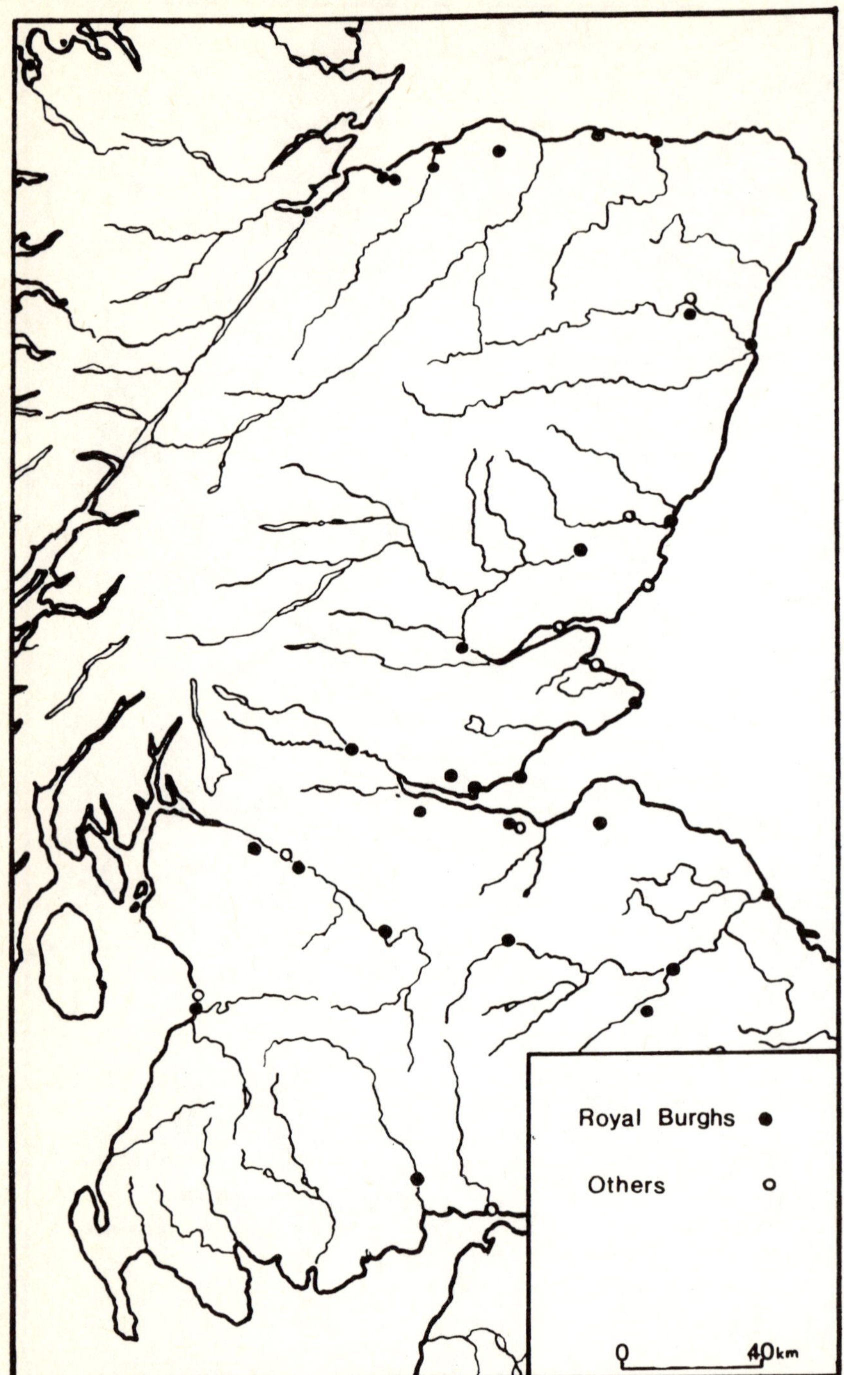

Fig. 2. Distribution of burghs recorded by 1214.

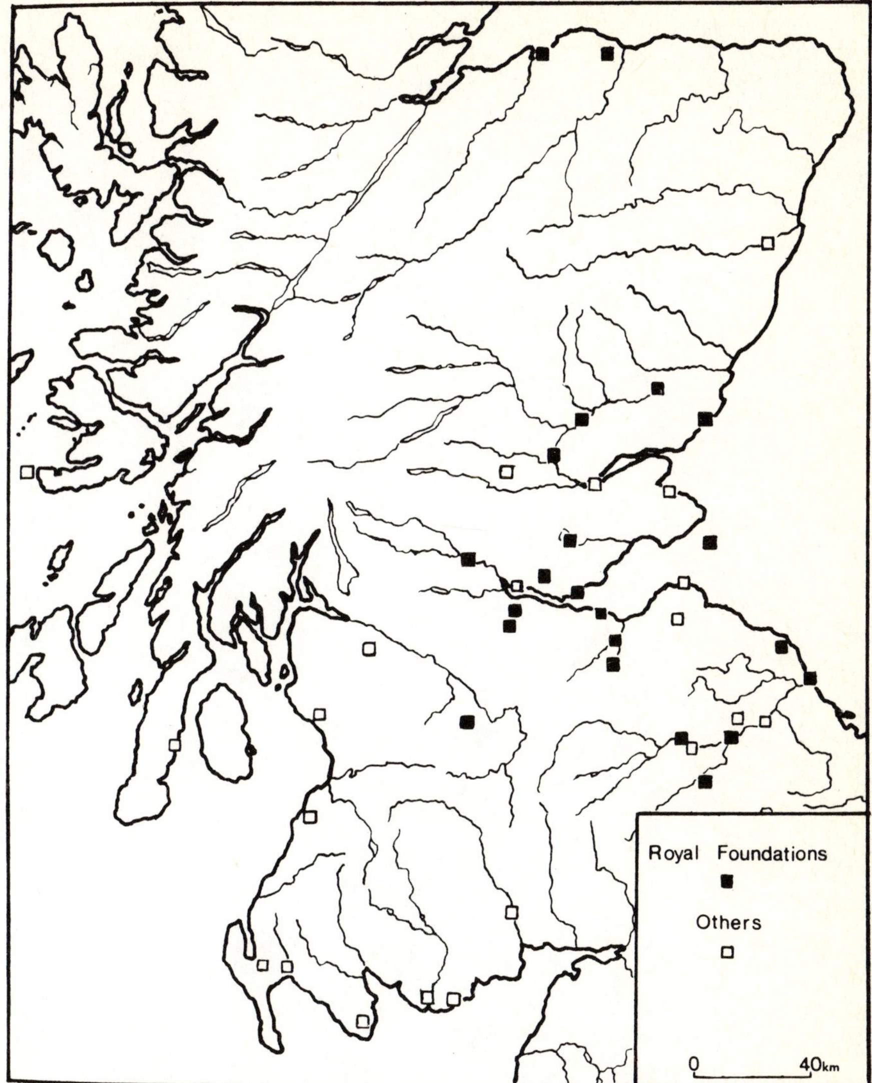

Fig. 3. Distribution of monastic foundations of all kinds recorded by 1214.

a site near the coast just over one mile to the north-west of Dirleton.[9] No motte can now be positively identified at Eldbotle, but it would clearly be worth looking for one by means of excavation or aerial photography. Lothian was a relatively rich and developed region, and it is possible that mottes did exist but were superseded fairly quickly by more up-to-date structures and have therefore been lost sight of.

If the two maps are considered together, it is clear that castles are common in the regions of firm royal control: there they may be a part of the general revolution we have described. But they are even more common elsewhere. The motte is a symbol

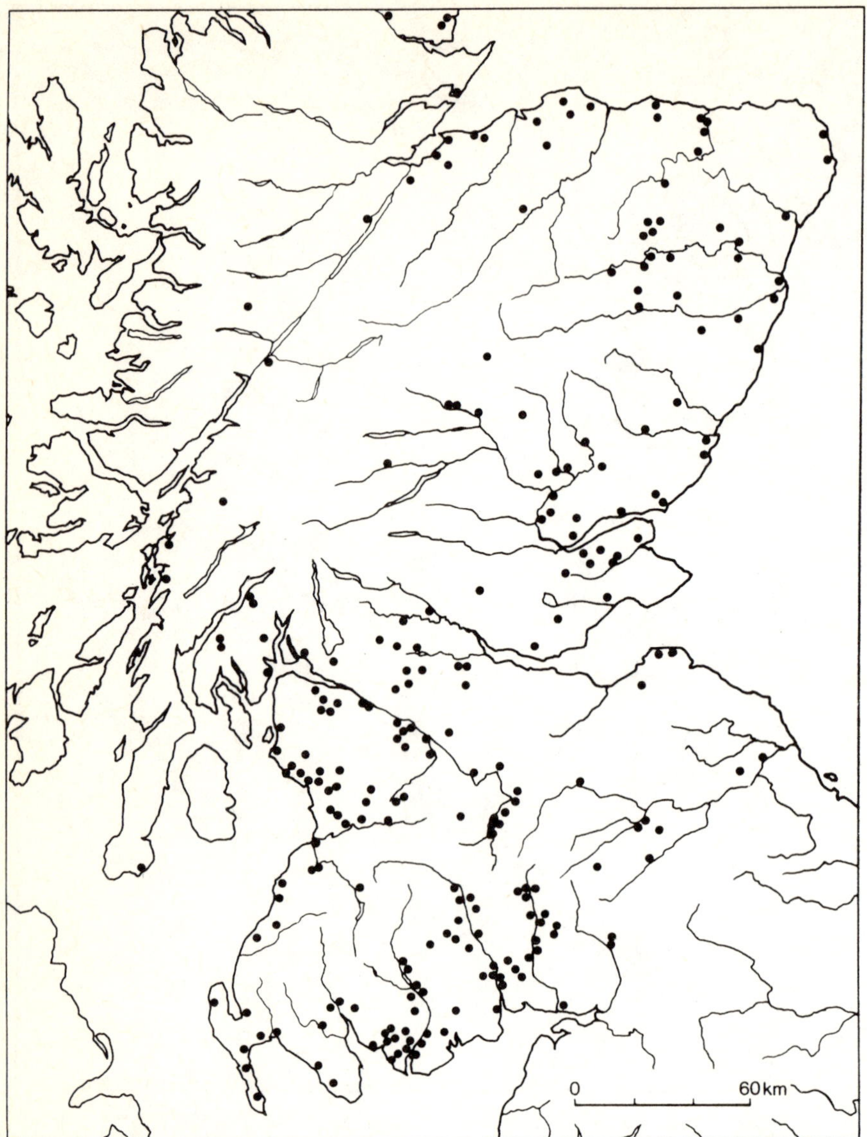

Fig. 4. Distribution of mottes in Scotland.

of alien authority, and these maps show how that authority extended far beyond the areas of direct royal control and also beyond the area for which written documents survive to give us a reasonable outline of what was happening. The mottes on the ground can reveal a story about which the documents may be silent. Mottes are common in Ayrshire, Annandale and Nithsdale, which were all areas where the crown depended for much of its authority on feudal control exercised by a great

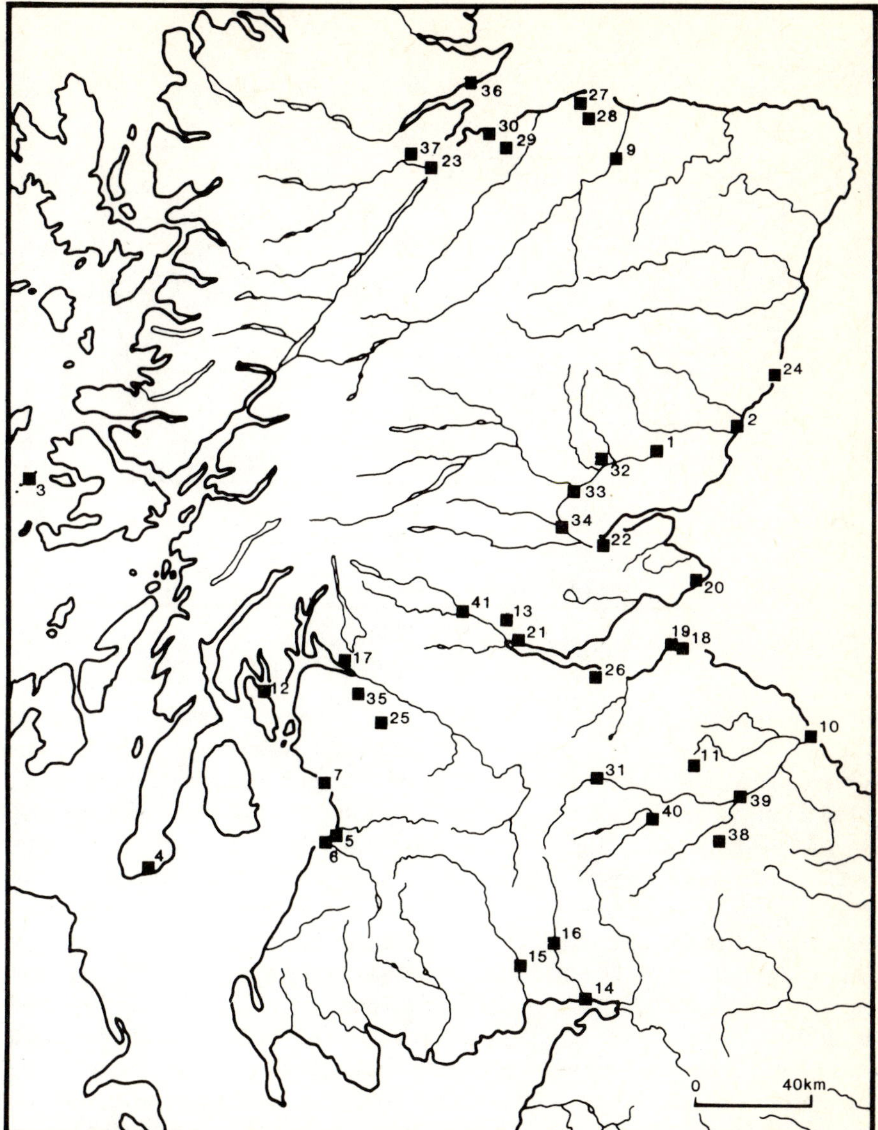

Fig. 5. Distribution of castles recorded by 1249.

magnate; and mottes are also very common in Galloway, which until well into the thirteenth century was notably independent and even rebellious.

This wide distribution of mottes raises the question of exactly how the castle fits into these various patterns of rule, varying from direct royal control to very considerable independence. To consider this, it will be best to limit the discussion to three areas, each of which illustrates a different situation.

The first is the Tweed valley (Fig. 6), where royal authority was firm and castles

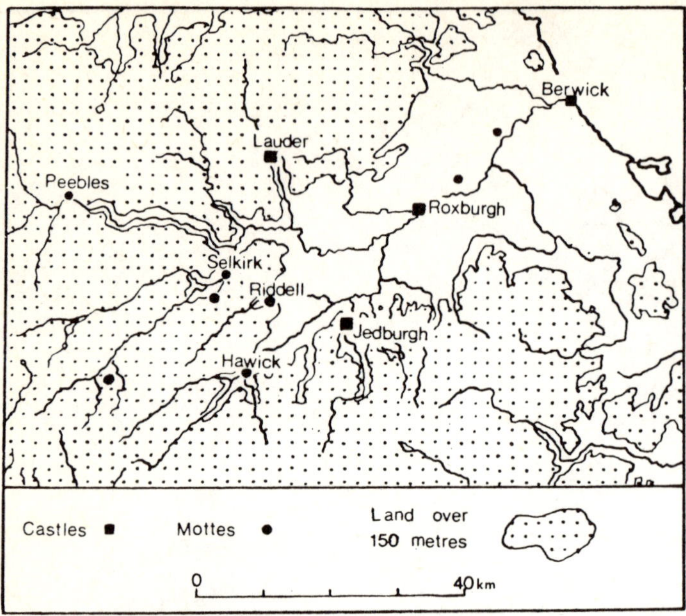

Fig. 6. The Tweed valley.

fit into a structure of royal administration. There were sheriffs, each with a castle, at Berwick, Roxburgh, Selkirk and Peebles, and a royal castle also at Jedburgh. The situation is very like that in Flanders in the mid-eleventh century, where the count ruled through a number of castellans;[10] and it is significant that all these castles have burghs attached to them. Roxburgh has a large empty and unexcavated burgh site; the others are modern towns. At Peebles the castle site is at the confluence of two rivers, and the main street of the town leads directly to the castle: a pattern which may suggest that the town was directly dependent on the castle. At Selkirk the castle site is on the fringe of the burgh, and this might imply that the castle was a later addition. Similarly, at Hawick, which was a private castle, the well-preserved motte is on the outskirts of the town.[11] All these castles were more than just individual structures. Royal or private, they were regional centres, the keys to the administration of their areas, and they were placed at the vital points where also the centres of population developed. There are a few other castles in the region: one at Lauder was the centre of the important Morville fief, and a motte at Riddell was probably the centre of a minor but early fief, which was held about 1150 by Walter of Ryedale (Riddell).[12] But above all this was an area of administrative castles.

Our second area, in the south-west, consists of Annandale and Nithsdale (see Fig. 7). Here we still find castles which act as regional centres, but there are far more which are the centre of a single fief or holding. Annandale was a great fief belonging to an Anglo-Norman family, the Bruces. Its first *caput* was at Annan, where there is not only the castle but also a town situated at a point suitable for crossing the River Annan. The castle is at the edge of the town, directly outside the boundary wall of

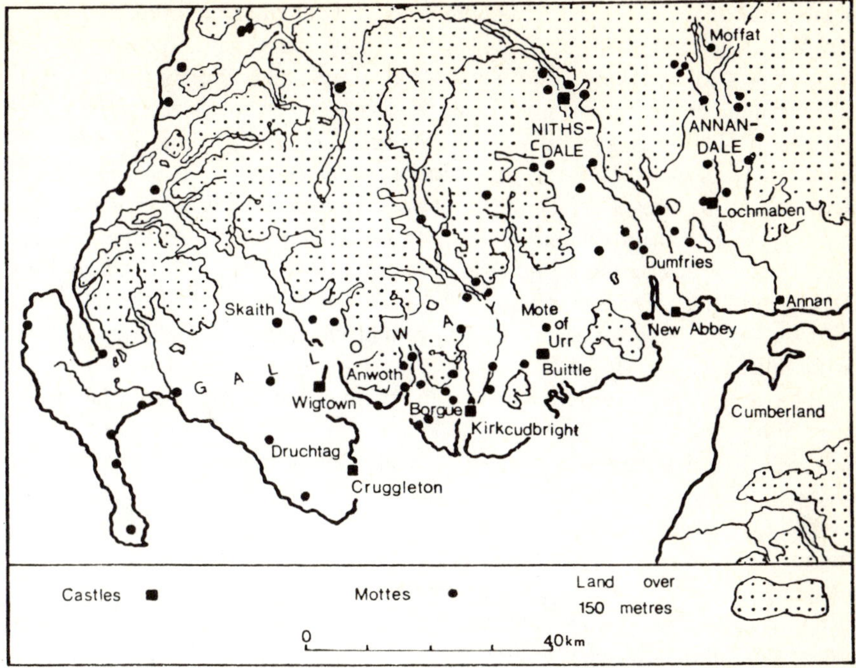

Fig. 7. South-west Scotland.

the burgh tenements. Later the centre of the fief moved to Lochmaben, about twelve miles away, where there was first a motte and then, close to it, an important stone castle erected in the later thirteenth century.[13] But the chief town remained at Annan and only a village existed at Lochmaben. The other mottes of Annandale represent the feudal holdings of the fief and are connected either with demesne lands, such as Moffat, or with sub-tenancies.[14] In Nithsdale there was a royal castle, sheriff and burgh at Dumfries.[15] The rest of Nithsdale was divided into a number of small fiefs, and the fairly thick scatter of mottes fits in with this tenurial structure. In contrast, therefore, to the administrative castles of Tweeddale, the majority of the castles of Annandale and Nithsdale belonged to individual barons of the second rank.

Galloway, on the other hand, our third area (see again Fig. 7), was an almost independent principality, ruled by its own lords. Down to 1161 its lord was Fergus, who is often called *princeps* and even *rex* of Galloway. The kings of Scotland seem to have encouraged in this area the infiltration of alien Anglo-Norman settlers, many of them from Cumberland in England, directly across the Solway Firth.[16] Between 1161 and 1185 Galloway was divided between two sons of Fergus, and in that period there appear in the few charters which exist for the area occasional references to outsiders. Borgue was held by an important family, the Morvilles, who had ties with English Cumbria but also held extensive fiefs elsewhere in Scotland; and at Boreland of Borgue there is one of the most striking mottes in the area.[17] The lands of Urr belonged to another Anglo-Norman, Walter de Berkeley, who was chamberlain of the king of Scotland from about 1171 to about 1190; and at Urr there is a large motte with a bailey.[18] At about the same time foreigners are also recorded at two other sites, Anwoth and New Abbey, and both have mottes.[19]

The chances are that a fair number of the mottes in Galloway represent similar settlement. There was a revolt in Galloway in 1174, and an English chronicler records that the Galwegians 'at once expelled from Galloway all the bailiffs and guards whom the king of Scotland had set over them (*omnes ballivos et custodes quos rex Scotiae eis imposuerat*) and all the English whom they could seize they slew; and all the defences and castles (*munitiones et castella*) which the king of Scotland had established in their land they besieged, captured and destroyed, and slew all whom they took within them'.[20] Clearly there were more foreigners in Galloway than the four families recorded in the charters, and it was perhaps at this time, to take two examples at random, that mottes such as the small one at Skaith and the larger one at Druchtag were built.[21]

In 1185 there was another upheaval in which one of the native line of lords of Galloway, Roland, a grandson of Fergus, seized the whole inheritance. It is recorded that he slew the most powerful men in Galloway and occupied their lands, 'and in them he built castles and very many fortresses' (*castella et munitiones quamplures*).[22] Some mottes must therefore belong to that period; and it is worth noting that according to this statement mottes were being erected by Galwegians themselves. In the thirteenth century the native line of lords ended in three heiresses, who were married to three powerful Anglo-Norman barons: a further move in the attempt to establish royal authority in the area. One of these, John de Balliol, acquired Buittle, where there are remains of an important castle.[23] Another, Roger de Quincy, earl of Winchester and Constable of Scotland, got Cruggleton, which may originally have been the site of a fort of the lords of Galloway. It is dramatically situated on a clifftop in a position unlikely to have appealed to a motte-builder. At some stage before 1292 a stone castle was built there which was still standing in the sixteenth century, although only a single arch now survives.[24] Sometime during the thirteenth century royal castles were erected at Kirkcudbright and Wigtown;[25] and it may be that by the later thirteenth century Galloway was entering a new castle-building phase and mottes were becoming a thing of the past. But that is little more than conjecture.

There is, therefore, an ample context for the Galloway mottes. Only one of them, Mote of Urr, has been seriously excavated in modern times. Unfortunately no more than an interim report has ever been published, but excavation did establish that the motte was built earlier than the thirteenth century, which is what we would expect.[26] The mottes at Borgue, Anwoth and New Abbey also have a documentary context and they should be next for excavation. For the history of the south-west of Scotland in the early Middle Ages, nothing could add so much to our understanding as a thorough programme for selective excavation of mottes in the area. But very little has yet been done, and our present aim is merely to indicate from the historical side the context into which they fit.

We have tried to show here the kind of conclusions that may emerge from the bringing together of documentary and archaeological evidence on the problems of our early castles. There are certainly many problems left. Are there really no more mottes in Lothian? If so, is there any better explanation than the one we have put forward? We have not tried to analyse the mottes into different types, and it might be that something would emerge if mottes with baileys were plotted in comparison with mottes without baileys. We have not discussed the dating of the mottes. We have tended to assume that they belong to the twelfth and perhaps also the thirteenth centuries, which seems to be the implication of the documentary evidence. But any adequate discussion of dating must wait for much more excavation. All we have tried to do is to provide a historical background against which that and other questions can in future be discussed.

NOTES

This study was first published in 1972. It seems to us that a major reappraisal of the issues is not yet appropriate, and we have therefore made only minimal changes for this reprint. A few phrases in the text have been altered to improve clarity, and up-to-date references have been inserted in the notes. Three short general surveys of the topic have appeared since 1972: Duncan, *Scotland*, pp. 433–43; G. Stell, 'Mottes', in *Historical Atlas of Scotland*, ed. P. McNeill and R. Nicholson (St Andrews, 1975), pp. 28–9; and E.J. Talbot's article cited below, p. 13, n. 1. Two local surveys are C.J. Tabraham, 'Norman settlement in upper Clydesdale: recent archaeological fieldwork', *TDGAS*, 3rd ser., liii (1978), pp. 114–28, and *idem*, 'Norman settlement in Galloway: recent fieldwork in the Stewartry', in *Studies in Scottish Antiquity*, ed. D.J. Breeze (Edinburgh, 1984), pp. 87–124. The following excavation reports are also relevant: G. Ewart, 'Excavations at Cruggleton Castle, 1978–81', *TDGAS* (forthcoming); G. Haggarty and C.J. Tabraham, 'Excavation of a motte near Roberton, Clydesdale, 1979', *ibid.*, 3rd ser., lvii (1982), pp. 51–64; H. Murray and G. Ewart, 'Two early medieval timber buildings from Castle Hill, Peebles', *PSAS*, cx (1978–80), pp. 519–27; M.E.C. Stewart and C.J. Tabraham, 'Excavations at Barton Hill, Kinnaird, Perthshire', *Scottish Archaeol. Forum*, vi (1974), pp. 58–65; and P.A. Yeoman, 'Excavations at Castlehill of Strachan, 1980–1', *PSAS* (forthcoming).

1. For fuller details of the changes here sketched in outline see Duncan, *Scotland*, Chs. 6–8; G.W.S. Barrow, *Kingship and Unity: Scotland 1000-1306* (London, 1981), Chs. 2, 3; *RRS*, i, pp. 27–56; ii, pp. 28–67.

2. S. Cruden, *The Scottish Castle*, revised edn. (Edinburgh, 1963), pp. 38–49. See also G.G. Simpson and R.W. Munro, 'A checklist of western seaboard castles on record before 1550', *Notes and Queries of the Soc. of West Highland and Island Historical Research*, xix (1982), pp. 3–7.

3. Barrow, *Era*, *passim*; Barrow, *Kingdom*, pp. 315–36; R.L.G. Ritchie, *The Normans in Scotland* (Edinburgh, 1954), *passim*.

4. The maps are based on Barrow, *Kingdom*, pp. 311–14; G.S. Pryde, *The Burghs of Scotland* (Oxford, 1965); and Cowan (Easson), *Religious Houses*.

5. The first scholar to establish conclusively that the Scottish mottes were Norman was Dr George Neilson, in an article which is still of great value: 'The motes in Norman Scotland', *The Scottish Review*, xxxii (1898), pp. 209–38.

6. D. Christison, *Early Fortifications in Scotland* (Edinburgh, 1898), pp. 1–54.

7. This map is based on a list of mottes compiled by Mr Geoffrey Stell. We are greatly indebted to him for allowing us to use his material, without which our studies would have been much more difficult; and we are pleased that he has agreed to publish his list as Appendix I, below. Fig. 4 excludes those mottes (or sites of mottes) which are listed in

Appendix I as 'possible' or 'doubtful', while no. 302, Langdale (Sutherland), does not appear.

8. Appendix II, nos. 26, 19, 18.

9. RCAHMS, *Inventory of East Lothian*, p. xli and no. 27.

10. For a brief account of the Flemish system of *castellania*, which has many parallels with the Scottish *vicecomitatus*, see F.L. Ganshof, *La Flandre sous les premiers comtes*, 3rd edn. (Brussels, 1949), pp. 104–6.

11. RCAHMS, *Inventories of Roxburghshire*, nos. 233, 905, *Peeblesshire*, no. 523, and *Selkirkshire*, no. 24. The whole question of the relationship of Scottish burghs to their castle sites requires investigation. On the lay-out of burghs see J.W.R. Whitehand and K. Alauddin, 'The town plans of Scotland: some preliminary considerations', *Scottish Geographical Magazine*, lxxxv (1969), pp. 109–21.

12. Lauder: Appendix II, no. 11. Riddell: *RRS*, i, no. 42.

13. RCAHMS, *Inventory of Dumfriesshire*, nos. 3, 445.

14. *CDS*, i, no. 706.

15. RCAHMS, *Inventory of Dumfriesshire*, no. 128.

16. *RRS*, i, p. 13 and n. 2.

17. Lawrie, *Charters*, no. 215; RCAHMS, *Inventory of Kirkcudbright*, no. 54; Appendix I, no. 190.

18. *Holm Cultram Reg.*, nos. 122–3; R.C. Reid, 'The Mote of Urr', *TDGAS*, 3rd ser., xxi (1936–8), pp. 14–17; RCAHMS, *Inventory of Kirkcudbright*, no. 489; Appendix I, no. 204.

19. *RRS*, i, p. 13, n. 2; Appendix I, nos. 181, 208.

20. Anderson, *Scottish Annals*, p. 256, translating from *Gesta Regis Henrici Secundi*, ed. W. Stubbs (Rolls Ser., 1867), i, pp. 67–8.

21. RCAHMS, *Inventory of Wigtownshire*, nos. 200, 389; Appendix I, nos. 316, 314.

22. Anderson, *Scottish Annals*, p. 288, quoting *Gesta Regis Henrici Secundi*, i, pp. 339–40.

23. RCAHMS, *Inventory of Kirkcudbright*, no. 74. On the division of Galloway see *Wigtownshire Chrs.*, pp. xxxix–xli.

24. R.C. Reid, 'Cruggleton Castle', *TDGAS*, 3rd ser., xvi (1929–30), pp. 152–60; RCAHMS, *Inventory of Wigtownshire*, no. 420.

25. RCAHMS, *Inventories of Kirkcudbright*, no. 262, and *Wigtownshire*, no. 541; Stevenson, *Documents*, i, p. 206.

26. B. Hope-Taylor, 'Excavations at Mote of Urr', *TDGAS*, 3rd ser., xxix (1950–1), pp. 167–72.

APPENDIX I

PROVISIONAL LIST OF MOTTES IN SCOTLAND

Geoffrey Stell

This census of mottes in Scotland is based principally on field identifications made by the former Archaeology Division of the Ordnance Survey and by the Royal Commission on the Ancient and Historical Monuments of Scotland. These have been supplemented by information from other sources, and this revision has benefited especially from the work of Eric Talbot of the University of Glasgow.[1] Most of the sites noted under the counties of Berwickshire, Dumfriesshire, East Lothian, Fife, Kirkcudbright, Peeblesshire, Roxburghshire, Selkirkshire, Stirlingshire and Wigtownshire have already been published in the relevant RCAHMS *Inventories*.[2] The lists for the three south-western counties were revised, however, and other identifications were made, particularly in Ayrshire and Lanarkshire, during marginal land surveys of field monuments in 1951–5 and 1956–8.[3] In addition, since the first publication of this list in 1972, mottes and other types of medieval earthwork have been included in the classified lists of field monuments published in the RCAHMS *Archaeological Sites and Monuments Series*, No. 1 (1978)– . I am much indebted to Peter Corser for extracting and arranging all the available information that has come to light as a result of this work. Most of the other material is contained on the Ordnance Survey Archaeology Division's unpublished record cards.

The aim of the census is simply to supply a provisional list of sites as a basis for further observations and research. Doubtful cases are indicated wherever possible, but many of the identifications are of course subject to confirmation and correction. No attempt has been made to distinguish between different motte-structures or to identify other types of defensive constructions, except for the ringworks noted mainly by Mr Talbot.

The term 'motte' has been mostly omitted from the titles, but the name of the parish has been included if required for an unambiguous identification. The sites are arranged by six-figure grid references within an alphabetical order of counties, and it has proved more convenient to maintain the arrangement of the pre-1975 counties in this revision. Uncertain identifications are indicated by a four-figure grid reference or are simply marked 'unidentified'.

1. E.J. Talbot, 'Early Scottish castles of earth and timber: recent field-work and excavation', *Scottish Archaeol. Forum*, vi (1974), pp. 48–57, esp. at pp. 54–6. An attempt has been made to bring the present list up to date in the light of this and other notices of mottes, but not all have been included here. Cf., e.g., the addition suggested in Barrow, *Era*, p. 110,

n. 113, the Cunnigar at Mid Calder, Midlothian, whose name and character, like that of another site in Midmar, Aberdeenshire, indicate a medieval rabbit warren or enclosure rather than a motte.

2. *Berwickshire* (1915); *Dumfriesshire* (1920); *East Lothian* (1924); *Fife* (1933); *Kirkcudbright* (1914); *Peeblesshire* (1967); *Roxburghshire* (1956); *Selkirkshire* (1957); *Stirlingshire* (1963); *Wigtownshire* (1912).

3. *Inventories of Selkirkshire*, pp. xiv–xviii, and *Stirlingshire*, p. xxv; R.W. Feachem, 'Iron Age and early medieval monuments in Galloway and Dumfriesshire', *TDGAS*, 3rd ser., xxxiii (1956), pp. 58–65.

ABERDEENSHIRE

1 Doune of Invernochty	**NJ 352129**
2 Parks of Coldstone (site)	**NJ 434054**
3 Peel of Fichlie	**NJ 459139**
4 Lesmoir Castle	**NJ 471281**
5 Kildrummy	**NJ 471169**
6 Auchindoir	**NJ 475245**
7 Cumins Craig	**NJ 478245**
8 'Castlehill', Auchindoir and Kearn parish (doubtful)	**NJ 513282**
9 Castlehill, Druminnor	**NJ 515287**
10 Huntly Castle	**NJ 532407**
11 'Roundabout', Alford parish	**NJ 555163**
12 Peel of Lumphanan	**NJ 577037**
13 Moathead, Auchterless parish (possible)	**NJ 715417**
14 Earthwork, Chapel of Garioch parish	**NJ 724262**
15 Bass of Inverurie	**NJ 782206**
16 Castle Hill, Kintore (probable)	**NJ 794163**
17 Dalforky Castle (doubtful)	**NJ 807336**
18 Pitfoddels Castle (probable)	**NJ 910030**
19 Tillydrone (probable)	**NJ 936089**
20 Earl's Hill, Ellon (probable)	**NJ 957304**
21 Moat Hill, Cruden parish (possible)	**NK 062368**
22 Castle Hill, Rattray	**NK 086574**
23 Inverugie	**NK 102487**
24 Gardybien, Glenmuick (probable)	**NO 444990**

ANGUS

25 Easter Peel, Lintrathen	**NO 264540**
26 Castleton of Eassie	**NO 333466**
27 Court Hillock, Kirriemuir (doubtful)	**NO 380542**
28 Kirriemuir Hill (possible)	**NO 392546**
29 Invergowrie	**NO 395307**
30 Castle Hill, Inshewan	**NO 445572**
31 Forfar (possible)	**NO 457505**
32 Old Downie, Monifieth	**NO 519365**
33 Barry	**NO 533347**
34 Gallowshill (possible)	**NO 573492**
35 Castle Hillock, Edzell	**NO 584688**
36 Brechin Castle (possible)	**NO 597599**

37 Glenskinno (possible) **NO 681608**
38 Maryton Law **NO 682556**
39 Redcastle, Inverkeilor **NO 689510**
40 Montrose (possible) **NO 717573**

ARGYLL

41 Ard Luing (possible) **NM 737066**
42 Staing Mhor **NM 814081**
43 Rera **NM 831207**
44 Carnasserie (ringwork) **NM 838009**
45 Dùn Mor, Bonawe **NN 012325**
46 Strachur (Strachur House) **NN 093016**
47 Strachur (Ballemenoch) **NN 103999**
48 Strachur (Strachurmore Farm) **NN 108008**
49 Otter Ferry (Ballimore) **NN 922833**
50 Macharioch **NR 726094**
51 Glendaruel, Achanelid (dun or rectangular motte?) **NS 005878**
52 Glendaruel **NS 006874**
53 Dunoon, Castle Crawford **NS 179787**

AYRSHIRE

54 Judge Mound, Skelmorlie Mains (possible) **NS 199663**
55 Dowhill **NS 203029**
56 Castle Knowe, Hunterston **NS 203508**
57 Green Hill, Halkshill, Largs **NS 207593**
58 Kelburne Park, Fairlie (possible motte or dun) **NS 212562**
59 Shanter Knowe **NS 219074**
60 Montfode Mount **NS 227438**
61 Knockrivoch Mount **NS 254451**
62 Auldmuir (possible) **NS 264499**
63 Dunduff (ringwork) **NS 272164**
64 Castlehill **NS 283432**
65 Court Hill, Dalry (site) **NS 292495**
66 Mote Knowe, Monkwood (possible) **NS 298002**
67 Kidsneuk, Bogside, Irvine (site) **NS 309409**
68 Ayr Castle (site) **NS 335222**
69 Alloway (ringwork) **NS 339180**
70 Chapel Hill, Chapelton **NS 344442**
71 Lawthorn Mount **NS 345406**
72 Woodlands (probable) **NS 346136**
73 Court Hill, Beith (possible) **NS 361540**
74 Lindston, Dalrymple parish (possible moated homestead) **NS 372168**
75 Carmel Bank, Kilmaurs parish **NS 387380**
76 Symington (possible) **NS 38 31**
77 Helenton, Symington parish **NS 393311**
78 Witch Knowe, Coylton parish (possible) **NS 399199**
79 Greenhill, Kilmaurs parish **NS 401392**
80 Barnweill Castle (probable) **NS 407301**
81 Law Mount, Stewarton **NS 411448**
82 Castle Hill, Riccarton parish (possible) **NS 417359**

83 Tarbolton	**NS 432274**
84 Dalmellington	**NS 482058**
85 Castlehill Farm	**NS 483388**
86 Witch Knowe, Hillbank Wood, Ochiltree parish (possible)	**NS 502217**
87 Castle Hill, Alton	**NS 503388**
88 Judge's Hill, Loudon parish (possible)	**NS 519386**
89 East Newton, Newmilns	**NS 519385**
90 Castle Hill, Burflat Burn, Loudon parish (possible)	**NS 546378**
91 Borland Castle, Old Cumnock parish (possible)	**NS 585174**
92 Castle Hill, Sorn parish	**NS 588263**
93 Main Castle, Galston parish	**NS 612346**
94 Carleton	**NX 134895**
95 Doune Knoll (possible)	**NX 185971**
96 Dinvin, Girvan	**NX 200932**
97 Mote Wood, Camregan (possible)	**NX 221994**
98 Mote Knowe, Colmonell parish (possible)	**NX 232818**

BANFFSHIRE

99 Ha'Hillock, Deskford	**NJ 509628**
100 Castle Hill, Cullen	**NJ 509670**
101 Kinnairdy Castle, Marnoch parish (doubtful)	**NJ 609498**
102 Craig o'Boyne Castle (possible)	**NJ 616661**
103 Castlehill Farm, Marnoch parish (site)	**NJ 644513**
104 Mount Carmel, Banff parish	**NJ 679626**
105 Ha'Hillock, Alvah parish	**NJ 689584**
106 Banff Castle (probable)	**NJ 689641**

BERWICKSHIRE

107 The Chesters (possible ringwork)	**NT 740474**
108 Bunkle Castle (ringwork)	**NT 805596**
109 The Mount, Castlelaw, Coldstream	**NT 814418**
110 Fair Field, Ladykirk (probable)	**NT 893477**

CAITHNESS

111 Ring of Castlehill (ringwork)	**ND 282618**

DUMFRIESSHIRE

112 Druidhill Burn, Penpont	**NS 810015**
113 Ballaggan	**NS 835014**
114 Enoch Castle	**NS 872027**
115 Garpol Water, Moffat	**NT 051040**
116 Auchencass	**NT 063035**
117 Coats Hill	**NT 072042**
118 Auldton, Moffat	**NT 094058**
119 Ingleston, lower motte, Glencairn	**NX 799899**
120 Maxwelton	**NX 817896**

121 Moatland	**NX 865857**
122 Morton Castle	**NX 891992**
123 Dinning, Closeburn	**NX 893902**
124 Benthead, Closeburn	**NX 922958**
125 Lochside, Lincluden	**NX 958774**
126 Castle Dykes, Dumfries (medieval castle earthworks)	**NX 975747**
127 Dumfries (possible)	**NX 973764**
128 Tinwald	**NY 003815**
129 Torthorwald Castle	**NY 034783**
130 Rockhall	**NY 054767**
131 Castle Hill, Lochmaben	**NY 082822**
132 Lochwood	**NY 085968**
133 Spedlins Tower	**NY 097876**
134 Applegarth	**NY 104843**
135 Castle Knowe, Saughtrees	**NY 125950**
136 Wamphray Place, Newton	**NY 132969**
137 Castlemilk (possible)	**NY 150775**
138 Hutton	**NY 164894**
139 Gillesbie Tower	**NY 172920**
140 Annan	**NY 192666**
141 Barntalloch, Langholm	**NY 352878**
142 Wauchope Castle, Hallcrofts	**NY 355842**

DUNBARTONSHIRE

143 Faslane (site)	**NS 249901**
144 Shandon (possible)	**NS 257878**
145 Balloch Castle	**NS 388826**
146 Catter Law	**NS 472871**
147 Peel of Kirkintilloch	**NS 651740**

EAST LOTHIAN

148 Gladsmuir (site)	**NT 46 73** (unidentified)
149 Tarbet Castle, Fidra Island (site)	**NT 515867**
150 Castle Hill, North Berwick	**NT 560801**
151 Eldbotle (site)	**NT 505857**

FIFE

152 Court Knowe, Gornogrove	**NO 205103**
153 Inchrye	**NO 272165**
154 Agabatha Castle (site)	**NO 284127**
155 Collessie (possible)	**NO 293134**
156 Parbroath Farm	**NO 324178**
157 Maiden Castle, Dunipace Hill, Markinch	**NO 349015**
158 Moat Hill, Cupar (site)	**NO 372148**
159 Castle Hill, Cupar (site)	**NO 37 14** (unidentified)

160 Newton (possible) **NO 403246**
161 Leuchars Castle **NO 454219**
162 Perdieus Mount, Dunfermline (site) **NT 091867**
163 Lochore Castle **NT 175958**
164 Hillside, Aberdour parish (possible) **NT 193855**

INVERNESS-SHIRE

165 Erchless, Cnoc an Tighe Mhoir (possible) **NH 410410**
166 Urquhart Castle **NH 530286**
167 Wester Lovat, Beauly (possible) **NH 540460**
168 Holm House (probable) **NH 653420**
169 Petty (possible) **NH 736497**
170 Old Petty **NH 738498**
171 Ruthven in Badenoch (possible) **NH 765997**
172 Cromal Mount, Ardersier **NH 782555**
173 Old House of Keppoch **NN 271808**

KINCARDINESHIRE

174 Castle Hill, Strachan **NO 657921**
175 Green Castle (possible ringwork) **NO 668765**
176 Castle Hill, Durris **NO 780968**
177 Dunnottar **NO 882839**

KIRKCUDBRIGHTSHIRE

178 Minnigaff **NX 410664**
179 Machars Hill **NX 470653**
180 Kirkclaugh **NX 534522**
181 Boreland or Green Tower **NX 585550**
182 Woodend, Anwoth **NX 585566**
183 Polchree Farm, Anwoth (possible) **NX 592584**
184 Polchree **NX 594584**
185 Roberton **NX 604486**
186 Moat Park, Cally **NX 606556**
187 Barmagachan, near Borgue **NX 613494**
188 Palace Yard (ringwork) **NX 613543**
189 Dalry **NX 618813**
190 Boreland of Borgue **NX 646517**
191 Balmaclellan **NX 653794**
192 Trostrie **NX 656574**
193 Culcraigie (possible) **NX 657575**
194 Twynholm **NX 659539**
195 Little Duchrae **NX 664696**
196 Dunnance **NX 674637**
197 Castle Dykes, Kirkcudbright **NX 677509**
198 Boreland of Parton **NX 694709**
199 Kirkland, Parton **NX 696697**
200 Culdoach **NX 706537**
201 Kirkcormack **NX 717574**
202 Lochrinnie **NX 728871**

203 Ingleston, Kelton parish	**NX 775580**
204 Urr	**NX 815647**
205 Cullochan Castle	**NX 921754**
206 Lincluden	**NX 967779**
207 Troqueer	**NX 974748**
208 Ingleston, New Abbey parish	**NX 982651**

LANARKSHIRE

209 Castle Hill, East Kilbride parish (possible)	**NS 589563**
210 Bishop's Palace, Glasgow (ringwork)	**NS 601655**
211 Carmunnock (ringwork)	**NS 613578**
212 Cawder House	**NS 613724**
213 Castle Hill, East Kilbride parish (possible)	**NS 612557**
214 Castlemilk (possible)	**NS 613598**
215 Rutherglen	**NS 623617**
216 Mains, East Kilbride	**NS 627558**
217 Laigh Mains, East Kilbride parish (possible)	**NS 627561**
218 Greenlees	**NS 638585**
219 Peelhill	**NS 643367**
220 The Tor, Torrance	**NS 649526**
221 Drumsargad Castle, Cambuslang (site)	**NS 665597**
222 Hamilton, Low Parks	**NS 727566**
223 Darngaber Castle	**NS 729500**
224 Cot Castle (possible)	**NS 739456**
225 Millfield, Cambusnethan parish	**NS 795573**
226 Ladle Knowe, Douglas	**NS 826294**
227 Castle Qua (ringwork)	**NS 873449**
228 Lanark	**NS 879433**
229 Abington	**NS 933250**
230 Moat Farm, Roberton	**NS 940270**
231 Castledykes	**NS 942287**
232 Bower of Wandel	**NS 951287**
233 Crawford Castle or Tower Lindsay (possible)	**NS 954213**
234 Couthalley Castle (possible)	**NS 971481**
235 Carnwath	**NS 974466**
236 Loanheadmill	**NS 992310**
237 Wolfclyde	**NT 019363**
238 Biggar	**NT 039377**

MIDLOTHIAN

239 Crichton (ringwork)	**NT 384618**

MORAY

240 Grant's Fort	**NJ 053316**
241 Kilbuiach	**NJ 097603**
242 Tor Chastle	**NJ 130526**
243 Duffus Castle	**NJ 189672**
244 Elgin Castle	**NJ 212628**
245 Knight's Hillock, Urquhart parish	**NJ 283651**

NAIRNSHIRE

246 Cantraydoune	**NH 789461**
247 Nairn Castle (site)	**NH 885566**
248 Auldearn, Doocot Hill	**NH 917556**
249 Hillend (possible)	**NH 932547**

PEEBLESSHIRE

250 Peebles	**NT 249403**

PERTHSHIRE

251 Tom-na-Curtaig, Kerrowmore	**NN 589467**
252 Tom na Chisaig, Callander parish (possible)	**NN 627079**
253 Carnbane Castle, Fortingall parish (doubtful)	**NN 677479**
254 Coney Hill, near Comrie	**NN 776224**
255 Tom an Tigh Moir, Blair Atholl parish	**NN 807654**
256 Struan	**NN 812653**
257 Aldclune, Blair Atholl	**NN 895643**
258 Glendevon (site)	**NN 904047**
259 Kindrogan	**NO 055638**
260 Castle Hill, Clunie	**NO 111440**
261 Motte, Scone parish (probable)	**NO 126295**
262 Cairn Beddie, St Martin's parish (site)	**NO 150308**
263 Castle Hill, Cargill	**NO 158374**
264 Blairgowrie (site)	**NO 179455**
265 Rattray	**NO 209453**
266 Law Knowe, Errol (probable)	**NO 232224**
267 Barton Hill, Kinnaird	**NO 244287**
268 Blair Drummond	**NS 724986**

RENFREWSHIRE

269 Pennytersal	**NS 337712**
270 Motte, Kilmacolm parish (site)	**NS 352661**
271 South Denniston (probable)	**NS 358683**
272 Castlehead, Paisley (ringwork)	**NS 381635**
273 Castle Hill, Ranfurly	**NS 384651**
274 Houston House	**NS 411671**
275 Castlehill, Renfrew (site)	**NS 509679**
276 Elderslie, 'The King's Inch', Renfrew (site)	**NS 514675**
277 Crookston (ringwork)	**NS 525627**
278 Pollok (ringwork)	**NS 555626**
279 Crosslees, Eaglesham (possible)	**NS 558536**
280 Camphill (ringwork)	**NS 577621**

ROSS AND CROMARTY

281 Dunscaith Castle	**NH 807690**

ROXBURGHSHIRE

282 Hawick	**NT 499140**
283 Riddell	**NT 520248**
284 Ruletownhead (possible)	**NT 617128**
285 Smailholm (ringwork)	**NT 640346**

SELKIRKSHIRE

286 Phenzhopehaugh	**NT 318127**
287 Howden	**NT 458268**
288 Selkirk	**NT 470281**

STIRLINGSHIRE

289 Woodend	**NS 555887**
290 Keir of Cashlie, Drymen (possible)	**NS 556929**
291 Craigmaddie (ringwork)	**NS 575765**
292 Fintry	**NS 611866**
293 Keir Knowe of Drum	**NS 636953**
294 Maiden Castle, Garmore	**NS 643784**
295 Sir John de Graham's Castle	**NS 681858**
296 Balcastle Motte, Kilsyth	**NS 701781**
297 Colzium, Kilsyth (possible)	**NS 734782**
298 Bonnybridge (Mote of Seabegs)	**NS 824798**
299 Slamannan	**NS 856734**
300 Watling Lodge (site)	**NS 862798**

SUTHERLAND

301 Borgie (possible)	**NC 670587**
302 Langdale	**NC 698449**
303 Invershin	**NH 572963**
304 Proncy	**NH 772926**
305 Skelbo Castle	**NH 792952**

WIGTOWNSHIRE

306 Castle Ban, near Mains of Airies	**NW 966678**
307 Culhorn, Inch parish (possible)	**NX 078594**
308 Innermessan	**NX 084634**
309 Balgreggan	**NX 096505**
310 Ardwell	**NX 107455**
311 High Drummore	**NX 130359**
312 Droughdool	**NX 148569**
313 Motte, Old Luce parish (probable)	**NX 194573**
314 Druchtag	**NX 349467**
315 Boreland	**NX 355584**
316 Skaith	**NX 382662**
317 Castle (site) near Appleby, Glasserton parish	**NX 401409**

APPENDIX II

PRELIMINARY LIST OF SCOTTISH CASTLES RECORDED IN DOCUMENTS OR CHRONICLES DOWN TO 1249

This list is based on a survey of standard sources, but does not claim to be comprehensive. It records only places which are specifically described by the words *castrum, castellum*, or, occasionally, *oppidum*. Various other words of less specific meaning may also denote a fortified site or structure. For example, *manerium* can mean a 'manor-house', and the *manerium* of Leuchars, Fife (*St Andrews Liber*, pp. 397–8, datable 1280 × 1297) is a motte (Appendix I, no. 161). The word *curia* can mean a house as well as a court, as it does in an unusually descriptive reference to a house at Lamberton, Berwickshire, perhaps of the reign of Alexander II (J. Raine, *The History and Antiquities of North Durham* [London, 1852], app., no. 649). An *aula* such as that at Congalton, East Lothian, probably *c.*1224 (*Dryb. Lib.*, no. 24), may represent what in architectural terms would be called a 'hall-house'.

	DATE	SOURCE
ANGUS		
1 Forfar	before 1197	*St Andrews Liber*, p. 354
2 Montrose	1165 × 1214	*RRS*, ii, no. 556
ARGYLL		
3 Cairnaburgh (More)	1249	Anderson, *Early Sources*, ii, p. 556; Duncan, *Scotland*, p. 551
4 Dunaverty	1248	*CDS*, i, no. 1865; Duncan, *Scotland*, p. 550
AYRSHIRE		
5 Ayr	1197	*Melrose Liber*, i, no. 103
6 Greenan	1175 × 1199	*Ibid.*, no. 34
7 Irvine	1184	*Gesta Regis Henrici Secundi* (Rolls Ser., 1867), i, pp. 312–13
8 Unidentified site probably in Carrick	1175 × 1199	*Melrose Liber*, i, no. 31
BANFFSHIRE		
9 Boharm	before 1242	*Moray Reg.*, nos. 23, 64
BERWICKSHIRE		
10 Berwick	1173	*Gesta Regis Henrici Secundi*, i, p. 47
11 Lauder	1173	*Ibid.*

	DATE	SOURCE
BUTE		
12 Rothesay	1231	Anderson, *Early Sources*, ii, p. 476
CLACKMANNANSHIRE		
13 Clackmannan	*c.*1248 × 1264	SRO RH 6/54
DUMFRIESSHIRE		
14 Annan	*c.*1124	Lawrie, *Charters*, no. 54
15 Dumfries	1175 × 1187	*Glasgow Reg.*, i, no. 50
16 Lochmaben	1173	*Gesta Regis Henrici Secundi*, i, p. 47
DUNBARTONSHIRE		
17 Dumbarton	1222	J. Irving, *History of Dumbartonshire* (Dumbarton, 1917–24), ii, p. 287
EAST LOTHIAN		
18 Dirleton	after Sept. 1219	*Dryb. Lib.*, no. 37
19 Eldbotle	probably late William I	*Ibid.*, no. 104
FIFE		
20 Crail	1153 × 1165	*RRS*, i, no. 289
21 Culross	1217	SRO Supplementary Register House Charters, *s.d.*
22 Lindores	1249	*Lind. Cart.*, no. 62
INVERNESS-SHIRE		
23 Inverness	1197	*Melrose Liber*, i, no. 103
KINCARDINESHIRE		
24 Inverbervie	1232 × 1237	*Lind. Cart.*, no. 18
LANARKSHIRE		
25 East Kilbride	1175 × 1190	*Glasgow Reg.*, i, no. 55; cf. *RRS*, ii, no. 249
MIDLOTHIAN		
26 Edinburgh	*c.*1127	Lawrie, *Charters*, no. 72

	DATE	SOURCE
MORAY		
27 Duffus	1203 × 1222	*Moray Reg.*, no. 211
28 Elgin	1160	*RRS*, i, no. 175
NAIRNSHIRE		
29 Auldearn	1185	*Liber Insule Missarum* (Bannatyne Club, 1847), no. 2
30 Nairn	1215 × 1222	*Moray Reg.*, no. 25
PEEBLESSHIRE		
31 Peebles	1152 × 1153	*RRS*, i, no. 104
PERTHSHIRE		
32 Alyth	1196 × 1199	*Ibid.*, ii, no. 410
33 Cargill	1189 × 1199	SRO Maitland Thomson Photographs, no. 6
34 Perth	1157 × 1160	*RRS*, i, no. 157
RENFREWSHIRE		
35 Renfrew	1163 × 1165	*Ibid.*, no. 254
ROSS and CROMARTY		
36 Dunskeath	1179	Anderson, *Early Sources*, ii, p. 301
37 Redcastle (Eddyrdor)	1179	*Ibid.*
ROXBURGHSHIRE		
38 Jedburgh	1147 × 1150	Lawrie, *Charters*, no. 189
39 Roxburgh	*c.*1128	*Ibid.*, no. 83
SELKIRKSHIRE		
40 Selkirk	*c.*1120	*Ibid.*, no. 35
STIRLINGSHIRE		
41 Stirling	1107 × 1124	*Ibid.*, no. 182

2

THE EARLDOM OF CAITHNESS AND THE KINGDOM OF SCOTLAND, 1150–1266

Barbara E. Crawford

As part of the mainland of Scotland the province of Caithness was implicitly recognised as Scottish territory by the Norwegians in the treaty of 1098 between their king, Magnus Barelegs, and King Edgar of Scotland.[1] Being, however, the only part of the mainland which was thoroughly settled by peoples of Norse extraction,[2] Caithness was in a totally different situation from any other part of the Scottish littoral. During the period of settlement the native population had been to some extent displaced and the Celtic language replaced by Norse, at any rate in the north-east quarter of the province. The nature of the land also made it very different from the west coast (where the Norse also had some influence), for it was more fertile, with excellent pasture and arable land; and it was this factor which had attracted the Norse settlers to the area from Orkney in the ninth and tenth centuries.[3] The earls of Orkney then claimed jurisdiction over the settlers and theoretically held the ancient Celtic province as an earldom of the kings of Scots. The fact that Caithness was part of the Scottish mainland was, apparently, not particularly relevant: seen from the middle of the Pentland Firth it was merely another stretch of territory along with the islands of Stroma, Hoy, or South Ronaldsay, and, after all, 'united' with them by water. Furthermore, the *Ness*, as the saga writer called the north-east of Caithness, is cut off from the land to the south (the *Sutherland*) by the central upland area of the county and the long sea journey round Duncansby Head, so that it was particularly closely linked with the islands across the Pentland Firth. Geographical and historical factors therefore provide the reason for the anomalous position whereby Caithness lay under the jurisdiction of the earls of Orkney, nobles who owed allegiance to the kings of Norway for their island earldom. These earls also owed nominal allegiance to the kings of Scotland as earls of Caithness. A short stretch of water united the two halves of their lordship, and during the period under discussion Caithness was linked, emotionally and economically, with the Norwegian earldom.

These factors made the situation in Caithness one which the Scottish kings did not willingly tolerate. Access to the political heart of the Scottish kingdom was more possible from the Scandinavian north down the east coast than from the west, where a protective mountain barrier helped to keep the Norse of the Hebrides at bay. It is not surprising, therefore, that for the whole of our period the kings of Scotland made repeated efforts to bring under firm control Caithness and its ruling earls. Two incidents from the very beginning and the very end of the period demonstrate the vulnerability of their northern shores to a foreign power. In 1151 Earl Harald

Maddadson was trapped in the harbour of Thurso by King Eystein of Norway and compelled to pay tribute:[4] that is, the overlord of Norway was far more at home in the waterways and harbours of Caithness than the king of Scotland could ever dream of being. In 1263 King Håkon Håkonsson made Orkney his naval base for several weeks before moving south to renew his sovereignty over the Western Isles; and while in Orkney he sent an expedition to Caithness which demanded peace-money from the inhabitants in order to keep them neutral in the warlike situation which prevailed.[5] He (or another Norwegian king) even communicated with them by letter, as we know from the record of *littera regis Norwagie missa Cataniensibus* which was at one time in the Scottish treasury,[6] a striking record of the continuing links between Caithness and the northern world. The Caithness farmers probably still spoke the language of the Norwegian king, and a witness to the continuation of their separate identity is found in the use of the name *bondi* (Old Norse *bondi* = 'free farmer') for them in another, near-contemporary document in the central Scottish records.[7] We can see therefore that Caithness was closely bound to the land of a foreign power throughout the hundred years under discussion. By the end of our period, however, the efforts of the Scottish kings had weakened the traditional bonds, as well as the power of the native earls, as can be seen from the success of their measures to keep a firm control over Caithness during the crisis years of 1263–6.[8]

Although the Orkneyinga Saga, which continues up to 1231, gives us a picture of a totally Scandinavian society in Caithness, we have very little documentary information from the thirteenth century to give us confirmatory details. Since, however, the area lay under the jurisdiction of the Orkney earls, the administrative and defensive arrangements for their territories must have extended across the Pentland Firth. In order to control this important waterway, they had to control the Caithness side as well as the Orcadian. All the evidence points to a high degree of organisation of this kind in Orkney, including the *huseby* system of administrative farms,[9] and the naval defence arrangements based on the ounceland and pennyland land-divisions, which later became converted to a means of taxation.[10] Caithness was also divided into ouncelands and pennylands.[11] In a land grant of the late thirteenth century, Earl John Magnusson gave to the elder Reginald Cheyne *totam nostram oratam terrae* at Nottingham in Caithness.[12] We may even have evidence from this same charter of the persistence of a monetary due connected with the ancient Norse naval system. The land carried with it a payment or *servitium domini regis quod vocatur Layyeld.* In the fourteenth century the same payment appears in the Scottish exchequer rolls as the rent of the assize *de Lawyeld* from the earldom of Caithness, which brought in £20 *per annum.*[13] This due would appear to have been Norwegian in origin, and the fiscal imposition to which it refers presumably dates from the period when the earls, and the Caithness *bondi*, were primarily Norse speakers (that is, pre-1231). If the first element of the word has been correctly Scotticised to 'law' in the fourteenth-century reference (from Old Norse *logr*), the second element is evidently Old Norse *gjald* = 'tribute', 'payment'. If this was some kind of judicial due, then it may have been laid on the earldom on one of the occasions when the earl submitted to a fine (1202, 1222, 1263 or 1266).[14] If, however, the first element were not 'law' — and the way that the word is spelt *layyeld* in Earl John's charter suggests that it may not have been — then it could instead have been the same as the payment of *lida gjald*, a tax levied in Norway for the provision of the navy.[15] If so, this would confirm that the ouncelands and pennylands of Caithness were indeed the basis of a taxation and naval defence system laid down by the earls. The Old Norse word *skatt* = 'tax' is rarely met with in medieval Caithness, unlike the Northern Isles, where *skatt*-payments continued to be of fundamental importance in the economy to modern times. Nevertheless, later references to 'skatlands' and payments of 'skat-malt' and 'skat-silver' in Caithness strongly suggest that Norse fiscal terminology had indeed been current at an earlier date.

Ecclesiastical influence was the inevitable complement to secular control, especially as the Church in Orkney was closely associated with the earldom. We can assume, therefore, that Caithness lay within the jurisdiction of the early bishops of Orkney, and that the establishment of the first Scottish bishop of Caithness prior to 1147×1151[16] would have been a very unwelcome intrusion into the sphere of the ancient bishopric of Orkney. The most important church in Caithness in this period was at Halkirk (Old Norse, *ha-kirkja* = 'high church') in Thurso dale, in that part of Caithness most closely associated with Orkney: Bishop Adam of Caithness had a residence there in 1222.[17] Its proximity to the earl's castle of Brawl, which was the most important comital seat in Caithness throughout the Middle Ages, is reminiscent of the situation in Orkney where the bishop's see and church (Christchurch) were established by Earl Thorfinn about 1060, adjacent to his own residence in Birsay.[18] The bishops of Caithness also had a castle at Scrabster, where Bishop John was maimed in 1201, and this is close by another important earldom castle, at Thurso, which was first mentioned in 1154.[19] The proximity of these comital and episcopal residences can be no coincidence, but shows the close association of earl and bishop — an association which must stem from the period before Scottish bishops appeared on the scene. Both earl and bishop had had residences by the best anchorages on the southern shore of the Pentland Firth because of their need to cross the Firth which divided their joint earldom and bishopric. Even in the sixteenth century the bishops of Orkney held estates in Caithness, which they would seem to have retained from an earlier period.[20] It would be surprising if there had not been trouble when Scottish bishops attempted to move in and interfere in the long-established preserve of an Orkney bishop acting under the protection of the earl. The running feud with the earl, and the two physical attacks the Scottish bishops had to suffer, are merely symptoms of a very difficult underlying situation,[21] which in the end proved sufficiently daunting for the bishops to move to a safer place in the south of the diocese. With Bishop Gilbert's reorganisations in the years after 1223 and with the replacement of Halkirk by a cathedral at Dornoch, there was an evident acknowledgement that the traditional forces in the north of the diocese were too well entrenched for the Scottish churchmen to contend with them. The Scots kings had to struggle to make their authority felt for the whole of the hundred years under review, and particularly to maintain support for the church they had established as a spearhead for the reincorporation of the ancient Celtic province of Cat within their kingdom. The success or failure of this policy will now be assessed.

Andrew, the first bishop of Caithness (1147×1151–84), was certainly in contact with his diocese in so far as he sanctioned a grant made by Earl Harald Maddadson to the papacy in the second half of the twelfth century.[22] King David's pretensions to authority in the area about this same time are rather remarkable. A brieve was issued by him for the protection of the monks at Dornoch, in which he addressed the men of Caithness *and* Orkney, and Earl Rognvald as earl of Orkney.[23] A second earl, given neither name nor territory, was also addressed, and this may have been Harald Maddadson, who was associated with Rognvald in the earldom of Orkney from 1139 (but who only came of age *c.* 1150). Indeed, there is a hint in the saga account of Rognvald's and Harald's struggle for the division of power that the Scottish king may have been involved in prevailing upon Rognvald to accept the half-Scottish Harald as his co-earl.[24] This is the first evidence of direct Scottish interference in the comital succession, which was going to prove the most successful method of controlling the earldom.[25] On this occasion, however, it did not have fruitful results for the Scottish cause, as Harald Maddadson was not enthusiastic about the policy of spreading Scottish influence in Caithness. Harald's bitter conflict with the second bishop, John, has been shown to have resulted from the bishop's interference in the earldom,[26] and in the struggle to preserve his independence and his control over ecclesiastical payments, Harald enlisted the support of Innocent III. The extent of the quarrel can be seen from its culmination a few years later in the attack on Bishop John at his castle of Scrabster, when he was maimed by a band from Orkney led by the earl. This attack, as will be discussed on page 32, gave the Scottish king justification for an expedition to the north.

Continuing tension between the local northern tradition and the new ecclesiastical authority in Caithness led to the murder of the third bishop, Adam, in 1222. This was a result of his attempt to force Caithness into line with the rest of the Scottish Church in respect of church rights and, in particular, as regards teinds.[27] From different sources it appears that two kinds of teinds were involved. The saga says that the freemen of Caithness were objecting to the raising of the teinds from the customary rate of one spann of butter for every twenty cows to one for every ten cows,[28] and this payment, in a Norwegian measure of weight, was no doubt long established. Although teinds were not imposed on the whole of Norway until 1164, they then replaced older renders,[29] renders which the bishops of Orkney are likely to have received from Caithness. From the Annals of Dunstable we learn that the earl had also been hit by increased demands for the teinds of hay, 'concerning which both he [the bishop] and the earl of Caithness had made promise to the king of Scotland'.[30] This is verified by a papal letter written after the murder of Bishop Adam, which says that an agreement over teinds had been reached by the mediation of certain ecclesiastical persons in the presence of the king, by which the bishop had at last been granted what was due to him.[31] And the decree which the bishop issued as a result of this agreement is said to have had appended to it both the royal seal and the earl's seal. The earl and people of Caithness were not alone in their refusal to pay teinds at this time, although the situation there appears to have been the only one where the outcome was so violent: in the very next year, 1223, Honorius III wrote to the people of the Hebrides ordering them to pay all their teinds of butter and cheese,[32] and two years later Duncan, lord of Carrick, promised the bishop of Glasgow and a large assembly of clergy at Ayr that he would pay his teinds in full and compel his tenants to do likewise. In the following year the earl of Lennox promised the same.[33] The extant documents which these two sealed were no doubt similar to that which Earl John had sealed — and which he then attempted to get back from the bishop.[34] Although the kinds of teind are not specified in these extant charters, we know that the hay-teind in particular was a problem in Scotland; a mandate of Innocent IV later complained of evil practices in the Scottish Church and mentioned that magnates had been preventing the payment of teinds of hay, pasture and mills.[35] Obviously hay was an important render in the pastoral regions of Scotland; indeed, there seems to have been general resistance throughout Europe to the payment of hay-teind, because we find land being given to the Church apparently in order to escape it.[36] The clash between Bishop Adam and the earl, backed up by the farmers of Caithness, was therefore only one instance of a general protest against teinds of which we have contemporary evidence not only from south-west Scotland but also from the diocese of the Hebrides which, it is important to note, lay in the jurisdiction of the archbishop of Trondheim. In Caithness the resentment inflamed an already very sensitive situation, for the earl's father and Bishop Adam's predecessor had long maintained a running feud. These events cannot simply be attributed to the turbulent nature of the earls; there is no evidence that their relationship with the contemporary bishop of Orkney was anything but friendly.[37] In 1222, moreover, the antagonism to the bishop of Caithness existed throughout the area: the earl and *bondi* were at one in their hatred of the bishop and all he stood for.

The two main sources for the events of 1222 differ in their apportioning of responsibility for the attack on the bishop. The author of the saga shows a close knowledge of events in Caithness and of the activities of the Caithness farmers. He appears to have got his knowledge first-hand, for he tells of what Rafn the lawman said when he communicated with the bishop, and he gives the impression that all the action leading up to the burning of the bishop was initiated by the *bondi*. In this account, the earl did not participate, although he was residing 'a short distance off'[38] (presumably at Brawl), and he simply refused to mediate in the affair. This would be quite enough to arouse those suspicions about his motives mentioned by the chronicler Fordun, who however adds later that the earl 'proved by the witness of good men that he was guiltless and had given no countenance or advice to those ruffians'.[39] The Annals of Dunstable, on the other hand, depict Earl John as being the prime mover, if not the actual murderer of the bishop, and many additional details are given in this source about the earl slaying the bishop's chaplain in his presence, wounding his nephew, and finally ordering the bishop to be bound in his kitchen and the house set on fire.[40] This laying of the main burden of guilt at the earl's door may be simply a monkish desire to find a scapegoat: the Melrose chronicler certainly has a similar view of the murder.[41] From the other evidence we have it looks rather as if the earls were beginning to learn a little caution, and also to fear the wrath of their Scottish overlord, even though their sympathies were at one with the *bondi*. There is, however, no reason to doubt the rest of the information in the Annals of Dunstable, which details the earl's dislike of the demand for hay-teinds and his participation in a royal attempt at reconciliation, as well as his attempt to get hold of the sealed charter from the bishop. Indeed, his sympathy with the action was all too evident and he was as a result compelled by King Alexander to carry out the harsh punishment pronounced for the *bondi*.[42] In this instance, no individual was forced to carry alone the weight of retribution as one 'Lombard' had been in 1202.[43]

This second manifestation of anti-episcopal and anti-Scottish feeling in Caithness seems to have brought home to the Scottish crown the need for a more military bishop, and for greater consolidation of Scottish influence, before any permanent advance could be made towards incorporating the far north within the Scottish ecclesiastical and administrative framework. King Alexander took an expedition north in 1223, and thereafter ensured that Gilbert de Moravia (Murray) was appointed as Bishop Adam's successor.[44] Earlier in the century, as archdeacon of Moray, Gilbert had been given by his relative, Hugh de Moravia, a grant of Skelbo and of all the land west of Fernbuchlin to Invershin and the borders of Ross.[45] This was a grant evidently made for defensive purposes, as the territory concerned was important strategically in the current state of Scottish advance into Sutherland. Once he had been elected bishop, Gilbert's attitude towards the problems of the north seems to have been essentially realistic. He was not going to risk the fate suffered by two of his predecessors, and so he reorganised the diocese by moving its centre south to Dornoch, building a cathedral there, and establishing a collegiate chapter for its service.[46] Sutherland was, by then, the firm seat of the Moravia family and soon to be well out of the control of the earl of Caithness. Gilbert took advantage of the security of his own and his relatives' territorial position there to use Sutherland as an operational base for his episcopal ministry. As has already been suggested,[47] this move was to some extent a recognition of the failure of previous attempts to solve the situation in the north. The Church was forced to retreat under the protection of the secular arm, and Bishop Gilbert acknowledged this, in establishing his own base near the new political authority in Sutherland; he thus sought the protection which had been refused to him by the earls of Caithness, who continued to regard the ecclesiastical situation as they knew it in the islands as the norm, and bitterly resented the new ideas and new political control from the south.

The attacks on Bishop Gilbert's predecessors provided the Scottish kings with the opportunities for punitive expeditions to the north. A show of royal force was needed as a preliminary to reducing the power of the earls. The first royal expedition was in 1196–7, although on this occasion it was not for the purpose of securing the Church in the north. The earl of the time, the famous and powerful Harald Maddadson, had been attacking feudal representatives of the new Scottish order, not the ecclesiastical hierarchy. Although Fordun alleges that Earl Harald had been 'a good and trusty man' previously,[48] a recent assessment sees him as having been troublesome to the king as early as 1179.[49] Certainly, he must have been closely concerned in Malcolm MacHeth's claims to Ross and Moray, for his second wife Gormflaith (Hvarflöd) was MacHeth's daughter.[50] Such a marriage would have had political reasons behind it, which in the circumstances are likely to have been the creation of a united opposition to royal ambitions north of Inverness. Fordun explains Harald's behaviour in 1196 as being due to goading from his wife, but there must have been some very particular reason why this earl should have been prepared to provoke his Scottish overlord in the year following a dramatic encounter with his Norwegian overlord, when his power in his Orkney earldom had been curtailed.[51] In 1196 Harald is said to have led a force into Moray, and either in that year or the next his son, Thorfinn, fought a battle with 'the king's vassals' near Inverness, one of the important royal centres in the province of Moray. This constituted a serious attack on royal authority, and King William the Lion led a retaliatory expedition north, the first substantiated royal expedition to Caithness.[52] Roger of Howden adds the comment that when King William entered Caithness, Harald did not wish to start battle against him.[53] The object of the earl's aggression would appear to have been primarily the king's vassals. All the sources state that Harald in the first place went into Moray, which Howden says he 'occupied'.[54] All this action in Moray must have involved the Moravia family, who were the most important participants in the Scottish king's plans for the northern part of the kingdom. They had been given the lands of Duffus about 1130;[55] since then they had been in the van of the measures to consolidate royal authority in Moray;[56] and after the great victory of Mam Garvia in 1187 we can be quite sure that they were closely involved in the advance to Cromarty.[57] The family's ambitions were to become only too clear in the period after Earl Harald's death, when they succeeded in establishing themselves in Sutherland, eventually acquiring it as an earldom detached from Caithness (see below, p. 33).

The retaliatory measures undertaken by King William were superficially successful in restoring the Moravias' authority and also in extending his own. He is said by Fordun to have subdued both provinces of the Caithness men, and Howden tells us how part of the king's army reached Thurso and destroyed Earl Harald's castle there.[58] The earldom was at first divided and then taken away from Harald altogether. Half of it was given to Harald Ungi (the younger), grandson of Earl Rognvald and rival claimant to the northern earldoms. The elder Harald was allowed to retain the other half on condition that he brought certain enemies to the king at a prearranged meeting at Nairn, but when he failed to bring the required hostages, Howden states that he forfeited the remaining portion and lost all his possessions in the earldom, so that Harald Ungi became sole earl of Caithness. However, it was not easy for the king to maintain the advance that he had made towards curbing the power of so long-established an earl as Harald Maddadson. In 1198, the elder Harald defeated and killed his younger namesake in battle near Wick.[59] William the Lion therefore looked to another member of the earldom family, and gave a grant of authority to Rognvald Gudrodson, king of Man.[60] The policy of replacing one holder of the earldom by another member of the same family was, no doubt, due to the inability of the Scottish king at this point to do other than to make use of a weakness in the Norse method of inheritance, by playing off one member of the *jarlsaetten*[61] against another in the attempt to weaken the power of a strong and dangerous earl. The elder Harald's unceasing struggle against Harald Ungi, and then against Rognvald Gudrodson, proved him to be still the most powerful figure in the north (despite an evident lack of support in Caithness). It was not until he made the mistake of antagonising the Church in 1201 that Earl Harald found it prudent to submit to King William, apparently of his own volition. The first expedition sent against him in that year was not successful, and a second one was only in preparation when, in the spring of 1202, the earl came to the king at Perth, accompanied by the bishop of St Andrews, and offered £2,000 worth of silver to win back his overlord's goodwill and with it, once more, official recognition of his status as legal earl.[62] He was apparently fully restored to his Scottish earldom which, for the remaining four years of his life, he held undisturbed by king or claimant.

It is difficult to see what permanent advantage the Scottish king had gained from this struggle. As far as we know Harald suffered no ultimate loss of land or rights: the imposition of heavy fines seems to have been used as the most effective form of punishment, rather than the confiscation of earldom land. The same pattern was followed after the burning of Bishop Adam in 1222. A retaliatory royal expedition was followed by John Haraldson's submission. He at first had to give up half of his earldom into the king's hands, as well as to bestow lands and money on the Church. But he was allowed to redeem his earldom the following year with a very heavy fine.[63] Those Caithness farmers who had been present at the burning suffered dreadful retribution, being physically maimed and also forfeiting their lands. But they or their families were, similarly, allowed to redeem them; the papal letter concerned with their punishment ordered the bishop to put the lands under interdict *usque ad satisfactionem congruam observari.*[64] Indeed, we know a document once existed in the Scottish records called 'a quitclaiming of the lands of the *bondi* of Caithness for the slaughter of the bishop'.[65] This may have taken the form of an annual fine of a certain number of cattle which, later in the century, we find the men of Caithness responsible for paying into the royal exchequer.[66] There are also references in the exchequer records to permanent fines which lay on the earls of Caithness, Sutherland and Ross (as well as on the bishop of Ross).[67] It has been suggested that they may be linked with the events of 1202 or 1222,[68] although this seems unlikely in the case of the earl of Sutherland or the earl and bishop of Ross since they had had nothing to do with either incident. But whatever the reason for them, these examples of fines support the suggestion that the Scottish kings preferred to impose fines for misdemeanour in the far north rather than to confiscate land which they would then have had the problem of administering.[69]

The history of Sutherland is a separate problem. It had always formed part of the province and diocese of Caithness, but gained a separate identity in our period and was later to become a powerful earldom in its own right. As already mentioned, it was the Moravia family who were entrusted with the thorny challenge of absorbing Sutherland into the kingdom of Scotland. The first member of the family known to have possessed lands in Sutherland was Hugh son of William, who granted Skelbo and most of Creich parish to his relative Gilbert de Moravia when Gilbert was archdeacon of Moray.[70] Hugh held a lot more of Sutherland than that, however, for his eldest son succeeded to his Sutherland estates, which thus appear to have been considered more important than the older family lands in Moray which the second son inherited. William, son of Hugh, was indeed called *dominus de Sutherlandia* in the confirmation of his father's grant to Archdeacon Gilbert (pre-1222),[71] from which we know that William certainly held the whole of Sutherland. It has been suggested that the Moravia family were granted this land in 1197–8, when Earl Harald Maddadson lost half his earldom.[72] But there is no evidence to show that the territory in Hugh de Moravia's hands was former earldom land, or that it had been acquired from Harald Maddadson, whose earldom was handed over to his rival Harald Ungi in 1197. Nor is it said anywhere that Earl Harald was not fully restored to all his previous rights and possessions in Caithness after his submission to King William in 1202. Saga evidence suggests, however, that most of Sutherland was in the hands of the family of Moddan in Dale in the mid-twelfth century; and the heir of this family was Eric Slagbrellir, who married Ingigerd, the only child of Earl Rognvald,[73] and whose son was Harald Ungi. The younger Harald is therefore likely to have had large family estates in Sutherland, and it is possible that it was *these* lands which, on Harald Ungi's death without heirs in 1198, were entrusted by King William to his frontiersman, Hugh de Moravia. The fifteenth-century 'Genealogy of the Earls' says quite clearly that Sutherland was taken away from Earl Magnus II by Alexander II;[74] yet from the indisputable evidence that William de Moravia was *dominus de Sutherlandia* before 1222 this appears to be misleading if not erroneous information. When, however, this William was created earl of Sutherland, probably in the 1230s,[75] the earl of Caithness may well have lost some rights over Sutherland, and no doubt prestige: this may be the basis for the statement by the fifteenth-century compiler of the Genealogy that he lost the earldom of Sutherland. But the earl of Caithness cannot have lost much land in an area which had been in Moravia hands for some time.

Despite the royal expeditions of 1196–7, 1202 and 1222 and the submissions of the earls which followed, despite the installation of members of the Moravia family in powerful secular and ecclesiastical positions, the Scottish kings had no more than shaken the tight grip which the earls possessed over Caithness. It was finally to be loosened by more pacific means, the tying of the earldom family into the Scottish nobility by marriage, so that when the direct male line died out (which appears to have happened twice), heiresses passed the title and lands — by the process of succession — to men who already had close ties with the Scottish king. This must have been the purpose behind the incident, recorded by Fordun, when the daughter of Earl John Haraldson was taken hostage by King William after he had dealt with a revolt in Moray in 1214.[76] There is no evidence that Earl John had participated in the revolt, although his relations with the king cannot have been very satisfactory, as a treaty of peace is said to have been concluded between them at the same time. This improvement in their relationship was no doubt meant to be strengthened by a marriage for the earl's daughter, which the king would arrange with one of his vassals. There is no evidence as to which one was chosen, although it may have been a member of the house of Angus, which later took over the title to the earldoms of Caithness and Orkney. This succession resulted from the murder of Earl John at Thurso in 1231, which provided the Scottish kings with their first real opportunity to organise the northern earldom to their own satisfaction. The earl had been murdered by rival claimants, who were brought to trial in Bergen in the summer of 1232.[77] In the autumn most of these kinsmen were apparently drowned, along with the best men from Orkney, in the loss of the *göđingaskip* on its return from Norway to Orkney.[78] On 7 October *M. comite de Anegus et Katanie* witnessed a charter,[79] which shows that Malcolm, earl of Angus, must at that date have been considered the nearest claimant to the earldom of Caithness. The title to both Caithness and Orkney was held finally, however, by Earl Magnus, a member of the Angus family whose name suggests that his mother had belonged to the Harald Ungi line of the Orkney earldom family.[80] Magnus was not given a grant of Caithness until 1235–6, for before that (apart from the reference to Earl Malcolm already mentioned) *Walt' Cumyn comit' de Menteth comit' (de) Katany* witnessed a charter on 7 July 1235.[81] From these fragmentary pieces of information, it is impossible to know for what reasons first Earl Malcolm, then Walter Comyn, and finally Earl Magnus were given grants of the earldom of Caithness, but we can guess that they were made by Alexander II as part of his policy of establishing a new regime in the north: at just about the same time, Sutherland was being erected into an earldom for William de Moravia.[82] The process had presumably been completed by 26 July 1236, when *M. com' de Angus* and *M. com' de Cathaness* witnessed a charter of Alexander at Inverness,[83] the first royal charter that we know of to have been witnessed by an earl of Caithness. Maybe it was completed during this same royal visit to the north.

What did the settlement consist of? Apart from taking Sutherland — or some rights in the area — away from Earl Magnus, King Alexander granted him the earldom of Caithness by charter. If the secondary information can be trusted, it appears that Magnus was given two grants: the earldom of North Caithness in one, the earldom of South Caithness in the other (for the former of which he had to pay £10 *per annum*).[84] That he was granted the two halves of the earldom separately in this way is not unlikely, since other evidence shows that the earldom was often so divided. The line of division must have been well established, for rival Norse earls had frequently divided their spheres of influence.[85] As we have seen, this occurred in Earl Harald's time, and subsequently with his two sons, David and John, between 1206 and 1214. Magnus, however, enjoyed the united earldom for only four years, as he died in 1239,[86] and with the second rearrangement which followed his death, the Caithness earls lost permanently half of their Scottish earldom.

The evidence for this comes from the appearance of *nobilis mulier domina Johanna*,[87] long known to historians because of her importance as an heiress and her possession of Strathnaver and half of the earldom of Caithness. These lands were divided between the two daughters of her marriage with Freskin de Moravia, a nephew of the new earl of Sutherland and yet *another* member of this family to be involved in the monarch's plans for the north of his country. Freskin's and Joanna's two daughters thus eventually held one quarter of the Caithness earldom each.[88] In attempting to trace Joanna's origins, historians have made her inherit her half of the earldom too early (in 1231), and have also given her a purely Norse parentage. She has been identified with the hostage daughter of Earl John and his heiress, as well as being identified with the other half (that is, Harald Ungi's half) of the earldom line.[89] Now, in the first place, Earl Magnus of the Angus line was granted the *whole*

Table 1. *Conjectural descent of the earldom and lands of Caithness in the mid-thirteenth century*

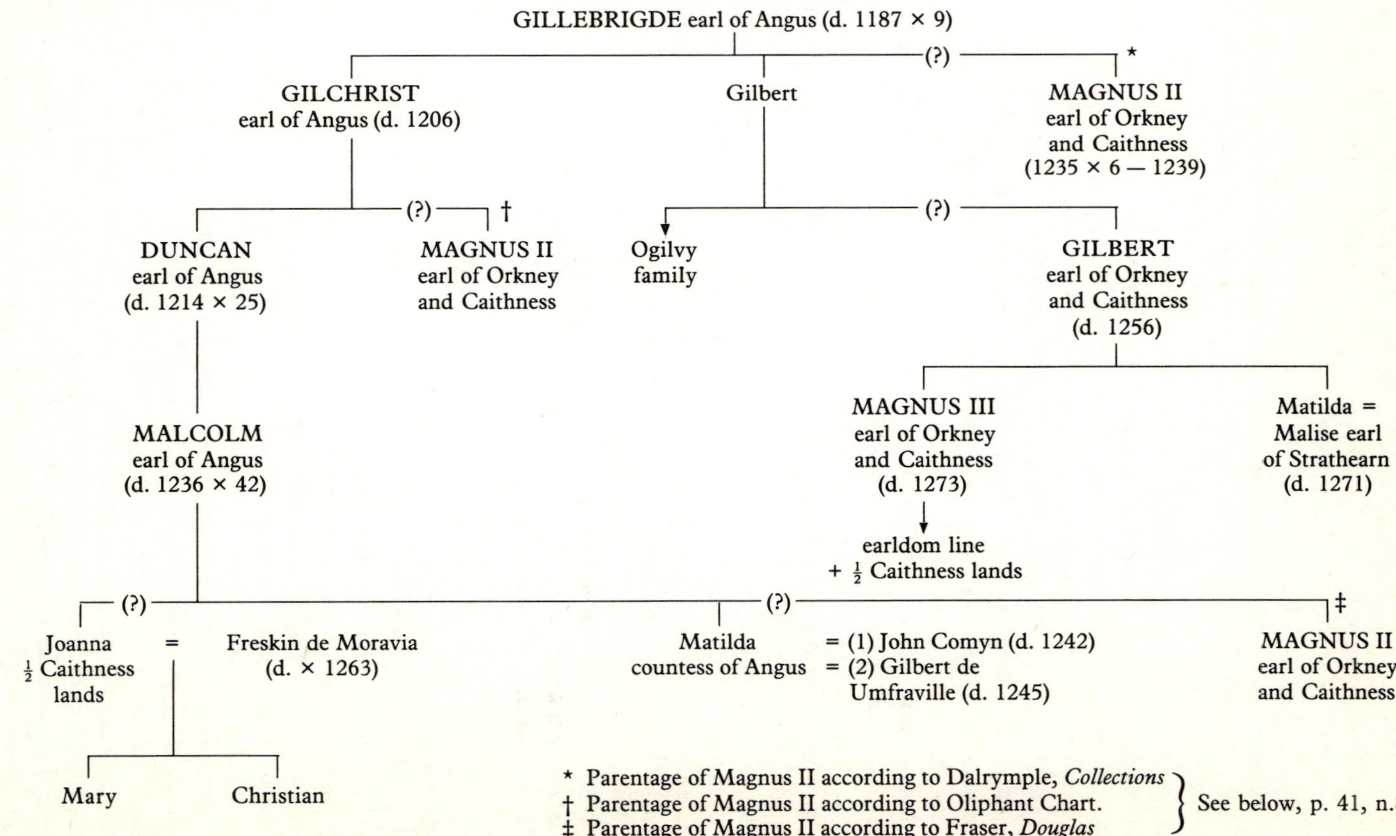

of the earldom, in two halves as has been discussed; any division of the earldom can only have taken place after his death in 1239. Secondly, there is one piece of evidence which suggests that Joanna was herself a member of the Angus family. This comes from a copy of a document, dated 1373, included in the fifteenth-century Panmure Codex, of which the 'Genealogy of the Earls' also forms part. Most tantalisingly, we have only the last few lines of this document as the preceding page of the Codex is missing; but there is sufficient to indicate — what has not been realised before — that this must have been an important explanation of the confused inheritance of the earldom of Caithness in the thirteenth century. All that remains of the document is this fragment: ... *per annum et dimedium, et obiit virgo sine prole, et sic comitatus revertebatur ad primas sorores Johannam et Matildam, quequidem Johanna soror senior nupta fuit domino Freskino ut supra notatum est. Scarmclath. 7 Augusti 1373.*[90] Joanna is here said to have inherited what must have been the earldom of Caithness along with a sister Matilda, after it had been held — apparently for one and a half years — by somebody else, who must have had a prior claim to it.[91] It would be surprising if such an important heiress as Matilda appeared nowhere else in the records of the period — when we know from other sources about Joanna — and it seems possible therefore that she can be identified with the Matilda, daughter of Malcolm, earl of Angus, who became countess of Angus in her own right after Malcolm's death, between 1236 and 1242.[92] This interpretation would mean that Joanna and Matilda were co-heiresses both to their father Earl Malcolm of Angus *and* to their relative, Earl Magnus of Caithness, who died in 1239. The crown appears to have awarded one earldom to each sister, Caithness to the elder and Angus to the younger. However, there remains the peculiar fact that Joanna in the end held only half of the earldom of Caithness, and her husband Freskin de Moravia never took the title of earl as far as is known. The title and half of the lands in fact passed to an Earl Gilbert, also earl of Orkney. We know very little about him; but it can be assumed that he was *not* the son of the preceding earl, Magnus (as the 'Genealogy of the Earls' makes no mention of any relationship between them), although we may suspect that he was another member of the Angus family.[93]

Why, then, was another individual given the title and half of the earldom lands when the right to the earldom is said quite clearly to have passed to Joanna and Matilda? The existence of the superior half of the lordship, the earldom of Orkney, probably had something to do with this problem, for no earl could rule Caithness without being accepted in Orkney and in Norway. In the first place, King Alexander may not have wanted Joanna's husband, Freskin de Moravia, to do allegiance to another overlord for a foreign earldom; and it was in any case very unlikely that he would have been accepted by a Norwegian king as earl of Orkney, through right of his wife.[94] Nor could Joanna herself hold the title of countess in her own right, as could her sister in Angus. A female member of the Orkney earldom family could pass only the right to claim inheritance of the earldom to her sons, as many of them did; but Joanna and Freskin had *no* male heirs. These factors may lie behind the anomalies involved in the inheritance, at this time, of the earldoms of Caithness and Orkney. In this situation another member of the Angus family had to be found who could receive the titles, and who was given half of the lands of Caithness. How long it took for the process to be worked out we do not know: indeed, the only positive information we have about Earl Gilbert is that he died in 1256.[95]

What do we learn from this involved rearrangement? Firstly, there is the evidence of royal interference in the inheritance of the heiresses of the earl of Angus, and the part played by the powerful Comyn family in the settlement would appear to have been important. One heiress was married to a member of the Comyn family (John Comyn, earl of Angus, who was killed in 1242)[96] and the other to a Comyn supporter (Freskin de Moravia), while Walter Comyn himself held the title to the earldom of Caithness for a short while in 1235.[97] Secondly, the success of the Moravia family in getting a grip on the northern earldom is a fitting climax to their role as right-hand men in the royal policy for the subjugation of the area. It may be, however, that Freskin was supposed to get the title to Caithness along with the hand of the elder co-heiress; and it would probably have suited the Scottish king very well if the union of Orkney and Caithness could thus have been broken. But, in this respect as in others, the strength of the influence from Orkney and the tie between the two earldoms meant that the inheritance customs of the Norwegian earldom proved pre-eminent.[98]

Nevertheless, the events of the next reign show that, by the mid-thirteenth century, Caithness had become to some extent an integral part of the Scottish kingdom. The successful way in which Alexander III tackled the threat presented by the Norwegian expedition to Scotland of 1263 is a vindication of his and his predecessor's policy. In that year, King Håkon Håkonsson led the last Norwegian effort to preserve sovereignty over the Western Isles. In this campaign the position of the northern part of the Scottish mainland was vital, and Alexander's harsh policy of preserving its loyalty by a campaign of monetary exactions and reprisals was very successful. The Norwegian expedition was itself a response to the attempt by Alexander to wean the Western Isles from their allegiance to the kings of Norway.[99] When King Håkon summoned his fleet to meet in Bergen in the summer of 1263, Earl Magnus Gilbertsson of Orkney and Caithness must have been summoned too, and he sailed westwards to Orkney, where the host remained for several weeks. Psychological war was waged on the people of Caithness by both sides. King Håkon, in Orkney, sent a force across to Caithness and laid a fine on the area in return for which peace was promised; he warned that if the men of Caithness refused to pay he would impose harsher terms on them.[100] For his part, Alexander took twenty-one Caithness hostages, as well as two from Skye, whose expenses were charged to the account of the sheriff of Inverness at 1d. and 1½d. a day respectively.[101] This was part of Alexander's attempts to ensure the loyalty of the men of Caithness. What can we deduce about Earl Magnus Gilbertsson's loyalty to his Scottish overlord? Since he joined the Norwegian expedition at Bergen, where he was given a long-ship by the king — a mark of favour — it looks as if he initially thought that loyalty to his Norwegian sovereign was paramount. The Norwegian king also trusted him sufficiently to leave him behind in Orkney when the fleet sailed on to the Hebrides, instructing him to follow as soon as he and his men were ready.[102] But thereafter the earl disappears from the saga account of this expedition, and that he failed to follow his Norwegian overlord is suggested by a statement in the late thirteenth-century official account of the Norwegian nobility, the *Hirđskraa*: there it is recorded that in the year following the treaty of Perth between Norway and Scotland (1267) he paid a visit to the Norwegian king and made terms with him.[103] Yet there is no evidence that Earl Magnus actively joined the Scottish king in defending Caithness against the Norwegians, and Magnus's authority in the area appears to have been superseded by a special royal commission to the earl of Buchan and to Alan Durward.[104] His passive loyalty was probably secured either by the taking of a hostage for his good behaviour or by his own imprisonment, and most certainly by the imposition of another heavy fine; in both 1263 and 1266 he paid fifty marks to the king, as part of the fines which he owed for those years, fines which clearly related in some way to the tense situation.[105]

Despite the failure of the Norwegian expedition, the tension between the two countries remained high until the treaty of Perth was drawn up in 1266, and in such a situation Caithness remained a front-line area. After the death of King Håkon in Kirkwall in December 1263, his successor sent Ogmund Krakadanz to the Orkneys and 'gave him authority over them for the defence of the land'.[106] This tells us that Earl Magnus was certainly absent from his Norwegian earldom, for he was by tradition appointed to protect it and organise it militarily. Like their earl, the poor men of Caithness were caught between the devil and the deep blue sea; we read that in the autumn of 1264 Alexander of Scotland sent an army north 'and they took much goods from the men of Caithness because King Håkon had laid a fine on the men of Caithness'.[107] It is possible that the exchequer rolls of 1265 contain a reference to the fruits of this raid: an entry records 200 cows of the fine of the men of Caithness, of which the bishop took his teind,[108] although elsewhere the story is told of how Lord Dougal of the Isles attacked the Scottish force which had laid the fine on the men of Caithness and, as it was returning, 'seized the great sum which they were carrying off'.[109] Twenty-one hostages from Caithness and Skye were still in custody in 1264 or 1265,[110] although by this date negotiations for peace were already under way. With the more peace-loving Magnus Håkonsson on the throne of Norway, Alexander's envoys were able to come to terms with the Norwegians at Perth in July 1266, which involved the cession of the Western Isles to Scotland, in return for 4,000 marks sterling and an annual payment of 100 marks.[111]

Thus, a dangerous situation had turned out successfully for the Scottish king, and in no small part this was due to the harsh policies of Alexander and his predecessors, who had never let an opportunity slip to enforce their authority over their northernmost earldom. They may not have been able to maintain any permanent evidence of Scottish royal authority in the shape of royal demesne or bailiffs or justiciars in the hundred years which we have examined; but by leading military expeditions north to make their presence felt, by cracking down with large fines when the opportunity gave them the moral justification, and by infiltrating vassals of their own choosing into the lands and title of the earldom when inheritance custom allowed them, they accustomed the earls — and also those 'men of Caithness' who are so frequently referred to in the records — to the heavy hand of

Scottish royal authority. When, therefore, a real crisis arose as it did in 1263, there does not seem to have been any will or ability among the turbulent *bondi* of Caithness and their earl to do other than submit.

NOTES

1. A.A.M. Duncan and A.L. Brown, 'Argyll and the Isles in the earlier Middle Ages', *PSAS*, xc (1956–7), pp. 193–4.

2. W. Nicolaisen, 'Norse settlement in the Northern and Western Isles', *SHR*, xlviii (1969), pp. 16–17.

3. *Ibid.*, p. 12.

4. *The Orkneyinga Saga*, ed. J. Anderson (Edinburgh, 1973 reprint), pp. 152–3.

5. Below, p. 37.

6. *APS*, i, p. 109. Is there any other example of a communication sent by a foreign king to the people of a Scottish province?

7. *Ibid.*

8. Below, pp. 37–9.

9. A. Steinnes, 'The *huseby* system in Orkney', *SHR*, xxxviii (1959), pp. 36–46.

10. H. Marwick, 'Leidang in the west', *Proc. of the Orkney Antiquarian Soc.*, xiii (1934–5), p. 23; *idem, Orkney Farm-Names* (Kirkwall, 1952), p. 210.

11. Ouncelands have not been traced in Sutherland, although pennylands appear to have existed as far south as the River Shin (information from lecture by M. Bangor-Jones to the Conference of the Scottish Society for Northern Studies, 1983).

12. SRO Dupplin Charters, bundle V, no. 138, ii. *Oratam terrae* = 'ounceland'. See also F. Thomas, 'What is a pennyland?', *PSAS*, xx (1885–6), p. 209.

13. *ER*, i, p. 570.

14. Below, pp. 32, 38.

15. *Kultur-Historisk Leksikon for Nordisk Middelalder*, x (Copenhagen, 1970), under *lide*. This term does not appear in any Orkney connexion but then nor does the word *leidangr*, which was however commonly used in Shetland (where it was corrupted to *leanger*) until the sixteenth century: see *Oppressions of the Sixteenth Century in the Islands of Orkney and Zetland* (Maitland Club, 1859).

16. Watt, *Fasti*, p. 62; G. Donaldson, 'Scottish bishops' sees before the reign of David I', *PSAS*, lxxxvii (1952–3), pp. 106–17.

17. Below, p. 29.

18. *Ork. Saga*, ed. Anderson, p. 43; B.E. Crawford, 'Birsay and the early earls and bishops of Orkney', *Orkney Heritage*, ii (1983), p. 104.

19. *Ork. Saga*, pp. 165, 196.

20. R. St Clair, 'The bishopric of Orkney: references to lands in Caithness', in *Old Lore Miscellany of Orkney, Shetland, Caithness and Sutherland*, iv (Viking Soc., 1911), pp. 17–19.

21. See B.E. Crawford, 'Peter's Pence in Scotland', in *The Scottish Tradition*, ed. G.W.S. Barrow (Edinburgh, 1974), pp. 20–1, for my interpretation of these events as a result of the clash between Norse and Scottish custom in the area.

22. *CPL*, i, p. 1; *Caithness and Sutherland Records*, ed. A.W. Johnston *et al* (Viking Soc., 1909–28), i, part one, p. 3.

23. Lawrie, *Charters*, no. 132; *RRS*, i, p. 44.

24. Harald's father was Earl Maddad of Atholl: see notes in *The Orkneyinga Saga*, trans. A.B. Taylor (Edinburgh, 1938), p. 388. From the saga account, the visit by Bishop John 'of Atholl' to Orkney would certainly appear to have been of an official nature, and a direct result of it was Rognvald's acceptance of Harald as co-earl. The only Scottish bishop of the period called John was bishop of Glasgow 1118–47: he had been King David's tutor and may well have come to Orkney after visiting Earl Maddad in Atholl.

25. Below, p. 36.

26. Crawford, 'Peter's Pence', pp. 19–21.

27. *Ibid.,* p. 21, where a brief account of the incident is given.

28. *Ork. Saga,* ed. Anderson, p. 200 (*not* for every thirty cows, as translated by G.W. Dasent in 'The Orkneyingers Saga', *Icelandic Sagas,* iii [Rolls Ser., 1894], p. 232).

29. K. Helle, *Norge Blir en Stat* (Universitetsforlaget, 1964), p. 41.

30. Anderson, *Scottish Annals,* p. 337.

31. *Caithness and Sutherland Records,* i, part one, p. 24; Theiner, *Monumenta,* no. 49.

32. *Diplomatarium Norvegicum,* ed. C.C.A. Lange and C.R. Unger (Christiania, 1849–1919), vii, no. 10.

33. *Glasgow Reg.,* i, nos. 139, 141.

34. Anderson, *Scottish Annals,* p. 337.

35. *Moray Reg.,* no. 260.

36. J. Dowden, *The Medieval Church in Scotland* (Glasgow, 1910), p. 173; J. Selden, *The History of Tithes* (London, 1618), p. 284.

37. This was Bjarne Kolbeinsson (Watt, *Fasti,* p. 250), said to have been a 'dear friend' of Earl Harald (*Ork. Saga,* ed. Anderson, p. 193). Harald was also a generous benefactor to the Scottish Church: Crawford, 'Peter's Pence', p. 19, n. 43.

38. *Ork. Saga,* ed. Anderson, p. 200.

39. *Chron. Fordun,* ii, p. 285.

40. Anderson, *Scottish Annals,* p. 337.

41. Anderson, *Early Sources,* ii, p. 479.

42. Anderson, *Scottish Annals,* p. 337; cf. *Chron. Fordun,* ii, p. 285; Anderson, *Early Sources,* ii, p. 452.

43. *Diplom. Norv.,* vii, no. 3.

44. Watt, *Fasti,* p. 58.

45. *RRS,* ii, no. 520.

46. Watt, *Fasti,* p. 62. Gilbert is said to have 'administered the affairs of government in the north, and superintended the building and fortifying of several royal castles for the security of the country': C. Innes, 'Records of the bishopric of Caithness', in *The Bannatyne Miscellany* (Bannatyne Club, 1827–55), iii, p. 11.

47. Above, p. 27.

48. *Chron. Fordun,* ii, p. 270.

49. Duncan, *Scotland,* p. 193; also P. Topping, 'Harald Maddadson, earl of Orkney and Caithness, 1139–1206', *SHR,* lxii (1983), p. 113.

50. *Ork. Saga,* trans. Taylor, p. 342.

51. *Ibid.,* p. 348.

52. See *RRS,* ii, pp. 15–16, for a chronicle of events. Surprisingly, the saga account does not appear to mention this expedition. It may be, however, that the account in *Flateyar Bok* of King William's later expedition of 1202 (*Ork. Saga,* trans. Taylor, pp. 347, 415) is in reality an account of the earlier expedition, for several features of it tally with the apparently devastating nature of that campaign.

53. Roger of Howden, *Chronica,* ed. W. Stubbs (Rolls Ser., 1868–71), iv, p. 10.

54. *Ibid.* P.A. Munch, *Det Norske Folks Historie* (Christiania, 1852–63), iii, p. 42n., suggested that Harald Maddadson rose in rebellion in 1196 because a rival had been granted part of the earldom and that therefore the older earl had a grievance. There is, however, no statement in the saga account or in any of the other sources that Harald Ungi (see below, p. 31) had been given part of the earldom before 1196. Nor is it likely that the older earl would have ravaged *Moray* to express his disapproval of such a grant. He took no such action in 1151 when an earlier rival, Erlend Ungi, had been given half of the earldom.

55. *RRS,* ii, no. 116.

56. The family's possession of shrieval authority in Moray became virtually hereditary: *ibid.,* pp. 40–1.

57. *Ibid.,* p. 12. The founding of the castle-burgh of Nairn ensured an easy crossing to Cromarty.

58. *Chron. Fordun*, ii, p. 270; Howden, *Chronica*, iv, p. 10.

59. According to the Icelandic Annals, this took place in 1198 (Anderson, *Early Sources*, ii, p. 350). Howden and Fagrskinna say this battle took place near Wick. How it came to be associated with Clairdon Hill near Thurso is unclear: *Ork. Saga*, trans. Taylor, p. 409; *ibid.*, ed. Anderson, p. 195, n. 1.

60. *Ibid.*, p. 195.

61. The *jarlsaetten* were all descendants of previous earls who had the right to claim the earldom in accordance with Norse custom. There are many earlier instances in the saga of claimants requesting the help of the Scottish king in granting them what they considered to be already their rightful inheritance.

62. *Chron. Fordun*, ii, p. 272.

63. Anderson, *Scottish Annals*, p. 337; *Chron. Fordun*, ii, p. 285.

64. *Caithness and Sutherland Records*, i, part one, p. 25.

65. *APS*, i, p. 110.

66. *ER*, i, pp. 19–20; below, p. 38. That this was a permanent imposition can be seen from a fragmentary, late thirteenth-century list of returns from the northern counties, which shows Caithness still obliged to return 200 cows: Stevenson, *Documents*, ii, p. 18, n. 1.

67. *ER*, i, pp. 13, 19.

68. *Ibid.*, p. lxi.

69. Annual fines had to be collected, of course, which presupposes the existence of some system of royal officials. Evidence of this from the thirteenth century is very meagre. Gilmakali, the *judex Catanie* who appears in 1225 × 1242, may represent the ancient position of a law officer who was attached to a Celtic province (Barrow, *Kingdom*, p. 74). But it seems unlikely that he would have been able to exercise any authority in northern Caithness (the above reference shows him witnessing a charter of the earl of Ross), where the Norse 'lawman' was still active: *Ork. Saga*, ed. Anderson, p. 200. A brieve of Alexander III is addressed *omnibus vicecomitibus, ballivis et ceteris hominibus suis de Moravia et de Catannie* (*Scone Liber*, no. 73). There were several sheriffs in the large province of Moray, and Caithness apparently came under the purview of Inverness. North of the Forth, sheriffs were confined particularly to areas where there were large quantities of royal demesne (*RRS*, i, p. 47), which makes it most unlikely that Caithness as yet had its own officer. By the end of the century, Caithness is called a *balliva*, although this reference probably dates from the period of English military rule (Stevenson, *Documents*, ii, p. 18, n. 1). This lack of evidence about royal officials in Caithness contrasts strongly with Orkney, where Earl Harald had to suffer Norwegian royal officials in his earldom after his participation in the rising of 1193. Indeed, the first indubitable royal bailiff we know of in Caithness was Sir Henry Sinclair in 1321: *Records of the Earldom of Orkney* (SHS, 1914), p. 7.

70. *RRS*, ii, no. 520; above, p. 30.

71. W. Fraser, *The Sutherland Book* (Edinburgh, 1892), iii, p. 2.

72. *Ibid.*, i, p. 9, quoting Lord Hailes. See also *ER*, i, p. lxi.

73. *Ork. Saga*, ed. Anderson, pp. 72, 188.

74. *Bannatyne Misc.*, iii, p. 77.

75. The date of the creation of the earldom is not known, but in 1275 there is a reference to *Willielmus clare memorie et Willielmus eius filius comites Sutherlandiae*: Fraser, *Sutherland*, iii, p. 7. William *dominus Sutherlandiae* was therefore created earl sometime after 1222, and perhaps in 1235 (*ibid.*, i, p. 12).

76. *Chron. Fordun*, ii, p. 274.

77. Anderson, *Early Sources*, ii, p. 483.

78. *Ibid.*, p. 484.

79. *Moray Reg.*, no. 110.

80. In two secondary sources Magnus is called son of Earl Gillebrigde (d. 1187 × 1189) (see Sir James Dalrymple, *Collections concerning the Scottish History* [Edinburgh, 1705], p. lxxiii), and son of Earl Gilchrist (d. 1206) (SRO Inventories of Titles, ii, Misc., Oliphant Family Charters). It is suggested by W. Fraser, *The Douglas Book* (Edinburgh, 1885), ii, p. 3,

that he was a son of Earl Malcolm, who was holding the earldom in 1232. The fact that he and two of his successors in the thirteenth century were all called Magnus strongly suggests that they were descended from the St Magnus half of the earldom, whose claim had been pressed by Harald Ungi against Harald Maddadson. A.W. Johnston thought that this claim may have passed to the Angus family through marriage with a sister of Harald Ungi (*Old Lore Misc.*, viii [1915], p. 52) rather than through marriage with the hostage daughter of Earl John mentioned above.

81. *Registrum Honoris de Morton* (Bannatyne Club, 1853), i, p. xxxv.

82. Above, n. 75.

83. C. Fraser-Mackintosh, *Invernessiana* (Inverness, 1875), facsimile, p. 29, where however the initials of the two earls have been misread as *E*.

84. SRO Invent. of Titles, ii, Misc., Oliphant Family Chrs., where it is said he was granted the earldom of *south* Caithness; and Dalrymple, *Collections*, p. lxxiii, where it is said he was granted the earldom of *north* Caithness. W.F. Skene, *Celtic Scotland*, 2nd edn. (Edinburgh, 1886–90), iii, p. 450, therefore thought that Magnus received only half of the earldom. See also *ER*, i, p. lxii, n. 1.

85. Lord Hailes, *Annals of Scotland*, 3rd edn. (Edinburgh, 1819), i, p. 164n., assumed that south Caithness was Sutherland, but this is unlikely since we know that Magnus lost all control over Sutherland. Moreover, we know that north Caithness owed £10 in annual rent, while in the next century the whole earldom owed £20, implying that south Caithness owed £10 also and was a separate entity: *ER*, i, p. 570.

86. Anderson, *Early Sources*, ii, p. 513.

87. *Moray Reg.*, no. 126.

88. Mary de Moravia married Reginald Cheyne *le fils* prior to 1269 (*ibid.*). Her sister Christian married William Federeth prior to 1286 (*ibid.*, no. 263). Their grandson gave his quarter of Caithness to Reginald Cheyne III: *RMS*, i, p. 601.

89. Skene, *Celtic Scotland*, iii, p. 450; J. Gray, *Sutherland and Caithness in Saga-Time* (Edinburgh, 1922), p. 106.

90. Printed in *Bannatyne Misc.*, iii, p. 43. P.A. Munch, *Symbolae ad Historiam Antiquiorem Rerum Norvegicarum* (Christiania, 1850), p. iii, described it as *ultimae linae diplomatis et ipsius genealogici ... comitum Sutherlandensium*.

91. Earl Magnus may have had a son or daughter who succeeded him for one and a half years and who died *virgo sine prole: Bannatyne Misc.*, iii, p. 43.

92. *Scots Pge.*, i, p. 166.

93. Earl Gilbert called his children Magnus and Matilda (*Bannatyne Misc.*, iii, p. 77), both of which were names in use by the Angus family, as we have seen. Earl Gilbert may indeed have been a member of the Ogilvy branch of the Angus family. His son Magnus witnessed a grant of land in free marriage to Alexander of Ogilvy prior to 1256: *Miscellany of the SHS*, iv (1926), p. 315, where however the editor has assumed, without any evidence, that this witness was Earl Magnus II. Gilbert's daughter Matilda had the patronage of the church of Cortachy in Angus (*Inchaffray Chrs.*, no. 86), which lay in Ogilvy territory.

94. There is only one instance — in the mid-fourteenth century — of the husband of an heiress being given the title, and he was a Swede: *Bannatyne Misc.*, iii, p. 77.

95. Anderson, *Early Sources*, ii, p. 587; cf. *Inchaffray Chrs.*, no. 86.

96. *Scots Pge.*, i, p. 167.

97. Above, p. 34.

98. Although Skene says the Caithness earldom's 'tenure was in accordance with the laws of Scotland' (*Celtic Scotland*, iii, p. 448), this was not so in the saga period. The eldest grandson of Malise, earl of Strathearn, Caithness and Orkney, is certainly said in the 'Genealogy of the Earls' to have succeeded (*c.* 1350) to the 'principall mans' of the earldom of Caithness 'be the law of Scotland and conswetude heritageble' (*Bannatyne Misc.*, iii, p. 79). But the situation in the second half of the fourteenth century was very different from that of the first half of the thirteenth century, when the inheritance customs governing the Orkney earldom were still prevalent. Moreover, this statement in the Genealogy is an attempt by the

fifteenth-century compiler to explain why the earls of that date no longer held the earldom of Caithness: see B.E. Crawford, 'The fifteenth-century "Genealogy of the Earls of Orkney" and its reflection of the contemporary political and cultural situation in the earldom', *Mediaeval Scandinavia*, X (1976), pp. 156–78.

99. K. Helle, 'Norwegian consolidation and expansion during the reign of King Håkon Håkonsson', *Orkney Miscellany*, v (1973), p. 8.

100. Anderson, *Early Sources*, ii, p. 615.

101. *ER*, i, pp. 13, 19.

102. Anderson, *Early Sources*, ii, p. 616.

103. *Norges Gamle Love indtil 1387*, 1 Raekke (Christiania, 1846–95), iii, p. 403.

104. *ER*, i, p. 20.

105. *Ibid.*, p. 19. As already mentioned (above, p. 32), it has been suggested that these amounts may have been connected with the events of 1202 and 1222. However, as they occur only in 1263 and 1266 — and appear moreover to represent a very heavy fine — they were more probably a contemporary means of ensuring loyalty.

106. Anderson, *Early Sources*, ii, p. 647.

107. 'The Saga of Hacon', trans. G. W. Dasent in *Icelandic Sagas*, iv, p. 375; Anderson, *Early Sources*, ii, p. 648.

108. *ER*, i, pp. 19–20.

109. 'The Saga of Hacon', p. 377; Anderson, *Early Sources*, ii, p. 649.

110. *ER*, i, p. 20.

111. *APS*, i, p. 420; *Diplom. Norv.*, viii, no. 9.

3

THE EARLY LORDS OF LAUDERDALE, DRYBURGH ABBEY AND ST ANDREW'S PRIORY AT NORTHAMPTON

Keith Stringer

It can easily be forgotten that the turbulent history of Anglo-Scottish relations in the later Middle Ages stands in sharp contrast to the many years of peace and friendly contact between the realms prior to Edward I's attempts to subdue Scotland in 1296. Despite occasional hostility and discord, Scots kings from David I to Alexander III enjoyed impressive personal and territorial connexions south of the Tweed, while a large minority of their lieges controlled estates in England and even in Ireland, Wales or France. In the twelfth century, it is indeed scarcely conceivable that the great advances set in train by King David I would have been possible unless he and his successors had been able to exploit fully their ties outwith the realm and attract into Scotland barons and knights, and churchmen and merchants, from England and other parts of the French-speaking world in order to strengthen and extend their rule. Remarkably, it is only in the last two decades or so that systematic scholarly attention has begun to be focused upon the seminal contribution made by this movement of peoples to the rise of the medieval kingdom of Scots. The rewards of this historiographical step forward are peculiarly valuable; and yet such concentration on the country of the colonists' destination has obscured the fact that the incoming lay dependants from England and northern France, though they generally lacked inherited riches, were often just as anxious to keep in close touch with the background from which they had sprung as they were to profit from their estates as tenants-in-chief in Scotland. Those royal vassals thus inclined were the forerunners, and sometimes the lineal predecessors, of the great Anglo-Scottish barons who were to play a major role in the life of England and Scotland in the thirteenth century, up to the 1290s the most formative period in the development of 'cross-Border' fief-holding. But just as there is a danger of underestimating the English or French attachments of the twelfth-century Bruces, Comyns, Giffards, Lindsays, Morvilles, Olifards, Stewarts, Vieuxponts and many others besides — and just as there is a risk of continuing to neglect the 'external' commitments of their often wealthier and better-documented counterparts after about 1200 — so we must not ignore the dynastic and tenurial links which families of native Scots descent were able to forge outside Scotland in a manner emulating that of the royal house itself. Although we have been taught that the Border had been stabilised along roughly its present line by the eleventh century, for such men the Tweed-Solway boundary was not the obstacle it would become during the years of protracted warfare from 1296. As this study will suggest, the Border can be shown to have been of little real significance in their private concerns and activities.[1]

One important aspect of the phenomenon of Anglo-Scottish proprietorship in both the twelfth and thirteenth centuries is that abbeys and priories on one side of the Border were endowed on the other with property for their own direct support, although as a rule these gains were at once modest and sited at considerable distances from the centres of their patrimonies. The following pages have their origin in the discovery of a series of *acta* among the muniments of two Northampton monasteries, the Cluniac priory of St Andrew and the Augustinian abbey of St James, which throw new light on the ecclesiastical ties that were developed in the wake of cross-Border feudal lordship.[2] These documents, edited in the Appendix to this chapter, help us to reconstruct in exceptional detail two interrelated stories, which share as their central theme the religious patronage of the Morville and Galloway families, as successive lords and ladies of Lauderdale. The first of these affairs was broached when Beatrice de Beauchamp granted the church of Bozeat in Northamptonshire to the influential Premonstratensian canons of Dryburgh, almost immediately after the abbey's foundation in 1150–2.[3] This, so far as is known, was the earliest interest Dryburgh would be offered in England, and it never became as prosperous there as its neighbours, the abbeys of Jedburgh, Kelso and Melrose, the priory of Coldstream, and the hospitals of Maison Dieu and St Edward at Berwick upon Tweed, whose respective English holdings included important assets just across the Border in Northumberland.[4] Bozeat church formed part of Beatrice's settlement in right of her marriage to Hugh de Morville, Constable of Scotland and Dryburgh's founder. But the Morville portion of Bozeat pertained to the great English honour of Huntingdon, which in the second quarter of the twelfth century was contested between the Scots crown and Earl Simon de Senlis II (d. 1153). Dryburgh was inevitably caught up in this controversy; and at about the time that Beatrice made her gift, Walter de Isel, a Senlis partisan intruded into Bozeat in an attempt to oust the pro-Scottish Morvilles, granted the same church of Bozeat to St James's abbey, Northampton.[5] Thus Dryburgh was in trouble over this remote Northamptonshire benefice from the start.

The abbey's subsequent connexion with Bozeat can be traced from the *acta* printed below. The surviving cartularies of St Andrew's priory, Northampton, supply the bulk of the relevant documents, including full versions of two important texts otherwise known only in the truncated form in which they appear in the late medieval Dryburgh cartulary, a poor and often unreliable manuscript. The St Andrew's cartularies also furnish us with the starting-point of our second tale. The endowments accumulated by the Cluniacs of Northampton, whose community had been established by the first Senlis lord of the Huntingdon honour in or shortly before 1100, were never sufficient to raise the priory to the level of a large ecclesiastical landowner, and it mostly depended upon local support of the kind that an unpretentious house of monks could usually expect to receive in medieval England. But one feature of its fairly meagre resources compels attention. Three of the priory's charters here published, as nos. 6, 7 and 8 in our series, show that St Andrew's attracted tiny gifts in south-eastern Scotland. In Berwickshire, Helen de Morville, the widow of Roland, lord of Galloway, bestowed upon the convent a ploughgate at Newbigging (in Lauder parish) between 1200 and 1210, and her son

Alan of Galloway (d. 1234) contributed an annual rent-charge of five marks to be drawn from Redpath (in Earlston), Glengelt (in Channelkirk) and *Grombelau* (unidentified). Helen's younger son, Earl Thomas of Atholl (d. 1231), added a yearly pension of two marks from 'Newland (*Nova Terra*) in Tweeddale', now represented by Harehope (in Eddleston), Peeblesshire.

These gifts of English property to Dryburgh and of Scottish property to St Andrew's provide an excellent illustration of the lack of concern for the Border in the affairs of two exceptionally prominent baronial dynasties in Scotland during the earlier Middle Ages; and in order to provide a fuller context for our documents we must delve into the history of the Morville and Galloway families, to uncover more about their activities and attitudes.[6]

We may begin early in the twelfth century when a small band of apparently landless Normans left their home at Morville, in the northern part of the Cotentin, in the hopes of making names for themselves on the other side of the English Channel. William de Morville crossed into Dorset under the patronage of the powerful Reviers-Vernon clan, his family's overlords in Normandy, and was installed as a minor landowner at Bradpole, between Lyme Regis and Dorchester.[7] Geoffrey and Herbert de Morville made a better move, setting themselves up in Yorkshire and the Midlands as prominent tenants of the honour of Mowbray.[8] Hugh de Morville was yet another of these Norman adventurers, and by far the most successful. His first notable appearance is about the early 1120s, when he was described in a charter by the future David I, king of Scots, as one of David's 'nobles and knights'.[9] King David secured for him a sizeable tenancy in the honour of Huntingdon, based on Bozeat and on Whissendine in Rutland. Hugh consolidated his local standing through his marriage to Beatrice, a daughter of the house of Beauchamp of Bedford; and rich rewards awaited him in Scotland itself, where David I raised Hugh up among the most prosperous and strongest lords of the kingdom, appointing him as *constabularius regis* and endowing him with the two great regional fiefs of Lauderdale, mainly in Berwickshire, and Cunningham in Ayrshire. Thanks to his attachment to the Scots monarch, Hugh had rapidly climbed from humble origins to the uppermost reaches of contemporary noble society.

As Hugh's career amply demonstrates, Scotland offered considerable opportunities to men of Norman-French stock in the first half of the twelfth century. Lauderdale comprises the whole valley of the Leader Water, and although that valley is for the most part narrow and steep-sided, it contains good, well-drained soils for cultivating grain and for rearing cattle and sheep.[10] This lordship, with the castle Hugh was to erect at Lauder and the abbey he was to found in Tweeddale at Dryburgh, a 'detached' portion of the Lauderdale fief, was no doubt the chief basis of his new-found substance; and it was at Dryburgh that Hugh would take the habit of a canon regular just before his death in 1162. Lauderdale, together with Cunningham and the Constableship of Scotland, then passed from Hugh to his son Richard, and subsequently to Richard's own son William. But in the case of the Morvilles, as of others, their swift rise to fame and power in Scotland did not mean that they automatically renounced their ties with the environment from which they had emerged. This is clearly seen in the marriage of Richard and the matrimonial careers of his sisters Maud and Ada, for all these children of Hugh the Constable married into the social milieu of Anglo-Norman England. By 1171 Ada was the wife of Roger Bertram, lord of Mitford in Northumberland;[11] and it is noteworthy, too, that the main stem of the Bertrams, though it first flourished in the Pays d'Auge, was strongly entrenched in the Cotentin, where it held property marching cheek by jowl with Morville, at Bricquebec and Magneville.[12] Maud's husband, William de Vieuxpont, was the senior representative of a Norman lineage which was already established in Scotland, but which also controlled several English fees; and William, it seems likely, eventually inherited his family's original home at Vieuxpont-en-Auge in Calvados.[13] By 1170 Richard de Morville had married Avice, daughter of William of Lancaster I, whose family, in spite of its Anglo-Scandinavian antecedents, had survived the Norman Conquest to occupy a position of weight in north-western England.[14] Moreover, if Avice was the product of William of Lancaster's second marriage, which is possible though by no means certain, she tied the Morvilles to one of the greatest Anglo-Norman dynasties, for in remarrying, William had allied himself to Gundreda, elder daughter of William de Warenne, second earl of Surrey (d. 1138).[15] It was Gundreda's younger sister, Ada de Warenne, to whom King David's son Earl Henry had been wed in 1139.

The point to stand out above all others, however, is that when Hugh de Morville had made his fortune in Scotland, he did not relinquish his existing, but far less imposing, possessions in England. For many years Hugh and his descendants retained this property in their own hands and lost no opportunity to augment it. In the medieval period marriage itself usually entailed a transfer of land, and with Avice of Lancaster Richard de Morville gained an estate, in the honour of Mowbray, in the West Riding of Yorkshire. It is difficult to gauge the true size of this establishment, but it was clearly a valuable accession. It embraced the manor, and presumably the castle, of Burton in Lonsdale and the large manor of Newby reaching across the foot of Ingleborough into Ribblesdale; the manor of Clapham, beside Newby, was probably within its bounds, while assets as far south as Eshton in Gargrave were possibly part of it. Richard's highly advantageous marriage thus confirmed not only his family's social but its territorial affiliations with England, and also had the effect of making him a near neighbour of his kinsmen who were already settled in the Mowbray honour.[16] Previously, Hugh de Morville, who had participated prominently in King David's invasions of northern England in the earlier part of Stephen's reign,[17] had received yet further substantial favour from the Scots crown when King David had endowed him with the lordship of the strategically vital district of north Westmorland. This interest of Hugh's had been forged in special circumstances, and it can hardly have seemed likely that it would survive an Anglo-Scottish *rapprochement*. Nevertheless, when in 1157 Malcolm IV surrendered Northumberland, Cumberland and Westmorland to King Henry II, the Angevin accepted Hugh's (? first-born) son and namesake as his tenant for the Westmorland fief, and made every effort to bind him closely in his service. In 1158 he gave the younger Hugh the mighty castle and manor of Knaresborough, one consequence of this being that just as Richard, Hugh's brother, was to become a neighbour of the Yorkshire Morvilles on one side of the Pennines, so Hugh became their neighbour on the other, for they held land at Bardsey, Collingham and Wothersome, within ten miles of Knaresborough.[18] From 1158 Hugh was assiduous in his attendance at the Angevin royal court in England and Normandy; he was commissioned as a king's justice in 1170, to hear the pleas of the crown at Carlisle and in Northumberland;[19] and when he entered the annals of general history as one of the assassins of Thomas Becket, he was described by Becket's chaplain and biographer, Herbert of Bosham, as a leading member of King Henry's baronial following.[20] Certainly, this son of an eminent noble family in Scotland had no difficulty in winning favour for himself — and eventual notoriety — under the English crown. But whether or not Hugh *junior* had originally been given both north Westmorland and Knaresborough as hereditary fiefs is unclear, and in any event his tenures were not fully incorporated within the family patrimony. Hugh the Constable's line was more successful in retaining its lands in Lonsdale and in the Huntingdon honour: it was this property that formed the core of the English inheritance of the Morville lords of Lauderdale.

The Yorkshire estates were far from the fees in the Huntingdon fief, and each of these enclaves was remote from Lauderdale and Cunningham. But there was no attempt to sell off or exchange the Lonsdale and Huntingdon possessions in order to strengthen the more valuable concentrations in Berwickshire and Ayrshire; there is no hint of a thorough reorganisation in the interests of greater economic and administrative efficiency. These holdings in England were obviously important to the Morvilles, and they maintained a firm stake in the English countryside by keeping some of the property in demesne. In Yorkshire, they seem to have controlled the castle at Burton in Lonsdale, to judge from its surviving motte, an exceptionally fine and commanding residence.[21] In the Huntingdon honour, they had a park, and doubtless a manor-house, at Whissendine.[22] We can reasonably suppose that Lauderdale, more so even than Cunningham, formed the nucleus of their estates, their principal sphere of influence and the economic centre of gravity of their wealth. But the Morvilles regularly travelled across the Tweed, conserving their lands in Lonsdale and in the English Midlands as carefully as they exploited their greater concerns in Scotland.[23] And before the family died out in the male line in 1196, all this property in the two kingdoms, no matter how acquired or how dispersed, had assumed the identity of a single complex of lordship, of one cross-Border inheritance.

War between the realms naturally threatened the unity of the estate. But that is far from saying that the intermittent bouts of Anglo-Scottish hostility in the twelfth century seriously disrupted this scheme of Morville landholding. Due to the wars of Stephen's reign, the Scots king had been dispossessed of the Huntingdon fief and the elder Hugh de Morville's fees in that estate taken from him. Yet it is instructive that about 1152 Beatrice de Beauchamp tried to dispose of property in the honour by granting the church of Bozeat to Dryburgh, for although her rights were at once challenged, the family was clearly not prepared to write off its Huntingdon manors as a total loss; and in fact Hugh was reinstated in them in 1157 when the honour was restored to Malcolm IV.[24] During the war of 1173–4 Richard de Morville also forfeited his English concerns. But after a new agreement had been reached between the crowns in the latter year, Richard managed to reclaim rents at Whissendine.[25] He and the Knights Templars reached an understanding on the assumption that his other Huntingdon assets would be recovered, and while it is true that Richard did not live to see this happen — he died in 1189 or 1190 — the delay was due more to the obstructive attitude of Earl David of Huntingdon than to continued disfavour at the English royal court.[26] In Yorkshire, he regained his 'land of Lonsdale' by redeeming it from the hands of William de Stuteville for 300 marks, a huge sum in those days and a measure of the high regard in which he held this property.[27] Thus whenever war undermined the predominantly peaceful relationship between the kingdoms, and the Morvilles were forced to opt for one side against the other, the English lands took second place to the Scottish. Yet in such circumstances they did not give up the Huntingdon and Lonsdale estates as lost for ever, and their landholding links with England, though temporarily parted, were not permanently severed.

A family's past achievements are not, of course, a firm guarantee of future prosperity, and if the Morvilles knew the sweetness of success, they also knew the bitterness of failure. The blow fell when William de Morville died in 1196 without issue to succeed him. In consequence, the continuity of his line was decisively broken, for William's nearest heir was his sister Helen, who carried the inheritance out of the family to her husband Roland, lord of Galloway. The Morville patrimony, both in England and in Scotland, was swallowed up within that of the Galloway dynasty. Nonetheless, it needs to be recognised that this merger of heritages represented a union between two families whose respective interests and concerns were basically identical. As the frontier of Norman expansion moved through Scotland, individual native magnates were won over to the new social order and incorporated within it. The lords of Galloway provide, even before 1196, an excellent illustration of how the personal and landed connexions of an old-established Scottish family were thereby extended, and of how closely these connexions could involve it with Anglo-Norman England. The bonds of kinship that undoubtedly existed between the Galloway line and the Norman and Angevin kings are best explained on the grounds that Roland's grandfather, Fergus, had married an illegitimate daughter of Henry Beauclerk.[28] Roland's father Uhtred had taken to wife Gunnilda daughter of Waltheof, lord of Allerdale in Cumberland, a marriage which placed at the family's disposal an estate at Torpenhow, between Cockermouth and Wigton.[29] The horizons of the lords of Galloway were not, therefore, confined to their own district of Scotland. They moved in the same social orbit as the Morvilles, sharing a similar outlook and the same disregard for the Border. In 1196 the Morvilles' Anglo-Scottish inheritance devolved into capable hands.

The creation of this new Morville-Galloway estate, one of the largest establishments ever to straddle the Tweed-Solway boundary, is of more than passing significance in the history of feudal Britain. The influence it carried was enormous, and Alan of Galloway, son and heir of Roland and Helen, had a memorable life in the two kingdoms. Although he was of Norse-Celtic descent on his father's side, and a great leader whose naval exploits on the western seaboard of Scotland won him respect in contemporary Norse circles,[30] Alan's deep absorption within the dominant Anglo-French milieu is not in question. It has been argued that he inspired and commissioned the Old French romance *Roman de Fergus*, and there is nothing inherently improbable in this opinion.[31] His wives were, successively, a sister of John de Lacy, constable of Chester and future earl of Lincoln, Margaret, eldest daughter of Earl David of Huntingdon, and Rose, daughter of Hugh de Lacy, earl of Ulster. In his public career, this lord of Lauderdale and Constable of Scotland was one of the sixteen named laymen by whose counsel King John claimed to have granted Magna Carta. His prominence in Anglo-Scottish politics also brought him the hope of an extensive Irish estate when John saw fit to deliver to his charge a huge block of territory in Ulster stretching from the River Foyle to the Glens of Antrim, together with Rathlin Island — although since this was a speculative royal grant, he may never have been able to stamp his lordship uniformly over these lands, and his tenure may not have lasted for very long. His brother Thomas, *jure uxoris* earl of Atholl, likewise gained importance as a proprietor in Ireland, and through John's grace became as much an English landowner as Alan, who himself added new estates in the southern kingdom, by marriage and in other ways, to buttress those which had descended to him from the Morvilles.[32] Such accumulations of wealth graphically demonstrate how the interests of a 'Normanised' Scottish family might transcend the land and sea boundaries between one part of the British Isles and another.

Let us move on a stage further. The Morville-Galloways were like any other medieval magnates in that the claims of family and of piety, and the need to attach to themselves a strong body of lay supporters, imposed recurrent demands upon their resources. Now, since distance and frontiers occupied no central place in the Morville mind, it does not surprise that the Morvilles readily involved others from outside Scotland in the organisation of their Scottish property. When Ada de Morville married Roger Bertram she brought to the Bertrams an interest at Nenthorn, and thus the lords of Mitford extended their concerns from Northumberland into Berwickshire.[33] Again, many were the Norman or English vassals who as Morville dependants shared in, and contributed to, the family's prominence in the Scots realm. Most notably, the great dynasties of Sinclair (St Clair) and Haig (Hague), whose origins lie in western Normandy, can trace their first advancement as Scottish lairds to Morville support.[34] Ralph Masculus and his family, ancestors of the Maules, were also intimately associated with the Morvilles in Scotland.[35] None of these three lineages can be linked directly with its patrons' estates south of the Tweed. But Alan of Clapham, another Morville follower in Scotland, took his name from the Yorkshire village of Clapham, in the shadow of Ingleborough, in which he held lordship and with which his family was still connected in the sixteenth century.[36] His father occurs as the priest of Clapham at about the time that Burton in Lonsdale and adjoining interests, which probably included Clapham, passed into Morville hands through Richard de Morville's Lancaster marriage, and Alan himself later gained rights at Addinston, four miles north of Lauder, by grant of William de Morville.[37] He succeeded Henry de St Clair as the baronial sheriff of Lauder; then, since he had prepared for his old age by buying himself into the spiritual fellowship of Furness abbey, he apparently retired to end his days as a monk of this Lancashire monastery.[38] But his descendants figure in Scottish sources and, as the Clephanes, they are still with us today.

It therefore seems quite plain that the Morvilles were more than prominent barons in Scotland who also had lands in England and ties with northern France, for they deliberately manipulated their network of contacts beyond the Scottish kingdom in order to attract others from the Anglo-Norman world to share in their own cross-Border concerns.[39] The information about Alan of Clapham, which appears to show how a vassal infeft in Scotland was recruited from the lord's property south of the Border, is especially enlightening. Furthermore, Beatrice de Beauchamp had had property settled upon her, as wife of Hugh de Morville the Constable, not only in the Huntingdon honour but also in Berwickshire.[40] These lords of Lauderdale regarded their estates as a single entity, and it was natural for them to create close bonds between their English and Scottish possessions.

The lords of Galloway, for their part, were simultaneously building up a clientage of English or Anglo-continental followers, some of whom, like Alan of Clapham, emerged as Anglo-Scottish landowners in their own right. These Galloway supporters — they included the Berkeleys, the Campanias and the Ripleys — did not hail from one region alone. But many (as may indeed be observed of the Morville entourage) were connected with English Cumbria: for example, Richard son of Truite, who had some claim to Gamblesby and Glassonby in Cumberland and who received a knight's feu at New Abbey in Kirkcudbrightshire from Uhtred of Galloway;[41] David son of Terri of Upper Denton on the Cumberland-Northumberland border, who gained Anwoth near Gatehouse of Fleet from Roland of Galloway;[42] and Thomas son of Cospatric, lord of Workington, whom Roland established at Colvend (formerly Kylwen, Culwen), from which holding Thomas's line was to take its family name of Curwen.[43] Moreover, after 1196 numerous Morville vassals or their kinsfolk passed into Roland's following, and many went on to serve in Alan of Galloway's. To pursue a particular case, the Maules in the person of Roger Masculus acquired half of Colvend through loyalty to their new masters, and it may well have been this connexion with south-western Scotland which enabled them to expand their interests into Ulster.[44]

These comments lead directly to an analysis of the ways cross-Border contacts were also extended and intensified by the Morville-Galloways in their capacity as patrons of religion, which serves in turn to provide the immediate context for detailed commentary on the *acta* appended to this study. Dryburgh abbey had itself been colonised by canons sent out from Alnwick in Northumberland;[45] subsequently, in 1218, the Gallovidian house at Tongland, another member of the Premonstratensian community in Scotland, was begun as an offshoot of the abbey founded by William of Lancaster II at Cockersand in Lancashire. Dryburgh's endowments as provided by Hugh the Constable, although they naturally comprised property mainly in his Scottish lordships, included assets at Great Asby and Maulds Meaburn in Westmorland.[46] Next to nothing is known about Tongland's resources: it cannot even be shown for certain that Alan of Galloway, the great-nephew of William of Lancaster II, was its founder.[47] But it is nevertheless evident that Alan's Galloway predecessors had distributed their pious gifts widely, and that several of their grants had involved English corporations in the possession of reserves in Scotland. The Knights Hospitallers in England, St Peter's hospital at York and two Cumberland monasteries, Holm Cultram abbey and St Bees priory — all these had acquired rights north of the Solway Firth by about 1200 thanks to the support of the lords of Galloway.[48] Conversely, Uhtred of Galloway had allowed Holyrood abbey to share in the benefits of his marriage to Gunnilda of Allerdale by granting to the canons the church of Torpenhow.[49]

Beatrice de Beauchamp's gift of Bozeat church to Dryburgh and the conveyances to St Andrew's priory at Northampton by Helen de Morville, Alan and Earl Thomas therefore belong to a well-established pattern of cross-Border religious patronage manifest in Morville and Galloway sources alike. We have already seen something of the circumstances of Beatrice's grant; and the steps leading up to the other benefactions can be elucidated in such detail as is remarkable in this period. In November 1200, after having accompanied William the Lion to a conference with King John at Lincoln, Roland of Galloway rode through the heart of the Huntingdon honour to Northampton, in order to prosecute the legal proceedings he and Helen had recently initiated, by offering 500 marks to have justice, in a bid to recover those lands in the honour sequestered from Richard de Morville in 1173–4.[50] But Roland died at Northampton a few days short of Christmas, and his servants, anxious for an immediate interment, arranged for his burial in the priory church of St Andrew.[51] In past years, St Andrew's had received important support from tenants of the Huntingdon estate, while the Senlis and Scottish lords of the honour cultivated the status of *advocati* or special protectors and feudal superiors of the priory.[52] But until Roland's death neither the Galloways nor their Morville predecessors had taken a direct interest in the house. It would, however, have been a perfectly normal reaction for Roland's wife and his sons to have made thank-offerings to St Andrew's for the honourable burial Roland had been given, and we may assume that their gifts in Lauderdale and Tweeddale were intended primarily for this purpose.

We have come a long way in pursuit of the early lords of Lauderdale, and the journey, beginning in *Basse-Normandie*, has taken us across almost every major boundary in Britain. The ability to amass important Anglo-Scottish interests is the central theme in their affairs, and here their activity matches that of other leading families in Scotland during this age. To look no further than their neighbours in Berwickshire, the house of Cospatric, earls of Dunbar, the Lindsays of Earlston, the Stewarts of Legerwood, and the Vieuxponts of Horndean and Langton not only were ensconced elsewhere in southern Scotland but also kept a tight hold of property in England, which they occasionally managed to extend through skilful exploitation of the marriage market and success in winning political rewards.[53] And if space permitted, it could be shown that in dispensing the patronage at its disposal this influential group of Anglo-Scottish landlords was as little concerned about the Border as were the Morville-Galloways.[54]

What seemed satisfactory to the patron was not necessarily a suitable arrangement for the grantee; but the practical strains these men sometimes imposed on their beneficiaries were not as severe as might be imagined. Lay lords, both great and small, were used to moving about their estates in the company of their followings, and if they wished to extend their itineraries in order to supervise directly remote assets in another country, and profit from the opportunities of future advancement which such perquisites offered, that could be done without too much hardship or inconvenience. An abbot or prior might find it difficult to visit isolated estates as frequently as a lay landlord, and in the last analysis his aim as an administrator was to mobilise forms of arable or pastoral enterprise to satisfy the needs of a community which obviously did not perambulate from one centre to another. But the problem of running possessions located at great distances from a monastery was by no means insurmountable. Direct management could be attempted by sending out personnel to oversee properties on the spot; sometimes a grange or monastic farm might be set up, and in especially favourable circumstances granges developed into small regular convents. By contrast, as many as possible of the difficulties of administration could be avoided by leasing out peripheral assets to some other proprietor for fixed annual payments in cash or in kind. All these methods of exploitation, which can be found in many large monastic lordships by the twelfth century, had a place in cross-Border ecclesiastical proprietorship.[55] Yet every now and then an isolated piece of real estate, or a rent-charge imposed on some far-distant property, was the cause of more trouble than it was worth, and administrative pressures forced monastic landlords to review their position.

Dryburgh abbey quickly found itself confronted by intractable managerial problems over its rights at Bozeat. Soon after Walter de Isel had disputed the convent's claims to the parish church by granting it to St James's abbey at Northampton, an understanding was arrived at whereby the benefice was to be held in perpetuity of Dryburgh by the English house, which undertook to pay, after the existing incumbent Edgar had died, a small annual pension. For as long as it was necessary to provide for Edgar's son Adelard, this was set at twenty shillings and one bezant, or a further two shillings in lieu; after Adelard's death, St James's was to render a perpetual rent of two and a half marks, which would be collected yearly by Dryburgh's messenger (App., no. 1).

Richard de Morville confirmed this agreement between 1162 and 1177 (App., no. 3);[56] and from the administrative viewpoint Dryburgh had some cause to be pleased with the compromise. A monastery would naturally have found it less impracticable to collect a predetermined emolument, however remote, than to deal at first hand with the revenues of a single living sited many miles away. Yet even the collection of fixed rents could be fraught with difficulties. Most obviously, non-payment often made their administration a costly and taxing business. When in about 1250 John of Plessey gave Coldstream priory forty shillings from the profits of his mill of Plessey (in Stannington), Northumberland, to be received in two annual instalments by the nuns' attorney, the priory took the precaution of stipulating that John and his heirs were to answer for its expenses in recovering arrears, should they withhold the money.[57] In about 1238, the legal advisers of the English order of Sempringham had recommended more elaborate safeguards over the forty marks owed to it each year by Paisley abbey. The master, canons and nuns of the order formally insisted upon a penalty payment for default of £20; that Paisley place itself under the jurisdiction of the bishop of Glasgow, who was empowered to coerce the abbey through spiritual sanctions; and that Paisley should have no right of redress 'except when there is such war in the land that the money cannot be carried safely'.[58] Furthermore, whenever revenue had to be collected from another centre a dependable envoy had normally to be found,[59] and the cost of dispatching such a courier could easily prove greater than the income at stake. Thus when in 1202 Kelso abbey relinquished to Lanercost priory its rights to the church of Lazonby in Cumberland for compensation payments of two bezants, it was at pains to avoid sending envoys on lengthy and difficult journeys across the Cheviots by arranging for Lanercost to hand over the money on St James's day at Roxburgh fair.[60] A little later, Lanercost itself struck a blow for effective management when it specified that the annual rent of one pound of cumin owed by Robert son of Walter de Conkilton for property at Fenton and Kingston, in the parish of Dirleton in East Lothian, should be paid at Carlisle fair.[61]

No arrangement such as this, however, could be reached by Dryburgh with St James's; and the difficulties caused by distance were posed in an acute form. The canons, well aware of their disadvantages, swiftly complained of having been 'often inconvenienced by the length of the journey to collect the pension in person' (App., no. 2). Nevertheless, efficient revenue collection was evidently important to the abbot and convent, and it is to their credit as administrators that an effort was made to minimise their problems. By the mid-1190s at the latest, they had appointed the abbey of Sulby as their agent in obtaining the Bozeat income each year (App., no. 2). The sources do not allow us to test the effectiveness of this device, but since Sulby was only fifteen miles north-west of Northampton, it was admirably placed to procure revenue from St James's on Dryburgh's behalf. We also know that this sort of administrative arrangement had its parallel elsewhere, perhaps especially among houses of the same religious order;[62] and here it is noteworthy that Sulby belonged like Dryburgh to the *ordo Premonstratensis*.

The Sulby expedient, then, may have helped to secure the Bozeat pension for Dryburgh. But in fact the abbey did not have to look far for an alternative and more efficacious solution to its difficulties. Since many English as well as Scottish monasteries were troubled by isolated assets across the Border, the possibility existed of individual houses combining to make mutually advantageous exchanges; and Dryburgh took a preliminary step in this direction in 1193, when the canons were able to use part of the Bozeat income to rid themselves of a dispute concerning one of their properties in Scotland. This controversy originated in Alexander de St Martin's gift to Dryburgh of Bangly (in Haddington), East Lothian, which had been made by 1174 at the instigation of Richard de Morville and in reconciliation with him for the death of his brother Malcolm, whom Adulf de St Martin had accidentally killed while hunting.[63] At the time of Alexander's grant, Richard had also insisted on the proviso that Dryburgh should pay ten shillings *per annum*, as a rent-charge on half a ploughgate in Bangly, to the Augustinian abbey of St Mary *de*

Pratis at Leicester, where Malcolm de Morville had been buried (App., no. 4).[64] Here, therefore, is yet another Anglo-Scottish tie to be attributed to the Morvilles; and once again we see the importance a family attached to a monastery chosen as a burial place for one of its number. But the Dryburgh canons subsequently neglected their obligations to Leicester abbey and held back their payments. The matter was ventilated on 22 February 1193 before a 'general chapter' of the Premonstratensian order in England, held at Newhouse abbey in Lincolnshire under the presidency of Abbot William of Licques (dép. Pas-de-Calais), who was then acting for the abbot of Prémontré as his duly appointed commissary. Leicester thereupon renounced its interest in Bangly, in exchange for a yearly render of five shillings, which Dryburgh instructed the abbot and convent of St James's to hand over to Leicester out of the Bozeat pension (App., nos. 4, 5).

In accepting this compromise, the Dryburgh canons had good cause for satisfaction. Firstly, they had reinforced their rights within a tenancy which, though not close to the abbey itself, was conveniently situated in an area of south-eastern Scotland where they were developing a substantial estate, particularly in and around Dirleton, Gullane and Saltoun.[65] Secondly, they had strengthened this valuable grouping at little cost to themselves, for although they were still duty-bound to pay rent to Leicester, albeit at half the original rate, this commitment was to be met in the future by means of part of a far-off and troublesome pension. Dryburgh had accordingly learned that the Bozeat income, distant though it was, could be of value in promoting its Scottish concerns; and this lesson was to be remembered in 1243, when the abbey all but put an end to its administrative difficulty in Northamptonshire.

The convent did so by agreement with St Andrew's priory at Northampton. No records exist to show how St Andrew's had earlier responded to the challenge of managing the ploughgate it had been given in Newbigging by Helen de Morville, and of drawing the annual rents conveyed by her sons. At Newbigging, where its interest was far too small to warrant the creation of a grange, the priory's arrangements were presumably similar to those of another Northamptonshire corporation, the hospital of St James and St John at Brackley, whose assets in Scotland were leased out for specified terms to local men, who thus bore full, though temporary, responsibility for administering and maintaining them.[66] But in 1243 St Andrew's gave in perpetuity to Dryburgh the Newbigging ploughgate, while the canons authorised the priory to take the entire Bozeat pension from St James's each year, to retain two marks for itself, and to deliver to Leicester abbey the five shillings' annual rent assigned to that house in 1193. The residue of twenty pence was to remain at Dryburgh's disposal, and await collection 'by a certain envoy of the abbot and convent' (App., no. 9). The abbot of Dryburgh completed the agreement by writing to the abbot of St James's and eliciting his undertaking to pay the Bozeat moneys to St Andrew's (App., nos. 10, 11). Regrettably, there is no means of telling whether or not the Dryburgh canons ever attempted to obtain the paltry twenty pence reserved for their future use. Nor do we know the fate of the Scottish rents given to St Andrew's by Alan of Galloway and Earl Thomas, which are not mentioned in the covenant with Dryburgh. It may be that both parties, in theory if not in practice, remained Anglo-Scottish proprietors and that they shared, despite all the drawbacks, a reluctance to liquidate wholly their rights beyond the Border. But each house had nevertheless acted decisively to reconstruct its accretions across the Tweed into more satisfactory units of lordship. In Dryburgh's case, the Newbigging property formed a serviceable addition to the canons' holdings in Lauderdale north of their *grangia* at Kedslie.[67] The major part of what remained out of a distant income in England had been exchanged for a new estate in land which constituted, as did Bangly, a useful extension of the abbey's patrimony; at small loss to itself, Dryburgh had virtually succeeded in substituting a viable administrative and economic proposition for one that was not.

The historian of baronial families in earlier medieval Scotland has often found it easy to neglect the concerns that many members of this group maintained beyond the Scottish kingdom. The assumption is that the Tweed-Solway boundary formed, to all intents and purposes, a sharp dividing line cutting across the range of baronial interests. This essay has attempted, albeit on a modest scale, to beat down this supposed barrier. While it does not pretend to provide a detailed history of the Morvilles and their Galloway successors, enough will have been said to show that these magnates were not only large landowners in Scotland. Their territorial power stretched deep into England, and Alan of Galloway's commitments in Ireland remind us of the wider opportunities that were open to ambitious men in thirteenth-century Britain. These lords of Lauderdale would not have regarded themselves as simply 'Scottish' barons. If anything, they belonged to a larger baronial society of Norman-French descent or inclination whose only frontier that clearly mattered was the one set by the limits of its own expansion. It is impossible to draw firm lines between their extensive concerns.

What does not mislead is to stress that England and Scotland represented the main area of activity of the Morville-Galloways; and something has been revealed of the Anglo-Scottish contacts forged in their shadow. Politically they were important figures, and favours were bestowed upon them by the kings of both realms. We have also seen that although periodic warfare threatened the Morvilles' position as landowners in the two kingdoms, it did not destroy their cross-Border estate. Ultimately it was the failure to produce male issue which caused the family's downfall, yet its widespread interests survived within the framework of a bigger Galloway patrimony. In 1234 Alan of Galloway also died without a male heir to succeed him and his massive lordship, excluding the Irish lands, was dispersed among his three daughters. Their husbands, Earl Roger de Quincy, John de Balliol and William de Forz, were consequently promoted to the very forefront of the Anglo-Scottish baronage of their day.[68] Thus, in the earlier Middle Ages the cross-Border bond could outlast a family's inability to ensure the continuity of its line as well as the intermittent warfare between the kingdoms; and once that bond had been established it was constantly being renewed through the exercise of patronage. To be sure, administrative problems might result in attempts to round off gains across the Border. But when Dryburgh abbey concluded its agreement with St Andrew's priory at Northampton in 1243, the canons had held on to their

Northamptonshire income, slight though it was, for nearly a hundred years; and where the difficulties of management were less pressing there was no need to resort to exchanges, or sales. It was only from 1296, when war between England and Scotland became more common than peace and the pulse of national feeling quickened on each side of the Tweed, that the tradition of proprietorship across the Border was really stretched to breaking point. And even then, although the baronial and knightly links generally proved to be less resilient than the ecclesiastical,[69] it would be wrong to envisage a sudden dislocation of the pattern. Jedburgh abbey, a Scottish monastery more richly endowed in England than Dryburgh, did not relinquish the church of Arthuret in Cumberland until 1333.[70] The canons retained rights at Abbotsley in Huntingdonshire until 1340, when they gave the advowson and an associated pension to William of Felton, 'for his faithful counsel and aid'.[71] They may not have finally lost possession of the manor of Lee Hall (in Bellingham), Northumberland, until 1375, and they still enjoyed other English holdings — unspecified in the sources — as late as 1400.[72] Admittedly, the sheer longevity of Jedburgh's Anglo-Scottish ties was exceptional; but it was not in fact unique. For almost two centuries after the outbreak of the wars of independence Durham cathedral priory battled with remarkable success to preserve its connexions with Berwickshire. Yet even the pertinacious Durham community was eventually obliged to recognise that times had changed, and in May 1462 the 'last English monks on Scottish soil' were at last ejected from their cell at Coldingham.[73] In the twelfth and thirteenth centuries many influences combined to draw England and Scotland close together, but the Anglo-Scottish bonds maintained and created by great lords like the Morville-Galloways could not survive a drastic breakdown in friendly political relations between the realms.

NOTES

1. I have attempted to take the main arguments of this essay a stage further in Stringer, *Earl David*, esp. Ch. 9.

2. My thanks are due to Dr Grant Simpson for helping to bring these sources to my attention, and for leave to print my edition of no. 8 below, a charter of Earl Roger de Quincy which was first edited by him in his unpublished Ph.D. thesis, Simpson, 'RQ'.

3. Lawrie, *Charters*, no. 219 (= *Dryb. Lib.*, no. 93).

4. *Northumberland Hist.*, vi, pp. 377–8; xi, pp. 117, 182–3, 189–90, 281–2; xii, pp. 85, 97; xiv, pp. 120–1; xv, p. 239; *Coldstream Chartulary*, nos. 27–8, 53–5; *CDS*, iii, no. 962.

5. BL Harl. Chart. 52.C.4. The extreme date-limits of Isel's grant, *c.*1150 × 1153, are determined by the foundation of St James's (J.C. Dickinson, *The Origins of the Austin Canons and their Introduction into England* [London, 1950], p. 125, n. 3) and by the confirmation charter of Earl Simon II (BL MS Cott. Tib. E. v, fo. 88r).

6. Professor G.W.S. Barrow's recent contributions to a history of the Morville lords of Lauderdale in *The Scottish Genealogist*, xxv, no. 4 (1978), pp. 100–3, and Barrow, *Era*, pp. 70–83, which are indispensable, have been cited sparingly. Normally, therefore, I have annotated my account of the Morvilles only where additional material is offered in evidence.

7. Barrow, *Kingdom*, pp. 323–4; Loyd, *Origins*, p. 70; *Book of Seals*, no. 178; *Cartulary of Buckland Priory*, ed. F.W. Weaver (Somerset Rec. Soc., 1909), no. 227.

8. The suggestion in *Charters of the Honour of Mowbray, 1107–1191*, ed. D.E. Greenway (London, 1972), p. xxxiv, n. 1, that the Morvilles of the Mowbray honour hailed from Morville, dép. Manche, is confirmed by the surname of one of their tenants in Warwickshire, Roger de Neuham (de Niweham), corrupted from Néhou, which lies seven kilometres south of Morville and was the *caput* of the honour of Vernon in Normandy. The tenurial link between Néhous and Morvilles in England was to be reproduced in Scotland: Barrow, *Era*, pp. 79, 189.

9. Lawrie, *Charters*, no. 46.

10. *Land Utilisation Survey*, ed. L.D. Stamp, part 14 (Berwickshire), by P.C. Waite (London, 1941), pp. 10, 16–17.

11. *Dryb. Lib.*, nos. 92, 150; *RRS*, ii, no. 65.

12. *Recueil des actes des ducs de Normandie de 911 à 1066*, ed. M. Fauroux (Mémoires de la Société des Antiquaires de Normandie, 1961), no. 205; *Cartulaires de Saint-Ymer-en-Auge et de Bricquebec*, ed. C. Bréard (Société de l'Histoire de Normandie, 1908), pp. 183ff. The senior Bertram line maintained a residence at Bricquebec, the headquarters of its Cotentin estates: F. Delacampagne, 'Seigneurs, fiefs et mottes du Cotentin', *Archéologie médiévale*, xii (1982), p. 195.

13. Stringer, *Earl David*, p. 128.

14. *Pipe Roll 16 Henry II*, p. 53; G. Washington, 'The parentage of William de Lancaster, lord of Kendal', *TCWAAS*, new ser., lxii (1962), pp. 95–100.

15. *Comp. Pge.*, xii, II, p. 362; *EYC*, viii, p. 10.

16. The main sources for reconstructing the dimensions of Richard de Morville's Yorkshire estates are *EYC*, ix, no. 43, and *Coucher Book of Furness Abbey*, ed. J.C. Atkinson and J. Brownbill (Chetham Soc., 1886–1919), II, ii, pp. 301–2, 304–5, 310–11, 334–7, 417. That adjacent lands, pertaining in fact to the Percy fee, were held by his kinsmen, one of whom was also called Richard de Morville, increases the difficulty of identifying the full extent of his property: see, e.g., *EYC*, xi, no. 253.

17. E.g., Lawrie, *Charters*, no. 119. Cf. also Richard of Hexham, *De Gestis Regis Stephani*, ed. R. Howlett in *Chronicles of the Reigns of Stephen, Henry II, and Richard I* (Rolls Ser., 1884–9), iii, p. 178.

18. For the younger Hugh de Morville as lord of north Westmorland see K.J. Stringer, *History of the Berwickshire Naturalists' Club*, xl (1974), p. 37; Barrow, *Era*, p. 73. For the Morvilles of Bardsey, etc., SRO RH 6/13; *EYC*, xi, no. 297; *Charters of the Honour of Mowbray*, ed. Greenway, no. 347 and p. 264.

19. R.W. Eyton, *Court, Household, and Itinerary of King Henry II* (London, 1878), pp. 33, 53, 68, 78, 145, 150; *Pipe Roll 16 Henry II*, pp. 33, 52.

20. Herbert of Bosham, *Vita Sancti Thomae*, ed. J.C. Robertson in *Materials for the History of Thomas Becket* (Rolls Ser., 1875–85), iii, p. 487.

21. S. Moorhouse, 'Excavations at Burton-in-Lonsdale: a reconsideration', *Yorkshire Archaeol. Journal*, xliii (1971), pp. 85–98.

22. *CurRR*, vii, p. 189. For the possible site of the Morville manor-house see *VCH Rutland*, i, p. 117.

23. Skeleton itineraries of Richard de Morville and Hugh, his father, can be compiled from the following: Lawrie, *Charters; RRS*, i; ii. They show them often travelling between Scotland and England in the Scots king's household, and we may be sure that both men were attending to their own concerns in the two kingdoms as well as to the concerns of the king of Scots.

24. Cf. *CurRR*, vi, p. 274.

25. *Ibid.*, vii, p. 189.

26. *Ibid*; Stringer, *Earl David*, p. 114.

27. Another private quarrel, that of Mowbray *versus* Stuteville, had complicated Richard's position: cf. *Charters of the Honour of Mowbray*, pp. xxviii–xxxi. Richard had raised the money shortly before he died by selling all the pasture of Birkwith and Selside, in the parish of Horton in Ribblesdale, to Furness abbey. See *Coucher Book of Furness*, ed. Atkinson and Brownbill, II, ii, pp. 334–5; but note the different terms in *ibid.*, pp. 335–7.

28. Barrow, *Bruce*, p. 36, n. 2.

29. *St Bees Reg.*, p. ix, n. 1.

30. Cf. *Konunga Sögur: Sagaer om Sverre og Hans Efterfølgere*, ed. C.R. Unger (Christiania, 1873), p. 332.

31. M.D. Legge, *Anglo-Norman Literature and its Background* (Oxford, 1963), pp. 161–2; adding *Arthurian Literature in the Middle Ages: A Collaborative History*, ed. R.S. Loomis (Oxford, 1959), pp. 377–9.

32. For further references and a fuller discussion of points raised in this paragraph see Stringer, *Earl David*, pp. 183–5.

33. *Dryb. Lib.*, no. 150.

34. Barrow, *Kingdom*, pp. 317–18, 324; *idem*, *Era*, pp. 79–80.

35. See Appendix, no. 3 and comment.

36. *Coucher Book of Furness*, II, ii, pp. 299–300, 306–7; H. Speight, *The Craven and North-West Yorkshire Highlands* (London, 1892), pp. 147–8.

37. *Coucher Book of Furness*, II, ii, p. 306; *Chartulary of Cockersand Abbey*, ed. W. Farrer (Chetham Soc., 1898–1909), III, ii, p. 968. An abstract of William de Morville's charter for Addinston survives in *APS*, vii, p. 153. The same source provides evidence of a further four charters in favour of Alan of Clapham, including a grant and a confirmation by Alan of Galloway.

38. Barrow, *Kingdom*, p. 298; *Coucher Book of Furness*, II, ii, pp. 306–7.

39. More fully on the Morville lay following see the works by Barrow cited at n. 6 above.

40. Lawrie, *Charters*, nos. 219, 238.

41. T.H.B. Graham, 'The sons of Truite', *TCWAAS*, new ser., xxiv (1924), pp. 43–9; *Wigtownshire Chrs.*, pp. xix–xxi.

42. *Ibid.*, p. xxiii.

43. *Ibid.*, p. xxv; F.W. Ragg, 'De Culwen', *TCWAAS*, new ser., xiv (1914), pp. 343–432.

44. *St Bees Reg.*, no. 60. One Richard Masculus, an associate of Richard de Morville and Roland of Galloway, occurs as an Irish landowner through the patronage of John de Courcy (*Melrose Liber*, i, nos. 94, 108; *St Bees Reg.*, pp. 521, 525). He can possibly be identified as the *nepos* of William Masculus, lord of Fowlis Easter in Angus, who is mentioned in *St Andrews Liber*, p. 41. Richard son of Truite's son and namesake also served Courcy in Ulster: *St Bees Reg.*, pp. xiii, 521. John de Courcy's links with Scotland include his marriage to a great-granddaughter of Fergus of Galloway and a connexion with Dryburgh abbey: see *ibid.*, p. xii, n. 2, with *Scots Pge.*, iv, p. 136; Appendix, no. 9, comment.

45. Eustace fitz John, who founded Alnwick abbey in 1147–8, had supported King David's invasions of northern England in the 1130s. It is interesting to find in Eustace's following, or at the side of his Vesci successors (Anglo-Scottish proprietors from 1193), men who were connected in one way or another with the Morvilles. Note Ralph Masculus and members of the families of Malchael, Maltalent (Maitland) and Ros: G. Tate, *The History of the Borough, Castle, and Barony of Alnwick* (Alnwick, 1868–9), ii, app., pp. viiiff. It seems probable that the Richard Maltalent who served as steward to the Vescis in Northumberland about the mid-thirteenth century was one and the same as the founder of the line of Maitland of Thirlestane, in the lordship of Lauderdale. This appears to have escaped the notice of the family historians, though it has been suggested, in *Scots Pge.*, v, pp. 278–9, that Richard Maltalent of Thirlestane was associated with Chevington, near Alnwick.

46. *Dryb. Lib.*, nos. 249–51, 253–4, with Barrow, *Scottish Genealogist*, xxv (1978), p. 102. It is unfortunate that Dryburgh's interest in these English properties cannot be traced further than the papal bulls confirming them to the abbey.

47. Cowan (Easson), *Religious Houses*, p. 103. Thomas son of Cospatric had founded Shap abbey in Westmorland, the full sister-house of Tongland, by 1201.

48. *Holyrood Liber*, no. 54; *CChR*, iii, pp. 91–2; *Holm Cultram Reg.*, nos. 120–1, 128; *St Bees Reg.*, no. 62.

49. *Holyrood Liber*, no. 24.

50. Roger of Howden, *Chronica*, ed. W. Stubbs (Rolls Ser., 1868–71), iv, p. 142; *Rotuli de Oblatis et Finibus in Turri Londinensi asservati*, ed. T.D. Hardy (Rec. Comm., 1835), p. 84.

51. Howden, *Chronica*, iv, p. 145; cf. Cambridge, Corpus Christi College, MS 281 (2) (Chronicle of St Andrew's priory, Northampton), fo. 24v.

52. Earl Simon de Senlis II is described as the *advocatus* of St Andrew's in *Facsimiles of Early Charters from Northamptonshire Collections*, ed. F.M. Stenton (Northamptonshire Rec. Soc., 1930), no. 55. Further, Barrow, *Kingdom*, p. 174.

53. The English estates of the earls of Dunbar have been extensively discussed in *Northumberland Hist.*, vii, pp. 29ff.

54. In catering for their spiritual welfare, the Stewarts made several gifts of Scottish property to English corporations: e.g., Walter son of Alan (d. 1177) endowed St Peter's hospital, York, with rights at Legerwood (*CChR*, iii, p. 90; *RRS*, ii, no. 103); and Alan son of Walter instructed Melrose abbey to pay to its sister-house of Warden in Bedfordshire four shillings annually from the rent he was owed for Mauchline, Ayrshire (*Cartulary of the Abbey of Old Wardon*, ed. G.H. Fowler [Bedfordshire Historical Rec. Soc., 1930), no. 311 [1189 × 1194]. See also below, p. 168.

55. Stringer, *Earl David*, pp. 203ff. More generally see D. Knowles, *The Religious Orders in England* (Cambridge, 1948–59), i, pp. 32ff; C. Platt, *The Monastic Grange in Medieval England* (London, 1969).

56. Shortly afterwards, the bishop of Lincoln confirmed Bozeat church to St James's *in proprios usus*: BL MS Cott. Tib. E. v, fo. 91v. Further, J. Bridges, *The History and Antiquities of Northamptonshire* (Oxford, 1791), ii, p. 161.

57. *Coldstream Chartulary*, no. 55.

58. G.W.S. Barrow, 'The Gilbertine house at Dalmilling', *Collections of the Ayrshire Archaeol. and Natural History Soc.*, iv (1958), pp. 62–4. Even these precautions did not prevent recurrent dispute and litigation between the Gilbertines and Paisley over the payment of this pension: see J. Edwards, 'The order of Sempringham and its connexion with the west of Scotland', *TGAS*, new ser., v, part one (1905), pp. 82–90.

59. When, probably in the early thirteenth century, the abbot and convent of Melrose put tenements at Carlisle on perpetual rent to their daughter-house of Holm Cultram for one mark yearly, reserving rights of lodging for Carlisle fair, the money was to be paid during the annual visitation by the abbot of Melrose, or when the visitation was customarily held (*Melrose Liber*, ii, p. 675; *Holm Cultram Reg.*, no. 40d). Compare the arrangement entered into in 1294 when Melrose farmed to the Cumberland abbey in perpetuity all its property at Rainpatrick (in Gretna), Dumfriesshire: *ibid.*, no. 95g; *Melrose Liber*, ii, pp. 671–2. The abbot of Melrose is found visiting Holm Cultram as late as 1472, to preside at the election of a new abbot and to issue a code of injunctions (*ibid.*, no. 577); long before then, however, the rents had probably lapsed.

60. M. Walcott, 'A breviate of the cartulary of the priory church of St Mary Magdalene, Lanercost', *Trans. of the Royal Soc. of Literature*, 2nd ser., viii (1866), p. 499.

61. *Ibid.*, p. 471.

62. E.g., by 1267 the monks of Kelso had been appointed as procurators of their mother-house, the abbey of Tiron (dép. Eure-et-Loir), responsible for collecting an annual income from the *firma burgi* of Perth (*Kelso Liber*, ii, no. 398). Similarly, note the use of merchants by Norman monasteries to secure revenues owed to them in England: D.J.A. Matthew, *The Norman Monasteries and their English Possessions* (Oxford, 1962), pp. 67–9.

63. *Dryb. Lib.*, nos. 94 (*Langelau*), 97 (*Langelaw*). The earlier forms for Bangly as given in the printed edition of the Dryburgh cartulary should probably be amended throughout to *Bangelau*, etc. Cf. *Calendar of the Laing Charters 854–1837*, ed. J. Anderson (Edinburgh, 1899), no. 2; Appendix, no. 4 with comment.

64. Further, Nichols, *Leicester*, I, ii, app., pp. 71, 74; A.H. Thompson, *The Abbey of St Mary of the Meadows, Leicester* (Leicester, 1949), p. 178. As is indicated by the place of burial, the hunting accident apparently occurred in Charnwood Forest, immediately north-west of Leicester, or in the Morville park at Whissendine. Dryburgh owed rent on Scottish property to another English house, the nunnery of Holystone in Northumberland: *Dryb. Lib.*, no. 148.

65. *Ibid.*, nos. 7, 8, 23, 34, 104; J. Morton, *Monastic Annals of Teviotdale* (Edinburgh, 1832), pp. 307–8.

66. Simpson, 'RQ', app. A, no. 15; *Inchaffray Chrs.*, app., no. 4.

67. For Kedslie, and on Dryburgh's principal acquisitions in upper Lauderdale by this date, see *Dryb. Lib.*, nos. 109–15, 123–32, 176–87. Cf. also Morton, *Monastic Annals*, pp. 306–7.

68. Cf. below, pp. 103, 155–6.

69. Cf. Stringer, *Earl David*, p. 207.

70. T.H.B. Graham, 'Arthuret, Kirklinton and Kirkoswald', *TCWAAS*, new ser., xxviii (1928), pp. 41–5.

71. Oxford, Balliol College, Abbotsley Deeds, E 7/2. Felton thereupon granted both the advowson and the pension to Balliol College: ibid., E 7/3–8; F. de Paravicini, *Early History of Balliol College* (London, 1891), pp. 167–72.

72. *Northumberland Hist.*, xv, p. 239; *CDS*, iv, nos. 238, 560.

73. R.B. Dobson, 'The last English monks on Scottish soil', *SHR*, xlvi (1967), pp. 1–25.

APPENDIX

(I first published most of the following *acta* in *The Innes Review*, xxiv [1973], pp. 139–47, and the remainder in *History of the Berwickshire Naturalists' Club*, xl [1974], pp. 47–9. They are reprinted here as originally presented, save for some additional commentary.)

Of the eleven documents edited below, the original of only one is extant (no. 1). Although this text was published by Joseph Stevenson in 1834, it has been included partly because Stevenson's edition was careless and partly for the sake of completeness. The other *acta* are drawn from the following sources:

BL MS Royal II B. ix. (Cartulary of St Andrew's priory, Northampton. xiii cent.). Nos. 6, 7, 8, 9.

BL MS Cott. Vesp. E. xvii. (Cartulary of St Andrew's priory, Northampton. xv cent.). Nos. 4, 5, 6, 7, 8, 9, 11.

BL MS Cott. Tib. E. v. (Cartulary of St James's abbey, Northampton. xiv cent.). Nos. 2, 3.

Bodl. MS Topographical Northants c. 5. (Transcripts of Dr John Bridges, *c.*1720, including material lost from preceding source in the Cottonian Library fire of 1731.) No. 10.

NLS MS Adv. 34.4.7. (Cartulary of Dryburgh abbey. xv cent.). Nos. 4, 9.

In this edition, abbreviated forms are usually extended, and the extension is in italics where it is uncertain. The spelling has not been normalised and scribal insertions are indicated by oblique strokes. The scribe's punctuation and capitals have been retained in editing the original; elsewhere, punctuation and capitals are editorial. Rubrics have been omitted except in one instance where a rubric provides additional information to the text which it describes. Where more than one copy of a text is known, the printed version is taken from the first MS cited, and major variants in the remainder are noted. In nos. 6, 7, 8 and 9 words and parts of words lost through injury to the preferred text are supplied from the second source cited and placed within square brackets.

1

Agreement between the canons of Dryburgh and the canons of St James's, Northampton, concerning the church of Bozeat (13 December 1152 × 1177, possibly × *c.*1173).

CYROGRAPHUM[1]

Hec est conuentionis ueritaS inter canonicoS ecclesie Sancte Marie de Drieburg[2] 7 canonicoS ecclesie Sancti Jacobi de Norhamtona[3] ⁛ Quod ipsi canonici de Driebu/r/g concedunt predictis canonicis de Norha[m]tona[4] ecclesiam de Bosgieta[5] cum omnibus pertinentiis suis[6] ad tenendum[7] de eis in perpetuum . reddendo annuatim in uita aoelardi post decessum[8] ædgari[9] patris sui ⁛ uiginti[10] solidos[11] . 7 unum bizanzium[12] . uel duos solidos[11] pro bizanzio[13] . post discessum[14] uero ipsius[15] aoelardi ? ipsi canonici de Norhamtona recipient ipsam ecclesiam suam[6] de Bosgieta[5] in manu sua liberam 7 quietam . 7 reddent prenominatis canonicis de Drieburg duas Marcas 7 dimidiam annuatim inperpetuum . 7 hoc post natale domini quando nuncium suum miserint[16] ad abbatiam sancti Jacobi[17].

Endorsed: Conuencio inter nos 7 Canonicos de Drieburc (contemporary with text); super ecclesia de Boseyat' (? xiv cent.); Drieburg (? xvii cent.).
Description: Original, not indented, measuring 13.2 × 14.4 cm., with foot folded to depth of about 1.5 cm. Single slits through foot and fold at five places; three tags remain but no seal survives.
Source: BL Cott. Chart. xxi. 13 (original). NLS MS Adv. 34.4.7, fo. 29v (copy of counterpart of original) = *D*. Printed above from the original, noting major variants in *D*.
Printed: *Illustrations of Scottish History from the Twelfth to the Sixteenth Century* (Maitland Club, 1834), p. 19 (from original, with errors). *Dryb. Lib.*, no. 90 (from *D*, with errors).
Notes: [1]Original only, letters cut through. [2]Driburgh', here and throughout, *D*. [3]Norththamton' (? with mark of abbreviation through first th), *D*. [4]m scratched out; Norththamtoun, here and subsequently, *D*. [55]Bosgitta, *D*. [6]Word omitted, *D*. [7]tenendam, *D*. [8]Corrected from disessum. [9]Algari, *D*. [10]vigentj, *D*. [11]sollidos, *D*. [12]bitantium, *D*. [13]bitantio, *D*. [14]decessum, *D*. [15]ipsis, *D*. [16]miserunt, *D*. [17]*D* adds etc.
Comment: The convent came to Dryburgh on 13 December 1152 (*Chron. Melrose*, p. 35), and Richard de Morville had confirmed this agreement by 1177, possibly by *c.*1173 (no. 3).

2

The convent of Dryburgh confirms that the abbot and convent of St James's should hand over the pension they owe annually for Bozeat church to the abbot of Sulby (1153 × 1177, possibly × *c.*1173).

Omnibus sancte matris ecclesie filiis, conuentus ecclesie sancte Marie de Driburg', salutem in Domino. Sciatis vniuersi quod nos concedimus et hac carta nostra confirmamu[s][1] vt abbas et conuentus ecclesie sancti Jacobi extra Norh'pt[2] tradant pensionem quam debent nobis singulis annis in purificacione sancte Marie de ecclesia de Bosegayt' abbati de Suleby vel alicui ex canonicis de Suleby portanti l*itt*eras abbatis sui extra sigillum, sepius enim grauaremur ex longinquitate itineris eandem pensionem per nosmet ipsos ab eis accipere.

Source: BL MS Cott. Tib. E. v, fo. 91v.
Notes: [1]s lost through damage. [2]Sic.
Comment: It seems probable that this arrangement was confirmed, with no. 1, in no. 3, which refers to the 'chirographs' between Dryburgh and St James's. Certainly no later than 1193 (see no. 5).

3

Richard de Morville, Constable of the king of Scots, confirms to the canons of St James's all the agreement between them and Dryburgh concerning Bozeat church (1162 × 1177, possibly × *c.*1173).

[Ri]*cardus*[1] de Mor*re*uill' constabularius regis Scott*orum*, vniuersis sancte matris ecclesie fil*iis*, salutem. Sciant posteri quam present*es* me concessisse et hac mea carta confirmasse can*onicis* ecclesie sancti Jacobi extra Norh' omnem illam conuencionem que facta est inter illos et can*onicos* de Driebruch[2] de ecclesia de Bosegaye, iuxta omnia que in cyrograffis inter illos factis continentur. Hiis test*ibus* Rog*ero* abbate de Drib', Auicia ux*ore* mea, Will*elmo* fil*io* et hered*e* meo, Rad*ulfo* Masculo, Hugon*e* capellano, Rog*ero* clerico, Herreberto clerico, Elfio vicecom*ite*, Rog*ero* Crasso et aliis.

Source: BL MS Cott. Tib. E. v, fo. 88r.
Notes: [1]Ri lost through damage. [2]Sic.
Comment: Issued after Morville succeeded his father as Constable in 1162 and before the resignation of Abbot Roger of Dryburgh, the first witness, in 1177 (*Chron. Melrose*, pp. 36, 42). Since, however, Morville lost Bozeat for his support of the Scots in 1173–4, the act may belong before *c.*1173, although it is by no means impossible that he continued to give charters for Bozeat after this date. The eighth witness, Elfius (? read Elsius, for Elsi [of Thirlestane]), seems to have been a baronial sheriff, responsible for the Morville lordship in Scotland: Barrow, *Kingdom*, pp. 298–9. Ralph Masculus (Maule) and Roger Crassus attested certain other acts of Richard de Morville (e.g., *Selectus Diplomatum et Numismatum Scotiae Thesaurus*, ed. J. Anderson [Edinburgh, 1739], no. 75a; *Melrose Liber*, i, nos. 94, 108); and Masculus is possibly to be identified with the man of this name who later occurs as a tenant of Earl Thomas of Atholl in the neighbourhood of Mount Lothian and Penicuik, Midlothian (*Registrum S. Marie de Neubotle* [Bannatyne Club, 1849], nos. 31–2).

4

Notification of the agreement made on 22 February 1193 whereby the abbot and convent of Leicester quitclaimed to Dryburgh half a ploughgate in Bangly (in Haddington, East Lothian), for an annual render of five shillings which Dryburgh has assigned to them from its rent at Northampton. 1193.

Nouerint tam posteri quam presentes quod facta fuit h*ec* conuencio anno quarto post primam coronacionem Ric*ardi* regis Angl'[1] in cathedra sancti Petri apostoli in capitulo generali ordinis Premonstracensis[2] apud Neuhous,[3] celebrato coram Willelmo abbate de Lesthys[4] et Roberto abbate de Neuhous[3] et vniuersis aliis abbatibus fere tocius Anglie eiusdem ordinis, inter abbatem et conuentum[5] de Legr'[6] et abbatem et conuentum de Dryeburg'[7] super loquela que vertebatur inter ipsos de redditu decem solidorum,[8] quos abbas de Legr'[6] clamauit versus[9] abbatem de Dryeburg'[10] ex dono Ricardi de Moruyll'[11] pro dimidia carucat*a* terr*e* in Banglaue[12] quam[13] canonici de Dryeburg'[14] tenent. Videlicet quod predicti abb*as* et conuentus[15] Legrec'[16] quietam clamauerunt terram illam prefatis abbati et conuentui de Dryeburgh'[10] pro redditu quinque solidorum,[8] quos eis assignauerunt de redditu suo apud Northampton',[17] quos canonici de sancto Jacobo de[18] North'[19] canonicis de Legrec' annuatim ad purificacionem beate Marie inperpetuum persoluent de redd*itu* xxij solid*orum*[8] quos canonicis[20] de Dryeburgh' pro ecclesia de Bosiate[21] persoluer*e* tenentur, ita quidem quod canonici de Legr'[6] nichil[22] amplius quam quinque solidos[23] a canonicis de Dryeburgh' de cetero nunquam poterunt exigere.

Vt igitur h*ec*[24] conuencio inperpetuum perseueret firma et inconcussa, vtriusque conuentus scilicet de Legr'[6] et[15] Dryeburgh' et abbatum[25] de Lesthys[26] et de Neuhous sigillorum appo*sicione* corroboratur.[27] Hijs testibus Jord*ano* abbate de Torrenton', Adam abbate de Wyleby,[28] abbate Adam[29] de Welleford, Galfrido[30] et Adam canonicis de Dryeburgh', Philippo et Willelmo can*onicis* de Legrec' et multis aliis. Hec carta fuit facta anno m°c°x°ciij, ciclo l*unari* xvj°.

Source: BL MS Cott. Vesp. E. xvii, fo. 253v = *B*. Ibid., fo. 82r–v = *C*. NLS MS Adv. 34.4.7, fos. 31v–2r (abridged) = *D*.
Printed: Dryb. Lib., no. 99 (from *D*, with errors).
Notes: [1]Anglie, *C, D*. [2]Followed by ad, expunged, *B*. [3]Neuhus, *C*; Newhus throughout, *D*. [4]Leskijs, *D*. [5]conuentum et abbatem, *D*. [6]Legrec', *C*; Laycest' throughout, *D*. [7]Dryburk, *C*; Driburgh' throughout, *D*. [8]sollidorum, *D*. [9]aduersus, *C, D*. [10] Dryburgh', *C*. [11]Moreuilla, *D*. [12]Bangelaw, *D*. [13]quas, *C*. [14]Dryeburgh', *C*. [15]*D* adds de. [16]Legr', *C*. [17]North', *C*; Nothhamtoun', *D*. [18]Followed by st, expunged, *B*. [19]Northhamtoun', *D*. [20]canonici, *D*. [21]Bosiathe, *C*; Bosiete, *D*. [22]nihill, *D*; followed by obliterated letter(s), *B*. [23]sollidis, *D*. [24]hec igitur, *C*. [25]abbatem, *C, D*. [26]Lysthes, *C*; ? Liskijs, *D*. [27]*D* has corroborantur and ends here with Testibus etc. [28]Wylebe, *C*. [29]Adam abbate, *C*. [30]Gaufr', *C*.
Comment: See generally H.M. Colvin, *The White Canons in England* (Oxford, 1951), pp. 198, 231–2. All the abbots mentioned are recorded in other sources; but hitherto Abbots Adam of Welford (*alias* Sulby) and Jordan of Thornton (Curtis), Lincolnshire, are not known to have reigned as early as 1193 (cf. *Heads of Religious Houses: England and Wales, 940–1216*, ed. D. Knowles *et al* [Cambridge, 1972], pp. 186, 197). That *Banglaue*, etc., lay in Haddington parish is shown by *Dryb. Lib.*, no. 98, where for *Langelaw* we should read *Bangelaw*. The name is now represented by Bangly Hill, west of the Garleton Hills. *Wyleby* and *Wylebe* are forms for Welbeck (Notts), where there was a Premonstratensian community from the early 1150s. In the dating clause, the lunar cycle is used in the sense of the *cyclus decemnovennalis*: see A. Giry, *Manuel de diplomatique* (Paris, 1894), pp. 148–9.

5

Abbot Alan and the convent of Dryburgh instruct Abbot W(alkelin) and the congregation of St James's to pay five shillings yearly to the abbot and convent of Leicester from the rent they owe Dryburgh for Bozeat church (1193).

K*arissi*mis dominis et amicis suis domino W.[1] abbati de sancto Jacobo de North' et eiusdem loci vniuerse congregacioni, Alanus abbas et totus conuentus de Dryeburgh', salutem in vero salutari.[2] Vniuersitati vestre notum facimus quod ex quadam conuencione inter nos et abbatem[3] de Legrec' facta super dimidia carucata terre in Banglaue eisdem[4] abbati et conuentui quinque solid*os* pro predicta terra singulis annis ad purificacionem beate Marie inperpetuum persoluere tenemur. Quo circa vobis mandamus et supplicamus quatinus loco nostro prefatis abbati et conuentui de Legr'[5] memoratos v[6] solid*os* ad predictum terminum absque contradiccione persoluatis de redditu quem nobis debetis pro ecclesia de Boseiate. Nec omittatis pro litteris quas de nobis habetis de redditu nostro abbati[7] et canonicis de Suleby[8] tradendo. Valeat in Christo dilectio[9] vestra.

Source: BL MS Cott. Vesp. E. xvii, fo. 253v = *B*. Ibid., fos. 82v–3r = *C*.
Notes: [1]Willelmo deleted before W., *C*. [2]Preceded by saluatori, expunged, *B*. [3]*C* adds de

Legrec' et conuentum, with first three words deleted. [4]eiusdem, *C*. [5]Legrec', *C*. [6]quinque, *C*. [7]*C* has et conuentui de, expunged. [8]Sulleby, *C*. [9]Preceded by superfluous d marked for deletion, *B*.

Comment: See no. 4 for date. Walkelin was apparently elected abbot of St James's in 1180, and died in 1205/6: *Heads of Religious Houses*, p. 178.

A poor abstract of this document, and notes on nos. 4 and 9, survive in an early sixteenth-century Leicester abbey source (Bodl. MS Laud misc. 625), whence printed in Nichols, *Leicester*, I, ii, app., p. 74.

6

Helen de Morville grants to St Andrew's, Northampton, one ploughgate of her demesne, with appurtenances, in the toun of Newbigging in Lauderdale (19 December 1200 × 7 January 1210).

[Uniuersis sancte] matris ecclesie filiis ad quos presens scriptum peruenerit, Helena de Moruilla, [salutem in Domino. Sciatis] me dedisse et concessisse et hac carta mea confirmasse pro anima [Rollandi viri mei et pro] animabus antecessorum et successorum meorum et pro salute anime mee Deo et ecclesie sancti Andree de Norh't et mon[ach]is ibidem Deo seruientibus vnam carucatam de dominio meo in ualle de Laued' in uilla Neubigginge cum toftis et croftis /qui fuerunt/ Liulfo et G[lede]wis, scilicet quatuor acras terre Sveinesbreche per altam uiam que uenit de Neubigginge uer[sus] occidentem usque ad exitum predicte uille et sic ascendendo inter capita croftorum usque ad proximum sichetum et ex altera parte uie predicte Morflat, scilicet a uia predicta uersus orientem usque ad proximum fontem et a uiridi uia que uenit de Egrehope uersus boream usque ad capud de Huntendon', et tres acras et dimid*iam* prati ad fontem iuxta Derimedue; habendam in liberam, pu[ram] et perpetuam elemosinam cum communi pastura eiusdem uille quantum pertinet ad vnam [ca]rucatam terre et cum omnibus pertinenciis eiusdem terre et cum omnibus libertatibus et cum o[mnibus] aysiamentis in bosco, in plano, in pratis, in pascuis et in omnibus locis. Quare uolo et [conce]do ut predicti monachi prefatam terram cum omnibus pertinenciis suis habeant et possideant inperpetuum ita honorifice,[1] libere et quiete ab omni exaccione et consuetudine sicut aliqua elemosina in regno Scocie liberius et[2] quietius et honorificencius datur et possidetur. Et ego et heredes mei prefatam terram predictis monachis contra omnes homines warantizabimus. Hiis testibus Fergus fratre domini Rolland*i*, Henrico de Ferlington', Alan*o* de Tirlestan, Petro de Hage, Willelmo de Cuningesburg, Thom*a* filio Rollandi, Artur de Ardros, Ricardo de Warewik, Ricardo de Wincestr', Alein de Chapham,[3] Willelmo de Hertesheued, Ailredo, Yuone clericis et aliis.[4]

Source: BL MS Royal II B. ix, fos. 102v–3r = *A*. BL MS Cott. Vesp. E. xvii, fo. 253r = *B*.
Notes: [1]*B* adds et. [2]*B* omits et. [3]Thus *A*; read Clapham as in *B*. [4]et multis aliis, *B*.
Comment: The occurrence of Roland's son Thomas without comital style and his low position in the witness-list indicate a date before 7 January 1210 (cf. *RRS*, ii, no. 489). For Fergus, brother of Roland, see *Scots Pge.*, iv, p. 138. Alan of Clapham, Peter Haig of Bemersyde and Alan of Thirlestane were prominent tenants and followers of the Morvilles

and subsequently of the lords of Galloway. Most of the remaining witnesses are lesser figures; but several attested for William de Morville, in particular Richard of Warwick (i.e. in Cumberland; cf. *Pipe Roll 22 Henry II*, p. 120) and Richard of Winchester: *Glasgow Reg.*, i, no. 46; *Illustrations of Scottish History*, p. 15; *Melrose Liber*, i, no. 99. William of Conisbrough (Yorks, WR) controlled Staplegordon, Dumfriesshire: *TDGAS*, 3rd ser., xx (1935–6), pp. 133–9. William of Hartside took his name from Hartside in Channelkirk, where William de Morville confirmed to him land on the eastern side of the road leading from Stow to Dere Street, to be held in feu and heritage of Soutra hospital (SRO RH 6/12). He also held lordship at Oxton in Channelkirk, and is perhaps identical with the William of Hartside who occurs as sheriff of Lanark 1225–6: *Kelso Liber*, i, no. 246; *Glasgow Reg.*, i, no. 129; *Selectus Diplomatum*, etc., ed. Anderson, no. 32. Of the place-names, *Huntendon'* is now Huntington in Lauder parish (Nat. Grid Ref. NT 535498). The location of *Egrehope* is indicated by Edgarhope Wood, on the left bank of the Earnscleugh Water, and Edgarhope Law (NT 567531). Cf. also *APS*, vii, p. 138.

7

Alan son of Roland, Constable of the king of Scotland, confirms no. 6 (19 December 1200 × 1234).

Uniuersis sancte matris ecclesie filiis presentibus et futuris, Alanus filius Rollandi constab*ularius* regis Scoc', salutem. Sciatis me concessisse et hac carta mea confirmasse pro anima Rollandi patris mei et pro animabus antecessorum et successorum meorum et pro salute anime mee Deo et ecclesie sancti Andree de Nor[thampton'] et monachis ibidem Deo seruientibus vnam carucatam terre de dominico meo in ualle de Lauwede, eandem scilicet quam E. de Moruilla mater mea eisdem monachis[1] dedit [vbi vti]lius et maius aisiamentum eis fuerit; habendam in liberam,[2] puram et perpetuam elem[osinam cum communi] pastura quantum pertinet ad tantam terram et cum omnibus pertinenciis eiusdem [terr*e* et cum omnibus] libertatibus et aysiamentis in pascuis et[3] bosco, in prato, in plano et omnibus locis. [Quare vo]lo et concedo ut predicti monachi prefatam terram cum omnibus pertinenciis suis [habeant et possi]deant inperpetuum ita honorifice, libere et quiete ab omni exaccione et consuet[udine sicut cart*a*] Helene matris mee testatur et confirmat. Hiis testibus Gilberto filio Co[spat*ricii*, Alex*andro* fil*io* Cosp*atricii*], Willelmo de la Mare, Thom*a* Anglico, Radulfo de la Ch[am]paygn', Jacobo decano, Hug*one* capellano, Ad*a* capellano, Waltero et Ethereldo[4] clericis meis et aliis.[5]

Source: BL MS Royal II B. ix, fo. 103r–v = *A*. BL MS Cott. Vesp. E. xvii, fo. 255r = *B*.
Notes: [1]Word omitted, *B*. [2]*B* adds et. [3]in, *B*. [4]Etheldredo, *B*. [5]et multis aliis, *B*.
Comment: The two leading witnesses were brothers of Thomas son of Cospatric, lord of Workington and Colvend, and the first named, Gilbert, held Southwick by Colvend (*Wigtownshire Chrs.*, p. xxv; *Holm Cultram Reg.*, no. 131). On William de la Mare (de Mara) as a follower of Alan of Galloway see also SRO RH 6/308; *Kelso Liber*, i, no. 246; *St Bees Reg.*, no. 42. Thomas Anglicus, a former supporter of William de Morville and Roland (e.g., *Illust. of Scott. Hist.*, p. 15; *Selectus Diplomatum*, etc., no. 81), was probably connected with Little Asby in Westmorland: cf. *TCWAAS*, new ser., xx (1920), pp. 66–96. Ralph de Campania, lord of Borgue in Galloway, took service with the crown as constable of Roxburgh (*Melrose Liber*, i, no. 282).

8

Roger de Quincy, earl of Winchester and Constable of Scotland, confirms to St Andrew's, Northampton, all the lands and rents granted by his predecessors, to be held according to the terms of their charters, which he has inspected at Halse (Northants) (February 1235 × 5 June 1250, possibly × 2 November 1243).

Omnibus sancte matris ecclesie filiis presens scriptum uisuris uel audituris, Rogerus de Quency comes Wint' constabular*ius* Scocie, salutem eternam in Domino. Nouerit vniuersitas uestra me caritatis intuitu et pro salute antecessorum et successorum meorum, assensu Helene ux*oris* mee, [conc]essisse et hac presenti carta quantum ad me pertinet confirmasse[1] Deo et ecclesie sancti Andree [de N]orhampton' et monachis ibidem Deo seruientibus omnes terras et redditus quos habent [ex] donis antecessorum meorum. Videlicet ex dono Alani fil*ii* Roll*andi* tres marcas de firma de Redepeth et viginti solid*os* de firma de Langeld et dimid*iam* marcam de firma de Grombelau, dimid*iam* ad festum sancti Martini et dimid*iam* ad Pentecosten;[2] de dono autem Helene de Moruilla vnam carucatam terre de dominio suo in ualle de Louedere in uilla que uocatur Neubigginge, cum toftis et croftis qui fuerunt Liulfi et Gledewis et cum communi pastura quantum ad tantum terre pertinet et cum omnibus libertatibus et aysiamentis in pascuis, in bosco, in prato, in plano et omnibus locis; de dono uero Thome filio[3] Rolland*i*, com*itis* Attholl', redditum duarum marcarum in uilla que uocatur Noua Terra in uilla[4] de Tuede de terra que fuit Ricardi de Moruille. Quare uolo et concedo et precipio ut predicti monachi omnes predictas terras et redditus cum omnibus pertinenciis suis habeant et possideant inperpetuum, honorifice, libere et quiete ab omni exaccione et consuetudine sicut carte predictorum donatorum quas inspexi apud Hausho melius [et] liberius protestantur. Hiis testibus Seero de sancto Andrea, Johanne Monaco, Bernard*o* de [Ryp]el', Ada decano de Brackele, Philippo seruiente, Ricardo de Elinton', Sim*one* Page, [Ric*ardo*] de coquina et multis aliis.

Source: BL MS Royal II B. ix, fo. 103v = *A*. BL MS Cott. Vesp. E. xvii, fo. 256r–v = *B*. *Notes:* [1]hac presenti carta mea confirmasse quantum ad me pertinet, *B*. [2]ad festum Pentecost', *B*. [3]Sic; read filii. [4]Thus *A*; read valle as in *B*.
Comment: Roger succeeded as earl of Winchester in February 1235, and his wife Helen was dead by 5 June 1250 (Simpson, 'RQ', p. 38). Since the agreement between St Andrew's and Dryburgh is not mentioned in this confirmation, it was possibly given before 2 November 1243 (cf. nos. 9–11). For the identification of *Noua Terra* in Tweeddale with Harehope (in Eddleston), Peeblesshire, see *Melrose Liber*, i, nos. 82–4. The first three witnesses figure in Dr Simpson's discussion of Earl Roger's *familia*, below, Ch. 5.

9

Notification of the agreement whereby the prior and convent of St Andrew's demised to Dryburgh all the land they have in Lauderdale by grant of Lady Helen de Morville, for a reddendo of two marks yearly to be received in perpetuity from the abbey of St James (1243 × 2 November).

[Sciant p]resentes et futuri quod hec est conuencio facta inter abbatem et conuentum [de Dryebu]r'[1] ex vna parte[2] et priorem et conuentum sancti Andree de Norh't[3] ex altera. Scilicet quod [predicti[4] prior et conu]entus sancti Andree concesserunt et dimiserunt prefatis abbati et conuentui de [Dryeburgh' totam] terram suam cum omnibus pertinenciis suis quam habent de dono domine [Helene de Moruylle[5]] in valle[6] de Laweder,[7] tenendam et habendam inperpetuum, libere et[8] quiete et[9] plenarie [et honorifice per omnia s]icut in carta eiusdem Helene dictis priori[10] et monachis collata contine[tur, redd]endo inde annuatim dictis priori[10] et monach*is* duas marcas argenti[11] ad festum pur*ificacionis* beate Mar*ie*[12] percipiendas[8] inperpetuum[8] de domo sancti Iacobi extra[13] Norh't, scilicet de duabus marcis et dimid*ia* quas abbas et conuentus eiusdem domus abbati[14] de Driburg pro ecclesia de Bosiate[15] annuatim soluere solebant. Et sciendum quod predicti abbas et conuentus de Drieburg assignauerunt prenominatis priori et monachis dictas dua/s/ marcas argenti et dimid*iam* annuatim percipiendas de prefatis abbate et conuentu sancti [Jacobi] ad festum purific*acionis* beate uirginis, ita uidelicet quod prior et conuentus de Norh't duas [marc*as*] ad opus suum proprium pro predicta terra retinebunt et pro predictis abbate et conuentu de Driebu[rgh' quinque] solid*os*[16] abbati et canonicis de Leicestr'[17] annuatim per proprium nuncium ad predictum terminum persoluent et residuos viginti[18] denar*ios* prefatis abbati et conuentui de Drieburg' per certum eo[run]dem[19] abbatis[20] et conuentus[21] nuncium mittendos reseruabunt. Si uero contingat quod predictus abbas et conuentus de Drieburg prefatam[22] terram cum pertinentiis et aysiamentis pro defectu defensionis[23] predictorum prioris et conuentus aliquo tempore amittant, liberum erit eis predictas duas marcas et dimid*iam* de domo sancti Iacobi sine[24] impedimento[25] et contradiccione[26] prioris et conuentus [sancti] Andree exigere et recipere sicut antiquitus solebant, dum tamen[27] nec dolus nec neglige[ncia][28] eorum in aliquo possit[29] deprehendi. Et si contingat quod predicti abbas et conuentus sancti Iacobi[30] a solucione predictarum duarum marcarum et dimid*ie* cessauerint, licitum erit predictis priori et conuentui de Norh't[31] totam terram eorum predictam de Lawed*er*dale[32] sine contradiccione[26] et impedimento[33] abbatis et conuentus de Drieburg reseisire[34] et[11] in pace possidere sicut ante predictam conuencionem quietius possidebant, dum tamen[27] nec dolus nec negligentia[28] eorum in aliquo possit deprehendi.[35] Vt autem h*ec* conuencio rata et stabilis in perpetuum permaneat, vtraque pars sigillum capituli sui presenti scripto apposuit.[36] Hiis testibus domino Ada abbate sancti Iacobi de Norh't, domino Willelmo abbate de Crakefergus, Roberto priore de Cou*er*sham, Osberto priore de sancto Jacobo, Warnerio[37] canonico, Roberto de Bouilla clerico domini epi[scopi Linc'], Simone fil*io* Sewardi, Henrico de Plumpton' clerico, Sampsone[38] de [Aula, Walterio[39]] de Stotesbiri,[40] Rogero de Alecestr'.

Rubric: Conuentio inter nos et conuentum sancti Andree de Northhamtoun' super terra de Newbygyn' in villa de Lawder, etc.[41]

Source: BL MS Royal II B. ix, fos. 103v–4r = *A*. BL MS Cott. Vesp. E. xvii, fo. 254r–v = *B*. Ibid., fo. 83r–v = *C*. NLS MS Adv. 34.4.7, fos. 29v–30r (abridged) = *D*.

Printed: Dryb. Lib., no. 91 (from *D*, with errors).

Notes: [1]Dryeburg(h)' throughout, *B*, *C*; Driburgh' throughout, *D*. [2]parte vna, *B*. [3]North' throughout, with one exception, *B*, *C*; Norththamto(u)n' throughout, *D*. [4]predictus, *C*.

[5]Moruilla, *D.* [6]villa, *D.* [7]Lawder, *D.* [8]Omitted, *D.* [9]Omitted, *B, C* and *D.* [10]priore, *D.* [11]Omitted, *B.* [12]*B, C* and *D* have virginis for Marie. [13]juxta, *D.* [14]*B, C* and *D* add et conuentui. [15]Bosgetta, *D.* [16]sollidos, *D.* [17]Laycest', *D.* [18]vigenti, *D.* [19]eorumdem, *D.* [20]abbati, *C.* [21]conuentuum, *B.* [22]predictam, *B.* [23]defentionis, *D.* [24]sine written twice, *B.* [25]inpedicione, *C.* [26]contradicione, *D.* [27]cum, *D.* [28]neggligencia, *B, C*; necligentia, *D.* [29]poterit, *C.* [30]sancti Iacobi omitted, *C.* [31]Northampton', *B.* [32]Lawerdedale, *B*; Laweder vale, *C*; Lauderdale, *D.* [33]inpedimento, *C.* [34]reserire, *D.* [35]reprehendi, *C.* [36]*D* ends here with Testibus etc. [37]Warin*ero*, *B, C.* [38]Samsone, *C.* [39]Waltero, *C.* [40]Stutesbury, *B, C.* [41]*D* only.
Comment: For date see no. 11, comment. The first witness, Abbot Adam of St James's, occurs 1241–66 (*VCH Northants*, ii, p. 130). The attestation of William, abbot of Carrickfergus, is noteworthy. His abbey, founded as a priory by John de Courcy, was a daughter-house of Dryburgh and apparently received support from Alan of Galloway: A. Gwynn and R.N. Hadcock, *Medieval Religious Houses: Ireland* (London, 1970), p. 204. Another Premonstratensian house, Coverham abbey (Yorks, NR), is represented by Prior Robert. Neither William nor Robert is listed in P.N. Backmund, *Monasticon Praemonstratense* (Straubing, 1949–56), ii, pp. 47–8, 148.

10

The abbot of Dryburgh notifies Abbot Adam of St James's that he has assigned to the prior and monks of St Andrew's the two and a half marks St James's used to pay Dryburgh for Bozeat church (1243 × 2 November).

Viris venerabilibus etc. Ad*e* abbati sancti Jac*obi* etc. H. abbas de Drieburg' etc. Noueritis etc. nos duas[1] marc*as* argent*i* et dim*idiam*, quas nobis ann*uatim* de ecclesia de Boseg' redd*ere* solebat*is*, prior*i* et monach*is* sancti Andr*ee* assignasse etc.

Source: Bodl. MS Topographical Northants c. 5, p. 365 (abstract).
Note: [1]MS has 2.
Comment: Abbots Henry and Hugh of Dryburgh occur in or about the 1220s (*Dryb. Lib.*, nos. 165, 251; *Glasgow Reg.*, i, no. 140; *Kelso Liber*, i, no. 259). But this text seems to belong shortly before 2 November 1243 (cf. no. 11); therefore we should probably read 'J' for 'H' as the initial of the abbot of Dryburgh's name (John): cf. *Chron. Melrose*, p. 87; *St Andrews Liber*, p. 330.

11

Abbot Adam and the convent of St James's acknowledge that they are required to pay two and a half marks yearly to St Andrew's in perpetuity (2 November 1243).

Uniuersis sancte matris ecclesie filiis, Adam Dei gratia abbas sancti Jacobi extra North' et eiusdem loci conuentus, salutem in salutis auctor*e*. Nouerit vniuersitas vestra nos, ex assignacione domini abbatis et conuentus de Dryburgh' et spontanea voluntate nostra, teneri priori et monach*is* sancti Andree de Northampton' inperpetuum ad annuam solucionem duarum marcarum argenti et dimidie, eis ad festum purificacionis beate virginis Marie reddendarum, quas prius abbati et conuentui de Dryburgh' ad eundem terminum reddere solebamus de ecclesia de Boseyate. Et in huius rei testimonium presenti scripto sigillum nostrum apposuimus. Teste capitulo nostro.

Source: BL MS Cott. Vesp. E. xvii, fo. 81v.
Comment: The date 2 November (All Souls' Day) 1243 is assigned to this act of Abbot Adam (1241–66) in the record of litigation of 1331 over areas owed by St James's to St Andrew's: ibid., fo. 81r; Bodl. MS Topographical Northants c. 5, p. 404.

4

THE CHARTERS OF DAVID, EARL OF HUNTINGDON AND LORD OF GARIOCH: A STUDY IN ANGLO-SCOTTISH DIPLOMATIC

Keith Stringer

The present study arises out of researches on the fifth Scottish earl of Huntingdon.[1] Earl David (1152–1219), a grandson of King David I and the younger brother of Kings Malcolm IV and William I, lived in an age when the two leading themes in the development of earlier medieval Scotland can be clearly perceived: the consolidation of the territorial kingdom through innovations on the Anglo-Norman model, and the largely successful struggle to secure *de facto* independence of the stronger English monarchy. His main importance as a Scottish baron lies in his role as a mighty landowner in remote districts where the crown was anxious to underpin and extend its authority. In 1174 he assumed charge of the earldom of Lennox and held it in the king's name until the 1180s or '90s. By 1182 he had gained imposing estates on Tayside and in mid-Aberdeenshire, where he controlled the vast compact fief of Garioch, his principal Scottish power base. He later acquired Ecclesgreig (St Cyrus) and Inverbervie in the Mearns, and — it is most probable — sizeable assets in the ancient episcopal centre of Brechin. This great lordship in eastern Scotland guaranteed Earl David's status as one of the foremost nobles of the kingdom; and just as he buttressed his local influence through administrative changes and his patronage of the Church and lay dependants, so he contributed decisively to the burgeoning strength of the crown.

But Scotland was not the whole of Earl David's world. Improvements in political exchanges between the Scottish and English kingdoms account for his acquisition in 1185 of the honour and earldom of Huntingdon, to which the Scots royal house had maintained rights or claims since the days of King David I. For more than thirty years the earl entered fully into the life of the two countries and was a weighty 'contact man' between them. He retained his positions of trust in Scotland at the centre and in the provinces; but as a prominent magnate of the English realm, he also gave general aid to the Angevin kings in England, and crossed and re-crossed the Channel on their service to Normandy, Maine and Anjou. He was a major focus for the reception of Anglo-Norman social and legal influence in Scotland; he forged 'cross-Border' property ties that in smaller ways reflected his own; and he was conspicuous in Anglo-Scottish diplomacy. He thus contributed in good measure to that peace between the governments enduring almost without interruption in his lifetime and, indeed, long thereafter, which was as vital to the rights and dignity of the Scots crown as was the firmer basis of political power upon which they had begun to rest.

The main source-collection for reconstructing Earl David's significance in Anglo-Scottish history undoubtedly comprises the extant charters passed in his name. These number fifty-five and have already been gathered together for critical edition.[2] All but one survive in a suitable condition for detailed study: twenty-three (including one facsimile) may be classed as original documents, and thirty-one (excluding No. 31 for Harrold priory) are known only as manuscript copies. For the latter, by far the richest single archive is the thirteenth-century cartulary of the abbey of Lindores in Fife, the earl's own foundation and the principal object of his piety. Although this source does not preserve a complete record of the charters he issued for the house, it furnishes a grand total of twelve of which the originals have been lost. The substance of Earl David's *acta* has been put to full use elsewhere. What follows is primarily a discussion of their form.

This approach seems justifiable on several grounds. The lack of interest in the diplomatic of medieval English documents was lamented many years ago by W.H. Stevenson and Hubert Hall.[3] Since then considerable attention has been paid to the productions of the English and Scottish royal chanceries in the twelfth and thirteenth centuries: notably by Bishop, Chaplais, Cronne, Davis, Delisle and van Caenegem on the one hand, and by Barrow and Harding on the other. In England, but not as yet in Scotland, momentous strides have also been made in the investigation of episcopal diplomatic, thanks to the foundations laid by Sir Frank Stenton and C.R. Cheney; and the corpus of published work has been embellished by critical editions and studies in depth of the *acta* issued by a number of Earl David's contemporaries, including Archbishops Theobald and Stephen Langton.[4] In addition, the British Academy has recently launched the series *English Episcopal Acta*, with the aim of systematic publication of bishops' acts, arranged by diocese, from 1066 to the thirteenth century.[5] By contrast with royal and episcopal chanceries, however, the written administrations of lay barons have received scant attention from English scholars. There are published collections of the charters of individual twelfth-century magnates, of which the editions of the *acta* of the earls of Hereford, the earls of Gloucester and the Mowbrays deserve special mention.[6] But while there is no doubt of the general value of such works for the history of the Anglo-Norman baronage, the commentaries by their respective editors on the actual diplomatic of the charters are surprisingly thin and uninformative. From the viewpoint of diplomatic, the state of English studies of baronial charters therefore remains much as Stenton left it in the 1930s.[7]

In the field of private charters, as of episcopal *acta*, Scotland lags farther behind England. When it is appreciated that the government records of the medieval Scots kingdom, by comparison with those of England, are very few, and that in their local powers the greater landowners remained much more of a force than their English counterparts, charter studies are clearly basic to the Scottish medievalist. But, with the notable exception of Dr Grant Simpson's hitherto unpublished analysis of the acts of Roger de Quincy, earl of Winchester and Constable of Scotland (d. 1264),[8] work on the formulas of non-royal Scots charters has yet to advance far beyond the inquiries of Thomas Ruddiman, Walter Ross and their Victorian continuators.

The other main justifications for the present undertaking stem from the importance of Earl David's activity in time and place. Chronologically speaking, it coincides with what is already recognised by English scholars as a formative period in the evolution of private business documents, one which heralded the emergence of the fully developed and highly stereotyped instruments of the mid-thirteenth century. Thus the earl's surviving English charters illustrate in microcosm the extent to which in England, between 1180 and 1220, baronial *acta* were beginning to progress from idiosyncracy and irregularity in composition to greater uniformity, due not least to the pervading influence of the legal reforms of King Henry II. But David was apparently as active issuing charters in Scotland as he was in England. Although the Scottish charter was by English standards a comparatively recent innovation, in each kingdom by *c.*1150 preference for the testimony of the written word had begun to triumph over faith in the sufficiency of the spoken word.[9] The coming together of the two realms in this regard seems to be neatly reflected in the earl's extant acts: twenty-seven were written for Scottish beneficiaries or relate to Scottish interests, while twenty-seven (discounting No. 36 for the Norman priory of La Chaise-Dieu-du-Theil) are exclusively to do with England. In a particular sense, two questions can immediately be posed. How far was there a resident body of household scribes professionally engaged in drafting and writing David's *acta*? How far do his Scottish charters conform in their physical features and *clausulae* to the English? These issues obviously have a bearing transcending the intrinsic interest of the individual documents themselves. Pursuit of both can confirm or modify our view of a crucial age of growing record-consciousness and preoccupation with the law, illuminating at once the nature of contemporary baronial lordship in the neighbouring kingdoms and the degree to which Scotland came under the influence of English legal practices.

But first a note of warning. For one thing, Earl David's *acta* existing solely as copies may not preserve the exact phraseology of the originals. Again, we can be quite sure that his extant acts represent only a tiny proportion of those actually passed under his seal, while it is evident that the number of charters which have chanced to survive is, by contrast with certain other collections, relatively small. For example, 111 full texts survive for Earl William of Gloucester (d. 1183), 118 for Count Robert of Meulan (d. 1204), 143 for Archbishop Stephen Langton (1207–28), and 162 for Count John of Mortain, the future King John of England.[10] Moreover, the information which can be drawn from the survivals in Earl David's name, taken in isolation, will naturally have a restricted value for discussing the evolution of private *acta*. Beside these negative comments, however, may be set others of a positive sort. Many of the charter-copies concerned are to be found in sources known to have a reasonably high degree of reliability. Compared to those of some great personages, such as his mother Countess Ada de Warenne,[11] Earl David's collected acts are many. And we can arrive at a closer understanding of the nature of baronial *acta* by setting the earl's documents against the broader background of the conventions of contemporary royal, episcopal and — wherever possible — private charters.

Second, a note on procedure. In order to provide full answers to the two basic questions already raised, it is necessary to address them in a fourfold way: by providing a fuller context for Earl David's charters; by discussing the ecclesiastical 'department' in his household; by considering the external appearance of the original texts; and, finally, by analysing in depth the internal features of both the originals and the copies.

The documents record that the earl has granted, quitclaimed or confirmed, normally in perpetuity, lands or rights on land. *Acta* expressly designed to protect exemptions, easements and other favours were cast not as mandates but as charters. Quasi-legal or administrative decisions, and explicit injunctions or prohibitions, were occasionally embodied as incidental items in otherwise straightforward *cartae*. There are no brieves directed to the earl's officials (although many no doubt once existed), no letters patent in the strict sense (although they had begun to be dispatched by some authorities), and no personal missives. All the instruments concerned were regarded by their recipients as title-deeds, and to classify them more precisely than as 'charters' (or 'writ-charters') would presuppose distinctions which did not exist in the minds of the scribes who penned them. In general, the emergence of multiple, standardised documents, which historians can justifiably categorise as Bonds, Charters, Grants, Notifications, Releases, etc., lay in the future. A fundamental distinction must be drawn, however, between the written act and the judicial act. A charter supplies evidential security to an existing legal situation. It is not integral to that situation, but merely puts in writing an anterior disposition effected by a public expression of will, supplemented where appropriate by a symbolic or actual transfer of possession. The *donatio*, the solemn oral declaration in the presence of responsible witnesses, was valid in itself; and without doubt there were still many transactions for which charters were never expedited.[12] But grants could often be the cause of uncertainty and conflicting claims. Thus in order to secure a more permanent and authoritative account of the facts than that afforded by the memories of witnesses, beneficiaries were increasingly anxious to safeguard their position with written titles. In England and Scotland the act of giving did not begin to merge with the act of affirmation until the later Middle Ages. But long before grants were actually made *per cartam*, the charter had become important as a legal proof, ready to be produced in the courts as an addition, or as an alternative, to testimonial proof.[13]

The extant *acta* fall, as is the case in other charter collections, into two main categories: those which announce grants by the lord himself and those which renew or confirm grants by other parties. It is only to be expected from the nature of surviving medieval records that the majority in each group should concern the rights and properties of religious houses. In Scotland, but not in England, Earl David was usually the author of the legal actions which his charters put in writing. This, too, is only to be expected. Although it is broadly true that by the last quarter of the twelfth century newcomers to Scotland from England or France found 'the best land allocated, the best places taken',[14] there was nevertheless rather more scope in the contemporary Scottish great estate than in the English for its lord to make pious donations and support expectant knightly followers. Indeed, whereas in David's English lands the process of alienation to mesne tenants had largely been completed, in his Scottish fief, where feudal practices were introduced through his own lordship, he was able to build up by patronage a clientage network whose interests were married to his own.

As a Scottish baron, therefore, Earl David exercised a strong control over the land as a source of service and loyalty. The world to which his charters belonged was a world where a lord enjoyed real powers and normally chose his own tenants, and where lord-man relations had genuine meaning. The thanes and native freemen dwelling on the earl's lands had no freehold that he need recognise. Unless he agreed to accept their homage, they lacked adequate title and warrandice, and no doubt some were displaced or otherwise disadvantaged by his grants to favoured Anglo-Frenchmen or to the reformed Church. Furthermore, once the tenurial structure had been fashioned, possession and heritability continued to lack the security of automatic protection under royal controls.[15] The strength of the lord in his own court is confirmed by No. 28 which graciously 'grants' Monorgan (in Longforgan), Perthshire, to one Gilbert (Gillebrigde), whose father had earlier held it, and, less directly, it is exemplified by the fact that whenever a tenant alienated property, the earl's express approval was required in order to make the gift valid.[16]

The situation in much-governed England was altogether different. In the English lands, encumbered by an old-established and far more complex system of dependent tenures, the ties between individual tenants and David were often weakly based. The earl's position seems to have been strongest with regard to the Church, for several monasteries recognised the importance of reinforcing their titles by acquiring his written assent to the continuation of tenures created for them by his predecessors.[17] If earlier grants were to be honoured, the normal contemporary practice was to issue charters of confirmation; but the notion of a lord's discretionary power was occasionally emphasised by expediting charters in the form proper to new gifts. Three of Earl David's English *acta* fall into the latter category (Nos. 58, 60, 78).

Elsewhere in England there is little to show that seisin, or succession, was at the discretion of the earl and his court. Whereas nine confirmations or re-grants were inspired by the anxiety of the religious to secure his renewal of his predecessors' gifts, no confirmation or re-grant is known to have been made by David to lay mesne tenants. A mere three confirmations are in favour of laymen, and all confirm property conveyed by mesne tenants to under-tenants. Nor do they relate to the kind of run-of-the-mill transactions that are otherwise well attested. Two concern sales, the third ratifies a grant made in fulfilment of a settlement in the court of the Huntingdon honour (Nos. 12, 13, 23). There are grounds for believing that none of these arrangements may have been fully secure without the superior lord's participation, which could have served to minimise the risk of claims by the grantor's heirs.[18] In each instance, therefore, the initiative probably came from the feoffee. Moreover, whereas a number of confirmations deal specifically with property granted to religious bodies by tenants, only two of these corroborate gifts made during the earl's period of lordship (Nos. 20, 33).

Allowance must obviously be made for the accidents of survival, but in fact such information as we have scarcely surprises. Earl David's charters were written when the decline of seigneurial power in England was far advanced. Lay vassals were now so well protected by the king's courts that the day had largely passed when 'the relevant rules were those of each lord's court, and the rights which they protected might depend to a greater or lesser extent upon the will of the lord'.[19] The vassal's undisturbed seisin was guaranteed not through successive gifts but because the lord had in essence lost the ability to expel him. His ownership was stressed because royal safeguards ensured that his heir entered as of right rather than by the lord's favour; and it was further underlined because he could dispose of property as if his control over it were complete. Mesne fees had accordingly ceased to be a source, first and foremost, of services to the superior. The lord was compelled to recognise that their holders were proprietors by common law, that they did not have to be personally acceptable to him, and that homage and fealty were being drained of meaning.[20]

'Every charter includes some description of the property to which it relates, whether that property consists of acres, churches, or men. These descriptions become steadily more precise, and therefore more elaborate, as time goes on.'[21] The subject-matter of Earl David's charters, even of those which show him as a benefactor in his own right, cannot be fully associated with the movement towards detailed topographical descriptions, which is predominantly a thirteenth-century development. No. 6, recording his grant of the whole davoch of Resthivet in Garioch as a feudal tenement, is exceptional for its full description of boundaries, based on the River Urie, a 'great marsh' and other natural features. The normal form is closer to that of No. 79 for Sawtry abbey which deals solely with land in *Hangres* (the Hanger of Tottenham, Middlesex), but without identifying the manor involved or the exact position of the property within it. Local knowledge and the memory of those who saw the donee put in possession were still of importance in the conveyancing illustrated by the charters in this collection.

That is not to say, however, that the recipients of real property had necessarily to rely wholly on the memory of the countryside with regard to the actual resources of their estates. Many of the acts which relate to David's gifts of land contain a clause granting the property 'in meadows and pastures, in ways and paths, etc.', and including a comprehensive phrase such as 'with all its rightful appurtenances'. Little attention has been given to whether these lists of rights were inserted into charters as routine clauses or whether they faithfully reported the main physical attributes of the tenancies concerned. Certain phrases, *in bosco et plano, in pratis et pascuis*, etc., were obviously relevant to any normal freehold and are encountered with monotonous regularity. There is, nonetheless, a suggestive variety between the content of any one list and that of any other in Earl David's charters.

Basically these lists range from the long (e.g., Nos. 6, 46) to the relatively short (e.g., Nos. 17, 54). *In bosco* is conspicuous by its absence from No. 53, but this is accounted for by a specific reservation of woods for the earl's own use. *In moris, in mosis* and *in maresiis* are applied to conveyances of arable tenements only where such features were prominent, as at Leslie in Garioch where today we find Bogs, Southbog and other names of this nature (No. 55). Nor does it seem that *in vivariis* and *in piscariis* had merely a general significance. They rarely figure, but always appear together (Nos. 6, 44, 46, 55). *In caciis* ('in chases') qualifies the ancillary rights dependent upon Fintry, near Dundee (No. 27). The appearance of this phrase in any collection is highly unusual and patently cannot be put down to common form. *In ecclesiis et capellis* is found only in No. 55, recording Earl David's grant of Leslie to Malcolm son of Bertolf. Since Malcolm's son Norman is known to have controlled Leslie church, which he later gave to Lindores abbey, and since David confirmed his grant (No. 50), it is a reasonable assumption that the church had passed to Malcolm as an integral part of the Leslie feu. Indeed, when David's son, Earl John, confirmed Leslie to Norman 'as my father's charter ... bears witness', he was careful to stipulate 'except the right of presentation to the church of Leslie, which Norman has given to the abbey of Lindores'.[22] In the *acta* of King David II (1329–71), the lists of appendages 'are not so much a careful list of rights and possessions actually involved as an attempt to include everything which might otherwise be held not to be included'.[23] A similar observation has been made concerning the fourteenth-century private charter in Scotland.[24] But in Earl David's *acta*, although they rarely contain a precise description of the principal properties, the scribes made some effort to catalogue and define in a realistic fashion the major physical appurtenances of the lands about which they wrote.

Yet who were these scribes? However natural it may be to think that the acts written in Earl David's name and presented for authentication with his seal were penned by his own officials, it would be dangerous not to suspect that at least some were prepared by the beneficiaries, to serve whose interests the charters were, after all, produced. Even so, four chaplains and twelve clerks, to a man certainly or very probably of Anglo-Norman origin, have been positively identified in the earl's service.[25] Not all these persons were in his employment at the same date, and while some spent much of their careers in his circle, others may have been mere birds of passage. Nevertheless, after David became earl of Huntingdon in 1185 his personal staff normally included two chaplains and at least two clerks, who travelled with him on each side of the Border as members of his household. There is little specific information on the duties of this ecclesiastical establishment. But, plainly, the earl was eager to have in his suite men of the requisite talent and responsibility for scribal tasks. In point of fact, two clerks were *magistri*, men of sound scholastic training, and both had entered David's service with experience of other administrations: Master Thomas de Paraviso was a former clerk of the Scots king, and Master Peter of Paxton, a legally minded clerk who boasted a personal library of law books, had served the Senlis lords of the Huntingdon honour. Individual clerks were also provided with parochial benefices to reward and retain their services, while in certain cases 'professional' advancement was secured. Through David's good offices, Robert *clericus* was offered the church of Aberdour in Fife; Master Thomas was supported with the rectory of Potton in Bedfordshire and may have enjoyed temporarily the living of Lindores (Abdie); Master Peter was vicar of Great Paxton in Huntingdonshire and succeeded Master Thomas at Potton. Their rewards speak eloquently of David's confidence in their skills. For Master Peter, who later became vice-archdeacon of Huntingdon, baronial service paved the way to higher preferment in the Church. Philip *clericus* remained in secular employment and attained executive office as the steward of Earl David's Scottish lands.

There are thus *a priori* reasons for supposing that one important duty of the clerks, and possibly of the chaplains as well, was the production of the earl's charters. Study of the external features of the surviving originals, though few in number, helps to advance the argument. As may have been anticipated, it is impossible to tell from physical characteristics whether an act was issued in Scotland or in England. Almost without exception, the *acta* are written parallel to the longer sides of the parchment. For the shorter documents, between 14 cm. and 16.5 cm. is a common breadth and from 11.5 cm. to 14 cm. a common depth. Degrees of consistency may also be found in the methods of sealing and in the choice of seal colour. Thus title-deeds of permanent value were normally dispatched *sur double queue*, and the seal is usually in green wax. Documents of ephemeral importance could be sealed *sur double* or *simple queue*, but the seal is usually in white wax. Collections of contemporary private, even episcopal, *acta* do not invariably exhibit such uniformity in these respects;[26] and it gives us an additional reason for believing that Earl David's administration was soundly based.

The evidence of the actual handwriting of the twenty-three original charters is, however, less clear-cut. Three *acta* written by the same practised hand at different times and for different recipients are without doubt to be attributed to an earl's clerk, possibly to Robert *clericus* (Nos. 27 [see plate 1], 28, 34). Conversely, two charters for Aldgate priory, executed in the same regular charter hand, were presumably 'external' productions (Nos. 3, 4 [plate 3]); and two charters for Clerkenwell priory, written in a crudely ornamental charter hand, were probably prepared by a Clerkenwell scribe (Nos. 19, 20). Elsewhere, eight *acta*, though possibly the work of as many different scribes, are nevertheless in closely similar hands. These display a fairly advanced level of writing, in the economical format of a cursive, businesslike style which would have come readily to men regularly engaged in written tasks, and which may indicate the existence of a distinctive 'office' script (Nos. 33, 36, 38, 53, 56 [plate 2], 66, 69, 79). But the calligraphy of other *acta* is conspicuously different from this series. The most impressive of all the originals is undoubtedly No. 51 for Lindores abbey. This especially solemn confirmation is the largest in size (21.8 × 29.1 cm.), and it preserves a fine example of bold, upright book hand, a type of script normally found in liturgical works and the like. The parchment is carefully ruled, the text has a minimal amount of abbreviation, and the charter was obviously produced with a high sense of occasion. It was probably executed by a Lindores scribe. No. 68 for Repton priory stands at the opposite extreme. Not only is it the smallest original (14.5 × 5.7 cm.), but it is a scrappy production, written in an incompetent and slovenly hand. This charter was clearly prepared in unusual circumstances: although its authenticity is unquestionable, it is hard to imagine why the earl or the priory should have employed so unprofessional a scribe. Of the remaining six originals, Nos. 23 and 55, both in favour of laymen, bear the same kind of mannered charter hand, though since the script is rather less fanciful in No. 23, it may be that each was written by a different person. The other four *acta* (Nos. 6, 17, 18, 76) provide three distinct specimens of book hand, modified in No. 76 for Sawtry abbey by elongated and flourished ascenders which ape those of a papal privilege, and one instance of especially pronounced cursiveness.

Palaeographical study, therefore, offers some instructive findings, but these obviously need to be extended by further examination of the charters. We must turn to systematic analysis of their internal features, for which the evidence of *acta* known only from copies can, if treated cautiously, be brought into play beside that of the originals. At the same time, space will be found for general observations, not least so that it may be suggested how these sources can elucidate contemporary mentalities on the exercise and reality of magnate power.

Initial Protocol

As contemporary English and Scottish charter practice dictated, Earl David's *acta* normally open with a superscription clause containing his style, an address and a greeting. The epistolary nature of this introduction emphasises the extent to which the twelfth-century charter had evolved from the private letter.

Style

David's style was developed into the form 'Earl David, brother of the king of Scotland (*or* of Scots)'. Consideration of the use of the word 'earl', *comes*, highlights one easily ignored fact: that an earl was not automatically accorded in written record the dignity to which he was entitled. *Comes* was apparently indispensable to the superscription after David had acquired the earldom and honour of Huntingdon in 1185, although even then he was not invariably described as an earl in charters issued by other authorities.[27] That earlier, at the dates when he had rights or claims to the Huntingdon honour (1173–4) and the earldom of Lennox, it was not usual for him to be styled *comes* provides a more striking illustration of how irregularly comital style might be employed.[28] It is also significant of his title from 1185 that the territorial designation, 'of Huntingdon', is rarely included. The qualifying words generally emphasise the special dignity of his birth, not his tenure of a particular *comitatus*. One superficially attractive explanation of this practice might be developed from the fact that the office of an earl in England had by now become essentially a personal rather than an administrative dignity: just as the regular addition of a territorial style can perhaps be taken as a sign of an earl's strong powers of local lordship,[29] so its rare use can perhaps be taken to underline that comital rank was merely honorific. There are, however, fundamental objections to this thesis. Certainly, the decline in their power does not seem to have deterred other earls in England from parading a territorial style, and may even have encouraged it.[30] Possibly David's practice was simply informed by that of his Scottish predecessors, who were rarely, if ever, known by territorial name as lords of the Huntingdon honour.[31] The first recorded 'earl of Huntingdon' is in fact their Senlis rival Earl Simon III, who was occasionally given the title during his lordship of the honour in 1174–84,[32] his preferred designation being 'earl of Northampton'.

Twelve originals abbreviate David's name to a conventional ~~DD~~ or d̄d̄. In the remainder it appears in full: *Dauid* or, less commonly, *dauid*. Copies generally have *Dauid*, which may often be an extension of an original ~~DD~~, etc. The style continues, in its typical form, *frater regis Scocie* (or *Scott'*). If, for safety's sake, only the original texts are taken into account, *Scocie* is most frequently encountered. *Scoc'* and *Scotie* both appear once. A single original has *Scottorum* and the abridged form *Scott'* is found in six others. An exceptional form, *Scocc'*, occurs in two acts, penned by the same (? Clerkenwell priory) scribe, while *Scot'*, standing for either *Scotie* or *Scotorum*, occurs in four others. The two styles 'brother of the king of Scotland' and 'brother of the king of Scots' could therefore be used interchangeably; but there is a slight tendency for English acts to take the former. Their scribes were perhaps influenced by the change in the English royal style about 1199 from *rex Anglorum* to the expressly territorial *rex Anglie*. By contrast, the Scottish royal chancery for long retained the form 'of Scots', one which preserved the archaic tribal and personal notions of kingship.[33]

The earl's charter style thus seems at first sight to be remarkable for its non-standardisation. But examination shows that the scribes were improvising upon one construction; and we must bear in mind that even in well-organised writing-offices such a basic element as the lord's name and title was not invariably drawn up according to a set form.[34]

Address

(i) *General address.* There are three distinct forms of the general address, and — allowance made for variations, many of which seem to have no real significance — these do show telling degrees of consistency in their respective constructions and applications.

A. This mode of address runs, in its basic form, *omnibus hominibus et amicis suis*: 'to all his men and friends'. The earl's style always precedes these words, as was the customary practice when a lord addressed subordinates.[35] *A* and its variants are carried by eleven *acta*. One or more of the following elements could be added:

(1) *presentibus et futuris* or *tam presentibus quam futuris*

(2) racial addresses

(3) *clericis et laicis.*

'Present and future', which occurs eight times, appears most often, and serves to emphasise how contemporaries viewed the functions of charters, which were primarily intended to supply a lasting record for posterity. The phrase 'clergy and laymen' is found on only three occasions. Racial addresses, although jettisoned from English and Scottish royal acts by the 1170s,[36] are carried by five of the eleven *acta* in question. Three relate to England and are directed to 'French and English'. No. 55, which concerns Leslie in Garioch, is addressed to 'French, English, Flemings and Scots'. The mention of Flemings is unusual but, in this context, readily understandable. Flemish settlement in the Leslie district is well attested, and the grantee, Malcolm son of Bertolf, may himself have hailed from Flanders.[37] French, English, Scots and Gallovidians figure in No. 27. This act deals with Fintry in Angus and there is, evidently, no logical reason for the inclusion of Gallovidians in its address. Professor Barrow has found similar anomalies in the *acta* of King Malcolm IV.[38] The probable explanation of this aberration is that the scribe — in this case one of the earl's clerks — was influenced by an exemplar, for he has repeated the racial terms incorporated in a royal charter issued earlier for the same beneficiary.[39]

A bears little immediate resemblance to any of the general address clauses current in the English royal chancery. Delisle, in his analysis of Henry II's *cartae*, noted only one charter with a comparable introduction.[40] But it was a convenient way of condensing the long list of ecclesiastics and laymen addressed in solemn royal charters to a simple, all-embracing formula. This consideration produced *omnibus probis hominibus totius terre sue*, the short address, not unlike *A*, commonly used in the *acta* of contemporary Scots kings, which royal scribes later adopted as standard in formal grants or confirmations of perpetuities.[41] It is in fact reproduced verbatim by the opening words of No. 55. Yet 'friends' is a most unusual form in Scottish royal diplomatic,[42] while the kings of England did not deign to qualify their addressees as *amici*.[43] Similarly, although a bishop might write to his men, notably in transactions concerning his temporalities, it is rare to find episcopal *acta* addressed to a bishop's friends.[44] It may be that the use of *amici*, as in Earl David's acts, was intended to evoke a spirit of chivalrous fellowship which was deemed appropriate to barons and knights, but not to kings or bishops.

Forms equivalent to *A* appear in half the known charters of Margaret de Bohun (d. 1197); but they occur much less often in Professor Stenton's magnificent collection of twelfth-century charters relating to the English Danelaw.[45] It would, however, be unwise to imagine that *A* and its variants were an irregular feature of the early private charter in England, or indeed in Scotland. That only three of David's eleven *acta* bearing *A* are for churchmen (Nos. 18, 68, 79) hints that the secular nature of the address was normally regarded as unsuitable for acts executed in favour of religious bodies. More significantly, the majority of Stenton's Danelaw charters are for the Church, and of these merely six per cent have an address like *A*. But of the *acta* he numbered 454 to 556, which are nearly all for laymen, some thirty-eight per cent have addresses which resemble it. A lord's men and friends obviously had a greater interest in the creation of new lay feus and similar transactions than in grants to religion, which were normally made in alms and free of secular services.[46] Nevertheless, *A* became increasingly less usual in private charters,[47] although it seems possible that this type of address, which is typically feudal in form, lost ground more quickly in England than in Scotland. Earl David's *acta* offer little in the way of positive conclusions. But if we turn, for instance, to *Sir Christopher Hatton's Book of Seals* only five English charters bearing *A* or its equivalents can be found which certainly date later than 1200.[48] The latest appears to be a confirmation by William, count of Aumale, which passed shortly after 1214, and its address was probably lifted from a confirmation of the same grant issued by William de Mandeville, earl of Essex, in 1181.[49] Thirteenth-century Scottish instances seem to lie more readily to hand. Without making a systematic search, I have found examples for, among others, the earls of Buchan, Dunbar, Fife, Lennox, Ross and Strathearn, and for the lords of Annandale.[50] Now, certain developments in diplomatic appear to have occurred in both kingdoms at much the same time, for scribes in Scotland responded swiftly to changing English usages. But they are likely to have been influenced, too, by their immediate background, a marked feature of which was the continuing significance of lord-man ties when in England these had for the most part become conventionalised.

B. The second type of general address appears in twenty-six charters and is therefore the most common construction. It is grounded on the phrase *omnibus* (or *universis*) *sancte matris ecclesie filiis*: 'to all the sons of Holy Mother Church'. One or more of the following elements might be included:

(1) *presentibus et futuris* or *tam presentibus quam futuris*

(2) *et fidelibus*

(3) *ad quos presens scriptum pervenerit.*

The third element, 'to whom this present may come', is added only once (No. 60). The second is found eight times. As with *A*, 'present and future' is the commonest addition, occurring in seventeen of the twenty-six addresses.

By the second half of the twelfth century, *B* and similar forms were regularly used in both English and Scottish private charters.[51] Their origin does not lie with royal scribes. Rather, they spread from episcopal chanceries.[52] In light of *B*'s ecclesiastical character, it does not surprise that all Earl David's *acta* adopting this form are in favour of the Church. Here again there is a close correspondence between the subject-matter of a document and the nature of its address.

In English episcopal acts it was normal practice towards the end of the twelfth century for the bishop's name and title to be placed after *B* and its variants.[53] The usage in the present collection is not entirely lacking in common form. In nine charters David's style is written before the address, but in the remaining seventeen the sequence is transposed.

C. The final category of general address is represented by No. 56 for Earl Gillecrist of Mar: *omnibus has literas videntibus et audientibus* ('to all seeing and hearing these letters'). A further six acts open in this fashion. *Hanc cartam* or *hoc scriptum* is substituted for *has lit(t)eras* in four examples. *Visuris et/vel audituris* may also be used as an alternative to *videntibus et audientibus*, and *presentibus et futuris* is once added to the address. There is only one instance of *omnibus ad quos presens scriptum pervenerit* running by itself (No. 47).

In England and Scotland by the mid-thirteenth century, formulas based on *C* had become the normal opening for private charters which were generally addressed.[54] The address of letters patent also developed out of its basic construction. It is interesting and somewhat remarkable that all but one of the examples in Earl David's *acta* are from charters directed to Scottish beneficiaries. As intimated earlier, it would be a mistake to suppose that just because a scribe wrote in Scotland he was unfamiliar with new currents in diplomatic practice. Furthermore, examination of the seven acts introduced by *C* in connexion with the business in hand shows that while three deal with real property, four record minor grants and exemptions of the kind characteristic of letters patent (Nos. 15, 45, 56, 72). It would therefore be worth considering if in Scottish private charters *C* first asserted its predominance in grants of ephemeral or temporary value.

(ii) *Particular address*. This also occurs in seven instances, and the relative infrequency by comparison with *A* and *B* is unremarkable. 'Specific greetings of any sort become steadily rarer in private documents as time goes on. Any private charter which opens in this way may at once be provisionally assigned to the twelfth century.'[55] Earl David's charters of this type all relate to the honour of Huntingdon.

There is a clear preference for the word *honor* rather than *comitatus*, and the earl's style precedes each special address. It is noteworthy that he takes precedence of the bishop of Lincoln, who was scarcely his social inferior. In every case, the individuals addressed were those who would have been particularly important in ensuring that the grant or confirmation was observed. The bishop of Lincoln had an obvious interest, as the diocesan, in No. 34, which confirmed the church of Great Paxton to Holyrood abbey. Elsewhere, the earl was primarily addressing his honorial court of the Huntingdon fief. The men of the honour addressed were 'all his barons, knights and *probi homines*'; or 'his steward and all his barons and *probi homines*'; or simply 'his steward and all his *probi homines*', or 'all his men'. The technical phrase *probi homines* — a difficult term to translate precisely — was always a much more pronounced feature of the addresses of Scottish charters than of English *acta*. It is especially characteristic of the acts of Scots kings, who from the reign of David I almost invariably addressed all their men who were 'good', in the sense of 'worthy' or 'honourable'. 'At its fullest the phrase no doubt covered all the king's free subjects; but essentially it referred to the king's substantial and responsible subjects, men of the landholding class, burgesses and beneficed clergy.'[56] Much the same can probably be said of Earl David's *probi homines*. In three instances they are expressly described as both clerical and lay (Nos. 54, 58, 76).

There are other similarities between the seven special addresses and the superscriptions of Scottish royal charters. If we take the extant *acta* of Malcolm IV and William I as lords of the Huntingdon honour,[57] the address clauses almost always include the honorial steward, the *probi homines* of the fief are regularly mentioned, and there are occasional references to the king's *barones*. There is also a marked tendency to write of an *honor* rather than of an earldom. The scribes of David's charters were apparently influenced by these forms. For example, the scribe of No. 34 for Holyrood abbey, who was in the earl's employ, evidently had access to an earlier confirmation of the same grant by King William. He copied exactly its address and, with minor variants, the main body of the text. For his part, the scribe of William I's confirmation had drawn upon the charter recording the original grant by Malcolm IV.[58] Clearly, therefore, not all Earl David's *acta* are of like value in illuminating contemporary diplomatic habits, or the traditions of a particular administration.

Salutation

The usual form is a simple *salutem*. There are only two exceptions: *salutem in Domino* and the elliptical *salutem quam sibi* (Nos. 59, 79). The way in which the greeting was to develop in episcopal (and indeed in private) charters can be seen by comparing the *acta* of Archbishop Theobald, in which the emphasis was upon *salutem* alone, with those of Archbishop Stephen Langton, in which *salutem* is almost entirely supplanted by more elaborate forms.[59] In this regard, as in others, Earl David's charters belong more to the traditions of the twelfth century than to those of the thirteenth.

Text

At this point we must turn from the formal protocol opening each act to the diplomatic of the main body of the document.

Notification

The most common form of notification, which occurs twenty-seven times, is *sciatis*, followed by an accusative and infinitive: *sciatis me dedisse*, etc. *Sciant* is used eleven times, and normally takes the same construction as *sciatis*. It is always accompanied by the phrase *presentes et futuri*, or its variants. Three examples are unaddressed notifications, there being nothing to suggest that the absence of a superscription was determined by the contents of the documents (Nos. 6, 49, 53).

Forms of notification based on *noscere* are less frequent. *Noverit universitas vestra* appears four times. *Noveritis* is used eleven times and is found twice with *universi*. *Noverint omnes tam presentes quam futuri* occurs in a single example. With one exception, all these introduce an accusative and infinitive construction.

As the evidence of this collection indicates, the *scire* forms seem to represent the commonest notification in the private charters of Earl David's day, with a preference for *sciatis* rather than *sciant*.[60] Here the practice follows that of royal chancery scribes, who made greater use of *sciatis* than *sciant* both in England and (to *c.*1170) in Scotland. In English episcopal *acta*, the *noscere* constructions prevail.[61] In this regard it seems significant that all save one of the sixteen *noscere* forms carried by David's charters belong to acts for religious beneficiaries. It can thus be shown that, whereas *scire* and *noscere* were used indiscriminately in his *acta* for churchmen, *noscere* was not freely used in his *acta* for laymen. We must guard against the temptation to see a rule where none may in fact have existed. It is interesting, though, that when a contemporary bishop of Lincoln dealt with secular business, *noscere* was often eschewed in favour of *scire*.[62] Whatever the reason for the variant usages, *scire* had apparently been largely abandoned in private acts by about the mid-thirteenth century. In Earl Roger de Quincy's charters, *noscere* holds the field.[63]

Dispositive clause

Since the purpose of a charter was to provide perpetual proof of a conveyance already made, the act of giving is always expressed in the past tense. The usual formula, one well established in diplomatic usage by the 1160s or '70s, is *dedisse et concessisse et hac presenti carta mea confirmasse*. It is found, with minor variants, in thirty-six *acta*. The construction adopts the indicative on four occasions, a form which is normally determined by the scribe's use of the notificatory phrase *sciant presentes et futuri quod ego*. The other main dispositive clause, *concessisse et hac presenti carta mea confirmasse*, appears — again with minor variants — seventeen times. The first person perfect is used twice. A release of neyfs has *dedisse, remisisse et quietos clamasse* (No. 56). Such formulas are not uncommon in contemporary acts of this type.[64]

The derivatives of *do, concedo* and *confirmo* were normally conjoined in charters affirming new gifts. *Do* was usually dropped for confirmations of earlier grants. Some exceptions to this practice have already been noted (above, p. 76), but the most interesting of the *acta* in which *dedisse* was strictly inappropriate has yet to be discussed. In No. 44 Earl David announced his foundation of Lindores abbey and 'granted' to the convent its rights and possessions. The nature of this charter, which the monks later called their *magna carta*, neatly exemplifies what has long been recognised: that monastic foundation charters belong to a special category of written *acta*.[65] Firstly, No. 44 drives home that a foundation charter, far from providing an accurate guide to the date of the event to which it testifies, could be issued several years after the beginning of the religious house in question. The act passed between 15 February 1198 and 17 March 1199; but Lindores had been established by March 1195, when Pope Celestine III confirmed its property and privileges, and other evidence indicates that preliminary arrangements for the endowment were in hand by 1189.[66] Secondly, the *magna carta* serves to demonstrate that a foundation charter was not necessarily the earliest document to be executed for a monastery by its founder. The text is lengthy, it deals with many individual grants, and its style is disjointed and repetitive. These features are consistent with the view that the scribe had not prepared a careful draft but simply took the main body of the charter from a group of *acta* given to Lindores by David beforehand. Indeed, the *magna carta* is almost certainly predated by seven of the earl's surviving Lindores charters; and it evidently replaced an earlier but now lost foundation charter (Nos. 37–43). To begin any monastery was to engage in a protracted business undertaking. Many individual gifts were necessary before a founder felt that his community was securely established. These would often be guaranteed in separate writings; but at some appropriate stage the entire process would be set down in a single charter of endowment. Then, perhaps after a lengthy interval in which fresh grants had been made, an improved version might need to be engrossed to serve as a definitive record of a monastery's rights and possessions, a record of which No. 44 for Lindores abbey provides a classic example.

Holding clause

The holding clause, giving details of tenurial obligations, is a standard feature of the thirteenth-century charter.[67] Of the fourteen *acta* with no specific clause of this type in the present collection, only one is certainly later than 1200 in date (No. 74). Moreover, since all but three concern grants or confirmations in alms, its omission may generally reflect a lingering desire to avoid the somewhat indelicate assertion that property conveyed to the Church *in elemosinam* is 'to be held' of the grantor.[68] Technically, however, such conveyances did establish a tenurial relationship between benefactor and grantee.

Tenendum introduces details of tenure on eighteen occasions; *tenebunt* is used once. *Habendum* occurs by itself solely in relation to grants of teinds or rents (Nos. 3, 4, 73), and the practice may anticipate the fourteenth-century distinction between a grant and a gift, seen most clearly in English conveyancing, so that beneficiaries may 'have' (or be granted) revenues, but because of their incorporeity may not 'hold' (or be given) them. 'Such incorporeal things could not be made the object of livery of seisin. Since they had no substance there was nothing which a donor could deliver.'[69] The scribe of No. 73 for St Andrews cathedral priory seems to have made a conscious distinction when he wrote that a toft in Dundee was 'to be held' (*tenendum*) and a rent in the same burgh was 'to be had' (*habendum*).

Habendum and *tenendum* are thrice run together. The order of these words varies, but according to no discernible pattern. It is later practice which clearly shows the preference of Scottish scribes for *tenendum et habendum* while their English counterparts generally adopted *habendum et tenendum*.[70]

The clause begins with older, more peremptory phrases nineteen times. The commonest injunction is *quare volo (et concedo)*, of which there are thirteen examples. *Quare volo et firmiter precipio* occurs twice, and the following are each encountered once: *unde volo et precipio; volo itaque; volo eciam et concedo*; and *volo itaque et firmiter precipio*. These and similar formulas are also to be found introducing separate injunctive clauses. There is a particularly emphatic expression of the earl's will in No. 37 for Lindores abbey, in the form of a final sanction: 'wherefore I will and firmly command that none of my successors cause any injury or annoyance to the abbey contrary to my gift'.

The mandatory phrases here described were derived from the words of command prevalent in twelfth-century English and Scottish royal *acta*. *Quare volo et firmiter precipio* is almost standard usage of both chanceries, and such forms had quickly spread to private *acta*, notably to those of men of high feudal standing.[71] But in England, 'long before the year 1200 the features appropriate to a royal writ had begun to disappear from the charters of even the greatest among the king's subjects'.[72] There are exceptions to prove the rule: in particular, the charters of the early thirteenth-century earls of Chester, whose scribes were among the pre-eminent imitators of English royal chancery style.[73] Yet the use of mandatory clauses, especially those softened to a simple *quare volo*, seems to have continued longer in Scotland than it generally did in England. This much is suggested by the fact that fourteen of the nineteen examples from the holding clauses in this collection are supplied by acts of Scottish provenance, and the point is worth some further illustration. The like may be found in twenty-three out of about one hundred contemporary private acts in the Melrose abbey muniments. In the same archive, *(quare) volo (et concedo)* occurs in sixteen of the eighty or so private charters of the reign of Alexander II (1214–49).[74] Comparable frequencies of occurrence may be detected in the records of Dryburgh abbey, Glasgow cathedral and Kelso abbey.[75] The continuing power of secular lordship in Scotland was such that the lordly will was not as firmly controlled from above as it was under the strongly institutionalised royal authority in England. Rights still depended more or less closely upon the actual *voluntas* of the lord, and this appears to have affected the manner in which his decisions were communicated in writing.

The conditions of tenure and service stipulated in the holding clauses of Earl David's acts do not vary from one country to the other. In each kingdom, he granted or confirmed property to the Church to be held in alms; property conveyed to laymen was normally to be held in return for knight-service. Always to be remembered, however, is that 'the language of diplomatic sometimes evolved and crystallized in forms which did not represent current political ideas or legal realities with precision or accuracy'.[76] There is no doubt that the stylised language of our charters conceals as well as reveals important divergences between the feudal societies of the two realms. In both lands, lay vassals were to hold their possessions in perpetual feu according to hereditary descent (*in feudo et hereditate*); but whereas in Scotland a lord was not bound to acknowledge the heir's claims, in England he could be compelled to admit him into seisin. In both lands, the formulas of the charters stress that the purpose of a grant to a layman was to secure service; but whereas in Scotland the personal element was still real, in England the emphasis was already being placed on those legal and economic aspects of the relationship which benefited a lord financially and which are not in fact mentioned in the charters, namely on scutage and the incidents of escheat, wardship, marriage, relief and aid.

In the *acta* recording Earl David's grants to the Church, the phrase *in liberam et puram et perpetuam elemosinam* is a fairly common jingle. The traditional assumption is that these words, 'in free, pure and perpetual alms', served several purposes, that 'free' secured immunity from the secular courts, 'pure' barred the donor from demanding earthly services, and 'perpetual' guarded against future deprivation. This view can be tested against the evidence of the earl's charters, which in turn must be examined in the context of recent work on the early development of tenure *in elemosinam*.

David's conveyances in alms were not invariably 'free and pure'. Their only standard feature is their 'perpetuity', the emphasis being, apparently, that neither he nor his successors should revoke the gift. Closer examination shows, however, that the variants encountered, whatever their original weight, by now had in practice little, if any, significance. The belief that the characteristic feature of tenure in alms was exemption from secular jurisdiction can no longer be sustained with confidence.[77] Indeed, if the word 'free' was redolent with meaning, it seems curious that in one charter a church is granted *in liberam et puram et perpetuam elemosinam* whereas in a duplicate charter issued later the same church is granted *in puram et perpetuam elemosinam* (Nos. 38, 40). Again, if *puram* was a technical term, it seems difficult to explain why alms which are first specified as merely 'perpetual' can also be 'quit of all service, custom and secular exaction' (No. 73). Similar difficulties are posed whenever it is possible to collate the conditions of a grant with those of its confirmation. A church is given to Lindores abbey *in liberam et puram et perpetuam elemosinam*; David's confirmation omits 'free'.[78] Conversely, land is granted to Lindores *in liberam et perpetuam elemosinam*; the earl's act adds 'pure'.[79]

Too much should not, therefore, be read into the pious terminology of the charters. Analysis supports the view that by *c.*1200 the essence of gifts in alms was that the donees be immune from temporal services to the grantors, irrespective of the variant charter forms. The removal of church property from the power of secular landlords is what ecclesiastical reformers had long fought for, and such an immunity is what they had won. Thus Earl David accepted that when he endowed the Church he should not seek to gain direct material profit, but should provide a full estate outside the framework of dependent lay tenures. Earthly services are never reserved and often explicitly renounced. Where a particular consideration is specified, the services to be performed are spiritual, as in No. 44 for Lindores abbey, in which David renounces all secular exactions and enjoins that 'none of my successors may presume to claim anything from the monks save only prayers for the salvation of the soul'. Such returns, precisely stated, served to reinforce the grantee's freedom from other demands. Earlier in the twelfth century it was perhaps common for gifts in alms to be liable to rent; and in thirteenth-century confirmation charters forinsec burdens may still be reserved. But in Earl David's *acta* 'we glimpse the consolidation of a tenure rooted in a spiritual tie between lord and tenant, in which the imposition of material services appears anomalous and may pose grounds for dispute in the courts'.[80]

'Sicut' clauses

Most of the confirmations carry a phrase such as *sicut carta A testatur*, normally embodied in the holding clause. This was a common usage in David's lifetime. English bishops were already experimenting with the *inspeximus*, which rehearsed in full the charter being ratified.[81] Certain private individuals were also quick to recognise the advantages of this class of document (below, p. 96); but these lords were obviously in a small minority, while it was not until the 1220s that in the English royal chancery the 'greater confirmation' finally replaced the *sicut* form.[82] In the Scottish, the lesser confirmation reigned supreme until the time of Robert I.[83]

A second type of *sicut* clause, which occurs in sixteen of the earl's acts of Scottish provenance, is more interesting and deserves fuller consideration. All save one of the documents in question are frankalmoign charters, and the formula concerned is almost invariably included in the holding clause. Thus in No. 5 for Arbroath abbey property is to be held in alms 'as any abbey most freely, quietly and honourably holds and possesses any alms in the kingdom of Scotland'. There are variations on this theme. In the charters Lindores abbey received for the churches of Conington in Huntingdonshire and Whissendine in Rutland, the location is appropriately rendered by the phrase *in episcopatu Lincolniensi* (Nos. 38–41). 'Alms', which sometimes occurs as the subject of the clause, may be replaced by the type of property actually conveyed, and the terms of comparison can be further restricted. No. 35 grants to the monks of Kelso abbey two benefices in Lennox 'as they most freely ... possess their other churches in the realm of the king, my brother'. By No. 43 the monks of Lindores were to control Mugdrum Island in the Tay estuary 'as they most freely ... possess their other lands by my gift'. A similar comparative clause, carried by a Scottish charter of infeftment, provides that the grantee should hold 'as that knight of mine who best ... possesses his feu' (No. 27).

These formulas are important, for although lacking in precision they illustrate a striving after at least regional uniformity in the tenurial relationship between grantor and grantee. They were, moreover, common legal parlance in Scotland. As in the present collection, the usual territorial term is the general phrase *in (toto) regno Scotie*, one which, from the reign of Malcolm IV, was clearly meant to embrace more than simply the original *Scotia* north of the Forth-Clyde isthmus.[84] Some random examples of the particular are, however, worth noting: *infra comitatum de Dunbar; in episcopatu Glasguensi; in tota Laodonia; in comitatu de Levenax; in episcopatu Sancti Andree.*[85] Pre-feudal Scotland had exhibited a marked diversity of law; this class of *sicut* phrases, general and particular, helps to show how Anglo-Norman settlement in the earlier medieval kingdom went hand in hand with the acceptance of standard legal customs. Furthermore, such phrases could be applied not only to gifts in alms or to the creation of knights' feus, but also to dowry-settlements, grants of burghal tenements, and even to the land a freeman might give to his son.[86]

There is only one comparable example in David's English *acta*: 'as any of my knights most freely ... holds his fee of the honour [of Huntingdon]' (No. 17). In point of fact, constructions of this sort never seem to have been a prominent feature of the English charter. 'As they held on the day King Henry was alive and dead' is a familiar sub-clause of King Stephen's confirmations.[87] English charters of enfeoffment can carry a phrase based on 'as *A* [the predecessor] best and most quietly held', the stress likewise being placed not upon uniformity over a particular area but, as was perhaps appropriate in an older-established feudal society, upon continuity from one generation to the next. Closer to Scottish usage is 'as any alms can best or most freely be had or held by the religious', a form which recurs in the Sixhills priory charters edited by Professor Stenton.[88] But, again, the terms of comparison are not expressed territorially. A charter issued by Robert, earl of Leicester, for Lire abbey in Normandy between 1191 and 1204 appears to be exceptional in this respect. The grant it records was made in alms, 'freely, quietly and honourably, as any alms may be most freely possessed throughout my land'.[89]

Final Protocol

The concluding elements of the *acta* are the warranty, corroboration, witness-list, date and valediction, although in no text are these all present. Only the naming of witnesses was deemed essential.

Warranty

'By the end of the twelfth century a charter generally contained a clause of warranty.'[90] 'An express clause of warranty became customary in charters of feoffment at the beginning of the thirteenth century. By the end of the century, such clauses had become almost universal.'[91] Despite these claims concerning English charters, there are only three cases of warranty and one instance where such an obligation is clearly understood in this collection (Nos. 6, 11, 53, 69). In each explicit example, the earl pledges himself and his heirs to warrant a grant to the grantee and his heirs. Warranty is given *contra omnes homines et feminas; contra omnes gentes*; and, less comprehensively, *contra omnes homines*.

'A warranty is primarily a duty to defend in his seisin a tenant who has vouched one to warrant him. ... a breach of this primary obligation raised a secondary obligation — an obligation to make *escambium* for the lands lost.'[92] The necessity to provide a suitable exchange if the warrantor failed to protect a tenant in his seisin is succinctly acknowledged in No. 53. The earl warrants the gift to the donee and his heirs, and promises that both he and his heirs will 'give them equivalent exchanges from our lands in England if we are unable to warrant those [lands]'. Similarly, No.

69 runs 'and if by chance I or my heirs are unable to warrant the aforesaid rent ... we shall give them an equivalent exchange in our lands in England'. These undertakings, however, served to restrict the warrantor's liability. Neither Earl David nor his descendants could be required to make *escambium* out of Scottish property, and accordingly no claimant would receive compensation if the lord ever ceased to be an English landowner. 'It is in grants for religious purposes that a clause of warranty first becomes a normal feature of a charter, it is rarely found in early grants for military service.'[93] All four instances of warranty noted here in fact belong to lay *acta*, three being knight-service charters. Only one relates to Scotland; the remainder concern property in the Huntingdon honour.

The obligation to vouch for a tenant's title was, of course, implicit in all grants, whether or not it was spelled out in charters. But an express warranty made the obligation more certain and enduring,[94] and emphasised the sense of heritable proprietorship. Did the notion of explicit warranty develop significantly more slowly in Scotland than in England? While Earl David's charters alone scarcely give grounds for assuming that warranty is more likely to be encountered in English than in Scottish *acta*, it seems possible that such was indeed the case. The following shows the occurrence of warranties in thirteenth-century private charters of grant preserved in certain ecclesiastical archives, with the total number of the relevant documents consulted in each collection given in brackets.[95]

England		*Scotland*	
Canonsleigh abbey	66 (99)	Dryburgh abbey	34 (70)
Lincoln cathedral	58 (65)	Kelso abbey	20 (54)
Luffield priory	66 (76)	Lindores abbey	16 (41)
Shrewsbury abbey	159 (208)	St Andrews cathedral priory	9 (39)

These figures may serve to counteract a recent argument that thirteenth-century Scottish feudalism had essentially no reality beyond that to be found in warrandice.[96] Indeed, only three out of a group of forty acts issued by the contemporary earls of Strathearn contain warrandice clauses.[97] In a general sense, the irregular inclusion of explicit warrandice can reasonably be interpreted as a reluctance to acknowledge that a tenant enjoyed a true ownership which should survive any change of lord. But that English lords were regularly bound to formal warranty surely came about in part because prospective tenants appreciated that a lord's decision was no longer conclusive and could easily be overturned in the royal courts by plaintiffs with a better right.[98] In Scotland, a tenant was 'in' provided he had the lord's support and was less likely to lose his lands by judgement. This observation needs to be toned down (though not wholly jettisoned) for the period after the introduction of the brieves of dissasine and mortancestor by the mid-thirteenth century.[99] On the other hand, however, a good lord was one who automatically maintained his men in their sasine and compensated them when need arose. It may well be that the continued strength of lord-man ties played a part in ensuring that for Scottish freeholders implied warrandice often sufficed in itself, and that this contributed in its turn to the seeming infrequency of express covenants in private charters by comparison with those of England.[100]

Corroboration

There are only four instances of the corroboration (Nos. 3, 4, 6, 58), and this small number is apparently to be expected. Although the corroboration-formula had become a characteristic feature of English episcopal charters by the third quarter of the twelfth century, it does not seem to have entered into general use in private *acta* until after Earl David's death.[101]

In three examples, the desirability of supplying proper authentication is stressed in elegant language, and the clause ends with a reference to the application of the earl's seal. The appearance of the terse phrase *in cuius rei testimonium*, copied from English royal letters patent, is of some significance, especially since it occurs in No. 6, a Scottish charter of infeftment.

Witness-list

Forty-nine texts bear a witness-list. Elsewhere, the omission of witnesses is due to abbreviation by copyists, who have made this clear by ending their transcriptions with *testibus*, etc. The extant lists are normally introduced by *hi(i)s testibus*. Because of the tendency of transcribers to abridge *acta*, only the evidence of originals is significant with regard to the number of persons actually named in these clauses. A Scottish formulary of the fifteenth or sixteenth century states that 'according to some, at least five and, according to others, two or three are adequate for an instrument of sasine'.[102] In this collection, the scribes apparently had no clear notion of how many should attest a document. The majority of the original *acta* have between seven and fifteen named witnesses. Four originals have less than seven, two have nineteen, and three have twenty or more. The smallest number in an original is four; the largest is twenty-two.

There is no evident relationship between the number of attestors and the importance of the act which they attested. The longest witness-clause belongs to a simple charter of infeftment (No. 17); two acts, each with twenty witnesses, concern minor grants of teinds and rents (Nos. 3, 4). It seems that the number of witnesses depended in fact not so much upon the magnitude of the business recorded as upon incidental circumstances. The lists appear to have been swelled if the acts to which they belong were given *in curia regis* or before some other gathering where the company present was unusually large. Perhaps the chief consideration, however, was the size of the sheet of parchment available for use.[103]

No women, not even Earl David's wife or his daughters, attested the surviving full texts, though there was no legal obstacle to female witnessing.[104] Laymen predominate. There is not a strong correlation between the subject-matter of a document and the background of its witnesses. Bishops and other high-ranking churchmen normally figure in charters made out for ecclesiastical beneficiaries. But they are also found attesting acts of secular import; and of the seven originals without any clerical witnesses, five are for the Church.

In the witness-lists of King Stephen's charters 'churchmen precede laymen and all are in due order of precedence according to the class of each witness and his status within it'.[105] Of early private *acta* it has been suggested that, by contrast, the listing of witnesses was in general subject to no logical order,[106] and study of Earl

David's charters tends to confirm this view. Whenever King William the Lion does David the honour of attesting, he is naturally accorded seniority. It is again true that bishops and abbots usually, but not invariably, take precedence of earls. Other laymen are placed below archdeacons and deans. These dignitaries always precede chaplains, who themselves are normally placed high in the lists; but chaplains may also be relegated to an inferior position beside laymen of humble social origins. On several occasions they are among the last to be named.

The lay witnesses beneath the status of an earl were from wide and often ill-defined social backgrounds. Only two scribes attempted to differentiate by appellation of rank between one member of this body and another. The practice of assigning the styles *dominus* and *miles* did not gain ground in England and Scotland until later in the thirteenth century,[107] when knighthood had become firmly entrenched as a mark of genuine nobility. Men who at one time served as David's estate stewards are commonly given a high place and sometimes appear above chaplains. But there was no hard-and-fast rule, and in some lists a serving steward of estates can be found lower than laymen of modest standing. In one original, the constable (? of Dundee) has seniority; in two others, the constable of Inverurie is nearly at the bottom of the list. Few laymen, however, are preceded by *magistri* or simple clerks. But the *clerici* are not always last or very low in the lists in which they appear; and Master William, parson of Yardley Hastings in Northamptonshire, is the first witness in a list of eighteen names comprising chaplains and many of David's intimate lay associates. Where a clerk does occur as the final witness, it is dangerous to assume that he was the scribe of the charter.[108]

To sum up: although scribes had little hesitation in giving priority to witnesses of manifest importance, it is plain that they did not observe a rigid ruling with respect to the positioning of individuals who enjoyed a less well-defined social prominence, namely chaplains, clerks and the majority of the earl's lay acquaintances.

However haphazardly their names were set down, the witnesses had a specific legal function. The emphasis was being shifted from oral to written memory. But although the charter, authenticated by its seal, was the more rational and enduring mode of validation, documentary proof was still a matter of testimonial proof. Thus the witnesses were obliged to testify to and corroborate the provisions of the charters in which they were named, and for that reason they 'ought to be freemen and of good repute'.[109] Interesting here is the fact that men of native Scottish ancestry very rarely appear in the lists. In Scotland as in England, those who were normally called upon to attest, and whose word was therefore generally thought to carry greater weight, were of Anglo-continental or English descent. Scribal terminology gives no hint that the witnesses had been present at the judicial actions which the charters recorded. So far as they go, the phrases used give the impression that they had attended at the issue of the written *acta*, which were not necessarily drawn up on the same occasion as that when the substantive transaction took place. Nevertheless, it was not yet a legal requirement for a witness to be physically present at either of these stages. A letter of Robert de Muscamp, lord of Wooler, can be added to the small body of sources which serves to illustrate this point. Between 1216 and 1222 Robert wrote to all those already named as witnesses in his charter for Melrose abbey concerning Hethpool (in Kirknewton), Northumberland: 'I wished you to be cognisant of, and witnesses to, my alms which I have granted to the monks of Melrose, wherefore I entreat you to be witnesses of my gift as is contained in my charter.'[110] Indeed, we may see something of the flexibility of contemporary practice in No. 44, Earl David's *magna carta* for Lindores abbey. It seems evident that when this text was engrossed the witness-list was simply lifted from the earlier foundation charter which it superseded.[111] If the witnesses had 'seen and heard' the previous act, they would not have been wholly ignorant of the new charter's provisions, and could still vouch for their authenticity. Even so, this example suffices in itself to show the difficulties of interpretation that charter witness-clauses can pose. No. 44, however, is probably the exception rather than the rule among David's *acta*. This statement cannot be proved incontrovertibly; but it finds some support in recent researches by English scholars who have based their investigations on the study of large groups of non-royal charters. 'By the 13th century it seems to have become usual for all to be present at the making of the charter — the witnesses being, in Giry's phrase, witnesses "de la documentation" rather than "de l'action".'[112]

Date

Private charters earlier than the late thirteenth century rarely bear a dating clause, and there is no example of a time-date in this collection. Only four acts, three of which are Scottish, contain a date of place, which was presumably the place of issue: thus, Markinch, Haddington, Roxburgh and the unidentified *Wanntona* (Nos. 28, 34–5, 68). (There is, of course, the chance of its omission by copyists in *acta* not surviving as originals.) Each place-date, introduced by *apud*, immediately follows the witness-list. It may be assumed that the influence here was primarily that of the Scots royal charter, which from the reign of King David I usually carried a date of place.

Valediction

Only two acts conclude with an expression of farewell, given in the form of a simple *valete* (Nos. 68, 73). (Again, other examples may have been lost through abridgement by copyists.) The use of *valete* is particularly noticeable in twelfth-century episcopal charters, though the practice declined towards 1200.[113] Later, as was appropriate to its epistolary character, *valete* appears as a distinctive feature of letters patent.

In western Europe generally the twelfth century was a period when government became more rational, more bureaucratic and more efficient. Nowhere is this seen more clearly than in the rise of the use of the written word in communicating orders and decisions. Whereas writing had once been unimportant or largely entrusted to monastic *scriptoria*, in France, England and Scotland the monarchs secured a permanent nucleus of officials to produce *acta* and disposed of increasingly well-organised chanceries as essential departments of state.[114] At the same time, bishops were concerned to mobilise effective secretariats of their own. The interrelationships between public and private *acta* are manifest. Can it be said with justification that even by *c.*1200 it is doubtful 'that magnates possessed organized writing offices or chanceries'?[115]

So far as Earl David is concerned, let us stress those points which suggest the absence of a regular body of trained scribes. Palaeographical study shows that some charters presumably did emanate from recipients, and the variety we have often encountered in analysing the internal features of the *acta* might seem to indicate the prominence of external production. But, then, many charters of Henry II of England and William the Lion were the products of beneficiaries' scribes.[116] This suggests that 'local' writing may tell us more about the strong scribal traditions of particular monasteries than about the nature of particular secular administrations.[117] Moreover, the period 1180–1220 was still one of experimentation in the drafting of written instruments. Increasingly, scribes submitted to rules imposed by the developing land law and office routine; but private *acta* especially had yet to become fully stereotyped. Even in episcopal chanceries, 'dictators or scribes ... took a special delight in providing variety within a uniform medium', so that they might ring the changes in a manner that was not governed by the subject-matter — although in itself 'variety of function dictated considerable variety of form'.[118]

What, on the other hand, are the reasons for believing that Earl David employed a permanent group of professional scribes? His lordship was closely bound up with writing. He was attended on his perambulations by household clerks. Not all these men were necessarily capable of writing charters; but we know that some could draw on experience of other administrations, that the earl often deemed their services worthy of reward, that a few were able enough to be promoted to higher employment, and that some were men of academic learning and knowledgeable of the law. Master Peter of Paxton had a collection of legal treatises ready to hand; others were entrusted with upholding David's interests as attorneys in the English royal courts.[119] It seems inescapable that a number of these literate men were regularly called upon to draft and write his charters, although in only one case does positive proof exist that a household clerk actually put pen to parchment (above, p. 79). Only two or three *clerici* may have served at the same time; but it has yet to be demonstrated that any more than five royal scribes were simultaneously employed by King Henry II.[120] The variations in the component parts of the *acta* co-exist with a certain uniformity in draftsmanship. And where the variants are not confined to minor points of wording, they are often rational, related to the nature of the business being dealt with.

Needless to say, the extent to which the observable homogeneity of structure and phrasing was due to legal requirements, to common currency, or to regular work for the same master, raises exceptionally difficult issues. We can, however, be quite clear that David's administration was not as advanced as that of his brother-in-law, Earl Ranulf of Chester (d. 1232). Earl Ranulf employed a chancellor, and his scribes used a formulary; they issued letters patent, final concords and judicial writs, and they adopted a system of enrolment.[121] No case can be made that David's arrangements mirrored those of Count John of Mortain, whose whole household was closely modelled on the departments of contemporary Angevin royal government. His chancery dispatched charters whose *clausulae* were firmly grounded upon those of English royal *acta*: most notably, they normally contained a place-date and (from 1195) a time-date; and their scribes were ahead of royal clerks in borrowing the *inspeximus* from episcopal diplomatic.[122] Nor did Earl David deploy a specialised clerical administration like that of his successors, the fourteenth-century lords of the regality of Garioch.[123] Nevertheless, the majority of his charters are marked by terse and lucid draftsmanship; their script is generally that of men who were used to dealing with documents and were expected to work at speed, while in other respects their external features reveal instructive degrees of regularity (above, p. 79). Scribes had access to earlier charters when they needed to refer to them, and we cannot assume that where *acta* were based on documents in a beneficiary's archive, they were therefore written outside the earl's household (above, pp. 81, 84).[124] This does, however, help to account for the variant diplomatic usages in Earl David's acts by factors other than external writing. The charter form was used for many different purposes. But the scribes were not entirely ignorant of new practices, which in any case had yet to become standard elsewhere. Beneficiaries could be supplied with duplicate charters in the same manner as by the Scots crown (Nos. 38–41).[125] The earl could demonstrate his authority by 'granting' rather than confirming earlier gifts (above, p. 76) — the use of *dedisse* indicating a strong control over the drafting and thus the involvement of household clerks. One text was produced in the form of a bipartite document, so that the earl and the grantee would each receive a copy (see plate 3). That strengthened its probatory force; but even though the beneficiary had very probably seen to the production of this *carta duplicata*, it may also show that the earl's administration was interested in preserving for its own purposes a record of his decisions, and this is the principle that lay behind enrolment. In short, Earl David did not have a fully-fledged chancery, but the indications are that he had access to fairly advanced secretarial arrangements, and that these acted as an important medium through which at the baronial level techniques of written business were disseminated in England and, not least, in Scotland.

The second main problem which we set ourselves at the outset was how far David's charters elucidate legal history. Inevitably, the *acta* are disappointingly uninformative about forms of process. But since charters were directed to the single goal of providing proof recognised by the courts, they had to submit to rules of contemporary law. And since charters, as legal documents, had to conform to legal rulings, it is a point of first importance that there are no major differences in form between the earl's English and Scottish acts. This study therefore gives some support to Maitland's claim that 'we may doubt whether a man who crossed the river [Tweed] felt that he had passed from the land of one law to the land of another'.[126]

But in their details the charters also provide us with due qualifications. In law, and in administration, the two countries came to share a common heritage, yet although their legal systems were thus founded upon the same basic principles, they evolved under different influences. The divergences, and the resemblances, between legal developments in the earlier medieval kingdoms have still to be fully worked out, and it is already clear that the contrasts flowing from the fact that royal justice had a less decisive impact upon local jurisdictions in Scotland cannot be detected solely from the formal phraseology of charters. But this analysis will have served its purpose if it has succeeded in emphasising how rewarding it can be to study legal and administrative history in an Anglo-Scottish setting without being bound by the traditional national divisions.[127]

NOTES

1. Stringer, *Earl David.*

2. *Ibid.*, app., nos. 3-6, 11-13, 15, 17-20, 23-4, 27-8, 31, 33-47, 49-51, 53-6, 58-61, 65-6, 68-9, 71-6, 78-9. In this chapter, further reference to Earl David's surviving charters is made in the form No. 3, etc.

3. W.H. Stevenson, 'An Old-English charter of William the Conqueror', *EHR*, xi (1896), p. 735; H. Hall, *Studies in English Official Historical Documents* (Cambridge, 1908), pp. 157ff.

4. A. Saltman, *Theobald, Archbishop of Canterbury* (London, 1956); *Acta Stephani Langton, Cantuariensis Archiepiscopi, A.D. 1207-1228*, ed. K. Major (Canterbury and York Soc., 1950).

5. The inaugural volume of this series is *English Episcopal Acta*: i, *Lincoln 1067-1185*, ed. D.M. Smith (London, 1980).

6. 'Charters of the earldom of Hereford, 1095–1201', ed. D. Walker in *Camden Miscellany*, xxii (1964), pp. 1–75; *Earldom of Gloucester Charters: The Charters and Scribes of the Earls and Countesses of Gloucester to A.D. 1217*, ed. R.B. Patterson (Oxford, 1973); *Charters of the Honour of Mowbray, 1107-1191*, ed. D.E. Greenway (London, 1972).

7. See above all his introductory remarks in *Gilbertine Chrs.*

8. Simpson, 'RQ', Ch. 4.

9. M.T. Clanchy, *From Memory to Written Record: England, 1066-1307* (London, 1979), is of seminal importance for an understanding of the general background, although it tends to underestimate the pace of the spread of documentary habits.

10. *Earldom of Gloucester Charters*; É. Houth, 'Catalogue des actes de Robert II, comte de Meulan', *Bulletin philologique et historique*, année 1961, pp. 499–543; *Acta Stephani Langton*; M. Jones, 'A Collection of the *Acta* of John, lord of Ireland and count of Mortain' (unpublished Manchester University M.A. thesis, 1949).

11. V. Chandler, 'Ada de Warenne, queen mother of Scotland', *SHR*, lx (1981), pp. 135–8.

12. For some evidence that certain lesser landowners in thirteenth-century Scotland may not have been used to committing their transactions to writing see *Coupar Angus Chrs.*, i, no. 37; *Dryb. Lib.*, nos. 196–7; *Liber Sancte Marie de Balmorinach* (Abbotsford Club, 1841), no. 25; *Lind. Cart.*, no. 71; *Scone Liber*, no. 95.

13. PRO JUST 1/341, m. 2d, furnishes an example involving a now lost charter of Earl David for Sawtry abbey.

14. R.L.G. Ritchie, *The Normans in Scotland* (Edinburgh, 1954), p. 378.

15. There is no adequate account of the interaction between feudal and royal law in Scotland to compare with the works of Professor Milsom cited below, but two fruitful contributions to such a study have recently appeared: R. Burgess, *Perpetuities in Scots Law* (Stair Soc., 1979), and H.L. MacQueen, 'Dissasine and mortancestor in Scots law', *Journal of Legal History*, iv (1983), pp. 21–49.

16. Nos. 42, 44, 47, 50; *Lind. Cart.*, no. 81.

17. Useful here is S.E. Thorne, 'English feudalism and estates in land', *Cambridge Law Journal*, xvii (1959), esp. pp. 204–6.

18. Cf. S.F.C. Milsom, *Historical Foundations of the Common Law*, 2nd edn. (London, 1981), p. 115.

19. *Ibid.*, p. 100.

20. *Ibid.*, Chs. 5, 6; elaborated in *idem*, *The Legal Framework of English Feudalism* (Cambridge, 1976).

21. *Gilbertine Chrs.*, p. xix; cf. *Fitznells Cartulary*, ed. C.A.F. Meekings and P. Shearman (Surrey Rec. Soc., 1968), p. cxliii.

22. SRO GD 204/23/2. Similar to No. 55 is a charter of Robert de Brus, datable *c.*1215, confirming land in Dryfesdale, Dumfriesshire, *in nemore et plano, in terra et aqua, in monasterio et molendino*, the word *monasterium* being used here in the sense of 'parish church' or 'minster': *TDGAS*, 3rd ser., xxxv (1956–7), pp. 14–19. Cf. also *TCWAAS*, new ser., xvii (1917), pp. 218–19 (charter of Uhtred of Galloway, 1162 × 1175).

It is noteworthy how canonical strictures were influencing the private charter: Norman granted Leslie church with its full appurtenances, as if it were a mere secular property at his disposal; by Earl John's day, it had begun to be recognised that the gift of a church was essentially the gift of an advowson.

23. *RRS*, vi, p. 20.

24. A.B. Webster, *Scotland from the Eleventh Century to 1603* (London, 1975), pp. 72–3.

25. For the following see Stringer, *Earl David*, pp. 151ff.

26. Cf. *English Episcopal Acta*, i, p. lviii; C.H. Hunter Blair, 'A note upon mediaeval seals with special reference to those in Durham treasury', *Archaeologia Aeliana*, 3rd ser., xvii (1920), pp. 257–8.

27. Stringer, *Earl David*, p. 214.

28. *Ibid.*, pp. 213–14.

29. Cf. J.-F. Lemarignier, *Le gouvernement royal aux premiers temps capétiens (987–1108)* (Paris, 1965), pp. 128–31.

30. Cf. R.H.C. Davis, *King Stephen, 1135–1154* (London, 1977 reprint), p. 130.

31. *RRS*, i, p. 99.

32. E.g., *Cartularium Abbathiae de Rievalle*, ed. J.C. Atkinson (Surtees Soc., 1889), no. 185; *Facsimiles of Royal and other Charters in the British Museum*, ed. G.F. Warner and H.J. Ellis (London, 1903), no. 54; *Rufford Charters*, ed. C.J. Holdsworth (Thoroton Soc., 1972–81), ii, no. 721.

33. G.W.S. Barrow, 'Das mittelalterliche englische und schottische Königtum: ein Vergleich', *Historisches Jahrbuch*, cii (1982), p. 379.

34. Cf. C.R. Cheney, *English Bishops' Chanceries, 1100–1250* (Manchester, 1950), p. 55, n. 2; *De oorkonden der graven van Vlaanderen (1191-aanvang 1206)*, ed. W. Prevenier (Brussels, 1964–71), i, pp. 363–4; *Actes des comtes de Namur ... 946–1196*, ed. F. Rousseau (Brussels, 1936), p. cxl.

35. A. de Boüard, *Manuel de diplomatique française et pontificale: diplomatique générale* (Paris, 1929), pp. 265–6.

36. Barrow, *Era*, p. 6, n. 25.

37. Stringer, *Earl David*, p. 84.

38. *RRS*, i, p. 74.

39. *RRS*, ii, no. 48.

40. L. Delisle, *Recueil des actes de Henri II concernant les provinces françaises et les affaires de France: introduction* (Paris, 1909), p. 208.

41. *RRS*, i, p. 73; ii, p. 76; vi, p. 20.

42. It appears in the addresses of only five out of the 163 full texts collected for Malcolm IV (*RRS*, i, nos. 131, 144, 146, 150, 207), while *amici* are never addressed in the surviving acts of William the Lion.

43. At least in the charters executed by royal clerks: T.A.M. Bishop, *Scriptores Regis* (Oxford, 1961), p. 19.

44. There are only two instances in *Durham Episcopal Charters, 1071–1152*, ed. H.S. Offler (Surtees Soc., 1968). Both *acta* (*ibid.*, nos. 12, 13) were written by the same scribe. No

example occurs in *English Episcopal Acta*, i, or in M.G. Cheney, *Roger, Bishop of Worcester, 1164–1179* (Oxford, 1980), app. I.

45. 'Charters of the earldom of Hereford', ed. Walker, nos. 90–109, 112–23; *Documents Illustrative of the Social and Economic History of the Danelaw*, ed. F.M. Stenton (London, 1920).

46. Cf. *Gilbertine Chrs.*, p. xviii.

47. *Ibid*; cf. *Fitznells Cartulary*, p. cxlii.

48. *Book of Seals*, nos. 116, 191, 298, 444–5.

49. *Ibid.*, no. 445 with notes.

50. *Aberdeen Reg.*, i, p. 14; *Coldstream Chartulary*, no. 7; *Miscellany of the SHS*, iv (1926), p. 311; W. Fraser, *The Lennox* (Edinburgh, 1874), ii, no. 4; *Moray Reg.*, no. 259; *Inchaffray Chrs.*, nos. 11, 12, 19, 25, 28, 34, 43–4, 58; *TDGAS*, 3rd ser., xxxv (1956–7), facsimile facing p. 14.

51. *Dryb. Lib.*, no. 97, a charter of Richard de Morville (d. by 1190) in which *A* and *B* are combined, must be regarded as an aberration from the norm. Parallel English examples in *Book of Seals*, nos. 143, 197.

52. Cheney, *English Bishops' Chanceries*, p. 68.

53. *Ibid.*, p. 69.

54. Cf. Simpson, 'RQ', pp. 176–8.

55. *Gilbertine Chrs.*, p. xviii.

56. Barrow, *Bruce*, p. 40.

57. *RRS*, i, *passim*; ii, nos. 41, 49–58, 146, 263.

58. *RRS*, ii, no. 41; i, no. 197.

59. Saltman, *Theobald*, p. 197; *Acta Stephani Langton*, p. xxvii.

60. Cf. *Earldom of Gloucester Charters*, pp. 21–2; 'Charters of the earldom of Hereford', nos. 93ff.

61. E.g., Saltman, *Theobald*, p. 210; *Acta Stephani Langton*, p. xxviii.

62. *English Episcopal Acta*, i, p. lvi.

63. Simpson, 'RQ', pp. 183–4.

64. E.g., *The Cartulary of Tutbury Priory*, ed. A. Saltman (Collections for a History of Staffordshire, 1962), no. 162.

65. V.H. Galbraith, 'Monastic foundation charters of the eleventh and twelfth centuries', *Cambridge Historical Journal*, iv (1932–4), pp. 205–22.

66. Stringer, *Earl David*, pp. 93–4.

67. *Gilbertine Chrs.*, p. xxviii.

68. Cf. *ibid.*

69. *Calendar of Antrobus Deeds before 1625*, ed. R.B. Pugh (Wiltshire Archaeol. and Natural History Soc., Records Branch, 1947), p. xxxvii.

70. Simpson, 'RQ', pp. 190–4; I.A. Milne, 'Land tenures in Scotland in the twelfth and thirteenth centuries' (unpublished Edinburgh University Ph.D. thesis, 1953), p. 266.

71. *RRS*, i, p. 82; *Gilbertine Chrs.*, p. xxxiii.

72. *Ibid.*

73. A.P. Duggan, 'The chancery of the Norman earls of Chester' (unpublished Liverpool University M.A. thesis, 1951), pp. 41, 62–5.

74. *Melrose Liber, passim.*

75. *Dryb. Lib*; *Glasgow Reg*; *Kelso Liber.*

76. C.R. Cheney, 'On the acta of Theobald and Thomas, archbishops of Canterbury', *Journal of the Soc. of Archivists*, vi (1978–81), p. 481.

77. A.W. Douglas, 'Frankalmoin and jurisdictional immunity: Maitland revisited', *Speculum*, liii (1978), pp. 26–48.

78. *Lind. Cart.*, no. 81; No. 50.

79. *Lind. Cart.*, no. 36; No. 42.

80. A.W. Douglas, 'Tenure *in elemosina*: origins and establishment in twelfth-century England', *American Journal of Legal History*, xxiv (1980), p. 111.

81. Cheney, *English Bishops' Chanceries*, pp. 90–6.

82. V.H. Galbraith, 'A new charter of Henry II to Battle abbey', *EHR*, lii (1937), pp. 70–3.

83. *RRS*, i, pp. 60–1; vi, p. 22.

84. Barrow, *Era*, pp. 153–4. But note *Cartularium Prioratus de Gyseburne*, etc., ed. W. Brown (Surtees Soc., 1889–94), ii, no. 1180 (charter by Robert Bruce, d. 1304): 'as any church of England or Scotland most freely and quietly holds any alms'.

85. Respectively, *Coldstream Chartulary*, nos. 22–3, 32, 34; *Registrum Domus de Soltre* (Bannatyne Club, 1861), no. 25; *Holyrood Liber*, no. 33; Fraser, *Lennox*, ii, no. 7; *St Andrews Liber*, p. 168.

86. E.g., W. Fraser, *The Melvilles Earls of Melville and the Leslies Earls of Leven* (Edinburgh, 1890), iii, nos. 4, 8; *Liber ... de Balmorinach*, nos. 21, 23, 25, 32; *Miscellany of the SHS*, iv, p. 316.

87. *Regesta Regum Anglo-Normannorum, 1066-1154*, iv, ed. H.A. Cronne and R.H.C. Davis (Oxford, 1969), p. 10.

88. *Gilbertine Chrs.*, pp. 1–38.

89. Évreux, Archives Départementales de l'Eure, H 438/16.

90. *Gilbertine Chrs.*, p. xxviii.

91. S.J. Bailey, 'Warranties of land in the thirteenth century', *Cambridge Law Journal*, viii (1944), pp. 275–6.

92. *Ibid.*, p. 284.

93. *Gilbertine Chrs.*, p. xxix.

94. *Registrum Monasterii S. Marie de Cambuskenneth* (Grampian Club, 1872), nos. 70–1, 73, show Cambuskenneth abbey securing 'improved' charters from Earl Saher de Quincy (d. 1219) concerning Abbots Deuglie (in Arngask), Perthshire, in order to obtain full warranty. A parallel example involving Earl Saher and the bishopric of Lincoln in *Registrum Antiquissimum of the Cathedral Church of Lincoln*, iii, ed. C.W. Foster (Lincoln Rec. Soc., 1935), nos. 873–4.

95. Sources as follows: *The Cartulary of Canonsleigh Abbey*, ed. V.C.M. London (Devon and Cornwall Rec. Soc., new ser., 1965); *Reg. Antiquissimum of ... Lincoln*, iii; *Luffield Priory Charters*, i, ed. G.R. Elvey (Northamptonshire Rec. Soc., 1968); *The Cartulary of Shrewsbury Abbey*, ed. U. Rees (Aberystwyth, 1975); *Dryb. Lib*; *Kelso Liber*; *Lind. Cart.* (excluding charters of Earl David); *St Andrews Liber*.

96. Duncan, *Scotland*, pp. 407–9.

97. *Inchaffray Chrs.*, nos. 86–7, 114.

98. For examples of Earl David's failure to warrant English tenancies to grantees see *CurRR*, vii, p. 213; *Pleas before the King or his Justices, 1198-1212*, ed. D.M. Stenton (Selden Soc., 1953–67), iv, nos. 4668, 4743, 4746.

99. MacQueen, 'Dissasine and mortancestor', pp. 21–49.

100. From 1290 allowance must be made for the encouragement given to express warranties in England by *Quia Emptores*, a statute to which there was no Scottish equivalent: cf. T.F.T. Plucknett, 'Deeds and seals', *Trans. of the Royal Historical Soc.*, 4th ser., xxxii (1950), p. 149.

101. Cheney, *English Bishops' Chanceries*, pp. 75–6; *Gilbertine Chrs.*, p. xxx.

102. 'De Composicione Cartarum', ed. J.J. Robertson in *Miscellany One* (Stair Soc., 1971), p. 87.

103. Cf. F.M. Stenton, *Anglo-Saxon England*, 3rd edn. (Oxford, 1971), p. 551; D.M. Stenton, *EHR*, lxxi (1956), p. 640. In the great majority of the originals the parchment is fully used up, so that very few have space for inscribing the names of additional witnesses.

104. W. Ross, *Lectures on the Practice of the Law of Scotland* (Edinburgh, 1792), i, pp. 125, 148; T. Madox, *Formulare Anglicanum* (London, 1702), p. xxxi. Even so, see *Cartulary of the Abbey of Old Wardon*, ed. G.H. Fowler (Bedfordshire Historical Rec. Soc., 1930), p. 9: 'women attest only in very early cases; neither in this nor in other cartularies has the editor found them to attest in the xiii cent.' Here is another subject worthy of fuller study.

105. *Reg. Regum Anglo-Normannorum*, iv, p. 9. Similarly, concerning the charters of Henry II, Delisle, *Recueil*, p. 225, and, concerning episcopal diplomatic, M. Parisse, 'Les chartes des évêques de Metz au xiie siècle', *Archiv für Diplomatik*, xxii (1976), pp. 290–2.

106. *Documents Illustrative of the ... Danelaw*, ed. Stenton, p. civ.

107. Cf. below, pp. 108–9.

108. J.H. Hodson, 'Medieval charters: the last witness', *Journal of the Soc. of Archivists*, v (1974–7), pp. 71–89.

109. 'De Composicione Cartarum', p. 87.

110. *Melrose Liber*, i, no. 306.

111. Stringer, *Earl David*, p. 94.

112. S. Bond, 'The attestation of medieval private charters relating to New Windsor', *Journal of the Soc. of Archivists*, iv (1970–3), p. 278. Further, *Fitznells Cartulary*, p. cxlvii; D.E. Greenway in *The Materials, Sources and Methods of Ecclesiastical History* (*Studies in Church History*, 1975), pp. 57–60.

113. Cf. *The Acta of the Bishops of Chichester, 1075-1207*, ed. H. Mayr-Harting (Canterbury and York Soc., 1964), p. 12; *Acta Stephani Langton*, pp. xlv–vi.

114. For France see G. Tessier, *Diplomatique royale française* (Paris, 1962); F. Gasparri, *L'écriture des actes de Louis VI, Louis VII et Philippe Auguste* (Geneva, 1973).

115. Clanchy, *From Memory to Written Record*, p. 40.

116. Bishop, *Scriptores Regis*, esp. pp. 9–10; *RRS*, ii, p. 70.

117. Cf. *Les chartes de l'abbaye de Waulsort: étude diplomatique et édition critique*, i, ed. G. Despy (Brussels, 1957), pp. 277–8.

118. *The Letters and Charters of Gilbert Foliot*, ed. A. Morey and C.N.L. Brooke (Cambridge, 1967), pp. 23, 26.

119. E.g., *CurRR*, i, pp. 73, 93; iii, p. 274.

120. Bishop, *Scriptores Regis*, p. 30.

121. Duggan, 'Chancery of the Norman earls of Chester'; G. Barraclough, 'The earldom and county palatine of Chester', *Trans. of the Historic Soc. of Lancashire and Cheshire*, ciii (1952), pp. 35–6.

122. Jones, '*Acta* of John, lord of Ireland', i, pp. 31ff.

123. *Aberdeen Reg.*, i, p. 167.

124. Cf. L.E. Boyle, 'Diplomatics', in *Medieval Studies: An Introduction*, ed. J.E. Powell (Syracuse, 1976), p. 86.

125. Cf. *RRS*, ii, p. 83.

126. F. Pollock and F.W. Maitland, *The History of English Law*, 2nd edn. (Cambridge, 1968 reissue), i, p. 222.

127. My colleague Dr P.D. King kindly read this chapter in typescript and made valuable suggestions for improvement.

5

THE *FAMILIA* OF ROGER DE QUINCY, EARL OF WINCHESTER AND CONSTABLE OF SCOTLAND

Grant G. Simpson

Roger[1] de Quincy, who died in 1264, belonged to a family of French origin, whose founder in England was Saher de Quincy I, a tenant about 1124–9 of land at Long Buckby (Northants) held of Anselm de Chokes.[2] It is virtually certain that Saher took his name from Cuinchy (cant. Cambrin, arr. Béthune, dép. Pas-de-Calais), on what later became the border of Artois and Flanders, as this place is less than sixteen kilometres from Chocques, the original home of his Northamptonshire overlord. Saher's second son, Robert de Quincy I, settled about 1165 in Scotland, then well known as a land of opportunity.[3] His advancement was evidently assisted by King Malcolm IV and King William I, who were his cousins: Robert's grandmother, Maud de Senlis the elder, had married as her second husband King David I, grandfather of Malcolm and William. Like many members of his family, Robert made a 'good marriage' by wedding an heiress, Orabile, daughter of Nes son of William, who brought to him extensive properties, mainly in Fife. The senior line of the family died out about 1191 and Robert himself died in 1197, after a distinguished career in Scotland which included a period from about 1170 to about 1178 as a royal justiciar of Lothian.[4] His son, Saher IV, also made a striking match by marrying, perhaps about 1190, Margaret de Beaumont, sister and co-heir of Robert 'Fitz Pernel', fourth earl of Leicester. Saher thus acquired considerable estates, particularly in the English Midlands, and a social position which led him into a busy and important public life. He served both Richard I and John, and as a reward was raised to the peerage as earl of Winchester about 1206–7. Earl Saher became a crusader, but fell ill and died at Damietta in 1219.

The family into which Roger was born, about 1195, as second son of Saher IV, was French in origin and background, although its Anglo-Scottish members presumably did not continue to hold French lands after the loss of Normandy in 1204. French influence was strengthened by Saher's marriage to one of the Beaumonts, who were among the greatest of Anglo-Norman families. French names such as Robert and Orabile are prominent in the Quincy family tree and the family was probably still French-speaking, although most of its members by Roger's time may also have known English. Yet although its roots were French, the family had become essentially Anglo-Scottish, and in assessing the influence of each of the three countries, we must give due weight to Scotland, since it provided the opening which enabled Robert I to raise the family into a position of some prominence. England was important since it gave them an initial impetus and since a family tradition of service to the kings of England quickly grew up and flourished. When Saher succeeded to part of the earldom of Leicester lands, the family's English interests widened considerably. 'While their feudal power was never sufficient to place them in the top rank of the English baronage, the Quincys played an important part for some six score years in the history of both England and Scotland.'[5]

French, English and Scottish strands are woven inextricably in the life of the Quincys. Their daily interests traversed three different countries and their outlook transcended national frontiers. It is not surprising that the family produced three crusaders: Roger's grandfather, father and younger brother. When Earl Saher became an English peer, the family became part of the aristocracy of Western Europe. Roger de Quincy was born a European.

As a result of his father's death in 1219, Roger acquired the Quincy lands in both England and Scotland. But his mother retained control of the former Leicester lands and along with them the title of countess of Winchester. Roger was not recognised as earl of Winchester until her death in 1235, when he inherited her lands; and it was natural in the circumstances that during his mother's widowhood he apparently took a great interest in Scotland and in his estates there. Following family tradition, he married, as the first of his three wives, a rich heiress, and a Scottish one at that. She was Helen of Galloway, eldest daughter of Alan, lord of Galloway, who succeeded on her father's death in 1234 to very considerable properties in southern, particularly south-western, Scotland. Roger also succeeded, in right of his wife, to the largely honorific position of Constable of the king of Scots, together with some scattered lands attached to that office. By 1235, therefore, Roger had acquired numerous, and notably widespread, estates throughout Scotland and England. In Scotland, indeed, he had become one of the great magnates of the realm, with his main properties in Perthshire, Fife, Lothian, Berwickshire and Galloway. His English lands were mainly in Leicestershire, Northamptonshire and Huntingdonshire, but outlying properties spread as far north as Cumberland and as far south as Dorset. Indeed, it was possible for Earl Roger to travel from Perthshire to the English Channel, and, except for a stretch of about a hundred miles in the north of England, never be more than thirty or forty miles at most from some piece of land in which he had an interest. He has been rightly described as 'one of the most widespread landholders in England and Scotland'.[6]

Yet, although his territorial standing was notable, Roger's political career was largely undistinguished; and his personal life was ultimately unhappy. He was summoned to take part in various English expeditions against the Welsh over the years from 1241 to 1264, and in 1242 joined Henry III's unfortunate expedition to Poitou and Gascony. He was involved in a few of the activities of the baronial party which opposed Henry III from 1258 onwards, but remained mainly in the background of these affairs. During the years 1257–61, he travelled frequently to Scotland as ambassador of Henry III to assist in dealing with the problems arising from Alexander III's minority; but again Roger appears rather as one of the supporting players than as a principal actor in the drama. His family life came to revolve around one tragic fact: he had no male heir to succeed him. His first wife, Helen of Galloway, bore him three daughters only and neither Maud, widow of the ninth earl of Pembroke, nor Eleanor, daughter of the fifth earl of Derby, whom he married secondly and thirdly, gave him any children at all. Matthew Paris notes that, on the death of Maud, he married his third wife with speed, 'still hoping to obtain from the Lord the favour of begetting a son'.[7] When he died on 25 April 1264, as the last male of his house, he must have been close to seventy, and although his personality remains to us largely a blank, we can at least be sure that — lacking a son — the old earl died a very disappointed man.

The fact that the Quincy family name died out with Roger has led many historians into the error of underrating the Quincys' considerable social importance in an Anglo-Scottish context over many decades. They lived on a par with four other major 'cross-Border' landowning families of the thirteenth century: the earls of Huntingdon, and the families of Bruce, Balliol and Comyn.[8] Indeed, this entire body of top-rank Anglo-Scottish magnates has until recently remained under-studied in print, and even misunderstood: national historians are sometimes prone to ignore those of a baron's activities which lie beyond one set of national frontiers.[9] Earl Roger demonstrates particularly well the milieu of the foremost Anglo-Scottish barons of the mid-thirteenth century, and it is vital to use evidence about him from both sides of the Border in order to draw a fully-rounded, not merely a one-dimensional, picture. To comprehend Roger and his position within the Scottish nobility of his time, his English background too must be carefully investigated.

The comparatively abundant source-material about him, mainly in the form of charters, makes it possible to study a number of aspects of his lordship — that lynch-pin of the entire social structure of his era. In particular, we can discover a certain amount about some of those who surrounded Earl Roger and can reveal something of their relations with the earl and with the rest of the world. Magnate followings prior to the fourteenth century have hitherto been given little detailed attention by historians of either England or Scotland.[10] The topic is worthy of notice, since each following had a pivotal role as a source of a magnate's social influence and prestige, and each following also represented the essential base of a lord's political and administrative activities.

None of the earl's household accounts has survived, and it is therefore impossible to draw a detailed picture of the administration of his household or to describe its daily routine, as can be done for a few other thirteenth-century households.[11] There are no explicit references to officials such as the steward of the household, the wardrober and the receiver-general, who are named in other households and may have existed in Earl Roger's. Some minor officers make occasional appearances. In Master Robert, the earl's doctor, who occurs twice as a witness, we have an official seldom mentioned in documents, yet of some importance to a great household.[12] Geoffrey the cook and Richard 'of the kitchen' (*de coquina*) appear as witnesses, and a deed about the earl's borough of Brackley (Northants) reveals that at least one burgess from there contributed the sum of 1½d. annually in support of the earl's kitchen.[13] One of the earl's tenants, Robert de Noveray, held his fee of Burton Overy (Leics) by the service of setting the first dish on the earl's table.[14] Such scraps of information are more tantalising than helpful. Equally frustrating is the absence of any specific reference to a baronial council, a body known to have existed in England as early as the twelfth century.[15] In the preamble of a charter about a disputed presentation to the church of Lathrisk in Fife, Earl Roger states that he and his *familiares* considered that the patronage of the church belonged to him.[16] This suggests little more than the informal consultation about business affairs which was part of everyday routine, and provides no proof that a council existed by that name.

The word *familiares* is significant, however, for if the evidence is insufficient for a comprehensive survey of household administration, it is certainly more abundant for a study of those who were attached to and intimate with the earl. A great man's *familia* was not merely his own family, although it would include some of his relations; in a sense it was an extension of his family.[17] It was not the same as his household: some household officers would be *familiares*, but domestic servants at the level of the laundress and the pantry-boy would not be.

Some of Roger's *familiares* can be traced in the extensive public records of England. But even here there are problems, for individuals closely attached to the earl may have had few occasions to deal with the central government and therefore few opportunities of being noted in the records by the ever-busy royal clerks. And it is often difficult to identify people. Was William de Bois who held half a knight's fee in Theydon Bois (Essex) in 1236 the same as William de Bois who held Nash (Bucks) in 1237–40?[18] Or the same as William de Bois who held one-third of a knight's fee at Finmere (Oxon) of the earl of Gloucester in 1242?[19] And was any one of them the same as Sir William de Bois, brother of Ernald de Bois, a frequent witness to charters by Earl Roger? It has proved difficult to establish a coherent sequence of biographical facts about some members of the *familia*. There is sometimes nothing to indicate whether a person with a particular name is in fact identical with a member of the *familia* so named or is some entirely different individual.

In the absence of household records, we must turn to the texts of Roger's acts for an answer to the question, Who were the important members of the *familia*? The charters are witnessed by a total of 315 persons;[20] and it is a reasonable assumption that the clerks who drafted the charters habitually named in the witness-lists persons who bore a significant relation to the earl on the occasion of his legal act which each charter records. The witnesses must frequently have been present when the act was passed, although the physical presence of a witness was not a necessity.[21] The clerks no doubt had a variety of motives in selecting appropriate witnesses. At the simplest, we find that John the chaplain of Tranent in East Lothian, who witnesses only one act of Earl Roger's, is witness to an agreement about teinds in the parish of Tranent.[22] It was convenient here to include a local cleric in the list; but no other clerk of any surviving charter chose to include John on any other occasion. His importance as part of Earl Roger's world was small, at least in the eyes of the clerks. On the other hand, those who witnessed frequently may be assumed to be those whom the clerks held to be significant personages in the context of the granting of the earl's charters. And on a practical level, those who appear often as witnesses must often have been present with the earl. By discovering the names of those who regularly witnessed his charters we can reveal those who mattered within his *familia*.

The frequency of occurrence of witnesses is shown in the accompanying table.

Table 2. *Frequency of occurrence of witnesses in Earl Roger de Quincy's extant charters*

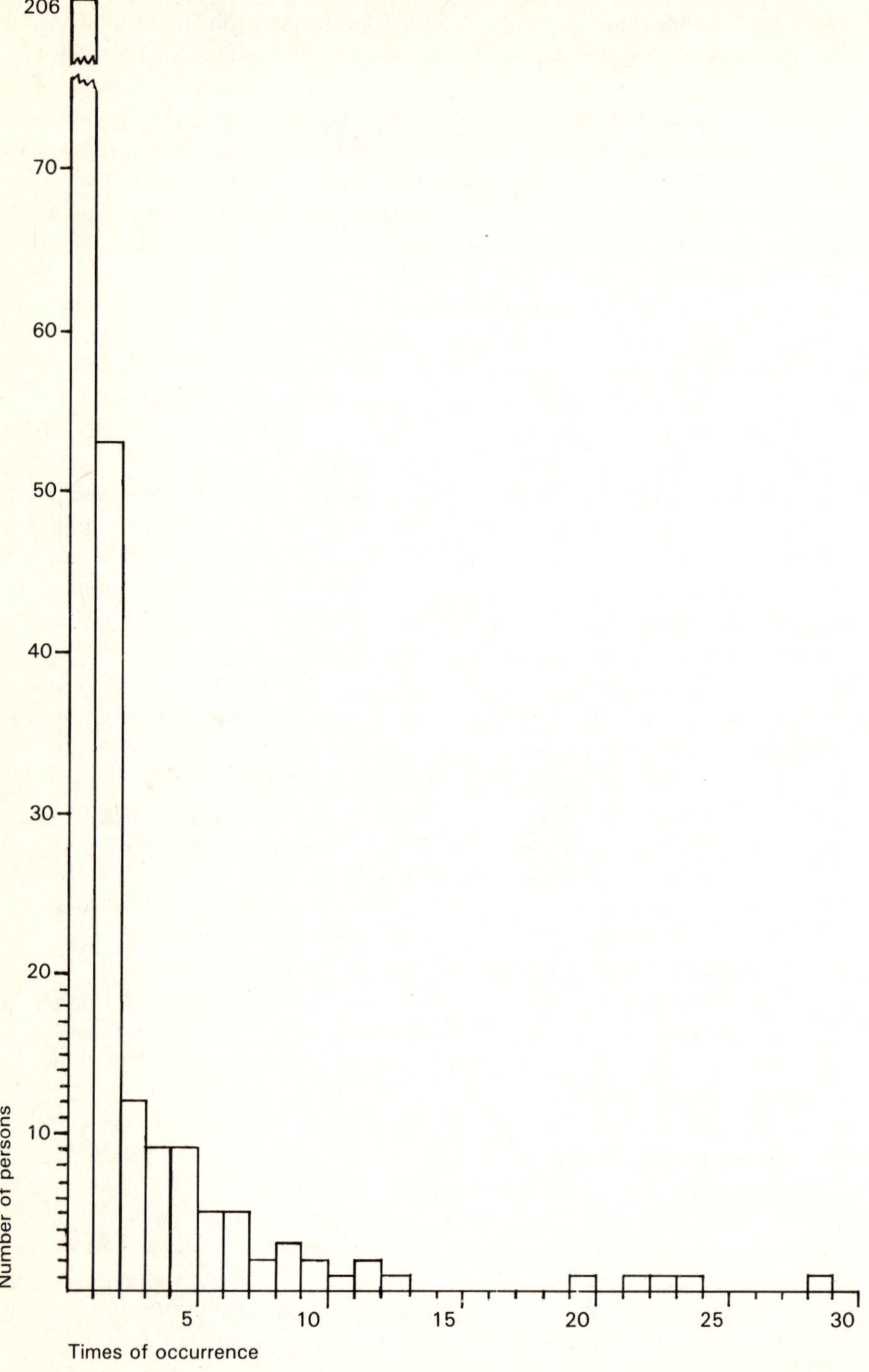

The chart covers a range from 206 persons who witnessed once only to one person, Saher of St Andrews, who witnessed twenty-nine times. It suggests that three groups of witnesses may conveniently be distinguished. Those who witnessed once or twice only are insignificant for the present purpose. Those who witnessed three, four or five times (twelve, nine and nine individuals respectively) have some importance; but the most significant group consists of those who occur six or more times. These last two groups can be labelled respectively the outer circle and the inner circle of the *familia*. The members of these circles can be listed in tables showing for each person his name, social position and number of appearances as a witness (see below, pp. 108–9). The two circles can also be classified according to social positions, as follows:

	Inner circle	*Outer circle*
Knights	15	13
Clerks/graduates	5	8
Burgesses	4	6
Chaplains	1	1
Uncertain	2	2
	27	30

The method here employed to isolate the important members of the *familia* does have certain defects. The surviving charters are only a fraction of those originally issued by the earl. We have no certain information about how long a particular individual remained within the *familia*. One man could have had considerable importance but only for a short period; and such a person would probably not appear within the inner circle as defined above. The division into inner and outer circles is of course merely a convention, introduced here simply for purposes of study. But this analysis is at least based on figures, not on guesswork, and it provides a skeleton which can now be clothed with flesh by examining the people involved, their social status, and their activities.

The social proportions of the inner and outer circles are very similar. In each circle about half of the persons listed are knights. Among the remainder, clerks and graduates predominate, burgesses are next in importance, and chaplains are the least prominent of all. In looking more closely at these classes, it will be convenient to deal with the chaplains first and then to work up the numerical scale to the knights.

The two chaplains, sir Eustace de Montivilliers and sir Maurice, were evidently members of the household. Eustace, who witnessed twelve times, appears at least as early as 1238 and as late as 1257.[23] What brought him into contact with the earl was apparently the manor of Arrington (Cambs). Earl Roger was mesne lord of a fee held there by Saher of St Andrews. In 1228, the abbess of Montivilliers (dép. Seine-Maritime) claimed one quarter of the manor from Saher of St Andrews and others.[24] It is conceivable that Eustace was a French clerk who first came to England on the

Table 3. *Earl Roger de Quincy's inner circle*

Sir John Becard	knight	20
Sir Henry Bisset	knight	8
Sir William de Bois	knight	25
Andrew Bonvallet	[burgess][25]	7
sir Brian[26]	clerk	23
Sir Philip of Chetwynd	knight	8
Sir John of Cranford	knight	23
Roger of Faffington	[uncertain]	6
Ernald le Goer	[burgess]	6
Sir Robert of Hereford	knight	7
sir Philip Lovel	[clerk]	11
John Mace	[burgess]	7
Mr Thomas of Man	graduate	10
Sir William de Montgomery	knight	9
sir Eustace de Montivilliers	chaplain	12
Sir John le Moyne	knight	10
Ralph de Nevill	[uncertain]	6
Sir Peter le Potter	knight	7
Sir Robert de Quincy	knight	8
Sir Robert of St Andrews	knight	12
Sir Saher of St Andrews	knight	29
Ranulf Sweyn	[burgess]	7
sir Peter of Syresham	clerk	7
Sir Warin of Thunderley	knight	9
Robert of Trafford	clerk	13
Sir Everard of Trumpington	knight	6
Sir Richard of Wix	knight	10

affairs of the abbess. Maurice the chaplain witnessed thrice only, and the extreme limit-dates of the texts in which he appears are 1245 and 1260.[27] The two men overlap as members of the household and witness together in Nos. 92 and 98. Both men served as successive rectors of the church of Laughton (Leics), where Eustace was in possession in 1235 and Maurice in 1250.[28] (It is possible that this benefice was a regular perquisite of members of the household, for the rector of Laughton about 1248–50 was sir Peter of Syresham, who was the earl's estates steward in England from about 1249 to 1252; and the rector in 1240 was Elias de Raveley, perhaps to be identified with Elias de Radeborg, who twice witnessed charters by the earl.)[29] Eustace may have been the principal household chaplain from 1235 and in the 1240s, and was perhaps replaced in this office by Maurice towards the end of the earl's life. It seems that the household normally included at least one chaplain, perhaps occasionally two.

There is also a hint that the household may have had another chaplain, one taken on the strength, as it were, when the earl moved to Scotland. 'William, our chaplain', witnessed two charters of Scottish provenance, datable respectively between 1234 and 1235 and between 1257 and 1264. William of St Edwards, chaplain, who witnessed another Scottish act, datable shortly before 1262, may be the same man, although the Christian name is too common to permit definite identification.[30] Yet another William could also be the same man: William, parson

Table 4. *Earl Roger de Quincy's outer circle*

Sir Robert de Betun	knight	5
Sir Ernald de Bois	knight	5
Sir John of Carlisle	knight	4
Sir Ralph Chamberlain	knight	4
Sir Gilbert of Colvend	knight	4
Sir Henry Engayne	knight	3
Henry of Faffington	[uncertain]	5
Robert Francis	clerk	5
Richard of Glen	[burgess]	3
Sir Richard de Harcourt	knight	3
Sir William de la Hay	knight	5
Mr Hugh	graduate	3
John of London	[burgess]	3
Sir William Lovel	knight	3
Roger of Luton	[burgess]	5
Mr Adam of Makerstoun	graduate	4
Hugh of Manby	clerk	3
sir Maurice	chaplain	3
Simon de Noisy	clerk	3
Sir William d'Oyly	knight	4
Richard of Radwell	clerk	3
Sir Bernard of Ripley	knight	3
Robert the vintner	[burgess]	4
Sir Michael de la Rose	knight	4
Mr Eustace of Shelford	graduate	5
Sir Duncan Sibald	knight	4
Elias Sweyn	[uncertain]	5
Roger of Trafford	clerk	5
Ernald Waryn	[burgess]	4
Thomas Waryn	[burgess]	3

of Heriot in Midlothian, who witnessed a Brackley deed about 1240, and who may have come south as part of the earl's entourage.[31] If these various Williams could be proved to be identical, then the earl had a chaplain in Scotland, presumably, from his surname, of English origin, who was remunerated by his possession of the church of Heriot, of which the Quincy family held the patronage, just as the English chaplains were supported by the church of Laughton.

It is at first sight surprising to find so many burgesses forming part of the earl's *familia*: four appear in the inner circle and six in the outer circle. But their presence is explained when we discover who they were. Almost without exception, they occur as witnesses only in those texts which concern the earl's Northamptonshire borough of Brackley.[32] The borough tenements of three of them are mentioned in one text: the houses of Robert the vintner and Ernald Waryn, and the four houses of Ernald le Goer.[33] These were men important in their own locality, farmers and bailiffs of their borough, and it was natural that they should attend upon the earl when he stayed at Brackley, or near by at his demesne manor of Halse, which he frequently did, and that they should act as witnesses when he granted charters about borough property, which he also frequently did. There is no means of knowing whether any of them lived with the earl at Halse when he was there, but their presence in witness-lists is so frequent that they must often have received entertainment in his hall as they waited upon him to discuss the affairs of his borough. They were, in fact, truly a part of the *familia*, but they probably did not itinerate with the household.

Clerks, on the other hand, are numerically more prominent in the list of *familiares* than the burgesses, and some of the clerks were certainly itinerant. They obviously took a vital part in the production of the earl's written acts,[34] and in the administration of his estates, but analysis of their social positions is also rewarding. (For convenience, university graduates have been included with the clerks.) Five clerks belong to the inner circle of the *familia*. These five include men who witnessed the earl's charters very frequently indeed: Brian the clerk witnessed twenty-three times, Robert of Trafford thirteen times, and Philip Lovel eleven times. Slightly less frequent are the appearances of Master Thomas of Man (ten times) and Peter of Syresham (seven times). Such men are the household servants closest to the earl in matters of business and administration, and it is no surprise to find that Philip Lovel and Peter of Syresham rose to be stewards of the earl's English estates and that Robert of Trafford acted as the earl's attorney in the king's courts.[35]

It is particularly hard to discern the social origins of people at this level of society, but obscure origins need not always be humble origins. No doubt Robert of Trafford acquired his name from Trafford, in the parish of Chipping Warden (Northants), a hamlet about eight miles north-west of the earl's demesne manor at Halse. The background of Master Thomas of Man is almost a complete blank, but he is perhaps identifiable with the individual so named who in 1246 was the second witness in a charter by Harald, king of Man and the Isles, granting land and privileges in Man to Furness abbey in Lancashire.[36] If so, Master Thomas's appearance in this context suggests not merely personal origins in the Isle of Man, but possibly also some degree of intimacy with the Manx royal family. Philip Lovel, who was to have a remarkable and flamboyant career as treasurer of King Henry III after he had left Earl Roger's service, may have had backing from prominent families in his early days. In 1253 he acted as a pledge for John Lovel of Minster Lovell (Oxon) when John did homage to Henry III, and this suggests that Philip may have belonged to that family.[37] Philip's first appearance on record is in 1231, when he was rector of Lutterworth (Leics), on presentation by a member of the Verdun family. Land in Lutterworth belonged to Rose de Verdun who was a tenant of Earl Roger at Bittesby, in the neighbouring parish of Claybrook.[38] It is difficult to delineate with certainty the early career of a clerk such as Philip Lovel, but it may not be too fanciful to conjecture that he was born of the Lovels of Minster Lovell, received his first advancement through the Verduns, and moved from their circle into the household of their feudal superior, Earl Roger.

Some of these clerks within the inner circle were, like the earl's chaplains, supported by livings in the earl's gift or under his influence. Peter of Syresham was rector of Laughton (Leics) and also occurs as rector of Syresham (Northants), the parish from which he took his surname.[39] Brian the clerk was rector of *Dersford* (perhaps Durford, Sussex), parson of Syston in Leicestershire, and parson of Leuchars in Fife.[40] The widespread patronage exercised by a major Anglo-Scottish baron here resulted in a clerk acquiring benefices in two separate realms. It is often impossible to say whether a clerk like Brian, who appears in possession of several benefices, was a pluralist or simply moved fairly rapidly from one to another. But the hint of pluralism suggests that such clerks must often have been non-resident. Perhaps, however, a clerk could look forward to semi-retirement on one of the earl's livings. Laughton may have been used thus;[41] and such a move may have been planned for Robert of Trafford, whose career as a clerk of the earl began in the 1220s and who, about 1256–7, was presented by Earl Roger to the church of Lathrisk in Fife. But if so the earl had to change his plans, for the prior and convent of St Andrews claimed that the patronage of the church was theirs and Roger had to revoke his presentation of Robert of Trafford.[42]

Since few of the earl's charters carry a place-date, it is difficult to demonstrate explicitly that these important clerks travelled about with the household. But the charters which they witness concern a wide range of places and are most likely to have been granted at a variety of locations. The clerks are quite unlike the burgesses of Brackley, who normally witness only charters about Brackley. Robert of Trafford and Master Thomas of Man witness acts of apparently Scottish provenance as well as English ones, and Philip Lovel is known to have accompanied the earl to Galloway.[43] The advancement of important clerks such as Philip Lovel and Peter of Syresham to the office of steward was a natural progression, for the steward also itinerated round the estates, sometimes joining the household, sometimes departing from it on a circuit of his own.

The eight clerks who fall within the outer circle of the *familia* do not form so homogeneous a group as those who were part of the inner core. Nothing has so far been found in the records to illuminate the activities of Hugh of Manby or Richard of Radwell. The only firm fact about Master Hugh the clerk, in addition to Earl Roger's designation of him as 'my clerk', is that he was parson of Leuchars in 1238.[44] Roger of Trafford was the brother of Robert of Trafford, mentioned above, and on three of Roger's five appearances as a witness he is in company with his brother.[45] The choice of the names Robert and Roger for the two brothers suggests a compliment paid by the Trafford family to the Quincys, who may have been their overlords or patrons. Roger of Trafford appears to have been a less important figure in the *familia* than his brother. But he also apparently travelled with the household, for he witnessed two acts of Scottish provenance, one of which was issued at Dysart in Fife.[46]

The remaining four clerks of the outer circle have strong local connexions, and this has not been a characteristic of any of the clerks so far discussed. Robert Francis, who witnessed five times, is an important figure, since his handwriting appears oftener in the earl's surviving charters than that of any other clerk but one.[47] Between about 1240 and 1260 his name, as a witness, and his handwriting occur very frequently in the deeds of Brackley hospital.[48] He is once described, by another clerk, as the son of Hugh Francis, who was the owner of a house in Brackley.[49] Although Robert Francis wrote charters for the earl about various estates, he witnessed only texts which relate to Brackley. The evidence suggests that he was a Brackley man, perhaps attached to the hospital there, and that he regularly gave professional service as a clerk when the earl came to Brackley.

The local connexions of the last three clerks in this group all lay within Scotland, and these men give the impression of being fairly important individuals who were drawn within the *familia* in Scotland just as Robert Francis was at Brackley. The most prominent of the three in contemporary society was Master Adam of Makerstoun, who was four times a witness, always in Scottish texts. From about 1240 until 1253 he was a member of the *familia* of David de Bernham, bishop of St Andrews, and he held office briefly as official of the diocese of St Andrews about 1259–60.[50] He was provost of the church of St Mary, St Andrews, from before 1250 until after 1280; and his appointment as a papal chaplain by Urban IV, about 1261–2, may have been a reward, at the instigation of King Alexander III, for his services on an embassy to England during the Anglo-Scottish dispute of 1257–8, in which Earl Roger himself took part as an ambassador of Henry III.[51] Adam of Makerstoun's closest link with Earl Roger was his tenure of the rectory of Collessie in Fife, to which he had probably been presented by the earl. When Roger proposed, about 1262, to grant this church to Lindores abbey, arrangements had to be made for Adam to resign his possession of the church.[52] By 1263 he had become parson of Ceres in Fife.[53] When the earl and his entourage arrived in Fife, the household could expect to be joined for a time by this busy ecclesiastic, who was evidently part of the Quincy interest in that region, but whose many other responsibilities would prevent him from travelling regularly with the earl to distant places.

Simon de Noisy, who witnessed three of Roger's acts, is so often mentioned in contemporary documents that one historian has suggested there must have been two persons so named. His name is French, possibly derived from Noisy-le-Roi, west of Paris.[54] He was a clerk of the French-born William Malvoisin, bishop of St Andrews, and evidently a member of his household. Simon frequently witnessed the bishop's acts during William's tenure of the see, from 1202 to 1238.[55] There are signs that Simon was a pluralist: in 1220 he was parson of Dysart, which was in the bishop's patronage, and he held, too, half of the patronage of the church of Lauder in Berwickshire.[56] He was also parson of Leuchars church.[57] As Earl Roger had land at Dysart, possessed half of the town of Lauder, and had one of his principal Scottish estates at Leuchars, it is evident that Simon de Noisy's career advanced under the earl's patronage. A fourth benefice in Simon's possession was the parsonage of Ormiston in East Lothian, which he held in 1238, and it again provided a link with the earl, as Ormiston is the neighbouring parish to Tranent, where Roger was the principal landowner.[58] Simon's social position is similar to that of Master Adam of Makerstoun: both were men of many interests, who combined their other activities with occasional attendance in Earl Roger's hall.

Master Eustace of Shelford, in contrast, is rather meagrely documented. He witnessed five acts, four Scottish and one English. No other facts about him are known, but it can be safely assumed that he was a member of a family of English origin which had settled on Earl Roger's Scottish estates.[59] Simon of Shelford, who was the earl's free tenant at Naughton in Fife, witnessed twice in the company of Master Eustace.[60] William of Shelford served in Scotland as a steward of Earl Saher and also of Roger himself.[61] Master Eustace of Shelford perhaps reflected the Anglo-Scottish interests of his own family by sometimes joining the earl's household on one of its Scottish circuits and sometimes journeying with it back to England.

The clerks who are to be found in Roger's *familia* have a variety of reasons for their presence there. Some are his closest advisers and busiest administrators; some are the men who wrote the acts by which his will was expressed on parchment; and some are men whose main interests lay elsewhere but who were drawn from time to time within the ambit of the earl. Among his principal clerks were men of experience, as is hinted by the earlier careers of some, and men of talent, as is demonstrated by the later preferment to higher positions which some achieved.

However important the household chaplain was for saying prayers or the household clerks for conducting the earl's business, the mere physical presence of the earl's knights must surely have been to the eye of a stranger the most impressive feature of Roger's entourage. Fifteen knights occur in the inner circle of the *familia* and another thirteen in the outer circle. These men were not like the clerks or the burgesses: Roger and his knights belonged to the same social class. Who were these knights?

Among the knights in the inner circle we can distinguish two groups. Some were landed men, and this group included two of the earl's relatives and two of his estates stewards. The other group was composed of probably landless knights, an important but poorly documented body of men.

Sir Robert de Quincy III, the earl's brother, was the one close relative within the *familia*. Robert witnessed eight of the earl's acts and possessed the Quincy manors of Wakes Colne (Essex) and Ware (Herts).[62] But the other kinsman was a more distant one and his affairs were more complex. This was Sir Saher of St Andrews, who witnessed twenty-nine times. The links which bound this significant man and his family to the Quincys require investigation in some detail.

Sir Saher of St Andrews had a brother named Sir Roger, and the two were nephews of Earl Saher.[63] Their close family connexion with the Quincys is reflected both by their Christian names and by Saher's seal, which bears the mascles which form the Quincy arms, plus a label to mark a junior branch of the family.[64] Saher and Roger were presumably the sons of a sister of Earl Saher, whose name is unknown, by an equally mysterious father who used *de Sancto Andrea* as a surname. We shall return later to the question of the family origins of the two brothers; but we must look now at their careers and their landed possessions. Their names first appear on record in the second decade of the thirteenth century. Both joined the baronial revolt against King John, and Roger was imprisoned in 1216–17. Saher returned to the king's faith in 1217 and recovered seisin of his lands in Northamptonshire and Nottinghamshire.[65] He had acquired these lands by marrying Matilda de Dyve, daughter and co-heiress of William de Dyve, who had died before 1185 and who was the representative of an old Anglo-Norman family.[66] In Northamptonshire, Saher got part of the manor of East Haddon, previously forfeited by the earl of Leicester and granted by the crown to William de Dyve before 1185.[67] The next parish to East Haddon was Long Buckby, where lay the original English estate of the Quincys. The influence of Earl Saher is perhaps visible here in an arrangement for marrying his nephew, who bore his name, to an heiress in the neighbouring parish. Saher's other acquisition along with his wife was part of the manor of Gotham (Notts). On the death about 1228 of his wife's grandmother, also called Matilda de Dyve, Saher succeeded to lands at Hinxton (Cambs), held in chief of the crown, and at Arrington (Cambs), held of Roger de Quincy as mesne lord, and apparently also to property in Sussex.[68] In Scotland, he acquired by some means not recorded land at Collessie, including an interest in the buildings and holdings belonging to the parsonage of the parish church.[69] In 1230 he served along with Roger de Quincy in the royal expedition to Brittany and was described on this occasion as a knight of Margaret, countess of Winchester. He was still alive in 1253, when he was involved in litigation about Dyve property at Corby (Lincs), but was probably dead by 1256, certainly by 1260, when his widow had quittance of common summons in Cambridgeshire.[70]

Saher's brother, Sir Roger of St Andrews, also acquired English property through Quincy influence. Before 1224 Countess Margaret granted to him all her land at Littlemore (Oxon), for one knight's service.[71] He was troubled by debts in 1227 and 1228, and it may have been for this reason that he granted the manor to the Templars, probably soon after 1235.[72] He had already, before 1235, made grants of Littlemore property to Garendon abbey and Brackley hospital. His brother Saher evidently also had interests in Littlemore, for he confirmed Roger's grant to Garendon and himself gave to the nunnery of Littlemore an annual rent of five shillings from his vill of Littlemore.[73] The two brothers' Scottish estates likewise overlapped: Roger too had land at Collessie, from which he granted an annual rent of forty shillings to Brackley hospital. Before 1235 the hospital surrendered this rent to Roger de Quincy, in exchange for his demesne at Gask in Perthshire.[74] Few details emerge from the records about the career of Roger of St Andrews. He also served in the Brittany expedition of 1230; but he is not known to have married, and is not heard of again after he had transferred his Littlemore estate to the Templars. He was almost certainly dead by 1249.[75]

The relations of the two brothers to Earl Roger, who was their cousin, present a contrast. Saher of St Andrews was evidently one of the earl's closest confidants: his frequent appearances as a witness cannot be explained solely on the ground that they were near neighbours in both Fife and Northamptonshire. Roger of St Andrews, on the other hand, did not witness any of the surviving acts. The contrast helps to illuminate the nature of the earl's *familia*: some men, such as Saher of St Andrews, were virtually permanent members of it, some joined it occasionally, but others, such as Roger of St Andrews, although perhaps attached to the earl by tenure and by blood as he was, had not, whatever the reason, any place within it.

The origins of the St Andrews family are an unsolved puzzle. Roger of St Andrews made grants in alms for the souls of Earl Saher and Robert de Quincy II, and of his own father and mother, whom he did not name.[76] This reticence is curious, and equally odd is the care which Saher of St Andrews took to confirm his brother's acts.[77] This suggests that they may have feared dispute over their possessions; and the marriage of their parents may well have been in some way irregular. The place from which the family derived its name is also obscure. This might have been St Andrews in Scotland, a well-known city and a place prominent in the affairs of the Quincys. But the name occurs frequently in France: the town of St-Andre de l'Eure, for example, is only fifteen kilometres from Pacy (dép. Eure), the *caput* of the Norman honour of the earls of Leicester.[78] From whom this branch of the Quincys took its origin we cannot at present say; but it is clear that the St Andrews family rose to be Anglo-Scottish landowners through Quincy contacts. The cross-Border links of a magnate family opened the way for similar bonds to be forged at a slightly lower social level.

We can now examine those other knights in the inner circle who possessed land but who were not related to the earl. There are five altogether, and two of these served the earl as land stewards in England: Sir John of Cranford, who witnessed twenty-three times, and Sir John le Moyne, who witnessed ten times. Cranford, as holder of only a small estate at Ashby St Legers (Northants), was the less notable of the two.[79] Sir John le Moyne, on the other hand, possessed the manor of Great Shelford (Cambs) in chief, by the serjeanty of supervising the making or repair of the royal crown, and had a public career of some prominence. After his time as Roger's steward, between 1235 and 1237, he served the English king in a variety of administrative positions, particularly as sheriff of Cambridgeshire and Huntingdonshire from 1253 to 1255 and again in 1265.[80] The stewards were semi-professional administrators, and the presence of several of them in the *familia* is to be expected. They were often close to the centre of affairs, along with the clerks, who shared with them the tasks of estate administration.[81]

One other landed knight also possessed professional expertise in estate matters: Sir Richard of Wix, who witnessed ten times. He was probably in the earl's service as early as 1248, when he witnessed an act issued in Scotland, at Dysart.[82] The fact that in 1261 he served along with one Richard of Hemington as steward of the bishop of Lincoln suggests that he had moved to another household, as estate administrators frequently did.[83] But he again took an important place in the running of Earl Roger's estates when, on the earl's death in 1264, Richard of Hemington and he were appointed by the crown to be joint keepers of the late earl's English lands. They acted in this capacity from July to November 1264, but were replaced early in 1265 by one of the king's escheators.[84] Sir Richard of Wix supported Simon de Montfort in the rebellion of 1265 and during the troubles of that time seized various manors in Suffolk. But he was pardoned in 1266 and his person, lands and possessions were taken into the king's peace. In the same year he returned to the profession of estates steward, taking office in that capacity with Edmund Crouchback, son of Henry III.[85] Although Sir Richard is not on record as a steward of Earl Roger, he belongs to the same category within the *familia* as those who were stewards: Sir John of Cranford and Sir John le Moyne.

The last two landed knights within the inner circle appear to be men of local importance rather than especially prominent figures in the *familia*. Sir Peter le Potter witnessed seven times, held a fee of the earl at Sibson (Leics), and is specifically described as 'our knight' on one of Roger's acts.[86] The known facts of his career seem to be few. In 1252 he had an exemption from service on assizes and in 1258 served as a knight from Leicestershire on one of the baronial commissions of that year. In 1272 he was threatened with loss of his lands at Sibson on suspicion of disloyalty to the crown, but proved that he was faithful and retained his property.[87] Sir Everard of Trumpington witnessed six times and held of the earl two and a quarter fees at Trumpington and Girton (Cambs) and half a fee at Chalton, in Moggerhanger parish (Beds).[88] The public records reveal him as a Cambridgeshire landowner of some substance. He had lands at Howe House (in Impington) and at Madingley in that county, as well as property in Bedfordshire and Leicestershire. He was active from the early years of the thirteenth century until at least 1251, when he was involved in a dispute with Henry of Bath, the justice, about a manor.[89] He occasionally took part in royal administration: as a justice in Cambridgeshire, and as one of those appointed to extend and partition the lands of John, earl of Huntingdon and Chester, who died in 1237.[90] Everard is found once in Scotland, when he witnessed a charter of Alexander II, datable between 1215 and 1220, confirming a grant by Earl Saher.[91] Earl Roger may have been his principal feudal superior, whom he served as one of the *familiares*, but Sir Everard had too many other activities on hand to be a permanent member of the earl's household.

These are the seven men who represent the landed interest in the inner circle of the earl's intimates: two relatives, Robert de Quincy III and Saher of St Andrews (both also tenants); two stewards, John of Cranford and John le Moyne, plus Richard of Wix, an administrator; and two tenants, Peter le Potter and Everard of Trumpington. Two features of their landholding are noticeable. They were not major landowners: as already shown, none possessed more than a few scattered manors. And their importance as landowners did not always depend entirely on lands which they held as tenants of Earl Roger. The links which bound them to the earl were mainly personal, as with relatives, or, presumably, financial: the estates steward, for example, would receive a regular fee.[92]

The other eight knights in the inner circle are apparently men who held no land, either of the earl or of anyone else. But they present a considerable problem because the evidence available about their activities is extremely sparse. About Sir William de Bois, for example, who witnessed twenty-five times, we know only that he was the brother of Sir Ernald de Bois of Thorpe Arnold (Leics), one of Earl Roger's principal tenants.[93] Presumably a younger brother of Ernald, William had followed the course taken by many landless younger sons by entering into service in the household of a major baron. Other knights apparently landless are difficult to identify with certainty. William de Montgomery witnessed nine of the earl's acts, but we have no means of discovering whether or not he was the knight of this name who is well attested as a landowner in Derbyshire, Nottinghamshire, Northamptonshire and Staffordshire between 1232 and 1269.[94] Similar doubts surround the names of Warin of Thunderley,[95] Henry Bisset,[96] Philip of Chetwynd[97] and Robert of Hereford.[98]

What can be said of such men, about whom the evidence is so negative? If they did hold land in England at all, they must have held very little, for the voluminous records of English government in the thirteenth century surely omit the names of very few landowners of any importance. We can be fairly certain that none of them held knights' fees of Earl Roger, for they do not occur in the feodary of his estates which it has been possible to compile.[99] It seems a reasonable assumption, admittedly based on negative evidence, that these semi-anonymous individuals close to the earl's own activities were in fact his household knights. 'The household knight is an elusive person. As he held no land, he naturally does not appear in the records from which our knowledge of feudal organization is mainly drawn.'[100] But of his existence within the social structure there need be no doubt. Messrs Richardson and Sayles have maintained that there were 'a good many landless knights of superior status, ready ... to take service with the king or anyone else willing to reward them for their service in an honourable employment'.[101] We can claim with some confidence to have identified a body of such men within the household of a great earl.

Two more seemingly landless knights have yet to be mentioned, and the known facts about them illuminate in a striking fashion our picture of the household knights. What reward could the household knight expect, in addition of course to the food, clothing and shelter supplied by his lord? Sir Robert of St Andrews, who witnessed twelve of the earl's acts, was a son of Saher of St Andrews, and received from Earl Roger, for homage and service, an annual fee of 100s. from the office of provost of the borough of Brackley, to be held until the earl gave him 100s. worth of land or rent in Scotland.[102] This grant is apparently a *fief-rente*, that is, 'a fief of which the object constitutes a yearly income assigned on a source of revenue other than an estate of land and of which the instalments are actually paid in kind or in money by the lord of the fief'.[103] Payment of household knights by this means was well known in the Low Countries, and was very occasionally used in the English royal household in the thirteenth century.[104] It was an eminently convenient method of providing salaries for those knights who were permanently in attendance on their lord and who had not yet succeeded in acquiring land. We do not know if Robert of St Andrews ever exchanged his *fief-rente* for land or rent in Scotland. By 1256 he had taken service in the household of Edmund de Lacy.[105] Whether or not he was the eldest son of Saher of St Andrews, he presumably succeeded to some of his father's lands, for at his own death in 1274 he held lands in Nottinghamshire, perhaps the family estate at Gotham in that county.[106]

One other presumably landless knight was the possessor of a similar rent. This was John Becard, who witnessed the earl's acts twenty times. He was killed at the battle of Evesham in 1265. He received from the abbey of Thame in Oxfordshire an annual rent of 100s., which passed on his death to his son and heir, Peter Becard.[107] There is no reference in the Thame cartulary to John Becard's annual rent, and we cannot prove conclusively by whose grant it originated or from which lands it was paid.[108] But two parallel grants by Earl Roger are suggestive. He gave to Reginald de Duno, who does not appear within the *familia* but did witness one of the acts, a yearly rent of 100s. in Sydenham (Oxon), to be paid by the abbot and convent of Thame. Roger also instructed the abbot and convent to pay to one Roger of Bushey five marks' annual rent due to himself, since he had granted it to Roger by charter.[109] The grant to Duno specifies rent from Sydenham, but the grant to Roger of Bushey mentions no place. But Sydenham is the only manor in which Thame abbey is known to have held land of the earl: in a complex series of transactions, he gradually transferred to it all that he held in an estate where in 1241 his demesne was worth at least £20.[110] He employed arrangements made with the abbey to remunerate Duno from Sydenham, and to remunerate Roger of Bushey, perhaps also from Sydenham. It seems a reasonable guess that the rent which John Becard, a prominent household knight, held from Thame abbey was the result of a grant by Earl Roger, possibly from Sydenham. These grants may not have been *fiefs-rentes* in the strict sense; but the evidence suggests that the earl made use of rents which lay within his control to remunerate certain followers, perhaps including one of his household knights.[111]

The fifteen knights of the inner circle of the *familia* present, therefore, an entirely comprehensible picture. Some were the earl's relations, others were his stewards and administrators; some were landed men in a modest way, others appear to be landless men perhaps receiving a form of salary. Some were transient figures who moved on to other households, others were fixtures who served in the earl's household for many years. What they were not is equally significant: none of the earl's major tenants was a knight within this circle of the *familia*.

Another thirteen knights occur in the outer circle. The same categories can be discerned within this group, and the numbers within these categories are similar. Only one of the thirteen was a relative of the earl. This was Sir Richard de Harcourt, who by marrying Orabile de Quincy II became Earl Roger's brother-in-law.[112] Besides being a prominent landowner in Leicestershire, Oxfordshire and Staffordshire, Richard was one of the earl's foremost tenants, holding of him three fees in Leicestershire.[113] Richard witnessed only three of the acts, two of which are from the period before 1235, and although part of the *familia* he cannot have been more than an occasional member of the household.

Within the inner circle it was possible to distinguish seven landed knights out of fifteen. In the outer circle the landed interest is represented by a further nine knights, of whom three were certainly Roger's tenants. Sir Richard de Harcourt was one of these, and a figure of equal prominence in contemporary society was Sir Ernald de Bois, who witnessed five of the earl's acts. Brother of William de Bois, one of the landless knights of the inner circle, Ernald was the head of a well-known Anglo-Norman family and was Earl Roger's principal tenant, holding some eighteen fees of the honour of Winchester in Gloucestershire, Leicestershire and Warwickshire.[114] One other landed knight in the outer circle was also a tenant of the earl, but was a much less distinguished figure than the two Anglo-Norman magnates, Harcourt and Bois. Sir William Lovel, who witnessed three times, had only half a fee at Chalton (Beds), held of the earl in 1242–3.[115] His activities have proved impossible to trace, since his name is so common, but he was certainly no more than a minor landowner.

A further four landed knights in the outer circle were apparently not tenants of the earl. Two of the four were English and two were Scots. Sir Ralph Chamberlain, who was the earl's estates steward in England at some time during the 1240s, witnessed four times. He was a Leicestershire landowner of moderate status, holding lands in that county as a tenant of the Basset family.[116] Sir Henry Engayne, who witnessed three times, was a tenant-in-chief of the crown, holding a knight's fee at Little Chalfield in Wiltshire,[117] a county where Earl Roger was the chief lord of numerous fees. The two Scots were Sir William de la Hay and Sir Duncan Sibald, who witnessed five and four times respectively. Hay was the brother of Gilbert de la Hay, third lord of Errol in Perthshire. William de la Hay received from his brother two ploughgates in Errol before 1251 and was the founder of the family of Hay of Leys. He was an ambassador sent by Alexander III to England during the Anglo-Scottish crisis of 1257–8, in which Earl Roger was also closely involved.[118] Duncan Sibald witnessed, along with William de la Hay and five other members of Earl Roger's *familia*, a grant by William de Malherbe to John of Kinloch, a tenant of the earl, about land near Pitlochie in Fife. Duncan Sibald, along with William de la Hay, was one of forty-one Scottish knights who about 1244 took an oath of good behaviour towards England on behalf of Walter Comyn, earl of Menteith.[119] Sibald may also possibly be identified with an Angus landowner of that name, who made a grant to Coupar Angus abbey in 1286.[120]

The last two landed knights of the outer circle are of particular interest because they were of Anglo-Scottish families; but both present problems, especially as it is difficult to provide firm evidence as to whether they were tenants of the earl or not. Sir Gilbert of Colvend, who witnessed four times, took his name from a parish in Kirkcudbrightshire, Galloway, near the mouth of the River Urr, in which Roger probably had land.[121] In 1262 Gilbert witnessed a charter about the church of Urr in the company of Sir Hugh de Beaumais, who was a witness to one of Roger's acts.[122] An estate at Colvend had been granted by an ancestor of Roger's wife, Helen of Galloway, to a family which also had land across the Solway Firth in England, at Workington in Cumberland.[123] Consequently, the family was known as both 'of Workington' and 'of Colvend' (latterly Corwen or Curwen), and Cumbrian historians have identified Sir Gilbert of Colvend as Sir Gilbert of Workington, who was active from about 1248 to about 1288 and was sheriff of Cumberland from 1278 to 1283.[124] It seems a reasonable presumption that Sir Gilbert was a tenant of Roger's at Colvend, but precise proof of this has not yet emerged.

Sir Bernard of Ripley, who witnessed three of the acts, had an English name but a Scottish background, again, as it happens, linked to Galloway. He was evidently a nephew of Bernard of Ripley, who flourished in northern England in the late twelfth century.[125] The name derives from a village and parish near Ripon, in the West Riding of Yorkshire. The Yorkshire Ripleys had already produced a Scottish offshoot in William of Ripley, to whom William the Lion had granted the estate of Dallas in Moray; and the second Bernard of Ripley, William's brother, at some date unknown married a Scottish heiress named Margaret and so acquired lands at Kirkandrews, in Borgue parish, Kirkcudbrightshire.[126] Earl Roger probably had land near by, at Senwick in Borgue, but proof that Sir Bernard was his tenant remains lacking.[127] He cannot have been other than an occasional member of Roger's household, especially as he proceeded to take service in the household of King Alexander II. Sir Bernard regularly witnessed Scottish royal acts from 1245 until the king's death in 1249;[128] but his attendance in the royal household may then have ceased, for he witnessed none of the acts of Alexander III.

The nine landed knights of the outer circle of the *familia*, therefore, were mainly landowners of lesser standing. Richard de Harcourt and Ernald de Bois are the exceptions. Three at least, possibly five, were tenants of the earl, notably Harcourt and Bois. We found that in the inner circle all the seven landowners were of lesser standing and only four were tenants. The conclusions are clear. The landed men who were regularly closest to the earl were men of modest substance and were sometimes, but by no means necessarily, his own tenants. Those two of his major tenants who appear within the *familia* were not particularly prominent members of it.

The outer circle of the *familia* also included a small group of apparently landless knights, possibly identifiable as household knights. They are four in number, and biographical details about them are almost entirely lacking. The name of Sir Robert de Betun brings before us again the place of origin of the Quincy family at Cuinchy, which is close to Béthune (dép. Pas-de-Calais). Another Robert de Betun had witnessed a charter of Robert de Quincy I, Earl Roger's grandfather, and the appearance in the Quincy family circle of two men bearing this surname suggests the possibility that the family still had an attachment of some kind to the area from which they originally sprang.[129] Sir John of Carlisle, who witnessed one of the four acts in which he appears as late as about 1259–60, seems unlikely to be identical with the man of that name who had his lands in Cumberland restored to him by the crown in 1217.[130] But it is possible that John of Carlisle was drawn into the earl's circle through contact with Roger's Cumberland properties. Sir William d'Oyly apparently occurs only once in the public records, on receiving a protection when crossing with the king to Gascony in 1253.[131] The last of these putative household knights, Sir Michael de la Rose, is a complete cipher.

Having identified, so far as possible, the knights within the earl's *familia*, and differentiated the known landowners from the rest, we can apply one more test to the documents which will help to illuminate the actions of these knights. As the earl's acts seldom record the places at which they were issued, we cannot normally discover which members of the *familia* were present at particular places. But the acts of English and of Scottish provenance are often distinguishable by their subject-matter; and beneficiaries petitioning the earl for charters must often have done so locally.[132] The habits of both landed and 'landless' knights in witnessing in England and Scotland, or in both, can be tabulated as follows:[133]

	Inner circle			*Outer circle*		
	England	*Scotland*	*Eng/Scot.*	*England*	*Scotland*	*Eng/Scot.*
Landed knights	3	–	3	5	3	2
'Landless' knights	–	–	8	1	–	3

The figures suggest two conclusions. The landed knights did not in general cross the Border very regularly. On the other hand, the 'landless' knights, with one single exception (Sir Michael de la Rose), are found with the earl in both countries. This is striking confirmation, from independent testimony, that these knights, about whom the sources reveal so little, are the household knights in the strict sense. Their ties were not to estates but to the earl's person. Like him and with him they were peripatetic. They were the core of his personal following.

We have now investigated all the main categories to be found in both circles of the *familia*.[134] What are the outstanding features of this body? Its composition is fluctuating and its members are frequently mobile. At its centre is a small group of long-serving followers, of whom the most prominent is Saher of St Andrews. Study of witness-lists will not reveal exactly how many men normally served within the earl's household, but the evidence analysed above suggests that at the heart of affairs there would regularly be at least half-a-dozen household knights, two clerks and a chaplain.[135] To these would be added estate officials, a few tenants and important local personages. Just as the king's court changed its character as it travelled up and down the country, so the earl's household drew in local men as it went on its way.[136] At Brackley, burgesses put in an appearance. In Scotland, prominent ecclesiastics such as Master Adam of Makerstoun or Simon de Noisy joined the entourage. The household lived physically on the move. But some members of the *familia* were also mobile socially. Several departed to other spheres: Philip Lovel entered English royal service, achieving both success and notoriety; Sir John le Moyne served the same monarch, at a more modest level; Sir Richard of Wix became steward of the bishop of Lincoln; Sir Robert of St Andrews entered the household of Edmund de Lacy and Sir Bernard of Ripley that of the king of Scots. Indeed, some of those who belonged to the *familia* may have been mere birds of passage. It is singular that the only knight who is noted in English official records as belonging to the earl's *familia* does not occur in our lists above. This was Sir Guy Pipard, a Worcestershire landowner, who in 1250 had a grant of freedom from service on assizes, juries or inquests so long as he belonged to the *familia* of Earl Roger.[137] He witnesses only two of the earl's acts and one issued by Roger's second wife, Countess Maud.[138] The pattern of the *familia* is kaleidoscopic and changes constantly as men are drawn into it and pass beyond it.

Tenants of the earl take only a small place within his *familia*. A few members of the inner circle were his tenants, but not all. Of his five major tenants, only two, Harcourt and Bois, were members of the *familia*, and they are in the outer, not the inner, circle. The great majority of tenants never appear in our lists at all and many do not witness even a single act. Robert de Noveray, a tenant who had the privilege of setting the first dish on the earl's table and might therefore be expected to occur as a member of the household, witnesses only one act.[139] His privilege must have been a formality, a piece of ceremonial for special occasions. So far as the evidence will take us, it appears that the *familia* and the tenantry were in separate categories which overlapped a little, but not much. The earl may have seen and heard his tenants in his courts, if he ever held these in person, but nearly all his daily companions and trusted administrators were a different group of men. Times had changed. Sir Frank Stenton pointed out that in the eleventh and twelfth centuries 'there can rarely have been need for a lord to take his knights, as such, into counsel. The advice which he needed, in time of peace, was not the advice of a military entourage, nor of the knights whom he had provided with land sufficient for their maintenance alone, but that of tenants with a substantial interest in his honour ... It was such tenants who formed the honorial baronage.'[140] Earl Roger's relations with his tenants were on a more formal basis than this. The feudal structure remained, but the habits of an earlier age had decayed.

The prominence of the household knights is perhaps the most striking feature of the whole organisation. Some were landowners, most were not, but all were closely attached to the earl. A similar body of men can be seen in other households of the period: in 1267, there were at least eighteen 'bachelors' in the service of Gilbert de Clare, earl of Gloucester and Hertford.[141] Apart from a few hints that some of them were remunerated with rents, such as *fiefs-rentes*, we do not know the exact terms on which such men were retained in Roger's household. The earliest indentures of retinue recording the terms of service to be rendered to an English magnate date from the late thirteenth and early fourteenth centuries.[142] But it cannot be doubted that Earl Roger supported what would eventually be called a retinue. 'The practice became a disease in later times, when it was systematized as "livery and maintenance".'[143] It is a long way from Earl Roger's following to the body of over two hundred knights, esquires and maids of honour who accompanied Gilbert de Clare, earl of Gloucester, and his countess in 1293, or to the livery roll of Lady Elizabeth de Burgh, compiled in 1343, which listed fifteen knights, ninety-three esquires, twenty-one clerks and numerous others.[144] But all these organisations have similarity. Earl Roger's entourage has developed somewhat from the simpler customs of the twelfth century and glances forward to the fossilised feudalism of the fourteenth century. Indeed, one historian of the fourteenth-century retinue system has maintained that what has been stigmatised as bastard feudalism 'may be most accurately described as the later medieval version of a more permanent feature of English social organisation: the grouping of servants and followers, household and retinue, noble and servile dependents, around the great estate, supported and attracted by its wealth and influence'.[145] Earl Roger's household and retinue, knightly in character but not over-elaborate, is at a half-way stage of development.[146]

One further characteristic of the *familia* is important: its members were mainly English. It is dangerous in a study of thirteenth-century society to decide a man's nationality on the basis of his name alone. But, certainly, in the inner circle of the *familia* prominent names such as Chetwynd, Cranford, Hereford, Trafford and Wix can be nothing but English. Only one member of this circle has through his name a specific French connexion: sir Eustace de Montivilliers, the earl's chaplain. The obscurity which surrounds the origins of the St Andrews family leaves it uncertain whether they should be credited to Scotland, England or France; but Saher of St Andrews's marriage and landownership gave him a particular attachment to England. Master Thomas of Man is rather an outsider, who presumably originated in the Isle of Man, which was a semi-independent kingdom during Earl Roger's lifetime but was added to the kingdom of Scotland in 1266. In the outer circle of the *familia*, Englishmen are still in the majority, but a little more national variety can be observed. Ernald de Bois and Richard de Harcourt were the heads of families which had remained Anglo-Norman until the loss of Normandy in 1204; and Robert de Betun bore a name of French origin. The Scottish element is slightly more prominent in this circle. William de la Hay and Duncan Sibald were landowning knights of Scottish birth; and Master Adam of Makerstoun took his name from a parish in Roxburghshire. Gilbert of Colvend had a Galloway name, but also English estates. Four men had mixed national backgrounds. Bernard of Ripley, Master Eustace of Shelford and Elias Sweyn had English names but Scottish careers and may be labelled Anglo-Scots. Similarly, Simon de Noisy can only be called a Franco-Scot.[147] The intermingling of Scottish, English and French elements which had for long been part of the Quincy family tradition is still reflected in the composition of Earl Roger's *familia*. But, as was natural for an earl whose richest manors lay in the English Midlands, Englishmen predominated among his *familiares*.[148]

NOTES

1. This study is a revised version of Chapter 3 of my unpublished Edinburgh University Ph.D. thesis (1965), Simpson, 'RQ'. References to the seventy-nine full charter texts edited in that work are given below in the form No. 23, etc. Since that edition was prepared, two additional texts have come to light and are calendared in the Appendix.

2. The fullest account of the family background and career of Earl Roger is in Simpson, 'RQ', Ch. 1, *q.v.* for references in support of factual statements herein. Details are also in *Comp. Pge.*, xii, II, pp. 745–54; see further S. Painter, 'The house of Quency, 1136–1264', *Medievalia et Humanistica*, xi (1957), pp. 1–9, and Barrow, *Era*, pp. 22–3.

3. *Ibid.*, pp. 7ff.

4. Barrow, *Kingdom*, pp. 102, 137.

5. Painter, 'Quency', p. 9.

6. Sir Maurice Powicke, *The Thirteenth Century*, 2nd edn. (Oxford, 1962), p. 580.

7. Paris, *Chron. Maj.*, v, p. 341.

8. For general surveys see Powicke, *Thirteenth Century*, pp. 579–82, 594, and Barrow, *Era, passim*; for specialist studies, Stringer, *Earl David*, and A. Young, 'The political role of the Comyns in Scotland and England in the thirteenth century' (unpublished Newcastle upon Tyne University Ph.D. thesis, 1974).

9. E.g., S. Painter, *Studies in the History of the English Feudal Barony* (Baltimore, 1943), p. 174, gave the annual income of the Quincy earls of Winchester as about £400, but took no account of revenue from their Scottish estates. Cf. Simpson, 'RQ', pp. 76–81.

10. See now, however, Stringer, *Earl David*, Ch. 8; C.J. Neville, 'The earls of Strathearn from the twelfth to the mid-fourteenth century, with an edition of their written acts' (unpublished Aberdeen University Ph.D. thesis, 1983), Ch. 4.

11. For a good, popular account see M.W. Labarge, *A Baronial Household of the Thirteenth Century* (London, 1965), based mainly on the household roll for 1265 of Eleanor, countess of Leicester, wife of Simon de Montfort; see further the valuable commentary in N. Denholm-Young, *Seignorial Administration in England* (Oxford, 1937), pp. 6–31.

12. Nos. 15 (*Lind. Cart.*, no. 131), 18 (*ibid.*, no. 135).

13. Nos. 39 (printed above, p. 68), 52 (*Brackley Deeds*, pp. 34–5); *ibid.*, pp. 27–8.

14. Nichols, *Leicester*, II, ii, p. 531.

15. Denholm-Young, *Seignorial Admin.*, pp. 25–31. For details of the permanent salaried council of the Clare family in the later thirteenth century, see M. Altschul, *A Baronial Family in Medieval England: The Clares, 1217-1314* (Baltimore, 1965), pp. 234–6.

16. No. 19 (*St Andrews Liber*, p. 336).

17. J.F. Niermeyer, *Mediae Latinitatis Lexicon Minus* (Leiden, 1976), defines *familia* as 'the aggregate dependants of different kinds subservient to a lord'. Note also the comment in Du Cange, *Glossarium* (Niort, 1883–7), iv, p. 410, that *familiares* were 'those whom kings and princes specially adjoined to their own family'. I have deliberately retained the Latin word *familia*, in preference to any English translation, since no one English word appears to

cover all the nuances required. 'Retinue' comes close, but has more overtones of 'military following' than seems appropriate for the thirteenth century. It is noteworthy that the Latin word *retenencia* (and its variants) = 'retinue' does not occur, at least in British sources, before *c.*1300, but becomes common thereafter: R.E. Latham, *Revised Medieval Latin Word-List* (London, 1965), p. 406.

18. *Fees*, i, p. 478; ii, p. 1447.

19. *Ibid.*, ii, p. 836.

20. Statistics of witnesses based on the texts in Simpson, 'RQ', plus the two additional deeds in the Appendix hereto.

21. *RRS*, i, pp. 78–9; E.L.G. Stones, 'Two points of diplomatic', *SHR*, xxxii (1953), pp. 47–51. See further above, pp. 93–4.

22. No. 30 (*Holyrood Liber*, no. 62).

23. No. 92 (*Brackley Deeds,* p. 37). (Full details of occurrence of witnesses can be found in the index of witnesses in Simpson, 'RQ', app. B.) Eustace witnessed an agreement made in the earl's presence in Scotland in 1238: *Inchaffray Chrs.,* no. 64.

24. *CurRR,* xiii, nos. 1009, 2365. Eustace witnessed No. 101 (*Brackley Deeds,* p. 23) as *de Mustervilers,* i.e., Montivilliers: A Dauzat and C. Rostaing, *Dictionnaire étymologique des noms de lieux en France* (Paris, 1963), p. 463

25. Burgesses are not specified as such in the witness-lists, but can be identified by the fact that they almost invariably occur only in charters about the earl's borough of Brackley (Northants). Some are described as 'of Brackley', 'bailiff of Brackley', etc.

26. The prefix *dominus* applied to clerks has been translated 'sir', while 'Sir' has been reserved for knights.

27. Nos. 92 (*Brackley Deeds*, p. 37), 98 (Oxford, Magdalen College, Brackley D. 247), 151 (*Brackley Deeds*, p. 30).

28. Nichols, *Leicester*, II, ii, p. 695.

29. *Ibid*; *Brackley Deeds*, pp. 31–2; Nos. 68 (Oxford, Magdalen College, Whitfield 159), 116 (*Brackley Deeds*, p. 22).

30. Nos. 15 (*Lind. Cart.*, no. 131), 18 (*ibid.*, no. 135), 36 (*Glasgow Reg.*, i, no. 169).

31. *Brackley Deeds*, p. 23.

32. Nos. 90–117, 152. There are two exceptions: Richard of Glen, a bailiff of Brackley, witnesses Nos. 63 (*HMC, Hastings*, i, p. 37) and 78 (BL Campbell Chart. iv, 10), which relate to Shepshed and Whetstone (Leics). But these deeds could have been granted at Brackley.

33. No. 98 (*Brackley Deeds*, pp. 32–4).

34. See Simpson, 'RQ', pp. 165–72.

35. Ibid., pp. 84, 87, 91; *ClR, 1256-9*, pp. 125–6.

36. *Book of Seals*, no. 428. I am grateful to Mr Basil Megaw for drawing this text to my attention and discussing it with me. Note also that a 'Master Thomas' was the second-last witness of a charter by Alan, lord of Galloway (d. 1234), to St Bees priory, Cumberland (*St Bees Reg.*, no. 42). It would be possible to envisage Thomas originating in Man, graduating in youth at a university so far untraced, entering the service of Alan, a magnate based not far from Man, and thence transferring to the *familia* of Alan's son-in-law, Earl Roger. But these remain speculations, not the proven details of a career.

37. *Excerpta e Rotulis Finium in Turri Londinensi asservatis, 1216–72*, ed. C. Roberts (Rec. Comm., 1835–6), ii, p. 149; *CIPM*, i, no. 269. For some details of Lovel's career in royal service see Simpson, 'RQ', pp. 87–8; Paris, *Chron. Maj.*, v, pp. 261–2, 270–1, 320, 345, 714–15, 719–20, 731; E. Mason in *The Church in Town and Countryside*, ed. D. Baker (*Studies in Church History*, 1979), p. 177.

38. Nichols, *Leicester*, IV, i, pp. 247, 265; *HMC, Hastings*, i, p. 331.

39. Nichols, *Leicester*, II, ii, p. 695; on Laughton see above, p. 108.

40. Nos. 52 (*Brackley Deeds*, pp. 34–5), 64 (*HMC, Hastings*, i, p. 37), 69 (*CChR*, i, p. 464).

41. Above, p. 108.

42. No. 19 (*St Andrews Liber*, p. 336).

43. Nos. 10 (*Scone Liber*, no. 79), 17 (*Lind. Cart.*, no. 137), 26 (SRO RH 6/54); Paris, *Chron. Maj.*, v, pp. 270–1. On problems of provenance see below, p. 120 and n. 132.

44. *Inchaffray Chrs.*, no. 64. Master Hugh is found in association with clerks of William Malvoisin, bishop of St Andrews, and may have been linked with his *familia* also: Watt, *Dictionary*, pp. 271–2. He is probably not identical with Master Hugh of Melbourne, a contemporary (*ibid.*, p. 387), and is not likely to have been the same person as Hugh of Manby.

45. Nos. 17 (*Lind. Cart.*, no. 137), 26 (SRO RH 6/54), 78 (BL Campbell Chart. iv, 10).

46. Nos. 17, 26, as in previous note.

47. Simpson, 'RQ', p. 167.

48. *Brackley Deeds*, pp. 25–56, *passim*.

49. *Ibid.*, p. 57.

50. For full details of Master Adam's career, with references, see Watt, *Dictionary*, pp. 370–3.

51. *CDS*, i, nos. 2126–7. Another of the Scottish ambassadors was William de la Hay, a knight who occurs in the outer circle of Roger's *familia* (see below, p. 119).

52. No. 15 (*Lind. Cart.*, no. 131); *ibid.*, nos. 142–3. It should also be noted that Makerstoun is the neighbouring parish to Mertoun, Berwickshire, in which Earl Roger had property: Simpson, 'RQ', pp. 262–3.

53. *CPL*, i, p. 391.

54. For evidence of Simon de Noisy's position and the suggested origin of his surname, see M. Ash, 'The administration of the diocese of St Andrews, 1202–1328' (unpublished Newcastle upon Tyne University Ph.D. thesis, 1972), p. 137 and n. Charter evidence does not support the contention in *Coupar Angus Chrs.*, i, p. 60, that there was more than one Simon de Noisy.

55. *St Andrews Liber*, pp. 161, 266; *Registrum Monasterii S. Marie de Cambuskenneth* (Grampian Club, 1872), no. 46; *Holyrood Liber*, no. 47; *Arbroath Liber*, i, no. 151.

56. *Dunfermline Reg.*, nos. 111, 125; *Dryb. Lib.*, no. 88.

57. No. 25 (*SHR*, ii [1905], p. 174). Simon de Noisy must be distinguished from Simon de Quincy, also parson of Leuchars: No. 22 (*St Andrews Liber*, pp. 256–7). On the career of the latter, whose relationship to the Quincy family is unknown, see *Coupar Angus Chrs.*, i, p. 44.

58. *Inchaffray Chrs.*, no. 64.

59. The surname derives from Shelford (Cambs). For details of the family, and its links with the Quincys, see Simpson, 'RQ', pp. 102–3.

60. Nos. 19 (*St Andrews Liber*, p. 336), 20 (*ibid.*, p. 337), 21 (W. Fraser, *History of the Carnegies, Earls of Southesk* [Edinburgh, 1867], ii, pp. 476–7).

61. *St Andrews Liber*, pp. 255–7; Oxford, Magdalen College, Whitfield 13 (1), (2).

62. Details of Sir Robert's career in Simpson, 'RQ', p. 24.

63. *Brackley Deeds*, p. 13; Oxford, Magdalen College, Whitfield 13 (1), (2).

64. BL MS Cott. Julius C. vii, fo. 235r.

65. *Rotuli Litterarum Patentium in Turri Londinensi asservati*, ed. T.D. Hardy (Rec. Comm., 1835), p. 189b; *Patent Rolls of the Reign of Henry III preserved in the PRO* (London, 1901–3), i, p. 19; *Rotuli Litterarum Clausarum in Turri Londinensi asservati*, ed. T.D. Hardy (Rec. Comm., 1833–4), i, p. 327b.

66. For pedigree of Dyve family see W. Farrer, *Feudal Cambridgeshire* (Cambridge, 1920), p. 160; and see also Loyd, *Origins*, p. 37. For pedigree, with some inaccuracies, of St Andrews family, G. Baker, *History ... of the County of Northampton* (London, 1822–30), i, pp. 160–1.

67. *CurRR*, xi, no. 2085; *Rotuli de Dominabus et Pueris*, etc., ed. J.H. Round (Pipe Roll Soc., 1913), p. 27 and n.

68. *CurRR*, xi, no. 2085; xiii, nos. 1009, 2365; *Excerpta e Rot. Fin.*, ed. Roberts, i, pp. 167–8; *ClR, 1227-31*, p. 18; *Liber Memorandorum Ecclesie de Bernewelle*, ed. J.W. Clark (Cambridge, 1907), p. 251; *CIPM*, i, no. 631. Saher later acquired land at Comberton (Cambs) and Corby (Lincs): Farrer, *Feudal Cambs*, p. 226; *ClR, 1251-3*, p. 445.

69. *Lind. Cart.*, no. 91, where *Serlo* is probably a scribal error for *Seherus*. This quitclaim by Saher of St Andrews is witnessed by Earl Roger and members of his household.

70. *Pat. Rolls of ... Henry III*, ii, p. 358; *ClR, 1227-31*, p. 450; *1251-3*, p. 445; *1259-61*, p. 454. J. Maitland Thomson stated that Saher was dead by 1256: *Inchaffray Chrs.*, p. 281. I have not traced the evidence for this statement, but have no reason to doubt its accuracy.

71. *Sandford Cartulary*, ed. A.M. Leys (Oxfordshire Rec. Soc., 1938–41), i, pp. 67–8. Fuller details of Roger's tenure of Littlemore in *VCH Oxon*, v, p. 208.

72. *Rot. Litt. Claus.*, ed. Hardy, ii, p. 191b; *ClR, 1227-31*, p. 81; *Sandford Cart.*, i, no. 91.

73. *Brackley Deeds*, p. 13; BL MS Cott. Julius C. vii, fo. 235r; *Monasticon Anglicanum*, ed. R. Dodsworth and W. Dugdale (London, 1655–73), i, p. 482.

74. No. 1 (*Brackley Deeds*, p. 14); Oxford, Magdalen College, Whitfield 13 (1).

75. *Pat. Rolls of ... Henry III*, ii, p. 358; *ClR, 1227-31*, p. 450; *Sandford Cart.*, i, no. 94.

76. *Brackley Deeds*, p. 13; Oxford, Magdalen College, Whitfield 13 (1).

77. BL MS Cott. Julius C. vii, fo. 235r; Oxford, Magdalen College, Whitfield 13 (2); *Sandford Cart.*, i, no. 93.

78. Loyd, *Origins*, pp. 28–9. A search has been made in charters granted in France by the earls of Leicester for witnesses named *de Sancto Andrea*, but has been unsuccessful.

79. *Fees*, ii, pp. 939, 1289.

80. *CIPM*, ii, no. 106; Simpson, 'RQ', pp. 86, 89.

81. For detailed discussion of Roger's English and Scottish estates stewards, see ibid., pp. 84–93. Only two of the seven known English stewards do not occur in the *familia* lists given above. None of the four Scottish stewards appears therein. On the prominence in the *familia* of men of English background see below, p. 122.

82. No. 17 (*Lind. Cart.*, no. 137).

83. *CPatR, 1258-66*, p. 144. On movement of stewards see Denholm-Young, *Seignorial Admin.*, p. 70.

84. *Excerpta e Rot. Fin.*, ii, p. 410; *ClR, 1261-4*, pp. 358, 407–9; *CPatR, 1258-66*, p. 403.

85. *ClR, 1264-8*, pp. 218–19; *Calendar of Inquisitions Miscellaneous (Chancery) preserved in the PRO* (London, 1916–63), i, nos. 882, 884, 898–9; *CPatR, 1258-66*, p. 555; *Calendar of the Liberate Rolls* (London, 1916–64), v, p. 241.

86. No. 65 (*CChR*, i, p. 429).

87. *CPatR, 1247-58*, pp. 137, 646; *Placitorum in Domo Capitulari Westmonasteriensi asservatorum Abbreviatio*, etc. (Rec. Comm., 1811), p. 183.

88. *HMC, Hastings*, i, p. 333; *Fees*, ii, p. 870.

89. *CurRR*, viii, pp. 70–1; xiii, nos. 1276, 1298; *Rot. Litt. Claus.*, i, p. 326b; W. Farrer, *Honors and Knights' Fees* (London and Manchester, 1923–5), iii, p. 262; Paris, *Chron. Maj.*, v, p. 213.

90. *Pat. Rolls of ... Henry III*, ii, pp. 216, 295, 449, 525; *ClR, 1234-7*, p. 547; *Excerpta e Rot. Fin.*, i, p. 318; *CPatR, 1232-47*, p. 234.

91. *Inchaffray Chrs.*, app., no. 4b.

92. Denholm-Young, *Seignorial Admin.*, p. 71, n. 2.

93. No. 143 (*Book of Seals*, no. 67). As Sir William de Bois was still alive on 6 March 1253 (No. 57 [*ibid.*, no. 15]), he is not identical with Sir William de Bois of Finmere (Oxon), who was dead by 29 October 1252: *Feet of Fines for Oxfordshire, 1195-1291*, ed. H.E. Salter (Oxfordshire Rec. Soc., 1930), p. 166. There is no evidence to suggest that Sir William de Bois was the owner of land in Essex or Buckinghamshire (see above, p. 105).

94. *ClR, 1231-4*, p. 124; *1264-8*, pp. 262, 270, 339; *1268-72*, p. 142; *CPatR, 1247-58*, p. 385.

95. Not identifiable as Warin of Thunderley who had lands in Essex in 1217 (*Rot. Litt. Claus.*, i, p. 340) and was a knight of Herefordshire in 1221 (*CurRR*, x, p. 171).

96. Presumably identical with Henry Bisset, a knight of Countess Margaret, who at one time held of her six yardlands in Whetstone (Leics), later granted to Stephen de Segrave (Nichols, *Leicester*, II, i, app., p. 117). There is no record of any holding there by Henry Bisset of Earl Roger. Presumably not identical with Henry Bisset who appears in Yorkshire in 1268: *ClR, 1264-8*, p. 499.

97. A Philip of Chetwynd who appears in 1277–96 must be another: *CPatR, 1272-81*, pp. 246, 430; *Calendar of the Fine Rolls preserved in the PRO* (London, 1911–62), i, p. 290; *Calendar of Chancery Warrants* (London, 1927), p. 54; *Placitorum ... Abbreviatio*, p. 237.

98. Although the name is presumably common, he might be identical with Robert of Hereford who acted as attorney for the abbot of Waltham and others in 1220, 1223 and 1234 (*CurRR*, ix, p. 59; xi, no. 222; *ClR, 1231-4*, p. 599).

99. See Simpson, 'RQ', app. D. Even here a caution is necessary: the fee held by Peter le Potter at Sibson (Leics) would have remained unknown if one text (n. 86 above) had not been discovered.

100. F.M. Stenton, *The First Century of English Feudalism, 1066–1166*, 2nd edn. (Oxford, 1961), p. 140.

101. H.G. Richardson and G.O. Sayles, *The Governance of Medieval England* (Edinburgh, 1964), p. 132.

102. No. 91 (R. Thoroton, *Antiquities of Nottinghamshire*, ed. J. Throsby [London, 1797], i, pp. 39–40).

103. B.D. Lyon, *From Fief to Indenture* (Cambridge, Mass., 1957), p. 16.

104. *Ibid.*, pp. 184–8. Lyon's statement (at p. 187) that 'not a record of this period shows the English barons granting *fiefs-rentes* to household knights' is contradicted by the example described above. He also maintains that by the thirteenth century household knights had all but disappeared in England. The two sources which he quotes in support of this statement contain no such suggestion; and the evidence discussed above points in the opposite direction.

105. *ClR, 1254-6*, p. 450.

106. *Cal. Fine Rolls*, i, p. 23. The important charter (n. 102 above) which records his *fief-rente*, although now lost, was apparently preserved in the eighteenth century in the archives of a Nottinghamshire family.

107. *CPatR, 1266–72*, p. 297.

108. *Thame Cartulary*, ed. H.E. Salter (Oxfordshire Rec. Soc., 1947–8).

109. Duno: No. 148 (*Book of Seals*, no. 95); witnesses No. 69 (*CChR*, i, p. 464) as *Reginaldo Daunou*. Bushey: No. 145 (BL Harl. Chart. 55.B.7); witnesses No. 58 (*Book of Seals*, no. 7).

110. No. 149 (W. Dugdale, *Baronage of England* [London, 1675–6], i, p. 688). For details of transfer of the Sydenham estate to Thame abbey see *VCH Oxon*, viii, pp. 117–18.

111. There is one example of an annual rent granted to a Scottish tenant, although not a *familiaris*, i.e. Saher of Seton, from lands at Tranent in East Lothian: No. 33 (BL MS Harl. 4693, fo. 10v).

112. *Cal. Inquis. Misc.*, i, no. 297.

113. *CIPM*, i, no. 411; *HMC, Hastings*, i, p. 330.

114. *CIPM*, ii, no. 222; Loyd, *Origins*, p. 51.

115. *Fees*, ii, p. 870.

116. *CPatR, 1272–81*, p. 349; *Fees*, ii, p. 949.

117. *Ibid.*, p. 736.

118. *Scots Pge.*, iii, p. 557; NLS MS Adv. 34.6.24, pp. 430–1; *ClR, 1256–9*, pp. 300, 329. A William de la Hay held of the honour of Winchester in 1277 two yardlands in Burton Overy, Leicestershire (*HMC, Hastings*, i, p. 326); but there is no evidence to show whether this was the Scottish knight of that name. The surname existed in England: William de la Hay was sheriff of Oxfordshire in the 1240s (*CDS*, i, nos. 1603, 1626).

119. *SHR*, ii (1905), pp. 173–4; *CDS*, i, no. 2672.

120. *Rental Book of the Cistercian Abbey of Cupar Angus* (Grampian Club, 1879–80), i, p. 344.

121. G.F. Black, *The Surnames of Scotland* (New York, 1946), p. 191; *RMS*, i, app. ii, no. 319: land forfeited by descendants of Earl Roger.

122. *Holyrood Liber*, no. 81; No. 81 (*Lind. Cart.*, no. 135).

123. *St Bees Reg.*, pp. x, 92 and n.

124. *Ibid.*, pp. 51–416, *passim*, esp. pp. 363–4; *Holm Cultram Reg.*, pp. 19–22, 25, 27, 39, 88.

125. *EYC*, i, pp. 399, 403–5; x, pp. 63, 65, 97–9.

126. *RRS*, ii, no. 576; J. Dallas, *History of the Family of Dallas* (Edinburgh, 1921), pp. 22–8; *St Bees Reg.*, pp. x–xi, 97–8. For further comment on the Ripley family see Barrow, *Era*, p. 192.

127. *CDS*, ii, no. 824(4). (The editor here reads *Sa'nayk'*, but the original has *Sanuayk.*)

128. J. Raine, *The History and Antiquities of North Durham* (London, 1852), app., no. 73; Fraser, *Hist. of the Carnegies*, ii, no. 25; *Scone Liber*, no. 81; *Arbroath Liber*, i, no. 266; *Melrose Liber*, i, no. 266; *Coupar Angus Chrs.*, i, no. 53; *Collections for a History of the Shires of Aberdeen and Banff* (Spalding Club, 1843), p. 299; J. Anderson, *The Oliphants in Scotland* (Edinburgh, 1879), no. 5; *Dunfermline Reg.*, no. 77; *Reg. Monasterii ... de Cambuskenneth*, no. 53.

129. Above, p. 102; *St Andrews Liber*, p. 354.

130. No. 152 (*Brackley Deeds*, p. 39); *Rot. Litt. Claus.*, i, p. 374b.

131. *CPatR, 1247-58*, p. 235. An important family named d'Oyly held Hook Norton and South Weston (Oxon) and died out in the main line *c.*1233 (Dugdale, *Baronage*, i, pp. 459–61; Farrer, *Honors and Knights' Fees*, ii, pp. 244–6). South Weston is three miles south-west of Sydenham, where Earl Roger had land in demesne; and Hook Norton is only fourteen miles from the earl's borough of Brackley.

132. Yet subject-matter is not an infallible guide to place of issue. For example, the terms of No. 39 (printed above, p. 68), which concerns lands in Lauderdale, Berwickshire, imply that it was issued at Halse (Northants), and this is confirmed by the presence of the rural dean of Brackley in the witness-list.

133. These figures are obtained by checking the apparent provenance of every text in which each knight appears as a witness in the edition in Simpson, 'RQ', plus the Appendix hereto. It is curious that all but one of the twenty-nine occurrences of Saher of St Andrews as a witness in the earl's acts are in documents of English provenance. But Saher did in 1238 witness an agreement of Scottish provenance made in the presence of Earl Roger and members of his *familia: Inchaffray Chrs.*, no. 64.

134. Among the four persons listed as of unknown social status, one deserves brief comment: Elias Sweyn, who witnessed five times and who was constable at Leuchars, the earl's principal 'manor-place' in Fife. He is also once designated 'of Shepshed', and appears to have been of some local position on that estate, one of Roger's Leicestershire demesne manors. Elias seems, therefore, to have had English family origins, but a Scottish career. See Simpson, 'RQ', pp. 93–4.

135. With the earl himself, this makes a total of at least ten, and this figure accords reasonably with the figure of twelve horses which could be accommodated in his stable at Clackmannan on his visits there: No. 26 (SRO RH 6/54).

136. For a description of fluctuations in the *curia* of Henry II and that of John, see J.E.A. Jolliffe, *Angevin Kingship* (London, 1955), pp. 139–65, esp. pp. 146–9, 156–7.

137. *ClR, 1247-51*, p. 260; *1234-7*, p. 467.

138. Nos. 94 (*Brackley Deeds*, p. 27), 107 (*ibid.*, pp. 22–3); *ibid.*, p. 30. The earl's marriage to Maud lasted from before 1250 until 1252 and, as Guy is described as belonging to the *familia* in 1250, it is possible that he was originally in Maud's employ, joined the earl's service for a brief period only, and thus came to seek the short-term exemption in which his name is mentioned.

139. No. 78 (BL Campbell Chart. iv, 10); Nichols, *Leicester*, II, ii, p. 531.

140. Stenton, *First Century*, p. 96.

141. *CPatR, 1266-72*, pp. 146–7. For an analysis of these bachelors, who may have been knights of lesser standing, see E.F. Jacob, *Studies in the Period of Baronial Reform and Rebellion* (Oxford, 1925), pp. 127–33.

142. Denholm-Young, *Seignorial Admin.*, pp. 23–4; M. Jones, *Journal of the Soc. of Archivists*, iv (1970–3), pp. 384–94.

143. Powicke, *Thirteenth Century*, p. 152.

144. Altschul, *A Baronial Family ... The Clares*, p. 236; G.A. Holmes, *The Estates of the Higher Nobility in Fourteenth-Century England* (Cambridge, 1957), p. 58. In 1313–14, Thomas, earl of Lancaster, granted liveries to seventy knights, twenty-eight esquires and smaller numbers of clerks and others (*ibid.*, p. 72); and it has been estimated that he regularly supported a retinue of between twenty-five and fifty knights: J.R. Maddicott, *Thomas of Lancaster, 1307–22* (Oxford, 1970), p. 45.

145. Holmes, *Estates of the Higher Nobility*, p. 83.

146. Cf. Denholm-Young, *Seignorial Admin.*, p. 30: 'private households had not yet developed into the complicated organisms which were common in the fourteenth century'.

147. For details of two minor families of French derivation who also became associated with the Quincys — the Cornets and the Chaumonts — see Simpson, 'RQ', pp. 104–5, with No. 30, notes.

148. I am indebted to Dr Keith Stringer for drawing to my attention the two texts calendared in the Appendix and for much other information and helpful advice.

APPENDIX

CALENDAR OF TEXTS OMITTED FROM EDITION OF ACTS OF EARL ROGER DE QUINCY IN SIMPSON, 'RQ'

1

Quitclaim by Roger, son of Saher de Quincy, earl of Winchester and Constable of Scotland, to Barnwell priory of all right to Chesterton (Cambs), promising warranty against claims of Margaret, countess of Lincoln. Witnesses: William de Ferrers, Robert de Quincy, William de Aubeni, Saher of St Andrews, Everard of Trumpington, Alan of Bassingbourn, Ferimeus (*sic*) of Caxton, John le Moyne and Peter de Brumford. (1235 × 1257).

Source: BL MS Lansdowne 863, fo. 96r; Bodl. MS Rawlinson B. 103, fo. 98.
Comment: The limit-dates of this act are those of Roger's assumption of the title of earl of Winchester and the death of Robert de Quincy III.

2

Quitclaim by Roger de Quincy, earl of Winchester and Constable of Scotland, to Belvoir priory of view of frankpledge and all suits of his court at Leicester or elsewhere, from two virgates in Waltham-on-the-Wolds (Leics). Witnesses: Sir William de Bois, Sir John of Cranford, grantor's steward, Sir Peter le Potter and Sir Robert of Hereford, kts. (1253 × 1259).

Source: Belvoir Castle, Rutland, MS Add. 105 (Cartulary of Belvoir priory), fo. 97r.
Printed: HMC, Rutland, iv, p. 166 (calendar).
Comment: The limit-dates of this act are provided by the period of stewardship of Sir John of Cranford (see Simpson, 'RQ', p. 91n.).

6

THE POLITICAL ROLE OF WALTER COMYN, EARL OF MENTEITH, DURING THE MINORITY OF ALEXANDER III OF SCOTLAND

Alan Young

The political role of the baronage in medieval Scotland, especially before about 1300, has been a strangely neglected subject. As a result, the view that Scottish barons in the earlier Middle Ages — and Anglo-Scottish barons are included in this category — were at best politically irresponsible aggressors and at worst political anarchists[1] has not been seriously contested. Concentration on periods of political crisis in Scotland has tended to emphasise the view that these barons played a largely disruptive role. This has been the case with studies of the minority of Alexander III, where emphasis has been laid on the Anglo-Scottish baronial family of Comyn performing 'the more fearful role of overmighty subjects'.[2] However, such judgements have generally been reached by viewing baronial activities in crisis from outside the baronial milieu. In order to achieve a more complete picture it is surely necessary to attempt an examination of a political crisis from inside. It is with this purpose in mind that the present study has been undertaken.

Several factors make the study of the role of Walter Comyn, earl of Menteith, during Alexander III's minority especially suitable for such treatment. The Comyns were one of the most powerful and politically influential families in thirteenth-century Scotland. An accurate assessment of their political role, however, has long been obscured by the anti-Comyn writings of Scottish annalists such as John of Fordun, or literary historians such as George Buchanan, who wrote when Stewarts had long held the throne and the traditions of Bruce and Wallace were deep-seated. The role of Walter Comyn, earl of Menteith, has especially suffered from extreme interpretations, largely as a result of his involvement in the minority crisis which both dominated and shaped his career between 1249 and 1258. In the attempt to understand his actions in these years two main views have emerged. Either Earl Walter has been seen as an unscrupulous and lawless political aggressor,[3] or else he has been regarded as the leader of a 'national' or 'patriot' party.[4] To look at Alexander III's minority from inside the baronial milieu, and especially from inside the Comyn family, is clearly desirable in order to put these interpretations into a proper perspective.

The sudden and unexpected death of Alexander II in 1249 brought a dangerous situation in Scotland because the heir, the late king's son by Marie de Coucy, was a boy of only eight years. One of the leading figures in the political crisis emanating from this situation was Walter Comyn, earl of Menteith. By 1237 Walter Comyn

K

was in a position of considerable political influence, as is shown by the treaty of York in that year when it was he alone who took the formal diplomatic oath on the king's soul when Alexander II renounced the centuries-old claim to the northern English counties.[5] This dominant position was based on his leadership of the Comyn family, perhaps the most powerful baronial family in Scotland at that time, with its effective control over the earldoms of Menteith, Buchan, Angus and Atholl,[6] as well as over the lordships of Badenoch, Kirkintilloch (Dunbartonshire) and East Kilbride (Lanarkshire). It was the very basis of this ascendancy, therefore, which was threatened in 1242 when the deaths of John Comyn, earl of Angus,[7] and Patrick, earl of Atholl,[8] removed two important earldoms from Comyn control. This twofold loss, together with the manner of Earl Patrick's death (the result of a plot laid because of the jealousy of the Bissets, a powerful Norman family),[9] provoked the Comyns, under Walter Comyn's leadership, to come to the forefront of the political stage in 1242, to claim and assure themselves of their position. Thus the 'challenge of the House of Comyn'[10] was, in fact, an attempt to stabilise the family's position rather than expand it, retaliation rather than unprincipled aggression. This is not to argue that the Comyns, in their pursuit of the Bissets, were not acting as overmighty subjects; but it should be noted that reaction against the Bissets was widespread and not merely restricted to the dead earl's relatives.[11] In 1242 there emerged *two* well-defined and powerful groups who separately launched attacks on the Bissets.[12] It seems that the Scottish king was unable to dominate either party, and Comyn control in northern Scotland was particularly evident.

The activities of the Comyns were also beginning to cause concern to the English crown. Although Henry III certainly had other reasons for marching north with an army in 1244,[13] it is clear that Walter Comyn's actions from 1242 to 1244 were regarded as a threat to the English king's northern territories. Walter had strengthened two castles in Galloway and Lothian,[14] and had also, before 1244, strengthened the castle of Tarset in Northumberland.[15] When there is added the possibility that Walter Comyn was involved in the harbouring of Geoffrey de Marisco,[16] one of the English king's enemies, it is evident that Walter must have appeared to be a real threat to Henry III.

The actions of the English and Scottish kings in 1244 recognised the desirability of curbing Walter Comyn's power. Henry III forced a treaty of friendship from the Scottish king and his magnates in 1244,[17] and also received a bond of good behaviour from the two powerful groups which had emerged in 1242 — the Comyn group led by Earl Walter and the group under the leadership of Patrick, earl of Dunbar.[18] Alexander II acted with similar intent, replacing the two Comyn-controlled justiciars — Robert Mowat and Philip de Melville — by Alan Durward and David de Lindsay.[19] It is noteworthy that neither of these men was in either of the two 'parties' which had emerged in 1242, and that from 1244 Alan Durward became Alexander II's chief adviser and head of a totally non-Comyn government. Walter Comyn must have resented the fact that this man, with little or no political influence prior to 1244, gained such an important position in government. Comyn resentment was most probably aggravated by the fact that the Durwards were their rivals in northern Scotland, especially in Mar and Atholl.[20]

The fact that the leader of the other main political group — Patrick, earl of Dunbar — was recognised at his death in 1248 as the leading magnate in the country[21] supports the view that the power of Walter Comyn had been effectively reduced.[22] However, Walter Comyn's decline in power was more apparent than real, and the political force of his 'party' was dormant rather than extinguished in the period 1244-9. Walter's prominence in the witness-lists of Alexander II's charters in this period[23] hardly denotes a full political eclipse. The nature of the Comyn following in 1244,[24] a tightly knit family group strong in both numbers and influence, whose three main branches, the Badenoch, Buchan and Kilbride lines, plus their connexions, supported Earl Walter, meant that Walter Comyn was still in a very strong position. As he had shown before 1244,[25] and was to show again afterwards, lack of formal political office was no real bar to his personal political influence.

Thus the actions of Walter Comyn should be judged from this position of strength. They should also be viewed in the light of the keen rivalry apparent, since about 1244, between the Durwards and the Comyns. Finally, they should be seen against the back-cloth of Henry III's interest and involvement in Scottish affairs in 1244. Certainly, Walter Comyn's actions from 1249 onwards cannot be judged solely in terms of Scottish politics. In fact, on Alexander II's death in 1249 there were three countries anxious to influence the young king — Scotland, England and France; and Scottish politics in these years should be viewed in the light of a change in Anglo-Scottish relations, with King Henry III then becoming the dominant figure in Scottish affairs.

The new situation in 1249 put Walter Comyn on his guard. The fact that there is no evidence of any formal arrangements having been made with regard to the government of Scotland during Alexander III's minority suggests that it was Alexander II's intention that Alan Durward should remain as head of the government.[26] He had been the king's chief adviser since 1244 and had, at about the same time, entrenched himself firmly in the royal circle by marrying Alexander II's illegitimate daughter, Marjory. This intensified the Durward-Comyn rivalry already existing as a result of their respective landed interests in northern Scotland. However, Walter Comyn was especially wary of Durward's royal connexion as it was the only real advantage which Durward held over him.

Alan Durward soon sought to formalise his position as head of the minority government, and make it more secure, by knighting the young Alexander before he was enthroned.[27] It has been suggested[28] that he did this because, in similar circumstances, Henry III had been knighted in 1216 by William Marshal, who was then asked by the English knights to take the office of *rector regis et regni.* The fact that Durward's supporters claimed that the future Alexander III should be knighted because it was 'Egyptian' day — the Egyptian theory of the origins of the kings of Scots countered the English theory that English kings were descended from Brutus of Troy — was certainly regarded as a mask to Durward's real purpose.[29] It soon became evident that the majority of Scottish nobles were suspicious of Alan Durward's plans and, perhaps more importantly, that Durward did not have enough authority over the Scottish nobility to carry his plans to a successful conclusion: *Et ecce statim postquam congregati fuerant, orta est inter magnates dissensio.*[30]

In contrast Earl Walter held the initiative from the outset. He had the political experience to see the parallel with the English king's minority and was quick to object to any further increase in Durward's control. Active in Scottish political circles since about 1210, Walter Comyn soon made his political presence felt in 1249, and his was the dominant voice emerging from the *dissensio,* with a clear challenge to Durward's plans. John of Fordun records:

> ... Walterus Cumyn comes de Menteth respondit, dicens se vidisse regem consecratum non tamen militem sed et saepius audisse reges consecratos, qui non fuerunt milites; et addidit inquiens: Quod regio sine rege procul dubio quasi navis est in mediis maris fluctibus sine remige seu rectore. Diligebat enim semper regem piae memoriae Alexandrum jam defunctum, sed et hunc etiam propter patrem. Ideoque quamcitius potuit ipsum puerum in regem sublimare proposuit, quia differre paratis semper nocet.[31]

It can be seen that the argument put forward by Walter Comyn against Durward's plans had little substance about it. In fact, it was little more than an opinion, but the important thing to note is that Walter Comyn was relying on his political weight in the country and on his political experience as a mainstay of Alexander II's government. Thus Earl Walter was not just giving *an* opinion — his objection represented *the* opinion and influence of the most powerful and most politically experienced member present. The fact that the majority of the Scottish nobility looked to Walter's political experience for guidance at this time is clearly shown, again by John of Fordun:

> Cuius consilio dicti episcopi, et abbas, necnon et magnates, omnis clerus et populus, *una voce,* ipsum in regem erigere consensum praebuerunt et assensum. Tu autem Domine.[32]

Walter's leadership was obviously highly valued. In contrast to Alan Durward's plan, Walter Comyn by a skilful piece of politics — 'this artful proposition'[33] — and by the weight of his political experience was able to mask his real intention to curb Durward's power yet also to keep the support of the Scottish nobility. The description of Walter Comyn emerging with dominance and authority from the argument — *quibus ponentibus, vir providus in consilio et perspicuus dominus Walterus Comyn comes de Menteth*[34] — is all the more valuable since it comes from a chronicler who was most acrimonious in his criticism of the later Comyn government: it gives an insight into Walter Comyn's qualities as a leader which, together with his large and tightly knit band of followers, made him such a dominant political figure.

Walter Comyn's authority was clear-cut. His advice was acted upon immediately and his leadership was generally accepted as he led Alexander to the throne,[35] successfully thwarting Alan Durward. The fact that Walter Comyn was still wary of Durward's place in the royal circle is shown by his apparent attempt to ally himself with Robert de Brus[36] who, if we can believe a partisan source, had been named as successor to Alexander II in 1238. Robert de Brus preferred to support Durward.[37] Nevertheless, although the Durward government was in office until 1251, Walter Comyn had shown in 1249 that, even without the justiciarships and control over the other offices, he was the dominant political leader. Despite the temporary setback in 1244, it is apparent that the political dominance of Walter Comyn and his party was *accepted* in Scotland. The fact that the government could not ignore his power in the period 1249-51 is shown by his attendance as a leading witness to several of Alexander III's charters.[38]

The intervention of Henry III in Scottish affairs in the latter part of 1251 is interesting in that it arose out of the Durward government's lack of control in the country. This in turn was largely due to Walter Comyn and his party's influence. Henry's intervention followed complaints that laymen were despoiling the priory of St Andrews and that the Durward government was affording it no protection.[39] These complaints to King Alexander were then followed by a complaint to the pope.[40] It is not clear whether the Comyns or the Durwards were responsible for the attacks on St Andrews priory, but it has been pointed out[41] that the canons were supported by the Durwards in their litigation with their neighbours in St Andrews, the provost and canons of the church of St Mary of the Rock, who usually looked to the Comyns for support. However, although the Comyns may not have been blameless, it appears that the clergy were complaining more of the lack of control of the Durward government and the consequent instability in church affairs. Certainly, the Comyns were closely involved with the clergy in sending a deputation to Henry III asking for aid and, more particularly, for Henry's intervention in Scottish affairs.[42]

The political skill and experience of Walter Comyn was shown here in two ways. On the one hand, his political knowledge at first hand of Henry III's intervention in 1244 had shown him the value of the English king's support, and he therefore sought this support in 1251. On the other, he realised the value of the clergy as a political, administrative and social force working for stability. Alan Durward had badly needed the support of the clergy in 1249, but it was the Comyn party which gained this support and thus added breadth and stability to their following. The Comyns had established a good reputation with the Church mainly through the munificence of William Comyn, earl of Buchan.[43] Walter Comyn, his son, was very careful to maintain this reputation.[44] In fact, the support gained from the clergy, especially after 1249, was a major reason for the prolonged nature of Walter Comyn's dominance.

Henry III proved very willing to accept the invitation, from both the Comyns and the clergy, to intervene in Scottish affairs. By Christmas 1251 this intervention was sealed by the marriage of the young king of Scotland to Henry's young daughter, Margaret, the couple being respectively ten and eleven years old. It soon became clear that Henry III took this new role as father-figure seriously, not only in regard to the welfare of the young couple but also to the welfare of the Scottish kingdom.[45] Hardly was the wedding ceremony over when Walter Comyn, showing his political opportunism to the full, accused Alan Durward of trying to set up himself and his family as rulers of Scotland by having his wife, the illegitimate daughter of Alexander II, legitimised.[46] The Melrose Chronicle shows that Alan Durward had sent messengers and gifts to the pope requesting him to 'legitimise' the daughters born to his wife, illegitimate half-sister of the new king, *ut si quid sinistrum regi*

Scotie eveniret ille tanquam heredes legitime ei in regno succederent.[47] Durward had clearly gone too far, and Walter Comyn was able to grasp the political opportunity which presented itself in 1251 to rid himself of his fear of Durward's royal connexions and gain control of the government offices for himself and his supporters.

After a brief inquiry into Walter's accusations, King Henry — in Alexander III's name — made changes in the government officers and placed the Comyns in power, Alan Durward being forced into exile.[48] Walter's plan was finally realised when Robert, abbot of Dunfermline and chancellor of the Durward government, gave up his seal and Gamelin became chancellor.[49] The Comyn party supporting Walter Comyn in government in 1251[50] had the same basic family nucleus as in 1244, with Walter Comyn at its head and with Alexander Comyn, earl of Buchan,[51] William, earl of Mar,[52] and John Comyn (d. *c.*1278) as his chief advisers. Still in the group from 1244 were Nicholas de Soules, John le Blund and Alexander Vinet (Uviet). Influential men gained from the Dunbar following after 1244 were David de Graham and Thomas de Normanville, both members of important baronial families. The most notable supporters of Walter Comyn's government in 1251, however, were the leading bishops of Scotland. Their importance was recognised in their high ranking among the Comyn supporters — they included William Bondington, bishop of Glasgow, Clement, bishop of Dunblane, Gamelin, bishop-elect of St Andrews, and William Wishart, archdeacon of St Andrews. With such a broad-based government it was clear that Walter Comyn had the general support of the country behind him, and it seems rather strange that Walter Comyn himself did not take on the most important position in government, the justiciarship of *Scotia*, which his father had held. Probably he had to placate his leading supporters by giving them the main offices. Thus Alexander Comyn, earl of Buchan, became justiciar of *Scotia* from, at the latest, 1253;[53] William, earl of Mar, was chamberlain in 1252;[54] Gamelin was chancellor by *c.*1254;[55] and Thomas de Normanville was justiciar of Lothian by *c.*1251.[56]

The years 1251-5 were to test Walter Comyn's political dominance over his own countrymen, and his leadership was to be tested also by the English king's involvement in Scottish affairs. Henry III was obviously aware, by his experience of 1244, of the power of Walter Comyn's party. However, he must have been impressed by the fact that the Comyns came to him in 1251 for his help and, moreover, that they had the support of the leading clergy and the majority of the Scottish nobility. This augured well for stability, and it was stability that Henry most of all wanted in 1251. Henry, too, must have thought that the restrictions he imposed on Walter's government would be adequate. He appointed two experienced Anglo-Scottish barons, namely Robert de Ros (King Alexander's cousin) and John de Balliol, as guardians of his daughter[57] and, no doubt, to safeguard his interests in Scotland. He also replaced the great seal, which was formally broken, by a small seal.[58] There is evidence, too, that Geoffrey de Langley was sent to Scotland as the queen's counsellor.[59] The fact that Henry intervened again in Scottish affairs in 1255, exactly on Alexander III's fourteenth birthday, also showed that he regarded the government as being subject to his overriding authority. By all these measures Henry III hoped to ensure that he had real control over the Scottish political scene.

In 1251, however, Walter Comyn, earl of Menteith, had finally achieved dominance in Scottish politics. He had used Henry III to get himself into this position, and his actions from 1251 to 1255 showed that he was not going to be restricted by the English king. As their history prior to 1251 had shown, Walter Comyn and his party were not content to be puppets. From the outset in 1251 Henry III clearly underestimated Walter Comyn as a political leader, and the years 1251–5 represent a victory for Walter's political leadership and diplomacy in overcoming Henry's schemes to direct affairs in Scotland, without actually provoking Henry by acting against English interests.

It is apparent that Walter Comyn was behind the scheme to remove Geoffrey de Langley, the queen's counsellor, from Scotland, again with common consent.[60] What importance Henry attached to Geoffrey's position is not certain, but it is clear that Henry regarded Robert de Ros and John de Balliol as guardians of the kingdom as well as of the young king and queen.[61] This was, however, effectively quashed by Walter Comyn — as is shown by the fact that the two guardians had no special precedence and little involvement in the government's activities. Although Robert de Ros, for example, appears several times in the records of the period 1251—5, his lowly position in witness-lists to Alexander III's charters is a reflection of his lack of status with regard to the Comyn government.[62] In contrast to the scarcity of the guardians' appearances in the acts of this government, and the lack of special precedence when they do appear, is the predominance of Walter Comyn's name and those of his chief supporters. The records certainly reveal the political reality of Walter Comyn's leadership in government. Walter's dominance over one of the guardians, John de Balliol, was demonstrated clearly by the Comyns' success in having their candidate, Henry, abbot of Holyrood, elected in 1253 to the bishopric of Galloway,[63] despite the opposition of John de Balliol in the name of the rights of the lordship of Galloway. The election of Henry was upheld at York in 1255.

As well as denying control to King Henry by dominating his two guardians, the Comyns under Walter's leadership were able to strengthen their own influence in a positive way. In 1254 and 1255 they pushed the successive claims of two of their supporters to the see of St Andrews.[64] Abel of Gullane contested the election of Robert de Stuteville in 1253, and was successful in 1254 when Robert's election was quashed by the pope. Abel was not only consecrated by the pope but was commended by him to the government in Scotland. More important, however, was Gamelin's election to the see of St Andrews in 1255 while he was royal chancellor. Gamelin, illegitimate by birth, had to be postulated by the pope. It is possible that he was a Comyn by birth, but it is in any case certain that he was a leading Comyn supporter.[65] It was, of course, part of Walter Comyn's political awareness that he realised the importance of the see of St Andrews. He showed the same concern in elections to this see as was shown regularly by twelfth- and thirteenth-century kings. In the elections of Abel of Gullane and Gamelin, Walter Comyn fulfilled a twofold objective: controlling the leading bishopric in Scotland and quashing the influence which his rival, Alan Durward, exerted in its cathedral chapter.

The black picture of the Comyn government painted by John of Fordun and Walter Bower has been seized upon by writers such as George Buchanan:

> The power of all things were mostly in the Faction of the Cumins. For they turned the Public Revenue to the enrichment of themselves, oppressed the Poor, and, by false Accusations, cut off some of the Nobles, who were averse to their humours and desires, and dared to speak freely of the State of the Kingdom.[66]

Certainly, although Bower's recommendation is true enough, his passage describing the government from 1251 to 1255 was strongly anti-Comyn:

> Sed quot fuerunt consules, tot fuerunt reges; quia videres illis diebus oppressiones pauperum, exheredationes nobilium, angarias civium, rapinas communium, sacrilegia decimarum, violationes ecclesiarum, ut merito dici posset: 'Vae terrae, cuius rex puer est.' Nihil in regimine magis convenit regi quam bonos consiliarios habere: quia si consiliarii sint falsi, sunt inimici regis capitanei; quia alia ei scienter suggerunt quam expedit eius statui. Et hi maxime sunt periculosi in communitate quacunque; quia, sicut in bonis consiliatoribus maxime consistit honor, salus et profectus regis et reipublicae, cuius caput est rex, ita in malis consiliatoribus maxime consistit confusio et subversio eiusdem.[67]

Walter and the Comyn government were guilty of hounding Robert of Kenleith, chancellor of the previous government, out of office, but Bower's description cannot be taken literally as an assessment either of Walter Comyn's leadership in government or of the government as a whole. The charges against the Comyns are riddled with inaccuracies. The charge that 'these councillors were so many kings' is contrary to the fact that Walter Comyn was accepted and recognised not only as leader of his 'councillors' but also as the head of a broad-based government. As events in 1249 had shown, his authority was accepted and he had the particular support of the clergy and the general support of the nobility in 1249 and 1251. Nor is there evidence that Walter and his party were working against the interests of the state. Walter certainly looked to his own and his family's interests, as we have seen. At the time, however, it was probably regarded as natural for the dominant party, especially in a royal minority, to secure stability by advancing its supporters. It was also probable that Walter Comyn, because of his already vast influence, had less need to pursue factional interest than his rival, Alan Durward, would have from 1255 to 1257. Thus Bower's description of Walter Comyn's government can be seen to be at best grossly exaggerated and at worst largely inaccurate. The description of the Comyns' excesses against the Church is illogical in view of the Church's support for Walter Comyn in 1249, in 1251 and, after the government's dismissal, again in 1255. Indeed, in contrast to what happened in 1251, the mainspring for the replacement of the Comyn government came from outside the country in the form of Alan Durward — a very different situation from the internally organised plot intended to oust Durward in 1251. Thus, given the climate of the time, there is no real evidence to suggest that Walter Comyn's conduct of affairs from 1251 to 1255 was more than usually culpable. Indeed, the lack of resistance from Alan Durward and his supporters in 1251 — with the exception of Robert the chancellor — backs up the opinion that the Comyn government and Walter's leadership were generally supported and were accepted in Scotland as being in the best interests of the state and the king. Later events were to show that Walter Comyn did not want to act against the king's wishes.

Walter Comyn seemed to have established a stable regime, yet he had a very strong and ambitious rival in Alan Durward, who well demonstrated his political skill in a political comeback. Like Earl Walter, Durward realised the necessity of Henry III's support and soon ingratiated himself by serving with the English king in Gascony.[68] By 1255 Henry III also had cause for complaint with regard to Scottish affairs. Yet his complaint was not that Walter Comyn's government was anti-English in its actions nor that Walter Comyn was working against the interests of either the Scottish king or the state. It stemmed rather from his resentment at the ineffectiveness of his two guardians, Robert de Ros and John de Balliol, whom he accused of failing in their duty.[69] Henry had obviously underestimated the political power of Walter Comyn in Scotland, and was using his two guardians as scapegoats for his own misjudgement; he was also very attentive to the young queen's complaints and to the physician Reginald of Bath's criticisms of the queen's treatment in Scotland with regard to her health.[70] Thus Henry III decided to intervene, and he supported Alan Durward in his counter-plotting by virtually giving a charter to rebel to Durward's supporters in Scotland, among whom were Patrick, earl of Dunbar, Robert de Brus, Malise, earl of Strathearn, and Alexander Stewart.[71]

The plan to overthrow the Comyn government was well worked out, involving a preliminary inquiry by Richard, earl of Gloucester, and John Maunsel; and it ended successfully about 4 September 1255, when the young king and queen were secured at Edinburgh[72] and brought to Roxburgh. The king and queen of England were waiting for them at Wark on Tweed.[73] The fact that the Durward party was able to capture King Alexander fairly easily from under the noses of the Comyns says much for the political skill and manoeuvring of Alan Durward; it also reveals a rather complacent attitude in the leadership of the Comyn government, for which Walter Comyn as leader of the Comyn 'party' should shoulder responsibility. For once Walter Comyn was unaware of the political situation, apparently convinced that his broadly based administration was secure. Hence their startled reaction when Earl Walter and his party found themselves suddenly out of government, politically isolated, and outmanoeuvred.[74] Walter was unable to prevent the assembly of seventeen lay and eight ecclesiastical magnates who approved the appointment of a new council of fifteen Durward supporters. The desire of Henry III to make more formal arrangements than in 1251 — a named council of fifteen to serve for seven years[75] — was a sign that Walter Comyn had exercised more political influence from 1251 to 1255 than Henry had intended.

The situation in 1255 was still critical, since King Alexander had not yet reached adulthood and the two leading parties were in dispute. Although one source attributes high principles to Alan Durward's actions in 1255,[76] the fact that the 1255 *coup* was a narrowly based movement rather than a national one is shown in the list of names of those supporting the removal of the Comyn government:[77] these names belonged to persons who were predominantly from the south-west of Scotland[78] and show a much narrower support than the more general support for Walter Comyn's government in 1251. Although the 1255 *coup* was backed up by powerful men in the persons of Patrick, earl of Dunbar, Robert de Brus and Malise, earl of Strathearn, the fact that the fifteen-strong council lacked either the presence or the backing of such senior bishops as those of St Andrews, Dunblane and Glasgow and also such 'national' figures as the earls of Menteith, Buchan and Mar meant it was very much a factional government dependent almost entirely on Henry III for its continuation. Its weakness, compared with Walter Comyn's government of 1251–5, is shown by the fact that only two bishops — those of Aberdeen and Dunkeld — were members of the 1255 council and only four abbots supported the Comyns' removal. It is apparent that the 1255 Durward government did not have general support and that Earl Walter had been ousted not by a more dominant or more popular power, as has been suggested,[79] but by stealth.

The new government soon showed that it could not control Walter Comyn. Indeed, Earl Walter and his party refused to put their names to the document setting up the new council.[80] Walter's position as the leading political figure in Scotland is shown, after the council had been set up, by the fact that — together with his entourage — he was granted a safe-conduct on 26 October to go to England to see the king.[81] Whether Walter Comyn was going to gain the king's support, lodge a complaint following the dissension among the Scottish nobility after Henry's departure[82] or, in fact, had been sent for by Henry because of these disturbances, is not known. Walter may have been reporting to the English king the political reality that Alan Durward lacked general support in Scotland. What is certain is that the English king was aware of Walter Comyn's position as the leading political figure in Scotland even after the *coup*.

Durward's fear of Walter's continuing power in 1255 was obvious in his attempts to discredit the Comyns for their actions in government.[83] He also tried to reduce Earl Walter's influence by reviving a claim to the earldom of Mar.[84] But the Comyn dominance in Scottish political circles was shown by Durward's failure to prevent the consecration of Gamelin, the Comyn government's chancellor, to the see of St Andrews.[85] In fact, Gamelin so won the pope's support that he was recognised as the rightful bishop of St Andrews and the Durward government, which had outlawed him, was excommunicated.[86] Thus Walter Comyn and his party still had the important backing of the clergy and, encouraged by Gamelin's consecration and angered by Durward's attempts to curb Comyn influence, Walter Comyn must have been able to exert great pressure on the government. The council eventually had to give way and consented in 1257 to pass on to Henry III a draft document:

> super quadam forma de qua comites de Menech, de Buchan, de Marr et Johannes Cumyn, una cum caeteris regni nostri magnatibus, pro bono pacis et regni nostri tranquilitate nobis instanter supplicarunt; de querelis, quas contra ipsos habemus, et etiam super aliis quae vestrae serenitati ex parte nostra plenius intimabunt.[87]

It is important to note that Walter Comyn was at this stage willing to work with the king of England and, indeed, saw Henry's help as necessary for his return to favour in Scotland. In this document, which no doubt advocated the reintroduction of

Comyn members to the Scottish government, Earl Walter was probably trying to show the relative stability of Scotland under his tested leadership and that of the earl of Buchan, the earl of Mar and John Comyn, compared with the insecurity and dissension under the Durwards. As a result, Henry III sent Roger de Quincy, earl of Winchester, to mediate,[88] but apparently with instructions not to change the rigid structure set up in 1255. Since Henry had previously sent John Maunsell north in 1256 to try to sort out the troubles in Scotland but without any positive effects, it became apparent to Walter Comyn that his tactics of working to regain power through the English king were failing. Thus the year 1257 was to mark a significant change in Walter Comyn's attitude. Having tried and failed after 1255 to persuade Henry III to intervene on his behalf, by 1257 Walter decided to use the power still at his disposal to achieve his ends. Members of the Comyn party seized the young Scottish king at Kinross and thus regained control over the government.[89] The Chronicle of Melrose claimed that the Comyns seized control because the leaders of the Durward government had been excommunicated and that, as a result, the Comyns feared that the country was dishonoured.[90] Undoubtedly the continued church support in Scotland for the Comyn party had a part in the *coup* of 1257, and the Comyn cause was certainly helped by the pope's disapproval of the Durward government. The Comyns' inability to gain Henry III's support, however, and their suffering at the hands of the Durward government,[91] played a more important part in Walter Comyn's decision to resort to force. Perhaps the most impressive aspect of the 1257 *coup* was the recognised leadership of Walter Comyn[92] and the unity and party-quality of his following.[93] One source, rather biased against the Comyns, begins the description of events in 1257 with an ironic comment on Walter Comyn's actions placed in the context of his previous political activities: *Walterus Comyn comes de Menteth, de quo non est modice mirandum.*[94] Nevertheless, this gives an impression of the scale and range of Earl Walter's achievements and aspirations on the Scottish political scene.

Walter Comyn's political acumen enabled him to realise that in the years 1257–8 Henry III — preoccupied with events in Sicily, worried at home by the baronial reform movement, the illness of the queen, and the successful rebellions of the Welsh — was in a difficult position. Walter Comyn was no doubt relieved by Henry's preoccupations, and these were probably taken into account when he organised the 1257 *coup* and again took positive action in allying with the Welsh in 1258.[95] Although it was the Welsh who seem to have taken the original initiative in seeking an alliance[96] — the first example of its kind between a body in Scotland and a body in Wales — it says much for Walter's political initiative that he played a significant role in bringing the two together. It soon becomes clear, however, that he was forced to exercise his initiative in this novel way because, in contrast with the position in 1251, he had neither the support of Kings Henry and Alexander nor that of the majority of the Scottish nobility. His supporters named in the treaty did include seven members of his old government of 1251–5, but there was apparently little support from magnates outside the Comyn family: the list of main supporters (Alexander Comyn, earl of Buchan, William, earl of Mar, John Comyn, now justiciar of Galloway, Aymer de Maxwell, John de Dundemor, David of Lochore and Hugh de Berkeley) had to be padded out with younger members of the Comyn family[97] such as William and Richard, brothers of John Comyn, and also William, earl of Ross, a relative[98] who had played little part in previous Comyn activity.

Still a powerful and closely knit group, this Comyn government, unlike that of 1251–5, nonetheless lacked real authority. Walter Comyn and his party had *de facto* command rather than real constitutional command. The comparative weakness in Walter's position was acknowledged by the Comyn leader in the terms of the Welsh treaty.[99] Walter Comyn and his associates agreed with Llywelyn, prince of Wales, and his supporters that they would make no truce with the English nor allow men from Scotland to fight against the Welsh. The Comyns also promised not to break the agreement unless they were compelled to do so by their king; indeed, they should try to persuade the king to enter the agreement. If the Comyns were compelled by their king to make a truce with Henry III, they were to try to promote Welsh interests. The terms give a strong impression that the Comyns did not control Alexander III and were desperately trying to win the support of their young king. Walter's political experience told him of the danger of an alliance between the young king of Scotland and King Henry, and the terms of the treaty suggest that he and his party had overreached themselves and were trying to draw back. His influence as the leader of a large and closely knit family unit was enough to secure his control of the government, yet Walter Comyn realised that this control would be short-lived unless he could win over the king and thus get a broader-based support. The alliance with the Welsh was therefore an inspired attempt to broaden the base of his government. Only three months after the alliance was made, however, the Welsh made peace with Henry III. The Comyn government's lack of effective control was seen when they lost the great seal, and is underlined by the freedom which King Alexander had in writing to King Henry and by the freeing of Queen Margaret from Comyn custody.[100]

Compromise was in the air in 1258, and in September, with King Alexander coming more into the political picture, a compromise council including four Comyn supporters, headed by Walter Comyn, and four Durward supporters was agreed upon.[101] Earl Walter, after going out on a limb in 1257, had shown by his actions in 1257–8 that he was unwilling to act unconstitutionally against the wishes of the king of Scotland. It is apparent that he was willing in September 1258 to take part in a compromise council as long as he had at least equal power with the Durwards.

Walter Comyn, earl of Menteith, must still have been the leading political figure in Scotland at his death in late October or early November 1258, as he was chief witness to a charter of Alexander III on 16 October.[102] The suddenness of his death and the reactions to it in both Scotland and England indicate the effect he had had on the political affairs of both countries. Messengers came to King Henry at St Albans on 22 November especially to report his death, and the nature of Matthew Paris's description of him at his death shows Walter Comyn's political importance in English eyes:

> Et dum ibidem moraretur, affuerunt nuntii asserentes quod Walterus Cumin comes in Scotia potentissimus, in fata concessit lapsus ab equo suo, ad quoddam offendiculum cespitante, et sic fractis cruribus, exspiravit.[103]

The frequent appearance of Walter Comyn at the centre of Scottish affairs from the second decade of the thirteenth century until 1258 meant that his death was bound to have important effects in Scotland. More particularly, the suddenness of his death and the loss of his leadership was a great blow to the Comyn 'party'. The fear that it would lose its dominant position in Scottish society was behind John Comyn's violent seizure of the earldom of Menteith from Walter's widow, Isabella, and her new husband, John Russell, between 1260 and 1261.[104]

After 1258 King Alexander III began to play a more active part in political affairs, and this year, in effect, marks the end of the minority. Walter Comyn's death undoubtedly facilitated Alexander III's emergence into the centre of political affairs, for the Scottish king was no longer obliged to maintain such a rigid balance between the Comyn and Durward parties. In practice he kept members of the Comyn family in the offices of central and local government, but added members of the Durward party to his council. Compromise was in the air in 1258; it was a reality in 1259 when Alexander Comyn, earl of Buchan, and Alan Durward, the leaders of the two main political groups in Scotland, acted as messengers of state and travelled to England to try to recover the document of September 1255 in which the Scots had agreed to the minority continuing under Henry III's overlordship until 1262.[105] This was a practical expression of the new political situation. The two main baronial parties were willing to work together and, what is more important, were willing to try to make a reality of their young king's plans for a more independent Scotland.

Undoubtedly the political experience gained by Walter Comyn since about 1212,[106] along with his personal ability, played a large part in his domination of Scottish politics in 1249–58. He was also the leader of the most powerful and tightly knit group in Scotland. The backing of such a large but compact group[107] and his personal qualities of leadership were, in fact, interdependent factors in both the nature and the length of his political involvement in Scotland. It would be inaccurate to describe his political role in the minority period outside the context of the Comyn family as a whole; above all, his actions must be assessed as those of a leader of a family 'party' caught up in a national crisis. Examples can be found, particularly in the period 1242–4, when Walter and his supporters used the power at their disposal in their own interests rather than those of the state. However, when judged from the viewpoint that family interests were threatened and that Walter's actions were, in the main, an attempt to stabilise the Comyn position rather than expand it, a clearer picture emerges. It would certainly be unwise to generalise about his political role in the minority crisis of 1249–58 by using the years 1242–4 as a guideline.

Study of the years 1249–58 does not leave an impression that Earl Walter was the unscrupulous leader of a resentful and unprincipled faction. After 1249 there is clear evidence that he was generally acting with majority support. Even the anti-Comyn annalist, John of Fordun, could scarcely disguise his admiration for Earl Walter's ability. And that ability and his political authority were certainly accepted by the whole Scottish nobility *una voce* in 1249, when Earl Walter successfully thwarted Alan Durward's plans to increase his personal power. It was also significant that Walter had the support of the Church in a joint appeal to Henry III to enlist his help in overthrowing the Durward government. Both Henry III and the Scottish Church regarded it as in the interest of Scotland that a Comyn government should be formed in 1251. That this Comyn government, supported by the majority of the Scottish nobility, by the Church, and by the king of England from 1251 to 1255, was so broad-based surely shows a general acceptance of Earl Walter's political leadership in Scotland. Undoubtedly, Comyn family interests benefited from this leadership, but majority opinion in Scotland obviously regarded Earl Walter's leadership as vital for national stability during a minority. The black picture of the Comyn government in 1251–5 painted by John of Fordun and Walter Bower, and especially their allegations of Comyn oppression of the Church, do not stand up to close inspection.

In fact, the only time that Earl Walter acted without majority support during the king's minority was when he usurped control of the young king himself in 1257 and once more took charge of Scottish government. The treaty which he made with the Welsh in 1258 clearly revealed the narrow base on which his power then rested. But the terms of the treaty show that he was keenly aware of the Scottish king's position in society and that he was unwilling, even when he had *de facto* command, to do anything without the young king's permission. This was hardly unprincipled leadership.

At the other extreme from the stigmatisation of Earl Walter as the unprincipled leader of a resentful faction is his elevation to the leadership of the 'patriot' party. Certain of his actions have been seized upon by writers who have subsequently seen him as upholder of the 'national' cause:

> ... possessed by high talents and a strong love of his country which enabled him to direct the great power thus lying in his hands for what he considered the interests of Scotland ... the patriotism of the Earl of Menteith was devoted to the preservation of the liberties of his country.[108]

It was probably Matthew Paris who first saw Walter Comyn's seizure of the king and government in 1251 as the wresting of power by native subjects from the hands of foreigners.[109] The fact that Walter Comyn's party was thus regarded as a 'native' party is certainly a tribute to the adaptation of the Comyns to Scottish society. On closer inspection, however, we see that Walter Comyn was not a fervent upholder of the 'national' cause. His attitude can best be judged in the period of Comyn government from 1251 to 1255 when he had the backing not only of the Scottish clergy but also of the majority of the Scottish nobility. In these very favourable circumstances, when he was the accepted and dominant political leader in Scotland and even pushed Henry III's two guardians very much into the background, it is most noticeable that he gave Henry III no real reason to intervene by the pursuit of aggressively Scottish policies. Indeed, when Henry III did eventually intervene in 1255, it was mainly because of his anxiety for his daughter's health and the mismanagement of his two guardians. It does not seem to have been due to the Comyn government's policies. Earl Walter's government accepted, apparently without much struggle, the allocation of taxes raised in Scotland for Henry III's crusading schemes in Sicily. If Walter Comyn had been the upholder of the 'national' cause it is probable that, enjoying popular support as he did, he would have pressed at the papal Curia for Alexander III's anointment at a coronation ceremony, and that he would also have tried to prevent taxes which had been raised in Scotland from being used by Henry III to further his own interests in Sicily. It is interesting to note in this connexion that these two matters were raised by the Durward government (stigmatised by writers as pro-English) and were major reasons for Durward's displacement by Henry III in 1251.[110]

Even the Scottish Church's support for Earl Walter cannot be used to show that his party had nationalist leanings.[111] Their alliance was based on a practical recognition by the leading bishops that Walter and his party were more capable of giving Scotland stability in a crisis than was Alan Durward. In the exceptional circumstances brought about by Alexander III's minority, it was a similar awareness of political realities which shaped Walter Comyn's attitude to the English king. It was realistic, and was in the interests of the stability of the nation, for both the Comyn and Durward parties to recognise that England was much stronger than Scotland and therefore to appeal to the English king for help. Also, in supporting his own political position, neither Walter Comyn nor Alan Durward could afford to be opposed to Henry III. In particular, Earl Walter had clearly learned from his experience of 1244 that King Henry's support was necessary. Astutely, he took care not to offend the English king while he managed cleverly to curb the influence of Henry's two guardians in Scottish politics between 1251 and 1255. Durward, on the other hand, although pro-Henry III for most of the crisis, took in Henry's view a too independent line at one stage in his government and was therefore removed from office in 1251. For his part, Walter Comyn acted against Henry III in 1257 only because he had first of all failed to win his support by pleading for the English king's intervention in Scottish affairs and because of his party's rough treatment at the hands of the Durward government after 1255. It would, therefore, be more realistic to describe the crisis in Scottish politics between 1249 and 1258 in terms of a pro-Comyn party and an anti-Comyn party than of a 'national' party and pro-English party. Henry III's support was necessary for any party in Scotland which hoped to remain in a powerful and influential position. Power for himself and his family and the maintenance of this power was Earl Walter's main motivating force during the minority. Political ideals such as 'nationalism' did not play a part in his thinking. Any connexion with nationalist elements was, therefore, purely incidental.

There is no doubting Walter Comyn's political weight, nor the ability and judgement in political affairs which enabled both him and his family to direct affairs in their favour for the greater part of the period of national crisis. Although family interests rather than political ideals guided his actions, he was not self-seeking to the detriment of the Scottish king and the interests of the Scottish kingdom, taking the period 1249–58 as a whole. Rather than as the unprincipled leader of a small, resentful faction, Earl Walter should be seen for the most part as a powerful leader prepared to work through the normal channels of government, despite a period of national crisis, and as acting with majority support in Scotland. His conduct in 1257 and 1258 formed an exception to the otherwise consistent pattern of behaviour, and even that exceptional conduct was embarked upon with reluctance.

NOTES

1. A.M. Mackenzie, *The Kingdom of Scotland* (Edinburgh, 1948), pp. 63–7, 113.

2. D.E.R. Watt, 'The minority of Alexander III of Scotland', *Trans. of the Royal Historical Soc.,* 5th ser., xxi (1971), p. 2. Duncan, *Scotland,* pp. 553–76, sheds further light on the general political scene in this important period without seriously disturbing this view of the Comyns' role.

3. *Chron. Fordun,* ii, p. 292; *Chron. Bower,* ii, p. 85; G. Buchanan, *The History of Scotland,* trans. J. Aikman (Glasgow and Edinburgh, 1827–9), p. 240.

4. W. Fraser, *The Red Book of Menteith* (Edinburgh, 1880), i, p. 18.

5. Stones, *Relations,* no. 7 (p. 50).

6. Walter Comyn held the title to the earldom of Caithness for a short while in 1235 (*Registrum Honoris de Morton* [Bannatyne Club, 1853], i, p. xxxv) and seems to have been involved in Alexander II's policy of establishing greater royal control in the north. The Comyn family appear to have exercised their influence in the inheritance of the earldom of Caithness. See further above, pp. 34, 37.

7. *Chron. Melrose,* p. 90. His relationship to Earl Walter is unknown. After his death in France, the earldom was under Umfraville control: *Handbook of British Chronology,* ed. F.M. Powicke and E.B. Fryde, 2nd edn. (London, 1961), p. 467.

8. Paris, *Chron. Maj.,* iv, p. 200. For Patrick's relationship to the Comyns see A.A.M. Duncan, 'The earldom of Atholl in the thirteenth century', *The Scottish Genealogist,* viii, no. 2 (1960). The earldom went to the Strathbogies via a daughter of David de Hastings and his countess.

9. Paris, *Chron. Maj.,* iv, p. 200.

10. Watt, 'Minority', p. 2.

11. *Chron. Bower,* ii, p. 73: *conquesti sunt omnes comites de combustione comitis Atholiae.*

12. *CDS,* i, nos. 2671–2.

13. Henry feared a Franco-Scottish alliance (Paris, *Chron. Maj.,* iv, pp. 358–61) and also desired the opportunity to bolster his prestige after his setback in Gascony.

14. *Ibid.,* p. 380. One castle was Hermitage in Liddesdale (*Chron. Bower,* ii, p. 74) — see RCAHMS, *Inventory of Roxburghshire,* i, p. 82.

15. *ClR, 1242–7,* p. 222. The earliest date usually given for Tarset is 1267. This development at Tarset, hitherto unnoticed by either Scottish or English historians of the period, adds extra weight to the role of Walter Comyn in these Border disturbances.

16. Paris, *Chron. Maj.,* iv, p. 380; F.M. Powicke, *King Henry III and the Lord Edward* (Oxford, 1947), p. 744.

17. Paris, *Chron. Maj.,* iv, pp. 381–2. In this treaty Alan Durward, David de Lindsay, Henry de Balliol and William Giffard swore on the king's soul to keep the terms of the agreement; cf. the treaty of York, in which Walter Comyn had alone performed this duty.

18. *CDS,* i, nos. 2671–2.

19. *Chron. Bower,* ii, p. 75. Robert Mowat certainly, and Philip de Melville probably, were in the Comyn following: SRO RH 1/2/32; *St Andrews Liber,* pp. 250–3.

20. *Aberdeen Reg.,* ii, p. 268; *Scots Pge.,* v, p. 573.

21. Paris, *Chron. Maj.,* v, p. 41.

22. Cf. Watt, 'Minority', p. 4.

23. *Melrose Liber,* i, nos. 231, 239; *Scone Liber,* no. 81. Cf. Duncan, *Scotland,* p. 550.

24. *CDS,* i, nos. 2671–2.

25. E.g., the Comyn control over the two justiciars, Robert Mowat and Philip de Melville, in 1241–4. See also n. 19 above.

26. Watt, 'Minority', pp. 6–7.

27. *Chron. Fordun,* i, p. 293. Fordun was writing in the 1370s or '80s; but there appears to be an otherwise unknown but self-consistent chronicle source in Fordun, providing information about political events in the mid-thirteenth century.

28. Watt, 'Minority', p. 7.

29. *Chron. Fordun,* i, p. 293.

30. *Ibid.*

31. *Ibid.*

32. *Ibid.* (my italics).

33. Lord Hailes, *Annals of Scotland,* 3rd edn. (Edinburgh, 1819), p. 195.

34. *Chron. Fordun,* i, p. 293.

35. *Ibid.,* p. 294.

36. *CDS,* i, no. 1763; cf. Watt, 'Minority', pp. 7–8. It has not been noticed, however, that the Comyns may have been interested in a Bruce alliance even before Alexander II's death: see *Lind. Cart.,* no. 41.

37. *CDS,* i, no. 2013.

38. See in particular SRO GD 175/1; also *APS,* i, p. 425.

39. *Concilia Scotiae,* ed. J. Robertson (Bannatyne Club, 1866), ii, pp. 241–2.

40. *Ibid.,* pp. 242–3.

41. Watt, 'Minority', p. 8.

42. *Chron. Fordun,* i, p. 295.

43. *Chron. Melrose,* p. 82.

44. He built a priory for Augustinian canons on the Isle of Inchmahome *c.*1238 (*Liber Insule Missarum* [Bannatyne Club, 1847], pp. xxix-xxxii); see also *Scone Liber,* no. 98, and *Moray Reg.,* nos. 76, 85.

45. Anderson, *Scottish Annals,* p. 368.

46. *Chron. Fordun,* i, p. 296.

47. *Chron. Melrose,* p. 110. Since there is no suggestion that these daughters were bastards, the chronicle presumably implied the legitimation of Durward's wife.

48. *Chron. Bower,* ii, p. 85.

49. *Chron. Fordun,* i, p. 296; cf. Watt, *Dictionary,* p. 211.

50. *CDS,* i, no. 2013.

51. Alexander was not mentioned in the bond of obedience of 1244 (*ibid.,* nos. 2671–2), but was certainly a leading supporter at the time.

52. William was not in the 1244 list. He became a prominent member of the Comyn party later. He married one of the daughters of William, earl of Buchan.

53. Having been preceded by joint justiciars *c.*1251, one of whom, Philip of Fedarg or Meldrum, was certainly and the other, Michael Mowat, was probably a member of the Comyn following (Barrow, *Kingdom,* p. 137).

54. *Handbook of British Chronology,* p. 178.

55. *Ibid.,* p. 174; Watt, *Dictionary,* p. 211.

56. Barrow, *Kingdom,* p. 137.

57. Anderson, *Scottish Annals,* p. 368. They were presumably chosen because they were Anglo-Scottish landowners and connected with the Scottish royal family.

58. *Chron. Fordun,* i, p. 296.

59. Anderson, *Scottish Annals,* p. 369.

60. *Ibid.*

61. Paris, *Chron. Maj.,* v, p. 501.

62. *Melrose Liber,* i, no. 336; *Dunfermline Reg.,* no. 84. John de Balliol does not make any appearance in the records evidencing government activities. For an alternative view of the role of Robert de Ros see Duncan, *Scotland,* p. 575; but the record evidence does not indicate that Ros played a leading role in that government or suggest that the Comyns co-operated with Ros and John de Balliol.

63. Watt, *Fasti,* p. 129.

64. *Ibid.,* pp. 292–3.

65. *CDS,* i, no. 2013. Note that on 13 October 1265 at Tynninghame in East Lothian, Alexander Comyn, earl of Buchan, announced that he had received at ferme from Gamelin, bishop of St Andrews, the land of Ellon in Buchan: *Collections for a History of the Shires of Aberdeen and Banff* (Spalding Club, 1843), pp. 311–12. On Gamelin see further Watt, *Dictionary,* pp. 209–10.

66. Buchanan, *History of Scotland,* p. 240.

67. *Chron. Bower,* ii, p. 85; cf. *Chron. Fordun,* i, pp. 296–7; ii, p. 292. The much-used scriptural quotation is from Ecclesiastes x, 16: 'Woe to thee, O land, when thy king is a child, and thy princes eat in the morning!'

68. *Chron. Melrose,* p. 111. Henry had great difficulty in England in getting men to undertake this campaign, and this thwarted his ambitions as an international potentate.

69. Paris, *Chron. Maj.,* v, p. 501.

70. *Ibid.,* pp. 501–2.

71. *Foedera,* I, i, p. 326.

72. *Chron. Bower,* ii, p. 90.

73. *Ibid; Chron. Melrose,* p. 112; *CDS,* i, no. 2002.

74. *Chron. Melrose,* p. 113.

75. Stones, *Relations,* no. 10.

76. *Chron. Bower,* ii, p. 89.

77. Stones, *Relations,* no. 10.

78. The south-west was dominated by Robert de Brus and his allies; names from the Perth and Stirling areas reflect Durward's influence there. For an alternative viewpoint on the nature of the 1255 party see Duncan, *Scotland,* p. 567.

79. Buchanan, *History of Scotland,* p. 241.

80. *Chron. Melrose,* p. 113.

81. *CPatR, 1247–58,* p. 429. A safe-conduct had also been granted to him on 4 September: *ibid.,* p. 424.

82. *Chron. Fordun,* i, p. 297.

83. *Ibid.*

84. According to papal mandates of 28 March and 4 October 1257: *CPL,* i, pp. 349, 351. Cf. Watt, 'Minority', p. 16.

85. *Chron. Bower,* ii, p. 90.

86. *Chron. Melrose,* p. 114.

87. *Foedera,* I, i, p. 353.

88. *CDS,* i, no. 2080; above, pp. 112, 119.

89. *Chron. Fordun,* i, p. 297. The great seal was also seized by the Comyns.

90. *Chron. Melrose,* p. 114. The Melrose chronicler supported the Comyns.

91. *Chron. Fordun,* i, p. 297.

92. *Chron. Melrose,* p. 114.

93. *Unanimiter consulti: Chron. Fordun,* i, p. 297.

94. *Chron. Bower,* ii, p. 91.

95. *Foedera,* I, i, p. 370.

96. John de Oxenedes, *Chronica,* ed. H. Ellis (Rolls Ser., 1859), p. 211.

97. *CDS,* i, no. 2155; cf. Watt, 'Minority', p. 17.

98. He was husband of Walter's sister, Jean.

99. *Foedera,* I, i, p. 370.

100. *CDS,* i, no. 2114.

101. There are two sources for our knowledge of this council: one version includes Earl Walter (*CPatR, 1258–66,* p. 2; also in *Foedera,* I, i, p. 378); the other omits Walter, and Earl Alexander heads the Comyn list (*ClR, 1256–9,* pp. 461–2; also in Stones, *Relations,* no. 11). The explanation for this discrepancy seems to be that one version was drawn up before the news of Walter's death, whereupon another version was prepared.

102. *Scone Liber,* no. 108.

103. Paris, *Chron. Maj.,* v, p. 724.

104. Theiner, *Monumenta,* p. 93; *Chron. Fordun,* i, p. 298. John Comyn was forced to give up the earldom to Walter Stewart and his wife, a politically sensible decision in which Alexander Comyn, earl of Buchan, took an important part. It was Alexander rather than John Comyn who was to lead the Comyn party during the next thirty years.

105. Paris, *Chron. Maj.,* v, p. 740.

106. For Walter Comyn as a witness to royal charters at the end of William the Lion's reign see *RRS,* ii, nos. 511, 513–14, 521.

107. *CDS,* i, nos. 2671–2 (for the 1244 'party'); *ibid.,* no. 2013 (for supporters in 1255); *Chron. Bower,* ii, p. 91 (for supporters in 1257); *CDS,* i, no. 2155 (for supporters in 1258). At one point in the thirteenth century there are said to have been thirty-two knights of the surname Comyn in Scotland: *Chron. Bower,* ii, p. 92.

108. Fraser, *Red Book of Menteith,* i, p. 18.

109. Paris, *Chron. Maj.,* v, p. 656.

110. Theiner, *Monumenta,* no. 142; Stones, *Relations,* no. 9; cf. Watt, 'Minority', p. 9.

111. The Church was the only section of the Scottish nation with a consistent and long-held desire for more Scottish independence, but its support for the Comyns in 1249, 1251 and 1255 was a practical one — the churchmen wanted stability.

7

THE BALLIOL FAMILY AND THE GREAT CAUSE OF 1291–2

Geoffrey Stell

The history of the Balliol family in France and Britain extends over eight generations, from the late eleventh century to 1364.[1] This widely ramified family obviously justifies detailed analysis and, as a first step towards a full-length study, this essay will relate some aspects of the family's background history to the momentous events of 1291–2, which brought the then head of the family to the forefront of Scottish political life, and ultimately to the kingship itself. For, as is well known, in November 1292 John Balliol or, to give him a fuller style, John de Balliol II, lord of Barnard Castle in County Durham and, since the death of his mother Dervorguilla in January 1290, lord of Galloway, finally emerged as the successful competitor in the adjudication by King Edward I of England concerning the vacant throne of Scotland.[2]

The Great Cause and its prelude are normally viewed in the context of Anglo-Scottish relations and as a stage in the developing sense of nationhood within the Scottish kingdom. With the benefit of hindsight, these events are also seen to mark a temporary setback in the rise of the Bruce family; the view from a Balliol standpoint has attracted comparatively little interest and sympathy, despite the fact that in their promotion to royal status in these islands the Balliols were unique among the feudal baronage of thirteenth-century Britain. In order to appreciate more fully the special circumstances in which John Balliol found himself in late 1292 there is, therefore, good reason for examining afresh from a Balliol point of view the question of rivalry between the Bruces and the Balliols, the effects on the family of the marriage of John de Balliol I and Dervorguilla of Galloway in 1233, through which the Balliol claim to the Scottish throne had initially stemmed, and, finally, the early life and career of John Balliol himself, later King John and then, unhappily, 'Toom Tabard'.

One feature that the Great Cause has always brought sharply into focus is the confrontation between the two strongest claimants, Bruce and Balliol, a central issue that is usually summed up as 'Bruce *versus* Balliol'.[3] Certainly, the petitions of these two parties do crystallise the opposed legal viewpoints of seniority as against nearness of degree in the transmission of the royal inheritance through the female issue of Margaret, eldest daughter of David, earl of Huntingdon (1152–1219). The arguments that were adduced in 1291–2 may have been presaged by the 'bitter pleading' between Bruce and Balliol that had evidently broken out at a time when John Balliol's mother was still alive, probably in the *colloquium* or parliament of

April 1286 within a month of Alexander III's death.[4] During the uneasy period of the Guardianship after 1286 the Bruces, lords of Annandale and earls of Carrick, mounted attacks on the royal castles of Wigtown and Dumfries, and on the *caput* of the Balliol lordship at Buittle, all in the south-west.[5] They then planned a takeover of the Balliol and Hastings share of the old Huntingdon lands in Garioch.[6] These actions can easily be construed as betraying a keen sense of rivalry and anticipation on the Bruce side, and perhaps a jealousy of Comyn political and territorial strength as well as an awareness of Balliol legal right. But whatever territorial aims the Bruces may have been nurturing, there is no evidence to show that the Balliols had similar, conflicting aims, or that the Bruces had ever seriously impinged on Balliol consciousness before 1286.

Indeed, aggressive or faction-forming activity on the Balliol side[7] does not emerge until after the death of the 'Maid of Norway' in September 1290, and even then, from what little we know of Balliol himself and his supporters during this critical period, John Balliol appears to have been somewhat detached from the political storm that was gathering on his behalf north of the Border. It is arguable, for example, that his assumption of the style 'heir of the kingdom of Scotland' on one occasion may have had much to do with the ambition of the beneficiary of the document in question, Anthony Bek, bishop of Durham.[8] Furthermore, whilst the auditors or sponsors who were later appointed for the hearing of the Great Cause may not have represented strict party divisions, the fact that John Comyn of Badenoch and Balliol together agreed to supply their quota of forty, and the fact that the names of the majority of lay persons in that list[9] mean far more to Comyn than to Balliol historians, clearly show the Comyn-based character of pro-Balliol support in Scotland at that time. It seems a reasonable corollary to suppose that the interests of the powerful Comyn family constituted the single most important influence on any political initiative directed against Bruce.

Despite these evident differences in attitude and involvement on the part of the Bruces and the Balliols, historians have been tempted to push the contest even further back in time. Placing the earlier histories of the two families in parallel at almost every juncture, they see the confrontation 'Bruce *versus* Balliol' as the culmination of an ancient rivalry of heroic proportions. This view presupposes that the recorded behaviour of the families had always been governed by similar conditions, and that their ambitions had always lain in the same general direction. Unfortunately, this more widely prevailing Bruce-oriented version of events runs the danger of misrepresenting the Balliols and presenting their history in a misleading light.

It is true that by marriage both parties had come into indirect contact by sharing in the division of the considerable Anglo-Scottish estates of Earl John of Huntingdon and Chester following his death in 1237.[10] The two shares that made up her mother's right ultimately fell to Dervorguilla de Balliol alone, including lands provided as compensation for the earldom of Chester, which was left undivided in English royal possession. Considering the many possible sources of friction it might have created, however, the partition of the congeries of lands, rights and rents that made up the honour of Huntingdon and the earl's Scottish estates seems to have been accepted more amicably than the rivalry thesis would lead us to expect. It is also true that the two families had married into the divided descent of Fergus of Galloway, but the Bruce marriage into the earldom of Carrick in about 1272 was comparatively recent, and the Balliols are not known to have contributed to the traditional Carrick-Galloway feud;[11] their lands and interests were mainly but not exclusively in eastern Galloway. The Balliols and Bruces also had neighbouring landed interests in the Cleveland district of north Yorkshire, in the wapentake of Sadberge in the Palatinate of Durham, and, to a lesser extent, in Cumberland.[12] After the first generation, however, the Yorkshire Bruces at Skelton followed a separate descent from the Scottish branch of the family, although the latter nonetheless retained a considerable interest in Hartness (Co. Durham) and in Guisborough priory, a Bruce family foundation. Furthermore, in contrast to the Balliols, the Bruces, lords of Annandale, became rooted in Scottish soil in the first half of the twelfth century.[13] The difference this made to the position of the two families at this date is well illustrated by chronicle accounts of events leading up to the battle of the Standard in 1138.

Richard of Hexham records that Robert de Brus (Bruce) and Bernard de Balliol went forward from the English royal camp at Thirsk in order to parley with King David I, who was then preparing to cross the River Tees into Yorkshire. Their efforts to dissuade him from this course of action were ineffectual. 'Therefore', wrote the chronicler, 'Robert returned to him [King David] the homage which he had done him, and Bernard the oath which on one occasion he had sworn him when he had been taken prisoner by him, and they returned to their comrades.' According to John of Hexham, 'Robert freed himself from the homage which he had done him for the barony which he held of him in Galloway, and Bernard freed himself from the loyalty he had long ago promised him', whilst Ailred of Rievaulx refers to Robert breaking the chain of fealty 'after the ancestral custom', but does not mention Bernard.[14]

These accounts show a clear and careful distinction between the homage for lands and the personal oath by which the two men were respectively tied to the king of Scots. The occasion of Balliol's capture and oath of fealty may have been David's rapid occupation of Northumberland in late 1135, but later commentators have assumed that, like Robert de Brus, he had already received from the king of Scots large tracts of land in southern Scotland.[15] However, the entries in the Kelso abbey cartulary to which they refer do not support the case.[16] The Balliol grant in question concerns a salmon-fishing on the Northumberland bank of the Tweed, at Woodhornstell near Tweedmouth. It was confirmed by King David in the last year of his reign when he was holding the earldom of Northumberland on behalf of his young grandson after the death of Earl Henry in June 1152.

Except during the troublesome episode relating to the bishopric of Durham after 1141,[17] Bernard was not inclined to support, or even to be on the same side as, the king of Scots. The family's normal pattern of military and political behaviour was exactly that, as Bernard's descendants demonstrated, and as successive kings of Scots learned to their cost, at Alnwick in 1174, when William the Lion was captured, and at Barnard Castle in 1216, when Alexander II tried to take the Balliol

Table 5. *The Balliol family in the twelfth and thirteenth centuries*

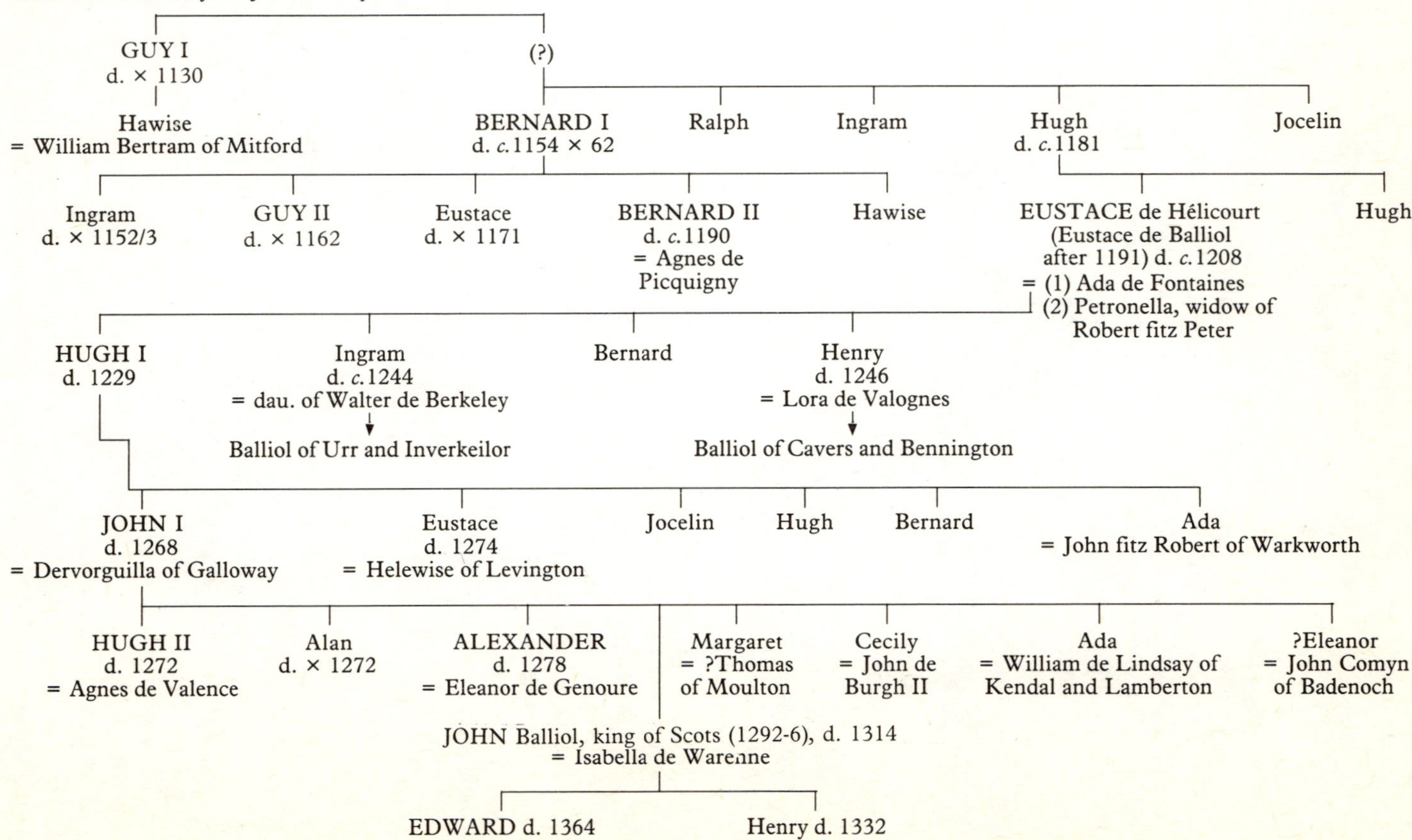

stronghold.[18] Indeed, as a bulwark against the Scots and a strong supporter of the English King John, Hugh de Balliol was the exception rather than the rule among the northern English barons in the early thirteenth century;[19] but the reasons for his behaviour and for his dependence on English royal favour lie outside the scope of this essay.

In fact, the earliest attachment to Scottish lands and interests by this family of Balliols, as opposed to the Balliols of Norman origin who appeared in Scotland under Warenne family auspices in the third quarter of the twelfth century,[20] was perhaps slightly before 1200. Ingram de Balliol, almost certainly the second son of Eustace de Hélicourt (*alias* Eustace de Balliol) and brother of Hugh de Balliol, made his first recorded appearance about this date, having married the daughter of Walter de Berkeley and through her succeeded to the lordships of Inverkeilor in Angus and Urr in Galloway.[21] Henry de Balliol, very probably his younger brother and Eustace's fourth son, followed his example with a marriage to Lora de Valognes. They were progenitors of the Balliols of Cavers in Roxburghshire and Bennington in Hertfordshire, occasional holders of the office of chamberlain of Scotland, Henry's second son, Alexander, later serving in this capacity for the Guardians and for his cousin, King John Balliol.[22] Ingram and Henry, the first of the family to be established in Scotland, were uncles of John de Balliol I, and the bonds of kinship appear to have been maintained. They were both parties to John's agreement with the bishop of Durham in 1231,[23] and it is not unreasonable to suppose that they may have paved the way for his marriage with Dervorguilla of Galloway two years later. Ingram, as lord of Urr, was particularly well placed, and as *E. de Ballelio* (i.e., *E* for 'Enguerrand', not for an otherwise unidentifiable 'Eustace' as has been suggested) he was first witness to a charter of Alan of Galloway, Dervorguilla's father, relating to the lordship of north Westmorland some time before 1226.[24]

The Scottish experiences of the Bruces and Balliols were thus dissimilar; they were also quite different in their cross-Channel connexions. The Bruces hailed from the Cotentin in western Normandy,[25] whereas the origins of the Balliol family lay beyond the eastern frontier of the duchy, within the adjacent counties of Vimeu and Ponthieu in Lower Picardy. Bailleul-en-Vimeu, Hélicourt and Hornoy, three of their four lordships, were grouped fairly close together between the Rivers Bresle and Somme, and the fourth, Dompierre, lay some distance to the north, on the River Authie.[26]

The family took its name from Bailleul-en-Vimeu, one of several Bailleuls in northern France that gave rise to the nineteen or so medieval families of the name known to Picard genealogists; and there were at least another dozen Balliol families in Britain. Prior to the Galloway marriage of 1233, the first five generations of the heads of this particular Balliol family had all taken wives of northern French origin. One spouse was evidently of the important family of Picquigny, *vidames* of Amiens, described as kinsmen of the Balliols in the early fourteenth century but apparently unrelated to the British Pinkenys, including those involved in the Great Cause.[27]

By contrast with most of the cross-Channel baronage, including the Bruces, the most remarkable feature of the Balliols' continental connexion was its sheer longevity, continuing long after the loss of Normandy in 1204 and almost unbroken into the fourteenth century. Reasonably full texts survive for rather more than twenty-five Balliol *acta* relating to their French estates before 1314, and a significant proportion of these date from the thirteenth century.[28] Unlike Normandy but like the independent county of Saint-Pol, Ponthieu (including Vimeu) for the most part remained outside the direct control of the Capetians in the first half of the thirteenth century. In 1254 the Lord Edward married Eleanor of Castile and, despite the existence of a son of Eleanor's elder brother, they jointly succeeded to the county of Ponthieu on the death of her mother in 1279.[29] Thenceforward the Balliol inheritance was as secure as Anglo-French relations would permit.

Not surprisingly, Balliol kinsmen, tenants and associates in Britain bear what can be described as a fairly considerable Picard imprint. Territorial surnames from the Balliol homeland found in England include Airaines (or Darreyns), Bouvaincourt, Domart (or Dummett), Rue and Fontaines; the last, like Grandsart, Vaudricourt and possibly Gourlay, found its way northward with the Balliols into Scotland.[30] The links made themselves felt in other ways too. By the terms of the Franco-Scottish treaty of 1295, for example, part of the money for the infant Isabel of Valois's dower was to be raised from Balliol's private landed interests in Picardy.[31] Less well known is King John's letter of protection issued in April 1293 in favour of the merchants of the city of Amiens coming to or staying in Scotland.[32] The main business of Amiens merchants in the later thirteenth century was the export of woad-dye, a lucrative trade which they had successfully directed towards the cloth-manufacturing areas of England. They had won for themselves special privileges at many of the major English seaports, and in Scotland they were obviously ready to take advantage of the exalted position of a man whom they could regard almost as a compatriot. As recently as June 1289, John had been amongst them in Amiens itself, confirming a sale of tithes by Walter de Grandsart to the college of Amiens.[33] Thus, although most of the private family transactions and alien personnel that emerged into Scottish public record during King John's reign were connected with his northern English possessions, a significant Picard element runs through the history of the family, distinguishing it from the Bruces and all other major members of the Anglo-Scottish baronage.

The Galloway marriage of 1233, upon which the Balliol claim ultimately rested, was also a major watershed in the private fortunes and public recognition of the family. It lifted the Balliols from the general ruck of the English baronage and, as later marriages with the Valences, the Warennes and Eleanor de Genoure (Geneva), a royal kinswoman, clearly showed, it placed them on a par with the English earls and on the edge of the English inner royal circle.

By 1233 John de Balliol I was over twenty-five years of age and had been for about four years in possession of the Balliol family inheritance. Dervorguilla, daughter of Alan of Galloway and his second wife Margaret, eldest daughter of Earl David of Huntingdon, was born some time after 1209, the date of her parents' marriage. Her highly distinctive name probably derived from an Irish connexion in the native Galloway line, possibly from a paternal aunt.[34] Despite the Lanercost chronicler's insistence that she was the 'senior' of her sisters, Dervorguilla was the lord of

Galloway's third daughter, his second by Margaret, a fact that was made abundantly clear at the time of the Great Cause. Margaret had been dead for at least five years before the marriage, and it was known that, since the loss of his brother in 1231, Dervorguilla's father was without legitimate heirs male. After his death on or about 2 February 1234 a partition was made in favour of Alan's three daughters against the claims of his natural son, Thomas, and was eventually enforced with Scottish royal support. It is unlikely that Balliol would have been advised of the desirability of the match in the first instance without expectations of some kind, although the gains that fortuitously accrued after 1234 through the deaths of Dervorguilla's uncle and sister must have gone considerably beyond what could have been foreseen.

Dervorguilla's paternal inheritance, which became more firmly secure after 1236, amounted to a third share in the Galloway lordship (principally, but apparently not exclusively, in the east), a share in the Morville inheritance in Cunningham and Lauderdale, and the dubious privilege of looking after her natural brother, Thomas, who was imprisoned in Barnard Castle.[35] Gains derived from her maternal inheritance quickly followed. As already intimated, upon the death of Earl John of Huntingdon and Chester in 1237, she and her elder sister, Christiana, succeeded to their mother's right in the Huntingdon honour and in John's Scottish lands, centred mainly in eastern and north-eastern Scotland, and to various properties in eastern England settled upon them in exchange for their claims upon the earldom of Chester.[36] Dervorguilla's share of this considerable Anglo-Scottish estate was substantially enlarged as a result of the successive deaths of Christiana (in 1246) and Earl John's widow. Christiana's share of the paternal inheritance was divided between Dervorguilla and her eldest (half-) sister Helen, wife of Roger de Quincy, earl of Winchester and Constable of Scotland; the details of the division are obscure but there may be reason for supposing that Dervorguilla's was the larger or more valuable share.[37]

In size and richness this massive accession of territories and rights of lordship dwarfed the ancestral estates of the family in northern and midland England, which were based upon Barnard Castle, Bywell in Northumberland, Stokesley in Yorkshire, and Hitchin in Hertfordshire. The bulk of the newly acquired properties had come into Balliol possession by the later 1240s, and the family estates in Britain reached their maximum extent between about 1246 and 1268. Unfortunately, John's death in 1268 was followed in quick succession by the deaths of his two elder sons, both of whom had married ladies with English royal connexions.[38] In addition to the vast inheritance and dower which the widowed Dervorguilla retained in her own hands, the family thus became encumbered with the provision of appropriate settlements for two more high-ranking widows. All three enjoyed long lives, and it was not until after Dervorguilla's death in 1290 that the family estates approached the extent and unity that they had attained in the middle decades of the thirteenth century.

Rough calculations based on officially declared incomes of later thirteenth-century date suggest that the total gross annual revenues from the Balliol lands (including the French estates) on the eve of the Galloway marriage might have been the equivalent of £500 in terms of the later figures.[39] Unfortunately, these figures do not provide a precise and reliable measure of the total increase in landed wealth for John de Balliol I. But by mid-century the family's annual income had probably at least doubled, and they were beginning to stand out among their contemporaries. Matthew Paris described John de Balliol I at this period as 'rich and powerful' and referred to Henry III's designs on the 'money which he had in abundance'.[40] Financial matters were never far beneath the surface of any major family's dealings with the reigning monarch, as John Balliol was to discover on the eve of the Great Cause. In May 1291 Edward I proceeded to distrain his goods and chattels for debts allegedly amounting to £1,224, in addition to the various claims that he had made in the previous decade.[41] Later, in 1293, Edward was also demanding an exorbitant payment of £3,290 as relief for John's succession to his mother's Scottish lands.[42] This high figure may have been part of a calculated programme aimed at John's financial and political discomfiture, but it is fastidiously precise and probably based on a genuine assessment. The seven-year period proposed for its repayment may give a clue, for a divisor of seven produces a realistic-looking figure of slightly less than £470 as a possible annual value of Dervorguilla's Scottish lands.

It had obviously not escaped Henry III's and Edward I's notice that the Balliols, enjoying what modern economists might term a high liquidity ratio, appeared almost always able to translate part of their wealth into cash. Indeed, John de Balliol I is known to have acted as moneylender not only to lay persons but also to Durham cathedral priory, an institution which acknowledged a debt to him through his executors of £1,000. Some other loans that he made are revealed among those deeds of Balliol College in which his executors obtained written confirmation of a miscellany of cash debts amounting to slightly less than £1,500, a sum that we know about simply by an accident of survival.[43] Dervorguilla was instrumental in bringing together the endowments and formulating the statutes of this eponymous house of scholars in Oxford, which was founded as an indirect result of transgressions committed by her husband against the bishop of Durham in 1255.[44] Balliol financial strength found physical expression elsewhere too. About 1420 Andrew Wyntoun composed a lengthy panegyric entitled 'How Dervorguil that lady spendyt hyr Tresoure devotly', and credited her with the foundation of houses of Friars Minor in Dumfries and Dominican Friars in Wigtown.[45] As in the case of the fifteenth-century bridge across the Nith that bears her name, her reputation for pious beneficence during her widowhood has gone beyond authenticated record. In 1273, however, she undoubtedly became the first and last member of the Balliol family to possess both the incentive and the means to be the founding patron of a full monastic establishment. In that year she founded in fond memory of her husband the Cistercian abbey of *Dulce Cor* or Sweetheart (Kirkcudbrightshire), a comparatively late foundation for that order and 'new' in relation to its mother-house of Dundrennan. The appearance and detailing of the monastery have little in common with Dundrennan, however; the substantial surviving remains are largely of English-influenced fourteenth-century character, the closest architectural parallel possibly being Netley abbey in Hampshire, which had no Balliol connexion.[46]

The family's increased wealth is also crudely measurable in other major items of building expenditure, most notably at Barnard Castle, their principal English residence and stronghold, named after the first Bernard. There, the earthworks and the two-phase twelfth-century stone castle received significant mid- and later thirteenth-century additions, including a large circular donjon.[47] Buittle Castle near Dalbeattie, the chief centre of their lordship in eastern Galloway, and Buittle Old Parish Church, one of the very few surviving parish churches of its date in the Stewartry, also betray Balliol architectural patronage in the later thirteenth century.[48] Except possibly for the church at Bellifontaine, however, the sites associated with the family in northern France do not reflect their proven ability to pay for high-quality stone building, and only the remains of earthworks have survived into modern times.[49] Endowments were made to local religious houses, but there was no Balliol monastic foundation on that side of the Channel.

Increased landed wealth gave John de Balliol I a platform for involvement in public life far beyond that of his predecessors, as can be gauged by his appearances in English government record from the mid-1240s onwards. He and his brother were the first members of the family to be appointed sheriffs; he served on various baronial parliamentary committees, and after 1258 was usually to be found among Henry III's select group of solidly royalist counsellors. Probably by virtue of his international interests, he was also a trusted envoy to both France and Scotland, although his role as joint guardian of the young king of Scots and his wife from 1251 to 1255 seems to have been largely nominal and subordinate to that of his partner, Robert de Ros of Wark and Sanquhar.[50]

Marriage is probably one of the most revealing indicators of changes in the level and direction of baronial ambition, however. By the 1270s three of John's sons in succession followed his example in claiming spouses of conspicuously high and noble status: the family was clearly edging its way into the social milieu of the English earls and the royal court.[51] Of his four daughters, two contracted marriages among the Anglo-Scottish baronage. The Balliol lady who married John Comyn (d. 1303), lord of Badenoch, justiciar of Galloway, and one of the Guardians of Scotland (1286–92), particularly attracted the attention of later Scottish chroniclers, for her spouse, one of the most powerful political figures in Scotland, and the future King John thereby became brothers-in-law. She was probably John's fourth daughter, and later chroniclers and Balliol genealogists refer to her variously as Mary, Margaret, or Marjory — a derivative but by this period evidently also a separate form of the name Margaret — whilst Joseph Bain and the *Scots Peerage* have suggested that she may have been called Eleanor. This identification is based on English record evidence of 1283 and 1284 relating to a John Comyn and his wife Eleanor, who were involved in judicial pleas in Yorkshire but at that time were staying in Galloway.[52]

Sir Thomas Gray in his fourteenth-century *Scalacronica* describes John de Balliol's eldest daughter, whom he chose to call Margaret, as lady of Gilsland.[53] Although from 1240 to 1293 that style strictly belonged to Maud de Vaux, who had brought Gilsland or Irthington (Cumberland) into the possession of the Moulton family, it would have been possible for a Balliol daughter during this period to have married one of two successive Thomas of Moultons, lords of Gilsland and Burgh by Sands.

The period of John de Balliol I's tenure of the sheriffdom of Cumberland between 1248 and 1255 is likely to have been the time that his first-born daughter reached marriageable age. In 1254 John's second brother, Eustace, was granted royal permission to marry Helewise of Levington, an important Cumbrian heiress to the barony of Kirklinton and half of Burgh.[54] Eustace himself served as sheriff of Cumberland and constable of Carlisle Castle during the critically important period of baronial rebellion between 1261 and 1265. As it happened, there were no known children of this marriage. Eustace outlived his wife by a couple of years, and was allowed to hold Kirklinton and half of the Burgh barony by 'the curtesy of England'.[55] The family links were strangely intertwined, however, for the heir to Helewise's moiety of Burgh was one of the Thomas of Moultons mentioned above. Moreover, Alexander de Balliol, John and Dervorguilla's third son, acquired before 1267 land at Thackthwaite in Cumberland, which was a royal re-grant of an escheat caused by the barons' wars.[56] The land in question was said to have belonged formerly to another Thomas of Moulton, grandfather of the man who may have been Alexander's brother-in-law. The acquisition was only temporary, and Alexander was obliged to renounce the land to Ranulf of Dacre.

This episode is yet another branch in the intriguing ramifications of the active but largely unrealised Balliol ambitions in Cumberland and around the Solway during the third quarter of the thirteenth century. Whilst the concept of building up estates into strategic territorial blocks may not have been an important part of contemporary baronial thought, John's career as sheriff of Cumberland could not have failed to make him aware of the geographical gap that lay directly between his two most important lordships in Britain, Barnard Castle on the one side and Galloway on the other. The attempt to bridge that gap in some measure is dimly perceptible, and the fact that it did not materialise makes it no less interesting.

From what has been said about his family background and from the fact that he had enjoyed possession of his Scottish inheritance only since 1290, there can be no gainsaying the verdict that at the time of the Great Cause John Balliol seemed 'a comparative stranger [to Scotland], a baron of great wealth and international connexions who yet remained an Englishman rather than a Scotsman'.[57] During his short reign he displayed few qualities of leadership and heroism, and afterwards there was little in the discredited and cashiered figure of 'Toom Tabard' to overcome the taint of Englishness and to endear him to later generations of Scots, especially if the recorded confession and denunciation of his former subjects that he made in the presence of the bishop of Durham on 1 April 1298 were authentic and unforced.[58] Despite this outburst, he has had some apologists who have judged him mainly on the question of appeals to Edward I and on the circumstances of his abdication. Their general conclusion is that he was merely an ordinary man, if perhaps a little weak and easily led, and that, as king of Scots, he had the misfortune to be confronted with a very difficult if not impossible political situation and with an extremely difficult English king. Given John's somewhat lack-lustre qualities, it is perhaps not surprising that, outside the relative limelight of his reign, he has remained among the least known kings in Britain of the high and later Middle Ages.

The obscurity surrounding the dates of his birth and death is typical. Three related inquisitions *post mortem* provide a birth-date ranging between 1248 and 1255;[59] 1248 × 1250 is probably an acceptable narrower limit, making him forty-two to forty-four years of age at his accession. Secondary accounts of his death demonstrate by their variety just how insignificant he became in his continental exile after 1299. His last recorded act was dated March 1314 and his death had occurred shortly before 4 January 1315, when Louis X of France was notified of the fact and was asked to accept the fealty of the proctor of Edward Balliol, John's son, for the Picard estates.[60] John probably lived long enough to have learned of the outcome of the battle of Bannockburn in June 1314, and possibly even of the Cambuskenneth parliament in the following November.

But it is John's early life and career that are least known, for virtually all assessments of his character and conduct have commenced with the events of 1290. The available biographical materials for the first forty years of his life are comparatively slight and fragmentary, but, when pieced together, some of this evidence casts him in a different light from that in which he has most often been judged.

The recital of the Balliol genealogy in the Great Cause confirmed that he was the fourth and youngest of the sons of John I and Dervorguilla. At the date of his father's death in 1268 he could have had few expectations of succeeding to the family estates, let alone to the kingdom of Scotland, but a sequence of deaths among his brothers brought the succession from eldest to youngest within ten years. Because of the assignment of dowers in favour of his mother and sisters-in-law, and because his mother retained her inheritance, it was a much-reduced English patrimony, centred mainly upon Barnard Castle, that he unexpectedly entered into in 1278–9. Upon his succession, he was subjected to demands for homage both by Robert, bishop of Durham, and by King Edward I.[61] Despite official acknowledgement of his rights as heir, however, there was a gap of almost a year between his third brother's death and John's active succession to the family estates. During the intervening period the family's Northumberland lands were taken into royal custody, and the contemporary chronicler Thomas Wykes recorded that John himself was in royal custody at about this time and was requiring royal consent for his marriage to Isabel, second daughter of John de Warenne, earl of Surrey.[62] The marriage probably took place in February 1281;[63] Wykes, apparently in error, placed it in February 1279/80, and, according to him, John, who was then over thirty, was *adolescens*, and Isabel, who was at least in her mid-twenties, was a young girl, *adolescentula*. The fact of royal custody was probably what was known to the chronicler, from which he then mistakenly deduced the exercise of wardship in a minority. The true reasons for this heavy-handed royal intervention are not at all clear, however. The recovery of relief payment and possibly moneys from a number of outstanding amercements and pleas may have been a consideration, but questions of finance are unlikely to have been the sole cause of this custodial treatment and the delay in his full succession.

Even within his own family's recent history, John was not unusual in allowing his marriage to wait until he had attained headship of the family. But in contrast to his brothers he does not appear to have pursued a career in English royal service —

military, crusading or diplomatic — in his early manhood. There may in fact be reason to believe that in the case of John, as the youngest son of an especially devout mother, his life up to the age of thirty may have been heading in an entirely different direction.

The most direct evidence in support of this hypothesis is the story recorded by Robert of Greystones within fifty years of the events that were described.[64] According to this account, in September 1290 there was a dispute between Ranulf de Neville, lord of Raby, and Richard of Houghton, prior of Durham, concerning the custom and protocol to be observed within the cathedral priory of Durham at the feast of St Cuthbert. John Balliol was evidently present at this dispute and was credited with a rebuttal of Neville's claims for precedence and privileges at the feast; he had, he said, for a long time attended the schools of Durham (*se in scholis Dunelmensibus perstitisse*), but had not heard of the ceremony which the lord of Raby claimed as his right. The only establishment in the monastic cathedral of Durham that would have fitted this description in the second half of the thirteenth century would have been the novices' school, whose detailed workings in the education of intending monks are known through a sixteenth-century manuscript, the 'Rites of Durham'; the almonry school and the public grammar school at Durham were fourteenth- and fifteenth-century foundations.[65] The evidence that Balliol had been destined for a monastic career is not conclusive, but it can at least be claimed that the general benefits of the religious education that he had received at Durham placed him among the more literate of Scottish medieval kings. For, as has recently been shown, there is a record of 1294 which testifies to his ability to read out a written petition in public (*ore proprio publice fecit*),[66] an educational attainment shared by few members of the secular nobility at that time.

NOTES

1. The fullest histories of the family are in *Northumberland Hist.*, vi, pp. 16–73, and G.A. Moriarty, 'The Baliols in Picardy, England and Scotland', *New England Historical and Genealogical Register*, cvi (1952), pp. 273–90, which is not without errors. The arrival of the family in Britain is usually ascribed to *c.*1093: for the source of this statement see J. Spearman, *An Enquiry into the Ancient and Present State of the County Palatine of Durham* (Edinburgh, 1729), p. 51, and Durham University Library, MS Mickleton and Spearman 32, fo. 11, citing 'MS Bowes, fo. (?9)', an untraced portion of the Bowes MSS formerly at Streatlam Castle, Co. Durham. For the terminal date, E.W.M. Balfour-Melville, 'The death of Edward Balliol', *SHR*, xxxv (1956), pp. 82–3.

2. Now fully documented in Stones and Simpson, *Great Cause.*

3. E.g., G. Neilson, 'Bruce *versus* Balliol, 1291–2', *SHR*, xvi (1919), pp. 1–14; Barrow, *Bruce*, Ch. 3, entitled 'Bruce *versus* Balliol'.

4. *Chron. Bower*, ii, p. 138; see A.A.M. Duncan, 'The community of the realm of Scotland and Robert Bruce: a review', *SHR*, xlv (1966), pp. 185–6.

5. Barrow, *Bruce*, p. 25; below, p. 172.

6. Barrow, *Bruce*, pp. 59–60.

7. Evidenced indirectly by, e.g., Bishop Fraser's letter to Edward I (Stones and Simpson, *Great Cause*, ii, pp. 3–4) and the so-called 'Appeal of the Seven Earls' (Stones, *Relations*, no. 14).

8. Stevenson, *Documents*, i, no. 125; see also *CPatR, 1281-92*, pp. 389, 414, and for Bek, C.M. Fraser, *A History of Anthony Bek, Bishop of Durham, 1283-1311* (Oxford, 1957).

9. List of auditors in *Foedera*, I, ii, p. 767, and Stones and Simpson, *Great Cause*, ii, pp. 84–5.

10. *CPatR, 1232-47*, pp. 206, 209–10; *ClR, 1237-42*, pp. 6, 12; *1242-7*, p. 104; *CDS*, i, nos. 1375, 1384, 1449. See also *Comp. Pge.*, iii, p. 169; vi, p. 647; R. Stewart-Brown, 'The end of the Norman earldom of Chester', *EHR*, xxxv (1920), pp. 36–8; M.F. Moore, *The Lands of the Scottish Kings in England* (London, 1915), pp. 11–12, 31–40.

11. Barrow, *Bruce*, pp. 36–7.

12. *EYC*, i, nos. 559–85; ii, nos. 647–776, and esp. pp. 11-16. See also *Cartularium Prioratus de Gyseburne*, ed. W. Brown (Surtees Soc., 1889–94), *passim*; Barrow, *Era*, p. 12. For the two families in the wapentake of Sadberge, C.M. Fraser and K. Emsley, 'Durham and the wapentake of Sadberge', *Trans. of the Architectural and Archaeol. Soc. of Durham and Northumberland*, new ser., ii (1970), pp. 71–82; for some Bruce interests in Cumberland, F.W. Ragg, *TCWAAS*, new ser., xiii (1913), pp. 199ff; M. Walcott, 'A breviate of the cartulary of ... Lanercost', *Trans. of the Royal Soc. of Literature*, 2nd ser., viii (1866), p. 500.

13. Lawrie, *Charters*, nos. 54, 199, with notes; *RRS*, ii, no. 80; Barrow, *Bruce*, pp. 28–30.

14. Anderson, *Scottish Annals*, pp. 192 and n., 195. Robert had already settled Annandale on his younger son, who remained loyal to King David.

15. E.g., *Northumberland Hist.*, vi, p. 22; R.L.G. Ritchie, *The Normans in Scotland* (Edinburgh, 1954), p. 148 and n; G. Chalmers, *Caledonia*, new edn. (Paisley, 1887–1902), ii, pp. 567–8.

16. *Kelso Liber*, i, nos. 25, 52 (= Lawrie, *Charters*, nos. 258–9).

17. A. Young, *William Cumin: Border Politics and the Bishopric of Durham, 1141-1144* (Borthwick Papers, no. 54, 1978), pp. 13–14.

18. Anderson, *Scottish Annals*, pp. 252–3, 333–4. It should be noted that Robert de Brus II of Annandale, deviating from his usual pro-Scottish position, supported Henry II in 1173–4, and as a result suffered temporary confiscation of his Scottish lands: *ibid.*, p. 247.

19. J.C. Holt, *The Northerners* (Oxford, 1961), p. 31; see also Paris, *Chron. Maj.*, ii, p. 533.

20. G.W.S. Barrow, *SHR*, xxx (1951), p. 48; *idem*, *Kingdom*, p. 328; *RRS*, ii, no. 3.

21. Ingram witnessed royal charters dating probably 1205 and 1211: *ibid.*, nos. 468, 496. For *acta* relating to the Scottish lands of this branch of the family see, e.g., *Arbroath Liber*, i, nos. 58, 293; BL MS Add. 33245, fos. 143v–4r; *Holyrood Liber*, nos. 70, 81; *Holm Cultram Reg.*, nos. 124–5, 147. For the subsequent history of their possessions, J.M.W. Bean, 'The Percies and their estates in Scotland', *Archaeologia Aeliana*, 4th ser., xxxv (1957), pp. 91–9. Moriarty, 'Baliols', pp. 285–90, provides other references, but mistakenly conflates the evidence for the Cavers and Inverkeilor branches.

22. For the Valognes connexion with Cavers and Melrose abbey see *Melrose Liber*, i, nos. 9, 150; Anderson, *Early Sources*, ii, pp. 405, 437, 543, 545 (= Ada, not Adam, de Balliol); adding J.H. Round, *The Ancestor*, xi (1904), pp. 129–36. For other references to this branch of the family and to the well-documented Alexander de Balliol of Cavers, see discussions in *Genealogist*, vi (1882), pp. 1–7; *ibid.*, new ser., iv (1887), pp. 141–3; *Notes and Queries*, 6th ser., v (1882), pp. 61–2, 142–3, 290–1, 389–90. Further, H.C. Andrews, *The Benstede Family* (Walthamstow Antiq. Soc., 1937), pp. 13–17; Moriarty, 'Baliols', pp. 285–90.

23. *Northumberland Hist.*, vi, pp. 41–2n.

24. Reproduced in facsimile in *TDGAS*, 3rd ser., v (1916–18), facing p. 258. See also *Holm Cultram Reg.*, no. 124, for Alan witnessing a charter by Ingram.

25. Barrow, *Kingdom*, pp. 322–3.

26. *Calendar of Documents preserved in France*, ed. J.H. Round (London, 1899), no. 1392; Loyd, *Origins*, p. 11; J.P. Maitland, 'The early homes of the Balliols', *TDGAS*, 3rd ser., xviii (1931-3), pp. 235–42.

27. For Agnes de Picquigny, wife of Bernard de Balliol II, see *Liber Vitae Ecclesiae Dunelmensis*, ed. A.H. Thompson (Surtees Soc., 1923), fo. 66r; *Cartularium Abbathiae de Rievalle*, ed. J.C. Atkinson (Surtees Soc., 1889), p. 66, no. 114. For Balliol connexions with

the *vidames* of Amiens, R. de Belleval, *Jean de Bailleul, roi d'Écosse et sire de Bailleul-en-Vimeu* (Paris, 1866), p. 84; *Treaty Rolls preserved in the PRO*, i (London, 1955), no. 537. See also F.I. Darsy, *Picquigny et ses seigneurs* (Abbeville, 1860), *passim*; F. Senn, *L'institution des vidamies en France* (Paris, 1907), pp. 113–14, 132–3, 139; and, for an account of the principal Pinkeny family in Britain, *Comp. Pge.*, x, pp. 521–6. Adam de Pinkeny, chaplain, was an attorney for John and Dervorguilla de Balliol in 1253: *ClR, 1251–3*, p. 452.

28. For published *acta* see, e.g., *Le cartulaire de l'abbaye de Selincourt*, ed. M.G. Beaurain (Société des Antiquaires de Picardie, 1925), nos. 112–13; *Recueil des documents inédits concernant la Picardie*, ed. V. de Beauvillé (Paris, 1860–82), i, p. 395 and n; Belleval, *Jean de Bailleul*, esp. pp. 99–104; *Recueil des chartes de l'abbaye de Cluny*, ed. A. Bernard and A. Bruel (Paris, 1876–1903), v, no. 4060 (cf. *Cal. Docs. France*, no. 1392). Principal sources of unpublished *acta* as follows: Amiens, Archives Départementales de la Somme, D 112 (Register of the college of Amiens), 2 H 4 (Cartulary of Saint-Martin-aux-Jumeaux abbey), 9 H 538 (Cart. of Saint-Laurent-au-Bois priory), 30 H 2 (Cart. of Valloires abbey); Arras, Arch. Dép. de Pas-de-Calais, H (Cart. of Saint-Josse-sur-Mer abbey); Metz, Bibliothèque Municipale, MS 1197 (Cart. of Dommartin, formerly Saint-Josse-au-Bois, abbey); Paris, Archives Nationales, S 5059, S* 5533 (Cartularies of the commandery of Fieffes); Paris, Bibliothèque Nationale, in Collections Baluze MS 38 (collegiate church of Longpré-les-Corps-Saints), and in Coll. de Picardie MSS 238 (Lazar house of Le Val de Buigny), 298.

29. H. Johnstone, 'The county of Ponthieu, 1279–1307', *EHR*, xxix (1914), pp. 435–52; R. Petit and A. Joron, *Le Ponthieu et la dynastie anglaise au xiiie siècle* (Études Picardes, 1969).

30. Airaines (cant. Molliens-Vidame, arr. Amiens): see esp. *Northumberland Hist.*, vi, pp. 176–89. Bouvaincourt (probably Bouvaincourt-sur-Bresle, cant. Gamaches, arr. Abbeville): *EYC*, i, no. 565; *Cart. ... de Rievalle*, ed. Atkinson, pp. 247–8n. Domart (Domart-en-Ponthieu, cant. and arr. Amiens): *Book of Seals*, no. 302; F.M. Stenton, *The First Century of English Feudalism, 1066–1166*, 2nd edn. (Oxford, 1961), pp. 159n., 276. Rue (cant. and arr. Abbeville): *Fees*, ii, pp. 1120–1. Fontaines (probably Fontaine-sur-Somme, cant. Hallencourt, arr. Abbeville): witnesses to Balliol transactions, e.g., *Northumberland Hist.*, vi, pp. 41–2n., and linked to Balliols by marriage; see Paris, Bibl. Nat., Coll. Baluze MS 38, fo. 216r–v. Grandsart (cant. Hallencourt, arr. Abbeville): *Registrum Palatinum Dunelmense*, ed. T.D. Hardy (Rolls Ser., 1873–8), ii, p. 801; Durham, Dean and Chapter Muniments, Misc. Chart. 6905; *RRS*, vi, no. 235. Vaudricourt (cant. Ault, arr. Abbeville): *Arbroath Liber*, i, no. 58. Gourlay ('seigneurs de Monsures', according to L. Goudallier, 'Écosse et Picardie (relations entre ces deux pays)', *Bulletin de la société des antiquaires de Picardie*, xxi [1904], p. 502): *Holyrood Liber*, no. 70; Barrow, *Era*, pp. 180–1.

31. *APS*, i, pp. 451–3.

32. A. Thierry, *Recueil des monuments inédits de l'histoire du tiers état: région du nord*, i (Paris, 1850), p. 300.

33. Amiens, Arch. Dép. de la Somme, D 112, fo. 6r.

34. E.G. Withycombe, *The Oxford Dictionary of English Christian Names*, 3rd edn. (Oxford, 1977), p. 83. For some Galloway family links with Ireland see J.R.H. Greeves, *TDGAS*, 3rd ser., xxxvi (1957–8), pp. 115–21; above, p. 50. For other occurrences of this name, C.T. Clay, *EHR*, lxv (1950), pp. 89–91; *CDS*, ii, no. 725; Stevenson, *Documents*, i, no. 65.

35. Anderson, *Scottish Annals*, pp. 340–2; *idem*, *Early Sources*, ii, pp. 492–8, 690; *Chron. Fordun*, ii, pp. 59–62; *Chron. Melrose*, pp. 83–4. For later negotiations concerning Balliol custody of Thomas of Galloway see *APS*, i, pp. 114–15; *Chron. Lanercost*, p. 116.

36. Above, n. 10.

37. See *Wigtownshire Chrs.*, pp. xxxix–xlvi; but cf. Paris, *Chron. Maj.*, iv, p. 563, where it is stated, without reference to Dervorguilla, that 'the large part of Galloway which pertained to her [Christiana] was transferred to the lot of the earl of Winchester, Roger de Quincy'.

38. *CIPM*, i, nos. 691, 773, 804. Hugh de Balliol married Agnes de Valence, niece of King Henry III, and Alexander de Balliol, Eleanor de Genoure, kinswoman of Queen Eleanor.

Agnes's dower-lands included part of the Balliol territory in Picardy: Amiens, Arch. Dép. de la Somme, D 112, fo. 6r. For Eleanor's dower-lands see, e.g., *CClR, 1272-9*, pp. 514, 550; *Calendar of the Fine Rolls preserved in the PRO* (London, 1911–62), i, p. 106; *CPatR, 1272-81*, p. 318; *Three Early Assize Rolls for the County of Northumberland*, ed. W. Page (Surtees Soc., 1891), pp. 262, 301; adding, for her later career, *EYC*, ix, pp. 60–2; *CIPM*, v, no. 237.

39. An approximate net figure calculated from the assessments of later inquisitions: e.g., *ibid.*, i, no. 691 (Bywell, Driffield, Hitchin); ii, no. 771; *CPatR, 1292-1301*, pp. 12–13 (Dervorguilla's possessions in England and Scotland); *Reg. Pal. Dunelm.*, ed. Hardy, ii, pp. 795–802; *CIPM*, v, no. 615 (lands in Co. Durham, Stokesley). See also *Kirkby's Inquest*, ed. R.H. Skaife (Surtees Soc., 1867), p. 133; *CDS*, ii, no. 736.

40. Paris, *Chron. Maj.*, v, pp. 507, 528.

41. Stevenson, *Documents*, i, no. 136 and p. 227n. See also *Cal. of Fine Rolls*, i, p. 322; *Calendar of Chancery Warrants preserved in the PRO* (London, 1927), p. 22; *CDS*, ii, nos. 254, 257.

42. *CPatR, 1292-1301*, pp. 12–13; *CDS*, ii, no. 670.

43. Durham, Dean and Chapter Muniments, Misc. Chart. 3585, 4463; *The Oxford Deeds of Balliol College*, ed. H.E. Salter (Oxford Historical Soc., 1913), nos. 592–605.

44. *ClR, 1254-6*, p. 217.

45. Androw of Wyntoun, *The Orygynale Cronykil of Scotland*, ed. D. Laing (Edinburgh, 1872–9), ii, p. 321; cf. Cowan (Easson), *Religious Houses*, pp. 121, 125–6.

46. *Calendar of the Laing Charters 854–1837*, ed. J. Anderson (Edinburgh, 1899), no. 46; *RRS*, vi, no. 235. Comparison with Netley abbey was suggested by Richard Fawcett in a lecture given at the Conference of Scottish Medieval Historical Research, 6 January 1979.

47. D. Austin, 'Barnard Castle, Co. Durham, first interim report: excavations in the town ward, 1974–6', *Journal of the British Archaeol. Assoc.*, cxxxii (1979), pp. 50–72. See also *ibid.*, cxxxiii (1980), pp. 74–96; T.W.U. Robinson, 'The castle of Barnard', *Trans. of the Arch. and Archaeol. Soc. of Durham and Northumberland*, i (1862), pp. 88–100; A.D. Saunders, *Barnard Castle, Co. Durham* (Official Guide, HMSO 1971 reprint); S.E. Rigold in N. Pevsner and E. Williamson, *The Buildings of England: County Durham* (Harmondsworth, 1983 edn.), pp. 85–7. An account of the castle is also included in the unpublished MSS relating to the Victoria History of Co. Durham, Darlington Ward (1914–15), bundle 218, pp. 34–78, deposited in the Institute of Historical Research, University of London. I am indebted to Mr C.R. Elrington for permission to consult this material.

48. RCAHMS, *Inventory of Kirkcudbright*, nos. 73–4, and refs. cited.

49. Maitland, 'Early homes of the Balliols', pp. 235–42.

50. Cf. above, pp. 136-7.

51. Above, n. 38; below, n.62. Documents relating to Balliol estates in Picardy show a mid-century change of style to *domini* or *sires de Bailleul*, apparently an indicator of noble rank for their Picard interests: cf. R. Fossier in *La noblesse au moyen âge, xie-xve siècles: essais à la mémoire de Robert Boutruche*, ed. P. Contamine (Paris, 1976), pp. 105–27.

52. *Chron. Fordun*, ii, p. 310; Wyntoun, *Orygynale Cronykil*, ii, pp. 312–13 (lines 1201–4), 314–15 (lines 1263–8); *CDS*, ii, p. lvi, nos. 228, 249. For a younger John Comyn who was a minor in 1279 but is unaccounted for in the 1280s see *ibid.*, nos. 168, 963; *Scots Pge.*, i, p. 507.

53. *Scalacronica, by Sir Thomas Gray of Heton Knight* (Maitland Club, 1836), p. 121.

54. *ClR, 1253-4*, p. 36; also T.H.B. Graham, *TCWAAS*, new ser., xii (1912), pp. 59–75.

55. *CIPM*, ii, no. 136; *CClR, 1272-9*, pp. 5, 138, 171; *Cal. of Fine Rolls*, i, p. 26.

56. *SHR*, v (1908), pp. 252–3. For other Balliol interests in north-western England see also, e.g., *CDS*, ii, no. 169, which refers to their claim to a share in the lordship of north Westmorland; in addition, Ada, youngest daughter of John and Dervorguilla, married William de Lindsay II, who succeeded to half of the barony of Kendal and to the lordship of Lamberton in the Merse: *CIPM*, i, no. 820; ii, no. 447.

57. Barrow, *Bruce*, p. 68.

58. Stones, *Relations*, no. 27; G.G. Simpson, 'Why was John Balliol called "Toom Tabard"?', *SHR*, xlvii (1968), pp. 196–9.

59. *CIPM*, ii, nos. 249, 771; Stevenson, *Documents*, i, no. 86.

60. Belleval, *Jean de Bailleul*, pp. 102–4 (original charter, Paris, Bibl. Nat., Coll. de Picardie MS 298, no. 114); *Treaty Rolls*, i, no. 537.

61. *CClR, 1272-9*, p. 579; cf. *Cal. of Fine Rolls*, i, pp. 102, 111; *CIPM*, ii, no. 249. His first recorded act, dated 29 July 1279, was issued from Sadberge, where the bishop exercised regalian rights: *Archaeologia Aeliana*, new ser., iii (1859), p. 78.

62. Thomas Wykes, *Chronicon*, ed. H.R. Luard in *Annales Monastici* (Rolls Ser., 1864–9), iv, p. 284.

63. *CClR, 1279-88*, pp. 75–6; *CDS*, ii, pp. 174–5.

64. Robert of Greystones, *Historia de Statu Ecclesiae Dunelmensis*, ed. J. Raine in *Historiae Dunelmensis Scriptores Tres* (Surtees Soc., 1839), p. 74 (also cited in J.R. Walbran, *The Antiquities of Gainford in the County of Durham* [Ripon, 1846], pp. 136–7n., and *Northumberland Hist.*, vi, pp. 53–4).

65. *VCH Durham*, i, pp. 365–8; *Rites of Durham*, ed. J.T. Fowler (Surtees Soc., 1903), pp. 62–3, 84–5, 91–2, 96–7.

66. Stones and Simpson, *Great Cause*, ii, p. 283.

8

JAMES FIFTH STEWART OF SCOTLAND, 1260(?)-1309

Geoffrey Barrow and Ann Royan

Of all the figures of major importance in Scotland in the medieval period, James, fifth hereditary Stewart of Scotland, who died on 16 July 1309, remains one of those about whom least has been written. Nevertheless, he played a notable part in government and politics between 1284 and 1309. Although his role in the first war of independence was never quite decisive, he was at all times a force to be reckoned with. Along with several other insufficiently regarded Scots leaders of his day (e.g., Sir John de Soules, with whom he was closely associated), James the Stewart deserves at least a brief biography. The essay which follows, the joint work of two authors who have each studied James's career independently, is an attempt to meet that need.

The date of James's birth is shrouded in mystery. The *Scots Peerage* makes the unsubstantiated statement that his birth occurred in 1243,[1] while that of his brother John is placed by Symson and Nisbet in 1246.[2] In 1965 G.W.S. Barrow argued for a birth date around 1253,[3] partly on the grounds that James's second son Walter was still (in Barbour's words) 'bot ane berdlas hyne' in 1314,[4] and partly because in 1252 James's father, Alexander of Dundonald, announced his intention of going on pilgrimage to the shrine of St James the Great at Compostella.[5]

It now seems more probable that James was born even later than that, perhaps around 1260. This suggestion may seem scarcely less arbitrary than the others, but it can be supported by two persuasive considerations. Firstly, James need not have been the first-born son. Among Alexander of Dundonald's known children the traditional Stewart names Walter and Alan are conspicuously absent. One might have been given at the baptism of an older son who died in infancy. James, with his distinctly unusual Christian name (rare in Scottish record before the later thirteenth century),[6] might have been merely the oldest surviving son. Secondly, the date of James's marriage before October 1296,[7] perhaps as early as about 1290, accords better with a man aged between around thirty and thirty-six than with one of thirty-seven to forty-three, especially bearing in mind that his official position as hereditary Stewart of Scotland and his dignity as one of the greatest feudatories of the realm called for him to have a direct heir. If moreover we shift the likely date of birth of his younger brother John from Nisbet's '1246' to about 1263, John's active leadership of young warriors on the field of Falkirk (1298) becomes easier to understand, and it would still have been possible for John to have fathered his family of several children.[8] As for the personal name James, its choice might well have been prompted by Alexander's pilgrimage to Santiago, but we should remember that the Stewart family's monastery at Paisley was dedicated to St James the Great, as well as to the Blessed Virgin and to the local St Mirren.[9]

The earliest documentary reference we have to James is in conjunction with his father as witness to a charter granted by Alexander III in January 1276.[10] James would then have been sixteen or seventeen, quite old enough to have been mentioned in a document, especially if he was by that time heir to his father. Indeed, if he had been as old as the *Scots Peerage* suggests, it is hard to see why he does not figure, with or without his father, in earlier record. Although the precise date of James's birth must remain a matter for speculation, it is more likely that he married while still in his thirties — and was therefore born about 1260 — than in his forties or fifties. If our suggestion is accepted, it would make James some twelve to fourteen years older than Robert Bruce (b. 1274), with whom and with whose family he was to be intimately associated throughout his later life.

It almost goes without saying that the Stewart owed much of his importance to his inherited position as one of Scotland's greatest landowners. The bulk of his estates derived from the liberal grant of lands made to his ancestor Walter son of Alan, the first of the Stewarts, by King David I and confirmed to him by King Malcolm IV in 1161.[11] The nucleus of the Stewart empire was formed in the time of this first Walter and consisted of the lordships of Renfrew, Mearns, Strathgryfe (including the coastal strip to the west of Strathgryfe proper), and north Kyle ('Kyle Stewart'). Stenton and Innerwick in East Lothian also came into the family's possession in this period,[12] as well as Birkenside and Legerwood in Berwickshire and (through Walter's marriage with Eschina of Mow, whose parentage has not been established) the lands of *Molle*, now Mow in Morebattle parish, Roxburghshire.[13] Renfrew, already made a burgh by David I,[14] formed the family's chief residence for a century or so, and it was originally at Renfrew that the first Stewart founded, around 1163, a priory for a colony of Cluniac monks drawn from Much Wenlock in Shropshire.[15] The monks were soon transferred to what were presumably more attractive quarters higher up the River White Cart at Paisley, probably a site with ancient religious associations. Over the years this monastery of the Blessed Virgin, St James and St Mirren was munificently endowed, chiefly by the Stewarts themselves, by their immediate followers and vassals, by the earls of Lennox, and by various western and Hebridean lords, including the lords of the Isles.[16] Despite their generous benefactions, however, the Stewarts were careful to reserve in their own hands the manor-house of Blackhall (*Nigra Aula*) in Paisley, along with its park and the extensive forest towards the south, originally (at least in part) the king's forest of Raise or Raiss.[17] In this forest the rights of the Stewarts as lords became more carefully defined, while the monks' liberties were correspondingly restricted.

Beside the great lordships in what became Renfrewshire and in the northern half of Kyle, James the Stewart inherited much other land in the west. Alan, second of the Stewarts, seems to have acquired Bute around 1200,[18] and in the time of Alexander of Dundonald the family gained ascendancy over Cowal and seem to have become patrons of its leading clan, the Lamonts.[19] In 1296 James the Stewart was known to have at his disposal large numbers of dependants, from Rothesay and the rest of Bute, and from Cowal, who had galleys and 'sea-power'.[20] As to land-power, quite apart from the considerable tenantry who held by military service there were a number of castles on the Stewart estates. Renfrew was evidently still viable enough in the 1290s for castle-ward to be demanded,[21] and in addition James possessed Rothesay,[22] Dunoon and Dundonald.[23] A memorandum of 1297 reported that James also controlled (by what authority is not known) the barony and castle of *Glasrog*, certainly in the west and perhaps to be identified with Glassary which at this time belonged to Master Ralph of Dundee, ancestor of the Scrymgeours.[24] A passage in the *Scotichronicon* mentions 'the impregnable castle of Helingerik', that is, Eilean Dearg near the mouth of Loch Riddon. If this had already been constructed before the end of the thirteenth century, it too would presumably have been under the Stewart's control.[25]

The Stewarts, through their ancestor Alan son of Flaald, had an old association with the county of Norfolk.[26] This English tie was kept alive in the thirteenth century through the interest shown by Walter II in the Cluniac priory church of St Andrew of Bromholm, on the Norfolk coast, which had acquired a relic of the True Cross. Pilgrimage to the Holy Rood at Bromholm was made fashionable by no less a person than King Henry III.[27] In an undated charter of between about 1282 and 1290 James the Stewart confirmed to the Cluniacs of Bromholm the gift made by his grandfather and confirmed by his father of twenty shillings annually, payable originally out of the burgh fermes of Renfrew.[28] James made a fresh arrangement whereby the annual charge would be laid upon his estate of Gorgie, west of Edinburgh, and payment would be made to the abbot of Holyrood who, presumably by no coincidence, was appointed Bromholm's perpetual procurator in Scotland.[29]

Stewart interests outwith Scotland gave rise to Irish as well as English connexions. By 1296, on his marriage to Egidia (Gelis) de Burgh, daughter of Walter de Burgh, earl of Ulster, James had acquired an estate near Coleraine in the north of Ireland, with the castle of the Roe, the borough and demesne of the castle, the lordship, service and rents of the lands of the English enfeoffed by the earl of Ulster in Keenaght (Ciannachta), and all the earl's land of Rennard.[30]

By the middle of the thirteenth century the duties of the hereditary Stewart (or Steward) of Scotland, *Senescallus Scotiae*, had become largely honorific. Nevertheless, the office gave its holder, in normal circumstances, access to the sovereign and a place on the king's council.[31] Since most of James's adult life was lived during constitutional or *de facto* vacancies of the Scots throne, it will be best to deal with this side of his activities in our discussion of his political career. But his position at the top of secular government cannot realistically be divorced from his participation in local government, which at the same time was linked to James's role as landowner and feudatory. Probably at the end of 1288 he secured appointment as sheriff of Ayr with command of Ayr Castle (the 'New Castle upon Ayr' as it was still known).[32] In this capacity he provided for the garrisoning and plenishing of the castle, spending forty marks 'for the defence of the country following upon the king's death'.[33] After the murder of his fellow-Guardian Earl Duncan of Fife in September 1289, he appears to have taken over the sheriffdom of Dumbarton with the keeping of its strategically important castle.[34] Thus a wide semi-circle of territory on the western seaboard of Scotland, broken only by Cunningham, would have come under the Stewart's control, either directly as lord of Renfrew, Kyle Stewart and other broad lands, or by the exercise of delegated royal authority in the case of the Lennox and Ayrshire.

The brief reign of King John saw the promulgation of a scheme, never in fact implemented, for reorganising the administration of the west Highlands.[35] The experience and standing of the Stewart, rather than any special trust or favour shown him by the new king, must have ensured the prominent position which the Stewart was assigned in this scheme. He was to take over a completely new sheriffdom comprising Bute, the Cumbraes, Kintyre and presumably Arran, to be known as the sheriffdom of Kintyre. Rothesay, with its strong castle, would certainly have made a suitable headquarters for the new administrative district, which specifically included the lands of the Lamonts in Lower Cowal. The Lamonts, Lochman son of Malcolm MacFarquhar and Angus son of Duncan MacFarquhar, and their kin, regarded James the Stewart, no less than his father, as their patron. On 23 July 1295, Malcolm Lamont (son and heir of Lochman son of Malcolm), then at Paisley, executed a deed sealed with the Stewart's seal as well as his own and witnessed by Master Gilbert of Templeton, parson of Rothesay, and Finlay vicar of Kilfinan (the Lamonts' church), described as the Stewart's chaplain.[36] No doubt when the new scheme of west highland administration was being considered in the parliament of 1293, king and council recognised the plain fact of the Stewart's great influence in this region of Scotland. But it was one thing to wield the power of a feudal lord, another to exercise royal authority on a large scale, as the holding of three adjacent sheriffdoms would clearly permit the Stewart to do. Had the scheme been put into force, the Stewart would have enjoyed little short of political and military dominance in the whole Firth of Clyde region at its widest extent. As it was, his power and influence in the area were demonstrated three years later when, at the outset of the war with England in 1296, he was in control of the whole of Kintyre with its chief castle — unidentified, but probably either Skipness in the north-east or Dunaverty at the south end — and disposed, as has been seen, of considerable sea-power.[37]

As already indicated, the office of Steward, which James inherited at his father's death in or about 1282,[38] automatically guaranteed its holder a place in the royal government of Scotland. The surviving evidence, however, suggests that James made a gradual entrance on to the national stage. He figures prominently in the acknowledgement of Margaret the Maid of Norway as heir to the throne, which was promulgated by the leading magnates of Scotland on 5 February 1284, at the Scone parliament.[39] The first thirteen names in this declaration are those of the earls, followed immediately by Robert Bruce, lord of Annandale. James the Stewart's name comes next, showing that although technically a 'baron' he ranked almost equal to the highest nobility of the realm. In the following year (26 January 1285), the Stewart was present at a parliament (*colloquium*) held in the hall (*aula*) of Edinburgh Castle. It is worth noting that of the three other leading men whose presence on this occasion was explicitly mentioned, Sir Walter Lindsay and Sir Reginald Crawford are subsequently found in association with the Stewart.[40] Later in 1285, on 13 July, James was again at Edinburgh in company with some of the greatest magnates of the realm, John Comyn of Badenoch, his cousin John Comyn 'of Buchan' (presumably son and heir of Earl Alexander), this John's younger brother Alexander, Sir David Graham and Sir Richard Siward, lord of Tibbers.[41] This is somewhat unusual company in which to find James the Stewart, and although we have no evidence that the king was at Edinburgh on this date, it may be that a session of the council was in fact the occasion of the meeting.[42]

Eight months later Alexander III, who in November 1285 had married Yolande of Dreux *en secondes noces*, died accidentally near Kinghorn while journeying through the night to join his new wife. The Maid of Norway was the apparent heir, although rumour had it that the king's young widow was pregnant. Parliament assembled in April 1286 and required at least the principal lieges to take an oath to keep and preserve the land of Scotland for their lady, the king of Norway's daughter, to swear fealty to her as their liege lady, and to keep the peace of her land.[43] The respect now accorded to James the Stewart and to his office is made clear from the fact that he was one of the six regents or Guardians (*custodes*, or in Andrew Wyntoun's verse-chronicle, 'wardanes') chosen at and by this parliament to govern the realm on the Maid's behalf. With that careful social symmetry which appealed so strongly to the public men of this period, the council of regency was composed of two bishops (St Andrews and Glasgow), two earls (Buchan and Fife), and two barons (Comyn of Badenoch and James the Stewart). Although, if our surmise as to his age is correct, James was still only in his middle twenties, it is doubtful whether he owed his election solely to the prestige of his office. Some balance of age may have been sought, since Buchan was a veteran, while Badenoch and the two bishops were in their middle years. Duncan III, earl of Fife, who held the premier earldom of Scotland, was also a young man. But contemporary gossip spoke ill of the earl's reputation,[44] while the Stewart appears to have enjoyed respect. Thus, he was singled out by the Norwegian government in the summer of 1286 as the appropriate Guardian with whom to lodge a complaint about the seizure of a Norwegian ship at Berwick.[45]

Few as they were, the six Guardians represented a nice compromise between rival factions and even between geographical regions which had deep roots in Scotland's past. Alexander Comyn, earl of Buchan, and his kinsman John, lord of Badenoch, were leaders of the old 'Comyn party', first discernible as a force in Scottish politics in the reign of Alexander II.[46] They were allied to William Fraser, bishop of St Andrews, an academic whose recorded career in the Church dated from the 1260s or earlier.[47] At the same time, the two earls and Bishop Fraser could be said to watch over the interests of historic *Scotia*, the country north of Forth and Clyde. Comyn of Badenoch (despite his highland lordship, a great landowner in the Borders and Tynedale), along with James the Stewart and Robert Wishart, bishop of Glasgow since 1271, could speak for the southern half of the kingdom, Lothian, Cumbria and Galloway. The Stewart and Wishart seem to have been close personal friends and allies, and the former was linked to the Bruce family by long-standing family ties.[48]

There is no evidence that any of the six rejected the Maid's claim to be queen of

Scots, but everyone was aware that she might not outlive her childhood and that if she died the two strongest claimants to the throne would be Robert Bruce of Annandale and John Balliol of Barnard Castle, heir to the ancient lordship of Galloway. For obvious reasons neither was made a Guardian, but it was no secret that the two Comyns and Bishop Fraser supported Balliol (whose sister was Badenoch's wife), while the bishop of Glasgow and the Stewart — and apparently the young earl of Fife also, albeit in a less committed fashion — gave their backing to Bruce. All told, the choice of Guardians appears to have incorporated a great deal of sophisticated thought.

Any personal contribution which James the Stewart may have made to the actual work of government would tend, inevitably, to be submerged beneath the collective agreements of the six. James must have assented to the despatch of the important mission to Edward I of England, sent after the English king had gone to Gascony in the summer of 1286.[49] He must also have played a part in the arrangements for the Maid to be brought to Scotland from Norway. In this period — whether in his capacity as lord of Kyle, sheriff of Ayr or Guardian is not clear — he required the tenants of Melrose abbey dwelling in Kyle Stewart (chiefly at Mauchline) to carry out wapinschaws (i.e., musters and inspections of arms) and give succour 'for the protection of public peace and of the realm, and to defend his lands and theirs' at a time when 'the tranquillity of the realm was disturbed and the state (*respublica*) was threatened by dissension' after Alexander III's death.[50] Behind this act there almost certainly lay some national provision made by the Guardians as a whole, for the earl of Strathearn raised tenants at this time within his earldom 'to maintain the peace and tranquillity of the realm of Scotland'.[51]

The council of regency was severely depleted in 1289 by the death of the two earls, Buchan dying at a ripe age, Fife being murdered near Brechin in pursuance of some family feud.[52] The crucially important decision to negotiate a marriage between Margaret of Scotland and Edward I's heir, Edward of Caernarvon, must have been taken by the four surviving Guardians, including the Stewart. The Guardians authorised the envoys who negotiated the treaty of Salisbury (November 1289)[53] and are named in the record of the treaty of Birgham (March-August 1290),[54] by which the marriage was provided for and its conditions stipulated in detail. It is noteworthy that the definitive treaty of Birgham, accepted by the Scots in July 1290 and ratified in the English parliament at Northampton,[55] was set in train by an exceptionally well-attended parliament summoned to assemble at Birgham in March. This parliament included, besides the four Guardians, no fewer than ten bishops, twelve earls, twenty-three abbots, eleven priors and forty-eight barons, claiming understandably to speak for the whole community of Scotland.[56] As we shall shortly see, the prominent role taken by the Stewart as one of the four Guardians throughout these negotiations was continued during the difficult period which followed the Maid's death in September 1290 — indeed, right through to the inauguration of King John in November 1292.

Before turning to the events connected with the Great Cause, the trial of claims to the Scots throne which occupied much of the years 1291 and 1292, it may be as well to make a general point concerning the Stewart's activity as Guardian and to refer to one episode in particular, the Turnberry Band, which shows him acting in a personal, or at least family, capacity.

Although surviving sources for thirteenth-century Scotland as a whole are scarcely voluminous, those for the period of the Guardianship from 1286 to 1292 are comparatively abundant. In his role as Guardian James the Stewart is mentioned in numerous brieves, the first to survive, dated 28 September 1286, dealing with an inquest into pasture rights on Salmond's Muir (*Salmanmor*), in the Angus parish of Panmure.[57] Given the difficulty of the situation, the Guardians appear in a highly creditable light, maintaining the smooth running of day-to-day government. Many brieves survive addressed by the Guardians to the chamberlain, giving instructions as to payment of fees.[58] These are among the records printed by Joseph Stevenson which provide evidence for the administration of justice and for the suppression of factional infighting, as well as for actual payments and receipt of fees.[59] In Scotland, such matters were to a large extent decentralised, although controversial cases were brought before assemblies of prelates and magnates at the king's court as a final resort.[60] A few of these prelates and magnates (e.g., Matthew Crambeth, bishop of Dunkeld, and Andrew Murray of Petty) seem to have been especially prominent in government, but in any case there was evidently a permanent council of magnates to assist the Guardians.[61]

It would be quite misleading to suggest that the death of Alexander III did not precipitate tension and conflict. Vigorously though the Guardians might strive to rule the Maid's realm in peace, aristocratic and regional rivalries never lay far beneath the surface. Within a few months of the king's death there was jockeying for position between the Balliol and Bruce factions. Bruce of Annandale and his son the earl of Carrick seized the royal castles at Dumfries and Wigtown and the lord of Galloway's castle of Buittle near Dalbeattie, obviously posing a most serious threat to Balliol's position as heir-apparent to the lordship of Galloway, still held at this time by his mother the lady Dervorguilla.[62] The uncertainty of the situation is reflected in the wording of the Turnberry Band entered into on 20 September 1286[63] by Robert Bruce, lord of Annandale, his son the earl of Carrick, James the Stewart and his brother Sir John Stewart of Jedburgh, Walter Stewart, earl of Menteith, and his sons, Patrick, earl of Dunbar, Angus Macdonald, lord of Islay, and his son, Richard de Burgh, earl of Ulster, and Thomas de Clare. By this 'band' or formal record of mutual allegiance the Scots magnates named undertook to support the earl of Ulster and Thomas de Clare in some unspecified venture. The band saves the fealties of all parties to the king of England (the feudal superior of Burgh and Clare as well as of the Bruces and Dunbar on the Scots side) and to whosoever shall be king of Scotland 'by reason of the blood of the late King Alexander' (the feudal superior of all the Scots who were parties to the band). An undue importance has been attached to this salvo. Such reservations were of course standard practice in all bonds or allegiances made among private subjects, and the only peculiarity of the Turnberry wording arises directly from the fact that at the time this band was made there was no duly inaugurated reigning sovereign of

Scotland, only the Maid of Norway, already styled queen but not yet (nor, as it happened, ever to be) formally installed as monarch. The wording would point to Margaret, Alexander's granddaughter, or perhaps to an as yet unborn child of the widowed Queen Yolande. It could only most indirectly and retrospectively point to Bruce or Balliol in whose veins the blood of the late king did not flow, for they claimed the throne by virtue of descent from Earl David of Huntingdon, great-uncle of the late king.

Although the precise purpose of the Turnberry Band must remain in doubt, it seems to have been satisfactorily explained by Sir Maurice Powicke. It was surely never intended to be a covert declaration of support for the Bruce claim to the Scottish throne, even if the Scots participants could be seen as a small but rather obvious rally of the Bruce faction. On the contrary, the wording of the band and the mention of Burgh and Clare (especially the latter) point to the pursuit of some enterprise to conquer land in the west of Ireland, probably in Connacht.[64] In view of the interest already shown in Irish settlement by families in the south-west of Scotland,[65] the participation of Bruces, Macdonalds and Stewarts does not appear surprising. Indeed, it may be that the Turnberry meeting was the occasion when marriage was mooted and agreed between James the Stewart and Egidia de Burgh. The band in any case underlines the close connexion between the Bruce family and the Stewarts, related by marriage and what by 1286 was evidently a long-standing tradition of friendship.

The death of the Maid of Norway in September 1290 precipitated a crisis without precedent in Scottish history, for the succession to the throne, although occasionally disputed, had not given rise to any serious and prolonged conflict since the eleventh century, when it was obviously governed by a body of law or custom different from what was acceptable in 1290. The contest would be between Bruce and Balliol, and the very real threat of civil war severely weakened the ability of the Scots leaders to stand up to an aggressive English king confronting them on the Border in May 1291 at the head of a respectable military force. At Norham on Tweed Edward I, completely reversing his 'softly, softly' policy of the previous year, embodied in the treaty of Birgham, demanded point-blank to be recognised as lord superior (*soverein seignur*) of the Scottish realm, sasine of which was to be given him by surrender of the royal castles. At first the Guardians played for time and, in conjunction with the castle-keepers, resisted Edward's demands.[66] But by 12 June, bowing to considerable pressure from Edward, who had shrewdly enlisted the competitors' support, they climbed down.[67] The castles were handed over, the Guardians accepted Edward's authority at least *de facto* and to the extent of allowing themselves to be reappointed with the addition of the English baron Brian FitzAlan of Bedale,[68] and the English king was effectively granted jurisdiction over the Anglo-Scottish tribunal set up to hear and determine the rival claims to the throne. As part of the process of taking control of Scotland, Edward I commanded all the substantial freeholders, lay and clerical, to take oaths of fealty to him as superior lord. The fealties from the south-east were evidently proffered at Berwick, but the rest of the country was divided into four areas, with a convenient centre for each, and three commissioners were appointed for each area to supervise the receipt of the fealties, while additionally every sheriff was ordered to take fealties within his sheriffdom. James the Stewart (along with the bishop of Glasgow and Sir Nicholas Segrave) was a member of the commission sitting at Ayr, presumably for the west of Scotland (excluding Galloway), and since he was also sheriff of Ayr and Dumbarton, his responsibility in these arrangements would have been considerable.[69]

The tribunal or court of claims included forty Scottish auditors (i.e., sponsors) for Bruce and forty for Balliol. Naturally, the Stewart and Bishop Wishart were among Bruce's auditors. By November 1292, after many adjournments, the court had given judgement in favour of John Balliol. The determined support which the Stewart and Wishart gave to Bruce was highlighted in the replies of the auditors when asked their opinion of the judgement. Most simply concurred, but the bishop said that while he now accepted the result, he had originally been convinced of the justice of Bruce's claim by many arguments and much evidence. The Stewart seems to have gone out of his way to answer that he agreed exactly with the bishop of Glasgow.[70] It is worth while casting forward to Robert I's first parliament held at St Andrews in mid-March 1309, which James the Stewart attended. The manifesto promulgated at that parliament declared that 'the loyal folk of Scotland always believed without hesitation, as they had understood from their ancestors and elders and believed to be true, that Robert Bruce the grandfather (i.e., the Competitor) was the true heir and was to be preferred to all others, after the death of King Alexander and of his granddaughter, the daughter of the king of Norway'.[71] Doubtless there were a number of influential persons present at the St Andrews parliament who would have been able to recall the events of eighteen years before; but hardly anyone who could have spoken with greater authority than the Stewart.

The Bruces and their followers must have been privately dissatisfied with the outcome of the trial, since they not only suffered a personal defeat but were forced to accept a king who, despite his lordship of Galloway, had closer connexions with England than Scotland. Nevertheless, Balliol was duly enthroned at Scone in the presence of the great magnates according to custom. There are very few records left of the legislation carried out during Balliol's short reign, but what we do find is the continuation of the Stewart involvement in government. From the king's first parliament there remains the brief ordinance for the construction of new sheriffdoms in the west of Scotland, where previously royal authority had been but sparsely represented. With its innumerable inlets and islands, the western coast of Scotland was strategically very vulnerable to outside attack, and, given that the Bruce stronghold in Scotland lay in the west, vulnerable also to civil insurrection. The proposed three new sheriffdoms, if they had been implemented, would have provided useful and important centres for royal authority at a local level. It was proposed that Lewis, Uist, Barra, Skye and the small isles were to be grouped with Wester Ross and Kintail to form the sheriffdom of Skye, under the jurisdiction of the earl of Ross. South of this, most of what is now Argyllshire, except for Kintyre, was to become the sheriffdom of Lorn, administered by the lord of Argyll, Alexander Macdougall, while James the Stewart, already hereditary lord of Bute and the Cumbraes, was to be sheriff of those islands together with Kintyre and presumably Arran, which were to be known as the sheriffdom of Kintyre.[72]

Though this appears a very wise political and strategic project, it never got under way because of the political upheavals which plagued Balliol's brief reign, effective for only three and a half years. King John's prestige in the eyes of his magnates received a bitter blow when he gave in to Edward I over the regulation of appeals outwith the kingdom. It appeared that the Scots, no longer retaining control in judicial affairs, had also lost their autonomy in military matters when in 1294 King Edward ordered King John to mobilise his troops in order to fight against Philip IV in Gascony.[73] Edward's demand for official Scottish military support (he had demanded service from the king, ten earls, and sixteen barons, including James the Stewart and Robert Bruce of Annandale) was met by a strong determination on the part of the Scottish magnates not to be included in English policies. Neither King John nor any of his barons answered the summons; instead, they made excuses[74] and, in preparation for further defiance, before December 1294 obtained absolution from Pope Celestine V for any oaths extracted from them under duress.[75]

The determination of the Scots magnates not to become a pawn in English policies hardened into a resolve to inaugurate a constitutional revolt to take over the actual government of the country themselves, while still acknowledging John Balliol as king. This extreme step was taken at the parliament held at Stirling on 5 July 1295,[76] where government was taken from Balliol's hands and put into those of a council of twelve selected magnates. Symmetrical representation of the magnates, foreshadowed in the period of Guardianship, is again revealed in the choice of four bishops, four earls and four barons. Once again James the Stewart represented his country's interests. We do not know what arguments were put forward for and against this revolutionary step, who supported it and who did not. All we can deduce from the list of the twelve councillors is that, firstly, they are representative of the two strongest factions, Bruce and Balliol, and secondly, the Bruce family themselves appear to have kept well clear of the fight. The actual membership of the council of twelve may be deduced from the first twelve magnates who fixed their seals to the treaty which Scotland concluded with France.[77] These (omitting heads of religious houses) were the bishops of St Andrews, Glasgow, Dunkeld and Aberdeen, the earls of Buchan, Mar, Strathearn and Atholl, and the first four of the eleven barons who affixed their seals: Comyn of Badenoch, James the Stewart, Alexander de Balliol and Geoffrey Mowbray.

From James the Stewart's past record it is no surprise to find him as one of the twelve councillors. Though tied by bonds of family alliance to the Bruces, the Stewart's foremost concern had always been the maintenance of stable government. During the period up to 1290 he was always associated with maintaining the normal flow of government activity. On the death of the Maid, unlike his two fellow-Guardians, Fraser of St Andrews and Comyn of Badenoch, he refrained from plunging into factional infighting. The Scottish magnates on the whole appear conservative in their notions of government and kingship, and although the English barons had set a precedent in 1258 by removing the reins of government from King Henry III's hands, it had taken another generation and a particularly acute combination of threatening circumstances for the Scottish magnates to follow suit. Only the realisation that under King John's ineffectual rule Scotland would become inextricably enmeshed within English affairs, losing both its customary privileges and independence, prompted the Scottish magnates to take over control of the realm.

The council of twelve were faced with two urgent tasks: to negotiate a French treaty and to put the country into a state of defence. Determination on the part of the Scots not to become an English satellite pointed clearly to an alliance with France. Though King Philip IV regarded the Scots as his enemies in March 1295, by May he spoke of them as his friends.[78] At the July parliament four commissioners were appointed to go to Paris, to negotiate an offensive and defensive alliance between King John and King Philip. This alliance was ratified by the Scottish king and parliament on 23 February 1296.[79] James the Stewart was not one of those appointed as negotiators, though as a member of the council he would have had a voice in the decisions. Negotiation and ratification of the treaty with France was tantamount to a declaration of war with England. The Scottish magnates, however, had yet to find out whether they could count on the support of the country. Calls for a wapinschaw and muster were sent out, the host being required to assemble on 11 March.[80] Amongst others, the Bruces refused to answer the summons and left the country, leaving their Scottish lands to be confiscated.[81] The council of twelve also ordered the removal of twenty-six English clerks from their benefices in St Andrews diocese.[82] Scotland was to be purged of English influence, and James the Stewart, together with the rest of the council, felt confident in their defiance of King Edward. The Border was in good hands, the key castles of Roxburgh, Berwick and Liddesdale being held respectively by James the Stewart, Sir William Douglas and Nicholas de Soules. And as we have seen James also controlled much land in the west, including the whole of Kintyre with its chief castle (Dunaverty?), as well as the barony and castle of *Glasrog*.[83]

The Scots, however, were over-confident. Edward I and his army swept into Scotland, taking Berwick by storm on 30 March and defeating the main Scottish army at Dunbar one month later. On 5 May James the Stewart surrendered Roxburgh Castle, following this up on 13 May by swearing fealty to King Edward.[84] Having become Edward's man, James the Stewart not only made sure that most of his own tenants followed suit, but was also employed by King Edward in receiving the surrender of the castles of Kirkintilloch and Dumbarton.[85] Sir Ingram de Umfraville handed Dumbarton over on 28 June, with his daughters Eve and Isabel as hostages. Kirkintilloch was surrendered about 10 June by Hugh Kennedy.[86] James the Stewart appears on the 'Ragman Roll' on 28 August as having formally sworn fealty and done homage to King Edward. Many of his tenants had done likewise, probably by proxy.[87] Vassals and associates of James the Stewart who came formally into the king of England's peace included clerks such as Master Gilbert of Templeton and Geoffrey de Caldecote, knights such as Sir John Stewart (James's brother), Finlay of Houston, William Fleming of Barochan, Arthur of Dunoon, Hugh Kennedy, Reginald Crawford and Robert Boyd of Noddsdale; and lesser laymen, Gilbert of Conisbrough, John Pride, Gillis of Eastwood, Patrick of Selvieland, Robert Cunningham, Walter son of Gilbert (Hamilton) and Thomas Brewster of the Forest of Paisley, to whom the Stewart gave a charter of Saucerland in Paisley, witnessed by Sir John de Soules and Sir Reginald Crawford.[88] Whilst these men and others listed in the Ragman Roll of August show a good cross-section of Stewart followers, there are a few notable exceptions. There is no sign of either Malcolm or William Wallace, or of any Sempills of Lochwinnoch, although Robert Sempill a few years later was serving James as steward of the barony of Renfrew.[89] Those men who submitted to King Edward received back their lands.[90] On 8 September the sheriffs at Ayr, Berwick, Edinburgh, Forfar, Lanark and Roxburgh were ordered to restore the lands and properties confiscated from the Stewart's tenants and sub-tenants.[91] Despite his submission, however, James the Stewart's position was appreciably weak. In the west, Alexander Macdonald of Islay seized his chance and wrested from the Stewart possession of Kintyre and *Glasrog*.[92] In the week 29 September–5 October 1296, the Stewart was commanded to hand over to Henry Percy (the English warden of Ayr and Galloway) all his hostages from that district, together with the castles of Kirkintilloch and Dumbarton.[93] The office of sheriff of Dumbarton with its rolls and brieves was also to be handed over.[94]

With the list of names from the Ragman Roll it is interesting to compare the list of the Stewart's closest friends and followers appearing in the attestation to James's principal charter for the family abbey of Paisley, issued at Blackhall on 9 January 1295.[95] Those witnessing this impressive document and appearing in the Ragman Roll are Bishop Wishart of Glasgow; the knights Sir John Stewart, Sir Andrew Fraser, Sir John de Soules, Sir Colin Campbell, Sir Reginald Crawford and Sir Arthur of Dunoon; the clerks Geoffrey de Caldecote, William Shaw, Alexander de Normanville and Patrick de Louwell; and the freeholders Gilbert of Conisbrough, John Pride, Gillis of Eastwood and Walter son of Gilbert.

1296 was not a totally disastrous year for James, for it was during this year that he contracted his marriage to Egidia (Gelis), sister of Richard de Burgh, earl of Ulster and lord of Connacht.[96] Sir Colin Campbell, Sir Walter Lindsay and Sir John de Soules were sponsors. This marriage, to the sister of one of Edward's supporters, not only gave James the Stewart substantial lands in Ireland but also the hope of a future heir. It seems rather surprising that James had not married earlier, and one is left to speculate on the reasons why he did not. Previous contracts may have been made, of which we have no record. What is fairly certain is that this was his first marriage, as there is no mention of any children other than those resulting from the Burgh alliance.

The precise timing of the explosion which was to come, and the extent of the preparation behind it, are hidden from our view. Both the Lanercost and Guisborough Chronicles say that James the Stewart and Bishop Wishart planned the rising of 1297 and instigated Wallace to acts of violence in which they would not join openly.[97] Probably in the winter of 1296–7 the Stewart and his friends kept 'a low profile' and made their plans. James spent Christmas 1296 at Blackhall with his brother John, who celebrated the feast with a gift to one of the great patron saints of the Border country, Waltheof of Melrose.[98] For the souls' weal of himself, his wife Margaret and their children, John Stewart gave two pounds of wax annually (or the equivalent market price) for a taper to burn at the saint's tomb in Melrose abbey. The grant was witnessed by James the Stewart, the abbots of Paisley and

Kilwinning, and the knights Reginald Crosbie, Walter and James Lindsay, and William of Abernethy (who had been in the Stewart's meinie the previous summer).[99] It was evidently men such as these who, as Walter of Guisborough tells us, attached themselves to Wallace — clearly with the connivance of their lords.[100]

The 'official' revolt, led by Bishop Wishart, the Stewart and the young earl of Carrick, Robert Bruce, lasted from May to July 1297, when it collapsed with the 'capitulation of Irvine'.[101] Sir William Douglas, a principal figure in the revolt and also a close collaborator with Wallace, surrendered and was imprisoned at Berwick. The bishop was detained in Roxburgh Castle. Bruce did not submit, and although the Stewart had surrendered conditionally under the terms agreed at Irvine, it is clear that he was not converted to an English allegiance. At Stirling in September, where the English under the earl of Surrey and Hugh Cressingham confronted the determined army of Andrew Murray and William Wallace, the Stewart and the earl of Lennox offered to pacify their compatriots, but we are told that they could not detach their own men from Wallace's force.[102] As soon as the battle of Stirling Bridge was won, the Stewart showed his true colours by ambushing the English as they fled, killing many and taking much booty.

Between Stirling Bridge (11 September 1297) and Falkirk (22 July 1298), there is little or no record of the Stewart's activities. At Falkirk his brother Sir John led the bowmen from Selkirk Forest and fell in battle beside them.[103] Wallace and the 'magnates of Scotland' fled to 'castles and forests'; it can be safely assumed that the Stewart was among them.[104] On 31 August 1298 Edward I, by now in control of southern Scotland, confiscated the estates of James 'late Steward of Scotland'.[105] Ironically, the estates were awarded to Sir Alexander Lindsay, the Stewart's former and future ally.

From 1298 to 1300 the guardianship, revived by Wallace only to be given up by him after the defeat at Falkirk, was shared by Bruce earl of Carrick and John Comyn the younger of Badenoch. In this period, and indeed in the five and a half years from Falkirk to the general Scots submission of February 1304, the Stewart took his full share in prosecuting the independence struggle. In 1299, shortly after the new bishop of St Andrews, William Lamberton, had returned from the continent, the Scots leaders carried out a bold raid into the heart of the Forest.[106] In addition to the two Guardians and the bishop, there were the earls of Atholl, Buchan and Menteith, James the Stewart, Ingram de Umfraville, William de Balliol, David Graham, David of Brechin and Robert Keith the marischal. With them, in Bruce's meinie, came Malcolm Wallace, William's elder brother. At a council held in Peebles, David Graham picked a quarrel with Malcolm Wallace by accusing his brother of going overseas without the assent of the community. In an instant Bruce and the Comyns were at each other's throats, and there were ominous cries of treason. This bitter quarrel, which might have split the patriots irreparably, was settled only by the Stewart and others coming between the two parties and pacifying them. Disinterested statesmanship between 1286 and 1296, duplicity at Stirling Bridge in 1297, good sense and moderation at Peebles in 1299 — both sides of the Stewart's character are revealed by the evidence of these years. After the Peebles council Bruce went to Annandale and Galloway, the Comyns retired to the north, and the Stewart went home to Clydesdale. It was about this time that he was reported to have been deeply grieved by an atrocity committed by the Northumbrian commander of English-held Lochmaben Castle, Robert Felton. Lochmaben's English garrison had suffered much at the hands of Robert Cunningham, a nephew of James's sister and a member of his own meinie, who at this time commanded Caerlaverock for the Scots. When Cunningham was killed, Felton had his head hoisted over one of the towers of Lochmaben.[107]

In May 1300 the Stewart was present at the parliament held at Rutherglen. Bruce was no longer Guardian, and Comyn resigned at the parliament because of disagreements with Bishop Lamberton. In this dispute, whatever was at the root of it, the Stewart and the earl of Atholl supported the bishop, and presumably with their approval Sir Ingram de Umfraville was brought in as Guardian to replace Comyn. The Comyns had not withdrawn from the patriotic struggle, for the young lord of Badenoch and his cousin, the earl of Buchan, were in the field in Galloway when Edward I launched his summer campaign and, in a two-day parley, put terms to the English king — the restoration of John Balliol to the Scots throne, recognition of his son Edward's right to succeed, and freedom for Scots magnates whom Edward had forfeited to redeem their estates from those to whom they had been regranted.[108] The terms were rejected by Edward, and when the subsequent military action proved inconclusive the English were compelled to retire from Scotland, with only the capture of Caerlaverock Castle to show for their pains. Early in 1301 the leadership crisis which was obviously affecting the Scottish war effort in this period was temporarily resolved by the appointment of Sir John de Soules as Guardian, evidently with the approval of the exiled John Balliol. A big military effort was staged by Edward I in the summer of 1301, chiefly aimed at the middle west where lay the bulk of the Stewart's lands. These were given by King Edward to Henry de Lacy, earl of Lincoln. There survives from the autumn or latter end of 1301 a letter to the English king from John Marshall, head of a family prominent among the Stewart's vassals, who was acting as the earl of Lincoln's bailie or steward.[109] In his letter Marshall asks for troops to be sent promptly, for the Guardian of Scotland, he reports, has occupied Cunningham and is threatening to invade Strathgryfe. Soules had in fact achieved a notable success in slowing down the English advance and in keeping his comparatively small but evidently highly mobile force intact, ready to strike at a moment's notice. The upshot of this brilliant military action, combined with assiduous diplomatic activity at the French and papal courts, was a truce to last from the end of January 1302 until the beginning of November.

In July 1302, however, the Scots' position was completely undermined by the crushing defeat of the French army at the hands of patriotic Flemish insurgents at Courtrai. So desperate did the Scottish patriots' prospects now seem that in the autumn of 1302 Soules himself, along with Bishop Lamberton, James the Stewart and Ingram de Umfraville, travelled to the French court in a bid to ensure Philip IV's continued support for their cause.[110] They stayed for almost a year, learning of the heartening victory achieved by Comyn of Badenoch and Simon Fraser at Roslin in February 1303 and sending at least one encouraging (but in truth too optimistic) despatch to their comrades at home. The Scots' fate seemed to be sealed by the peace of Paris made between Philip IV and Edward I on 20 May 1303, from which John Balliol and his kingdom were excluded.[111]

At the end of 1303 or early in the following year most of the Scots notables who had been at the French court returned home and, in line with the general submission negotiated between the English and Comyn of Badenoch at Strathord north of Perth in February 1304, came into King Edward's peace and allegiance.[112] Edward's attitude towards the Stewart was understandably harsher than it had been in 1296. At first severe conditions were imposed, for example, that he would have no safe-conduct until Wallace had been captured.[113] His estates were again in the hands of the earl of Lincoln. James did not recover them until November 1305, when he was made to seal an abjectly humble instrument of submission to the English king's will and pleasure.[114] In the same way his friend and colleague Robert Wishart, bishop of Glasgow and by now well advanced in years, received stern treatment at first, being threatened with two or three years' exile 'because of the great evil he has caused'.[115] Yet King Edward must have been persuaded to soften his attitude, for the bishop at least was brought into the scheme for reorganising the government of Scotland which was eventually promulgated in the Westminster parliament in the autumn of 1305.[116] The Ordinance outlining the reorganisation names two of the Stewart's associates, his kinsman Sir John of Menteith, who had in fact been keeper of Dumbarton for the English since 1304,[117] and — as a person still under suspicion — Sir Alexander Lindsay of Barnweill.[118]

In February 1306 Bruce's murder of Comyn of Badenoch at Dumfries set the whole of Scotland ablaze. Despite his years, Bishop Wishart was deeply implicated in the plot to place Bruce on the throne. It is almost certain that the Stewart, too, was committed to Bruce's cause, in line with all his own conduct since 1286 and with family tradition. Yet he refused to come out as an active combatant, possibly through infirmity. Edward I, understandably enough, did not trust him and confiscated his estates, once again granting them to the earl of Lincoln.[119] On 3 October 1306, at Lanercost priory in Cumberland, where King Edward lay on his sick-bed, James the Stewart made his final submission to the English king, swearing a complicated oath of fealty on the two holiest crosses in Edward's possession as well as on the more usual Consecrated Host, gospels and saints' relics.[120] The penalty for breaking the oath was to be immediate excommunication. On these terms, rather surprisingly, his estates were restored. In the meantime, his son and heir Andrew, who had been placed in the charge of Bishop Lamberton, had been handed over to Bruce by the bishop, much to Edward I's indignation.[121] Nothing further is heard of Andrew Stewart, who may not have survived the fearful hardships endured by the new king of Scotland and his companions in the months following the rout at Methven. It is not known who had the custody at this time of Andrew's brother Walter, who succeeded his father as Stewart; but the closeness of the ties between King Robert I and the Stewart family is shown very strikingly in 1315, when the king gave his daughter Marjorie — at that time his sole progeny — to Walter Stewart in marriage. One may speculate whether this match had been arranged between Bruce and James the Stewart several years before.

During the years 1307 to 1309 King Robert slowly won the initiative and vindicated his claim to the throne by the most commonly accepted test of the age — military success. A number of the men who helped him to achieve this success belonged to James the Stewart's own circle of dependants and friends: his nephew James Douglas, Neil (son of Colin) Campbell, Reginald Crawford, Robert Boyd and Alexander Lindsay. Some time after 3 October 1306, and perhaps at the time of Edward I's death on 7 July 1307, James the Stewart threw off English allegiance for the last time and joined King Robert. At the end of his life he could look forward to the future with hope, confident that under its brilliant young leaders his country would regain the independence it had enjoyed under Alexander III. The Stewart's last public act was his attendance at the parliament which Robert I held at St Andrews in March 1309.[122] That parliament approved a bold declaration of Robert I's right to the throne, dismissing Balliol's claims as invalid, and linking the legitimacy of Robert's kingship with the pristine liberty (i.e., independence) of the Scottish kingdom. It also resumed vitally important diplomatic relations with the king of France, who certainly recognised Bruce as king of Scots by July 1309.[123] Nine days after the date of Philip IV's letter to Edward II from which we learn of this recognition, on 16 July, James the Stewart died.[124]

Typically, our knowledge of the Scots baronage in the thirteenth and fourteenth centuries is derived either from charter-material with little or no support from narrative sources (compare the Hays of Errol or the Morhams of that Ilk), or from chronicles and English record evidence with little support from charters (compare Walter Comyn, earl of Menteith). In the case of James the Stewart we are fortunate to possess both kinds of source-material which, although never abundant, are sufficient to give us a fairly well balanced picture of the man as politician, statesman and feudal landowner. In the first two of these capacities James figures continually, if seldom with special prominence, in the record of Alexander III's last years and of the subsequent interregnum. It is possible to trace his career in the plentiful sources for the Anglo-Scottish war from 1296 onwards, although there are some notable gaps. His presences and absences in this surviving archive suggest a man of action rather than words. He did not take part in the negotiations for the marriage of Alexander, heir to the Scots throne, to Margaret of Flanders in 1281,[125] or for the treaty of Salisbury in 1289,[126] or for bringing Margaret of Norway to Scotland in 1290,[127] or for the Franco-Scottish treaty of 1295.[128] He took a back seat in the protracted dealings of 1300–1302 aimed at restoring King John and convincing the papacy that Scotland was an independent realm. Only at the close of 1302 was the Stewart directly involved in major diplomacy, when he formed part of the large Scots delegation at the French court. One gets the impression that James's presence was to act as ballast, as a name to impress King Philip, rather than for his skill in negotiation.

As landowner and feudal lord, James the Stewart can be seen as one of the foremost members of his class in Scotland more from our knowledge of the sheer extent of his vast estates, and of the numbers of men who were in one sense or another his dependants, than from estate records as such (non-existent), or even from charters. Nevertheless, a handful of his charters does survive, and from these we can see that he was concerned to define his own obligations and those of others, and that he was a conventional but hardly devoted son of the Church. We have already noted his confirmations for the Cluniacs of Bromholm and Paisley,[129] the latter being of course the special foundation of his ancestors and thus likely to receive his favour. But the Stewart's sole fresh privilege for the monks of Paisley seems to have been his order prohibiting any fish weirs on the Black Cart Water issuing from Lochwinnoch (Castle Semple Loch) which might spoil or interfere with their established weir at an unidentified place called *Lyncleyft*.[130] The Stewarts had also traditionally shown favour to Melrose abbey, but James merely freed the Cistercians of that house from a feu-ferme rent of ten shillings yearly, which they had hitherto paid from land held of the Stewarts in the barony of Innerwick.[131] During the interregnum of 1286–92, James issued a declaration in favour of Melrose to the effect that when he levied military service from the monks' tenantry at Mauchline in Kyle it was for the emergency only, was contrary to the monks' eleemosynary tenure, and would not form a precedent.[132] James's apparent indifference towards the Cistercians of Melrose is all the more surprising in view of the fact that contemporaries were aware of his family's traditional friendship. This we know from a grant to Melrose by Thomas Randolph the elder (*c.*1282 × 1285), made explicitly for the souls' weal of 'Alexander late Steward of Scotland and of James his son and heir'.[133]

Too few of James's charters for laymen or clerical individuals have survived to allow any generalisations about the internal polity of the Stewart lordship between 1282 and 1309. William son of John of Preston was given land in Tranent resigned by Simon Fleming at a parliament in Edinburgh Castle on 26 January 1285.[134] The Stewart's ownership derived from an exchange made between his father and Alexander Comyn, earl of Buchan, involving *Murcheley*, and the Stewart interest in that estate, wherever it was, is not clear. About 1290 James confirmed to Sir Henry Graham, interestingly enough 'with the advice and consent of his council', the estate of Tarbolton in Kyle, which had been held by Gilbert son of Richer (de Biéville).[135] Thomas Brewster (*braciator*) of the Forest of Paisley, whose fealty to Edward I is recorded in 1296,[136] had perhaps two charters of Saucerland in Paisley, one of which, dating to *c.*1294–5, is printed in full below from a notarial copy of the sixteenth century.[137] The grant to Thomas is strongly oriented towards his own occupation of brewing and towards other crafts, tanning, butchery and milling. William surnamed 'del Schaw', a clerk, got a charter of lands in the vicinity of Dundonald Castle (of which this document gives the earliest known mention), dating before 22 July 1298.[138] Possibly in the Stewart's later years, he gave a charter to the Renfrew burgess Stephen son of Nicholas of land between the burgh and the point of *Ren*, where Gryfe (as it was then called) falls into Clyde, previously granted to Patrick of Selvieland, to be held in feu-ferme for twelve pence a year.[139] Sir Adam of Fullarton, knight, son of umquhile Alan of Fullarton, had a charter confirming Fullarton with the land of Gailes, a fishery in the Irvine, and four and a half marks yearly from Shewalton.[140] An original charter of land in Largs for John Erskine, grandson of Sir John Erskine, knight, is briefly and faultily noticed in a report of the Historical Manuscripts Commission.[141] It has been successfully traced by Ann

Royan to the Scottish Record Office (GD 124/1/1112), and is of such interest that it is also printed below. It cannot be later than Bishop Wishart's imprisonment in 1306 and probably dates to *c.*1300.[142]

NOTES

1. *Scots Pge.*, i, p. 13.
2. D. Symson, *A Genealogical and Historical Account of the Illustrious Name of Stewart, from the first original to the accession to the Imperial Crown of Scotland* (Edinburgh, 1726), p. 60; A. Nisbet, *A System of Heraldry* (Edinburgh, 1816), i, p. 48. For James's birth 'in or about the year 1243' cf. Symson, as above, p. 74.
3. G.W.S. Barrow, 'James the Stewart of Scotland', *The Stewarts*, xii, no. 2 (1965), p. 77.
4. John Barbour, *The Bruce*, ed. W.M. Mackenzie (London, 1909), bk. xi, lines 216–17.
5. *Paisley Reg.*, p. 90.
6. An early instance is Jamis (*sic*) de Ramsay, for whom see *The Scottish Tradition*, ed. G.W.S. Barrow (Edinburgh, 1974), p. 39; *Highland Papers*, ed. J.R.N. Macphail (SHS, 1914–34), ii, p. 124.
7. Stevenson, *Documents*, ii, no. 401.
8. *Scots Pge.*, i, p. 13; Symson, *Genealogical and Hist. Account*, pp. 64–5.
9. The Stewarts' devotion to St James may be shown by the dedication of the parish kirk of Mow, Roxburghshire, to this saint: *Kelso Liber*, ii, p. 511.
10. Symson, *Genealogical and Hist. Account*, p. 58; *RMS*, i, no. 508.
11. *RRS*, i, no. 184.
12. *Ibid.*
13. *Ibid.*, no. 183. See also Barrow, *Era*, p. 65.
14. *Glasgow Reg.*, i, no. 66.
15. Cowan (Easson), *Religious Houses*, pp. 64–5.
16. *Paisley Reg.*, *passim*.
17. *Origines Parochiales Scotiae* (Bannatyne Club, 1851–5), i, pp. 70–1. The forest of *le Rase* is referred to in James the Stewart's charter of Saucerland to Thomas the Brewster (below, p. 192); called the king's forest in a note of this or a related charter in NLS MS Adv. 34.6.24, fo. 122v.
18. *Paisley Reg.*, p. 15.
19. Barrow, *Era*, p. 68.
20. *Rot. Scot.*, i, p. 31b.
21. Below, p. 193.
22. Barrow, *Era*, p. 69.
23. John, constable of Dunoon, witnessed a Lamont charter with Walter II son of Alan, the third Stewart (*Paisley Reg.*, pp. 132–3); for Dundonald see *Collections of the Ayrshire Archaeol. and Natural History Soc.*, vii (1966), p. 33.
24. Stevenson, *Documents*, ii, no. 445 (p. 191); *Highland Papers*, ii, pp. 115–17. See also Alexander of Islay's letter of 1296 reporting that the Stewart had taken control of Kintyre together with its castle (Skipness or Dunaverty?). This is printed in *SHR*, l (1971), pp. 16–17 (from PRO SC 1/18/147).
25. *Chron. Bower*, i, p. 46. There was also a castle at Inverkip in 1301, 1306 and 1307 (*CDS*, ii, nos. 1224, 1235, 1807; Barbour, *Bruce*, bk. viii, lines 98–9). This may have been in the Stewart's hands in the 1290s.
26. Barrow, *Era*, pp. 14–15, 65 and n. 20.
27. F.M. Powicke, *King Henry III and the Lord Edward* (Oxford, 1947), pp. 80–1, 135, 190.
28. *Holyrood Liber*, no. 78.
29. *Ibid.* It is not known how the Stewart acquired possession of Gorgie.

30. Stevenson, *Documents*, ii, no. 401.

31. The Stewart's presence at Alexander III's court is evidenced on 17 June (corrected date) 1284 and on 13 and 15 November 1285 (*RMS*, ii, no. 1791; iii, no. 2308; *HMC, Reports*, ii, app., p. 166). He is also found as witness to a safe-conduct issued by King John on 8 November 1295: *Historical Papers and Letters from the Northern Registers*, ed. J. Raine (Rolls Ser., 1873), p. 119; *Register of John de Halton, Bishop of Carlisle*, ed. T.F. Tout (Canterbury and York Soc., 1913), i, p. 56.

32. *ER*, i, pp. 38, 47.

33. *Ibid.*

34. *Rot. Scot.*, i, p. 1; Stones and Simpson, *Great Cause*, ii, pp. 105, 112.

35. *APS*, i, p. 447.

36. *Paisley Reg.*, pp. 138–9.

37. *SHR*, l (1971), p. 17; *Rot. Scot.*, i, p. 31b.

38. *HMC, Reports*, v, p. 624, shows James already Steward on 4 October 1282. Since Alexander the Stewart is not mentioned among the Scots magnates who sponsored the marriage of Alexander, heir to the throne, to Margaret of Flanders in 1281, it may be that he was by then already a sick man (Stones and Simpson, *Great Cause*, ii, p. 189).

39. *APS*, i, p. 424.

40. *Deeds relating to East Lothian*, ed. J.G. Wallace-James (Haddington, 1899), pp. 7–8. See Appendix I at the end of this chapter.

41. J. Hodgson, *A History of Northumberland* (Newcastle upon Tyne, 1820–58), II, iii, p. 327. The Stewart's title *Sen(escallus)* is wrongly rendered as *Men*'.

42. G.G. Simpson, *Handlist of the Acts of Alexander III*, etc. (RRS, 1960), nos. 159–61, shows the king in Fife in June 1285, near Perth in August, and at Edinburgh at the end of October.

43. Palgrave, *Docs. Hist. Scot.*, p. 42.

44. *Chron. Lanercost*, p. 127.

45. *Regesta Norvegica*, ii (Oslo, 1978), no. 444: letter from Alv Erlingsson to James Stewart as Guardian of Scotland. It is worth noting that an envoy from King Eric, Bjarne Erlingsson (presumably related to Alv), spent the winter of 1286–7 in Scotland, evidently to promote the interests of Eric as father of the queen-designate. See P.A. Munch, *Det Norske Folks Historie* (Christiania, 1852–63), IV, ii, p. 148. (We have to thank Mr John Simpson for help in translating these Norwegian references.)

46. Above, Ch. 6.

47. Watt, *Dictionary*, pp. 203–6.

48. G.W.S. Barrow, 'Early Stewarts at Canterbury', *The Stewarts*, ix, no. 3 (1953), pp. 230–3. A marriage between Walter II son of Alan and Euphemia, daughter of William de Brus and sister of Robert de Brus, may be indicated by record of 1261: *Northumberland Pleas from the Curia Regis and Assize Rolls, 1198–1272* (Newcastle upon Tyne Records Committee, 1922), no. 652; cf. *CDS*, i, no. 2302. Probably during the period when Bishop Wishart and James the Stewart were Guardians they were first witnesses of a charter given to his son by Richard of Glen of land at Glen, near Traquair (Peeblesshire), and several of the Stewart's vassals were also witnesses, e.g., Sir William Fleming of Barochan, Alexander of Kirkintilloch and (probably) John Erskine: *Rot. Scot.*, i, p. 11a–b.

49. Barrow, *Bruce*, pp. 22–3.

50. *Melrose Liber*, ii, no. 396.

51. *Inchaffray Chrs.*, no. 117.

52. *Scottish Tradition*, ed. Barrow, pp. 37–8.

53. Stevenson, *Documents*, i, no. 75 (p. 106).

54. *Ibid.*, nos. 92, 108 (where, however, it is to be noted that the Stewart was not one of the two Guardians who negotiated with the English plenipotentiaries: *ibid.*, p. 163).

55. *Ibid.*, no. 108.

56. *Ibid.*, no. 92.

57. *Ibid.*, no. 14. The pasture went with the land of Scryne.

58. *Ibid.*, nos. 22, 23 etc., up to no. 208.

59. *Ibid.*, *passim.*

60. Duncan, *Scotland*, pp. 608–11.

61. *Illustrations of the Topography and Antiquities of the Shires of Aberdeen and Banff* (Spalding Club, 1847–69), ii, pp. 129–30.

62. Palgrave, *Docs. Hist. Scot.*, p. 42; *ER*, i, pp. 36, 39.

63. Stevenson, *Documents*, i, no. 12.

64. G.H. Orpen, *Ireland under the Normans 1169-1333* (Oxford, 1911–20), iv, pp. 66–76, 112, 139–40; Sir Maurice Powicke, *The Thirteenth Century*, 2nd edn. (Oxford, 1962), p. 598 and n. 1.

65. Above, pp. 50–1; R. Greeves, 'The Galloway lands in Ulster', *TDGAS*, 3rd ser., xxxvi (1957–8), pp. 115–21. Mr Kenneth Nicholls, University College, Cork, has kindly supplied references to a charter by Duncan (earl) of Carrick granting the town (*villa*) of Ulderford, i.e. Larne, to Thomas de Mandeville (Dublin, PRO Ireland, Press Copies of Certified Copies, I, fo. 121), and to a claim to land at Drumaliss, Larne, by Duncan grandson of Alexander of Carrick, as held by Duncan (of Carrick?) in the time of King John (Irish Record Commission, Repertory of Plea Rolls, vol. x, pp. 241, 375).

66. Barrow, *Bruce*, pp. 45–7, 50–1.

67. Stones and Simpson, *Great Cause*, ii, pp. 97, 102.

68. *Ibid.*, p. 102. Edward I intended to recompense the Guardians, among them James the Stewart, for their labours and losses between 1286 and 1291 by granting them each £100 worth of land from wardships and escheats, but this was superseded by alternative compensation (*Rot. Scot.*, i, p. 3b).

69. Stones and Simpson, *Great Cause*, ii, pp. 122–3.

70. *Ibid.*, p. 220. James's closeness to Bruce in this period is shown by his witnessing the important agreement which Bruce made with Florence, count of Holland, on 14 June 1292: Stevenson, *Documents*, i, no. 255 (p. 321).

71. Stones, *Relations*, no. 36 (p. 281).

72. *APS*, i, p. 447. In John's first parliament, James the Stewart and John de Soules formally handed over to the king all the lands and tenements which Bernard de Balliol, King John's uncle, had held in Nenthorn, Berwickshire (*ibid.*, p. 449).

73. *Foedera*, I, ii, p. 804.

74. Walter of Guisborough, *Chronicle*, ed. H. Rothwell (Camden Soc., 1957), pp. 243, 270.

75. *Ibid.*, p. 270.

76. *APS*, i, p. 453.

77. *Ibid.*

78. Stevenson, *Documents*, ii, nos. 334–5.

79. *APS*, i, pp. 451–3.

80. *Chron. Lanercost*, p. 169.

81. Guisborough, *Chron.*, pp. 269–70.

82. Barrow, *Kingdom*, pp. 237–8.

83. Guisborough, *Chron.*, pp. 275, 279; *SHR*, l (1971), pp. 16–17; Stevenson, *Documents*, ii, p. 191.

84. *CDS*, ii, no. 737 and p. 193.

85. *Ibid.*, p. 224; *Rot. Scot.*, i, pp. 29–36 *passim.*

86. *Ibid.*, p. 32a.

87. *CDS*, ii, no. 812 and pp. 203–5, 211–13; cf. Barrow, *Bruce*, pp. 107–9.

88. *HMC, Reports*, iv, app. p. 528. A copy of the full text of this charter adds the witnesses: see Appendix II, no. 1.

89. *Miscellany of the SHS*, iv (1926), p. 321.

90. *Rot. Scot.*, i, pp. 29–33 *passim.*

91. *Ibid.*, p. 30a.

92. Stevenson, *Documents*, ii, no. 445.

93. *Rot. Scot.*, i, pp. 34b–6b.
94. *Ibid.*, p. 36b.
95. *Paisley Reg.*, pp. 92–6.
96. Stevenson, *Documents*, ii, no. 401.
97. Guisborough, *Chron.*, p. 296; *Chron. Lanercost*, p. 190.
98. *Melrose Liber*, i, no. 348.
99. *Rot. Scot.*, i, p. 32.
100. Guisborough, *Chron.*, p. 299.
101. *Ibid.*, pp. 297–9; Stevenson, *Documents*, ii, nos. 447, 452; Palgrave, *Docs. Hist. Scot.*, pp. 197–8.
102. Guisborough, *Chron.*, pp. 299–300.
103. *Ibid.*, p. 328.
104. William Rishanger, *Chronica*, ed. H.T. Riley (Rolls Ser., 1865), p. 387; Bartholomew Cotton, *Historia Anglicana*, ed. H.R. Luard (Rolls Ser., 1859), p. 304.
105. *CDS*, ii, no. 1006.
106. Barrow, *Bruce*, pp. 150–3, which see for the passage which follows.
107. *Ibid.*, p. 158; *CDS*, ii, no. 1101.
108. Rishanger, *Chron.*, pp. 440–1.
109. *CDS*, ii, no. 1121 (PRO SC 1/19/107); G.W.S. Barrow, 'Lothian in the first war of independence', *SHR*, lv (1976), pp. 167–8.
110. Barrow, *Bruce*, p. 117.
111. *APS*, i, pp. 454–5; Powicke, *Thirteenth Century*, pp. 653–4.
112. Barrow, *Bruce*, pp. 182–3.
113. Palgrave, *Docs. Hist. Scot.*, pp. 276, 281.
114. *CDS*, ii, no. 1713. It may be to the winter of 1305–6 that we should assign an undated charter of Alan, earl of Menteith, for Sir William de le Akynhewyde knight, witnessed by (among others) James the Stewart, Malise, earl of Strathearn, Alexander of Abernethy and John of Menteith. But it might belong to some date in the period 1297–1302 (W. Fraser, *The Red Book of Menteith* [Edinburgh, 1880], ii, p. 223).
115. Palgrave, *Docs. Hist. Scot.*, p. 284.
116. *Memoranda de Parliamento, 1305*, ed. F.W. Maitland (Rolls Ser., 1893), p. 293; *Rotuli Parliamentorum* (Rec. Comm., 1783–1832), i, p. 160.
117. Stones, *Relations*, no. 33 (pp. 246, 248).
118. *Ibid.*, pp. 253–4.
119. *CDS*, ii, no. 1857. On 26 August 1307 James the Stewart borrowed 500 marks from the earl of Lincoln, his sureties being John Moubray and Richard Lovel; the debt had not been repaid by June 1309: *ibid.*, iii, nos. 56, 98.
120. *Ibid.*, ii, no. 1843; *Foedera*, I, ii, p. 1001. In 1306 the Stewart had a gift of two tuns and one pipe of wine from the English king's store at Carlisle, worth £6. 13s. 4d. (*CDS*, iv, p. 488).
121. *Ibid.*, ii, nos. 1818, 1826.
122. *APS*, i, p. 459; Barrow, *Bruce*, pp. 261–6.
123. *APS*, i, p. 459; *Gascon Register A*, ed. G.P. Cuttino with the collaboration of J.-P. Trabut-Cussac (London, 1975–6), ii, no. 71 (p. 354), where the unnamed king of Scots must be Robert I. This letter is dated 7 July (1309); as recently as 19 April 1308 the French king had paid 333l. 6s. 8d. to John Balliol as king of Scotland: *Les journaux du trésor de Philippe IV le Bel*, ed J. Viard (Paris, 1940), no. 5917.
124. *Chron. Bower*, ii, p. 242.
125. Stones and Simpson, *Great Cause*, ii, p. 189.
126. Stevenson, *Documents*, i, no. 75 (esp. p. 106).
127. Surviving evidence shows only part of these negotiations, but nowhere does James the Stewart's name appear: cf. *CDS*, ii, nos. 417, 423, 428, 442, 445–6, 448–9; *Foedera*, I, ii, pp. 706, 713–14, 758.
128. *APS*, i, p. 451.

129. Above, pp. 168, 177.

130. *Paisley Reg.*, p. 254.

131. *Melrose Liber*, ii, pp. 687–8.

132. *Ibid.*, no. 396.

133. *Ibid.*, p. 685.

134. *Deeds relating to East Lothian*, ed. Wallace-James, pp. 7–8.

135. W. Fraser, *The Lennox* (Edinburgh, 1874), ii, pp. 17–18; *The Scottish Genealogist*, xxv, no. 4 (1978), pp. 106–7 and esp. n. 104.

136. *CDS*, ii, p. 213 (*le Breuester*).

137. Appendix II, no. 1, from a notarial copy among the muniments of the family of Shaw-Stewart of Ardgowan and Blackhall. Our thanks are due to Mr Alan Borthwick for providing a reference to National Register of Archives (Scotland), Survey 1847, which enabled us to trace this document to Strathclyde Regional Archives.

An early eighteenth-century collection, NLS MS Adv. 34.6.24, fo. 122v (p. 244 in old pagination), has a note of a charter by James, Stewart of Scotland (wrongly identified as James I before accession), to Thomas Browster of the lands of 'Sacerland beside Paisley', which may refer to a different charter, since it mentions licence and power to cut green wood in the *king's* forest of Raise as much as necessary for Thomas to build *houses* for his own use. This could not be derived from the text printed below, unless it was read and summarised carelessly.

138. *Collections of the Ayrshire Archaeol. and Natural History Soc.*, vii (1966), pp. 32–4, witnessed by John Stewart who fell at Falkirk.

139. *Misc. of the SHS*, iv, pp. 320–1 (Strathclyde Regional Archives, TD 829/1). In this charter Gilbert of Conisbrough is apparently called 'the father', implying that his son and heir was then of age. Patrick of *Selvenland* gave fealty to Edward I in 1296: *CDS*, ii, p. 204.

140. Walter Macfarlane, *Genealogical Collections concerning Families in Scotland* (SHS, 1900), ii, p. 333.

141. *HMC, Mar and Kellie, Supplementary Report*, pp. 2–3. In this abstract the beneficiary is wrongly styled 'Sir John Erskine' and the witness Walter Logan appears as 'William'.

142. Appendix II, no. 2. The Stewart's lordship at Largs is puzzling, for the estate seems to have belonged to Dervorguilla de Balliol, as heiress to Alan of Galloway and the Morvilles, *c.*1272–7 (*Glasgow Reg.*, i, no. 230). James's son Walter granted the church of Largs to Paisley abbey in 1318 (*Paisley Reg.*, p. 237), and his charter is witnessed by Robert Sempill, to whom Robert I granted the land in the tenement of Largs which had belonged to umquhile John de Balliol knight (King John?) (*RMS*, i, no. 52).

APPENDIX I

BENEFICIARIES AND WITNESSES IN THE CHARTERS OF JAMES THE STEWART

Witnesses include those appearing in (1) the agreement between Paisley abbey and John son of Roger of Auldhouse, 5 December 1284, which bore James the Stewart's seal (*Paisley Reg.*, pp. 65–6); (2) Malcolm Lamont's charter to Paisley, 23 July 1295, which also bore the Stewart's seal (*ibid.*, pp. 138–9); and (3) John Stewart's charter to Melrose abbey, 25 December 1296 (*Melrose Liber*, i, no. 348). Their occurrence in these documents is denoted by the dates 1284, July 1295 and 1296 respectively; other dated occurrences are given as 1285 and Jan. 1295. Witnesses to *Cartularium Comitatus de Levenax* (Maitland Club, 1833), pp. 20–1, a charter of Earl Malcolm of Lennox also witnessed by James the Stewart, are indicated by asterisks.

(1) *Beneficiaries*
Bromholm priory, Norfolk
Melrose abbey
Paisley abbey
Thomas Brewster (*braciator*) of the Forest of Paisley
John Erskine (de Yrskyn) grandson of Sir John Erskine knight
Adam son of Alan of Fullarton
Henry Graham
Stephen son of Nicholas burgess of Renfrew
William del Shaw clerk
William son of John Preston

(2) *Witnesses*
(a) *Lay*
Sir William of Abernethy knight (1296)
Alpin son of Donald
Robert Boyd knight
*Sir Nicholas (= Colin) Campbell knight (Jan. 1295)
*Gilbert of Conisbrough lord of Aberdalgie (1284, Jan. 1295)
John Crawford
*Sir Reginald Crawford knight (Jan. 1295)
Sir Reginald Crosbie (1296)
*Sir Hugh of Dennistoun knight
*Sir Arthur of Dunoon knight (1284, Jan. 1295)
Gillis of Eastwood (Jan. 1295)
Sir Ralph (of) Echline (1284)

Sir John Erskine (de Yrskyn')
Duncan Fleming
Sir Simon Fleming (1284)
Sir William Fleming knight of Barochan (for title *dominus* see *Rot. Scot.*, i, p. 11b)
Andrew Fraser knight (Jan. 1295)
Sir Simon Fraser knight (1284, 1285)
Thomas of Fulton (1284)
Sir Patrick Graham knight
*Sir Finlay of Houston knight
John of Knoc (1284)
Sir Alexander Lindsay knight
Sir David Lindsay knight
Sir James Lindsay knight (1296)
Sir Walter Lindsay knight (1284, 1296)
Walter Logan
Sir Herbert Maxwell (1284)
John of Menteith
John Pride (Jan. 1295)
Sir Thomas Randolph knight the elder
Robert of Roberton knight
Robert Sempill steward of the barony of Renfrew
Sir John de Soules knight (1284, Jan. 1295)
Sir William de Soules knight justiciar of Lothian (1284, 1285)
John Stewart knight (brother of James the Stewart) (Jan. 1295, 1296)
Walter Stewart earl of Menteith (1285)
Nicholas Wallace
Walter son of Gilbert (Jan. 1295)
John Wishart

(b) *Clerical*

Bernard abbot of Kilwinning (1296)
Geoffrey de Cald(e)cote clerk (Jan. 1295)
Finlay chaplain of James the Stewart, vicar of Kilfinan (July 1295), parson of Dunoon
Hugh parochial chaplain of Paisley, vicar of Kilmacolm (July 1295)
Stephen of Kent vicar of Inverkip (July 1295)
Lambert clerk (1285)
Patrick de Louwell clerk (Jan. 1295)
John Morton vicar of Inverkip
Alexander de Normanville clerk (Jan. 1295)
Ralph the chaplain (1285)
Robert. *See* Wishart.
William del Schaw clerk (Jan. 1295)
Stephen abbot of Paisley (1285)

Mr Gilbert of Templeton parson of Rothesay (July 1295)
Walter abbot of Paisley (1296)
Robert Wishart bishop of Glasgow (Jan. 1295)
Roger Wythirspon clerk

(c) Clergy associated with James the Stewart in a letter (1286 × 1295) to Laurence bishop of Argyll on behalf of Paisley abbey anent the church of Kilkerran in Kintyre (*Paisley Reg.*, p. 127).

Robert treasurer of Glasgow cathedral
Mr Thomas (son of Nicholas) of Dundee subdean of Glasgow (afterwards bishop of Ross)
Mr Alexander Kennedy (chancellor of the king of Scots *c.*1295–6)

APPENDIX II

TWO HITHERTO UNPUBLISHED CHARTERS OF JAMES THE STEWART

In editing these two charters, the use of u, v, i and j has been rationalised; otherwise the spelling and punctuation of the original charter have been retained, while the punctuation of the copy is editorial. The copyist has generally used the æ diphthong in words such as *præsentes*, but not invariably and never in *heres*. In all such cases, e is printed in our text.

1

James, Stewart of Scotland, grants heritably to Thomas called Brewster, for homage and service, all that land beside Paisley called Saucerland, by marches specified, with pasture for four cows with two calves not more than one year old within donor's park of Blackhall, with free ish and entry by one gate to be made at the side of the park adjoining Saucerland; with liberty to have brewhouses, abattoir, mill and tannery, with facilities to carry on trade, and with use of the Water of Cart saving the rights of the monks of Paisley; also grants pasture for twelve oxen and cows within common pasture of Raise, with liberty to make shielings; penalty for twelve beasts straying in donor's forest one penny; penalty for beasts straying in park of Blackhall two pence. Thomas and his men may have timber from growing wood under supervision of donor's forester, and firewood; also right to dig and dry peats in donor's peatmoss of Thornly. Also grants maximum fines of three shillings in donor's court of the barony of Renfrew, and that goods seized shall be paid for, before being seized, at reasonable market price. Performing forinsec service of one bowman for one day a year at donor's castle of Renfrew, if reasonably forewarned; rendering at Blackhall one penny yearly at Whitsun in name of feu-ferme. (*c.* 1294 × 1295 [all the witnesses also witness the Stewart's principal charter for Paisley abbey, 9 January 1295]).

Sciant presentes et futuri quod nos Jacobus senescallus Scotie dedimus et concessimus et hac presenti carta nostra confirmavimus Thome dicto braciatori et heredibus suis, pro homagio et servitio suo, totam[1] illam terram iuxta Passeleth que vocatur Sauserland, per has divisas: incipiendo de parco nostro Nigre Aule, descendendo per rivulum de Espedare usque ad rupem que est divisa monachorum de Passeleth, et per illam rupem ex transverso usque ad in aquam de Kerth', et sic per illam aquam de Kerth ascendendo usque ad quoddam fossatum quod est prope ianuam dicti parci nostri, et sic per latus eiusdem parci sicut tempore huius donationis nostre stetit, usque ad rivulum de Espedare predictum. Dedimus etiam et concessimus predicto Thome et heredibus suis pasturam ad quatuor vaccas, cum duobus vitulis dummodo de etate unius anni extiterint, infra parcum nostrum de

Nigra Aula, cum libero introitu et exitu de dicta terra sua usque in predictum parcum nostrum, per unam ianuam in latere predicti parci Nigre Aule faciendam ubicunque infra latus eiusdem parci iungens ad dictam terram pro se melius viderit expedire. Et si contingat predictum parcum nostrum per nos vel heredes nostros a loco quo tempore confectionis huius carte stetit removeri vel omnino deleri, volumus et pro nobis et heredibus nostris concedimus quod predictus Thomas et heredes sui pasturam predictarum quatuor vaccarum cum vitulis earundem, ut superius dictum est, in eodem loco pasturam habeant pro dictis quatuor vaccis cum duobus vitulis sine aliqua perturbacione. Tenendam et habendam predicto Thome et heredibus suis de nobis et heredibus nostris in feodo et hereditate, libere, quiete, bene et in pace, cum libertate habendi bracinas, carnificium, molendinum, tanatorium et omnes alias commoditates et libertates infra predicta terra, secundum quod ipse et heredes sui melius et utilius et commodius sibi viderint expedire; et ad omnimodas marcimonias exponendas et exercendas cum aisiamento aque de Kert quantum ad dictam terram de iure debeat spectare, salvo iure monachorum in dicta aqua prout habere solebant, et cum omnibus aliis libertatibus et aysiamentis ad predictam terram spectantibus vel aliquo tempore de iure spectare valentibus. Dedimus et concessimus predicto Thome et heredibus suis pasturam ad duodecim animalia, videlicet boves et vaccas, infra communem pasturam del Rase, cum libertate faciendi scalingas pre[dictis][2] animalibus suis infra communem predictam. Et quod si animalia dicti Thome vel heredum suorum vel hominum suorum infra divisas foreste nostre fuerint capta, pro duodecim animalibus [predictus Thomas][3] et heredes sui seu eorum homines dabunt unum denarium pro portagio quocienscunque fuerint attachiata. Insuper autem concessimus quod si quecunque animalia predicti Thome vel heredum suorum aut hominum suorum infra eandem terram inhabitantium fuerint capta· in parco nostro Nigre Aule, ipse Thomas et heredes sui et eorum homines dabunt duos denarios pro portagio quotienscunque dicta animalia capta fuerint in parco nostro prenominato, salvis tamen quatuor vaccis suis prescriptis cum duobus vitulis. Dedimus etiam et concessimus predicto Thome et heredibus suis et hominibus eorundem dictam terram inhabitantibus meremium in dicta foresta nostra, per visum forestarii nostri, de viridi ad edificandum ad sua necessaria super predicta terra, et de mortuo bosco ad comburendum, sine destructione. Insuper vero concessimus predicto Thome et heredibus suis et hominibus eorundem dictam terram ut prediximus inhabitantibus quod habeant communam in petaria nostra de Thornyley ad petas sibi fodiendas et dissiccandas, et cum libero introitu et exitu de predicta petaria ad altam viam que se extendit versus Passeleth sine perturbacione cariendas. Dedimus etiam et concessimus predicto Thome et heredibus suis et hominibus eorundem predictam terram inhabitantibus quod si in curia nostra vel heredum meorum baronie de Renfru quibuscunque querelis fuerint amerciati, pro quolibet amerciamento solvent tres solidos tantummodo, salvis nobis et heredibus nostris eschaetis vite et membrorum. Concedimus et pro nobis et heredibus nostris predicto Thome et heredibus suis quod nullus nomine nostro vel heredum nostrorum bona dicti Thome vel heredum suorum aut hominum suorum infra eandem terram inhabitantium aliquo modo capiat nisi pro valore quo dicta bona alibi in patria rationabiliter vendi possint, et hoc mediante pecunia in manu persolvenda antequam predicta bona de eadem fuerint remota vel deducta. Faciendo inde forinsecum servicium, ipse et heredes sui nobis et heredibus nostris, ad Castrum nostrum de Renfru, per architenentem uno die per annum, cum rationabiliter super hoc fuerint premuniti. Et reddendo nobis et heredibus nostris, pro omni servitio, warda, relevia, maritagio, auxilio regis, secta curie, et omnibus aliis consuetudinibus, exactionibus et secularibus demandis, ipse et heredes sui, apud Nigram Aulam, unum denarium ad penthecosten, nomine feodifirme. Nos vero et heredes nostri predicto Thome et heredibus suis predictam terram[4] cum omnibus pertinentiis suis, libertatibus et aysiamentis, et cum omnibus concessionibus et donationibus nostris, universis et singulis, in ista carta contentis, prout superius prenominatum est, contra omnes homines et feminas warrantizabimus, acquietabimus et in perpetuum defendemus. In cuius rei testimonium presenti scripto sigillum nostrum apposuimus. Hiis testibus Domino Joanne de Soulys, Domino Reginaldo de Crauford, Domino Arthuro de Dunon', militibus, Galfrido de Caldecotis, Johanne Pride, Gilberto de Cunigburg', Willelmo del Schaue clerico et aliis.

Note at foot: Hec est vera copia principalis cartae suprascriptae copiat*a* et collationat*a* de verbo in verbum nil addend*um* nec diminuend*um*. Transcript*a* per me Patricium Mosman notarium publicum, testan*tibus* meis signo et subscriptione manualibus

Patricius Mosman

(Monogram and notarial sign)

Source: Glasgow, Strathclyde Regional Archives Office, T-Ard 1/6/3 (Shaw-Stewart of Ardgowan and Blackhall Muniments). Undated notarial copy in italianate hand, apparently xvi cent. Patrick Mosman is recorded as a Paisley-based notary working in the Firth of Clyde area 1587–95 (*The Register of the Privy Council of Scotland*, ed. J.H. Burton *et al* [Edinburgh, 1877–], iv, pp. 200, 729; v, pp. 626, 654) and was sheriff-clerk of Dumbarton in 1600 (*ibid.*, vi, p. 634). We thank Dr John Durkan for this reference.

Printed: HMC, Reports, iv, p. 528 (abstract only).

Notes: [1]MS tota. [2]MS omits. [3]Supplied conjecturally. [4]MS predictarum terrarum.

2

James, Stewart of Scotland, grants to John Erskine, son of John son and heir of Sir John Erskine, knight, all the land which donor had and held in the tenement of Largs, heritably, with all pertinents, saving to donor the two marks of land held by Walter son of Richard, to which Sir John gave the liberties of a barony, and saving also to donor the right of patronage of (the kirk of) Largs; saving also to William son of Sir John Erskine two marks of land in the said tenement of Largs which the said Sir John resigned to donor with rod and staff, in which land the donor has infeft the said William. To be held for performance of forinsec service of the tenth part of the service of one knight. Grants also that John Erskine may have in the said land six brewhouses if convenient for him. Warrandice. (1283 × 1306, probably *c.*1300).

Omnibus Christi fidelibus hanc cartam visuris vel audituris . Jacobus Seneschallus Scocie Salutem in domino sempiternam. Noveritis universitas vestra nos dedisse . concessisse . et hac presenti carta nostra confirmasse Johanni de Yrskyn filio

Johannis filii et heredis domini Johannis de Yrskyn militis pro homagio et servicio suo totam terram quam in tenemento de le Larges habuimus et tenuimus. Tenendam et habendam sibi et heredibus suis de nobis et heredibus nostris . libere quiete et hereditarie cum omnibus pertinenciis libertatibus et aisiamentis ad predictam terram pertinentibus vel de iure pertinere valentibus sine aliquo retinemento . salvis nobis et heredibus nostris imperpetuum duabus marcatis terre quam Walterus filius Ricardi tenuit quam scilicet dictus dominus Johannes fecit in predicta terra de le Larges cum libertatibus ad baroniam pertinentibus. Et salvo nobis et heredibus nostris iure patronatus de le Larges. Salvis insuper Willelmo filio domini Johannis de Yrskyn' duabus marcatis terre in predicto tenemento de le Larges quam predictus dominus Johannes cum fusto et baculo nobis sursum reddidit . de qua terra nos predictum Willelmum infeodavimus . faciendo nobis et heredibus nostris forinsecum servicium de predicta terra quantum pertinet ad decimam partem servicii unius militis. Concessimus etiam pro nobis et heredibus nostris predicto Johanni de Yrskyn' filio Johannis filii et heredis domini Johannis de Yrskyn' militis . et heredibus suis quod libere habeant in predicta terra . sine omni molestia et gravamine sex bracinas si sibi viderint expedire. Et nos et heredes nostri predictam terram cum suis pertinenciis prenominato Johanni de Yrskyn' filio Johannis filii et heredis domini Johannis de Yrskin' militis et heredibus suis in omnibus sicut prescriptum est contra omnes homines et feminas warantizabimus acquietabimus et defendemus in perpetuum. In cuius rei testimonium presentem cartam sigillo nostro fecimus roborari. Hiis testibus domino Roberto dei gratia Glasguensi episcopo . domino Reginaldo de Crauford' . domino Johanne de Yrskyn' Waltero Logan Johanne Wyscard' Gilberto de Coningisburg' et multis aliis.

Written below at left-hand side, so as to be hidden by the fold, in pale ink, in hand contemporary with that of text but not identical: Doncano Macc Seweny'

Endorsed: No early endorsement.
Robert was Bishop of Glasgow from 1272 to 1316 some time between which this charter has been granted (xviii cent., second half)
3.

Description: Original, measuring 22.7 cm. × 15.2 cm., with foot folded to depth of about 4.5 cm. Extremely slender tag, slit for seal, but no seal survives. It seems doubtful whether it could have borne more than a small seal.

Hand: Characteristically rounded and decorative hand of later xiii-earlier xiv cent. Apart from the loss of the seal and one or two minor injuries, the document is in excellent condition and the writing is very legible.

Source: SRO GD 124/1/1112 (Mar and Kellie Muniments).

Printed: HMC, Mar and Kellie, Supplementary Report, pp. 2–3 (abstract only).

9

THE SCOTTISH MEDIEVAL CASTLE: FORM, FUNCTION AND 'EVOLUTION'

Geoffrey Stell

The[1] numerous castles and towers in the Scottish landscape prompt a variety of aesthetic, academic and practical responses. They can be appreciated in many different ways, but it is possible to distinguish three main underlying attitudes towards them.

Firstly, for over two centuries the Romantic viewpoint has evoked the medieval castle's dramatic, mysterious and legendary qualities, its grand and rugged features often making a perfect match with the magnificence of its original surroundings and the highly charged events in Scottish history with which it has been truly or allegedly associated.[2] The castle's majestic appearance and setting (see plate 4) provided much of the inspiration for the castellated mansion-building fashions of the late eighteenth and nineteenth centuries, and have continued to inspire and reward even the most arduous works of restoration. Eilean Donan Castle (Ross and Cromarty), the late medieval stronghold of the MacKenzies of Kintail and their MacRae constables, is to many *the* archetypal Romantic castle, not only by reason of its picturesque situation, but also because of the destruction that it suffered as a Jacobite outpost in 1719, coupled with the devoted efforts that lay behind its twentieth-century reconstruction.[3]

Secondly, given that the castle at its simplest definition was a strongpoint for the securing and exercise of feudal lordship, the study of castellated architecture has long had a specialist military bias. The more warlike aspects of castle history and function have been emphasised, and a close correlation has been postulated between castle-design, weaponry,[4] siege-warfare and private armies. These views have undoubtedly been influenced by interpretations of medieval technology and warfare embodied, for example, in the works of Viollet-le-Duc (plate 5); at different periods in modern times, they have also been conditioned by contemporary military thinking.[5] The seminal studies on castles in Britain that were published in and around the two World Wars earlier this century were not immune from these influences,[6] but they continue to provide the foundations on which the modern study of Scottish castles and fortified houses is constructed. By the nature of their approach, military and architectural historians alike have created a trend towards the classification and subdivision of the castle 'genus', hence the appearance of 'species' such as 'enclosure-castles', 'courtyard-castles', 'shell-keeps', 'keep-gatehouses', 'tower-houses' and 'hall-houses'[7] when medieval man appears to have referred only to castles, towers, fortalices and manor-places.

Everyone is aware that medieval kings, nobles and lairds did not spend their everyday lives permanently stationed behind high walls or in gloomy cheerless towers lowering at would-be combatants outside. There is thus a third viewpoint which seeks to emphasise architectural manifestations of the 'domestic' and public facets — residential, ceremonial and institutional — of these multi-purpose buildings:[8] the number, size and lay-out of the halls and chambers for the household, staff and retainers; the catering and service facilities required to match the numbers and lifestyles of the castle inmates; other basic amenities such as heating and window-glazing that made life bearable for those whose bodies seemingly had a greater tolerance of cold and draughts than centrally-heated twentieth-century man; and the cycle of fashions for applied decoration in or on stone, wood and plaster, the stylish embellishments that transcended the more fundamental necessities of life in the late medieval and early modern periods.[9] Although providing a much needed corrective to the military view, this approach also has an inbuilt bias insofar as it encourages a progressive or 'Whig' view of architectural history.[10] It assumes a process of Darwinian-like evolution in which the medieval castle is transformed through a semi-fortified stage into the recognisably modern house. Since Renaissance concepts of house-design and matters of taste approximate to what is today regarded as a civilised norm, the transformation is taken at its face value as an accurate, visible reflection of a corresponding 'improvement' in the behaviour and outlook of 'warlike' medieval man.

Some aspects of this transformation probably do reflect real changes in lifestyles. With the advent of a clearer functional division between private house and fortress in the sixteenth century there is no mistaking the unambiguously military purpose of engineered fortifications for use with and against artillery.[11] Likewise, where Renaissance features have been grafted on to an older fabric, the marked contrasts in style and appearance are very much heightened. This is certainly true of the remarkable Italianate facade with its diamond-faceted stonework introduced into Crichton Castle (Midlothian) by Francis Stewart in about 1585, which includes the first arcade of its kind and, more significantly in the long run, one of the first scale-and-platt stairs in Scotland (plate 6).[12] Even though there was little general advance over medieval technology in matters of water supply and sanitation,[13] there is no gainsaying the real improvements in stair- and window-design, and to some extent in domestic planning, during the course of the seventeenth century.

But paradoxically, perhaps, these developments in domestic architecture were accompanied by intermittent warfare of an unprecedented scale and intensity. The security-consciousness that this turbulence engendered may indeed explain the continuation of tower-building until the middle decades of the seventeenth century.[14] However, it is by no means certain that the chronology and distribution patterns of these later towers, particularly numerous in the north-east, Fife and the Borders, correspond with the incidence or aftermath of real violence,[15] and whether the pattern of more pacific 'domestic' building (evidenced in the initial stages, for example, by ground-floor halls)[16] tells the opposite story. The indications are that architectural behaviour in these respects is at best a somewhat uncertain, confused and erratic barometer of contemporary conditions.

Contemporary remarks and inscriptions also provide equivocal testimony. Battlements constituted one of the prime distinguishing features of a fortified residence,[17] and the battlement at Ancrum House in Roxburghshire was still regarded in 1632 as 'the grace of the house, and makes it look lyk a castle ...'[18] Even later, 'about the year 1666', repairs and additions were made to Newbigging House which, in the opinion of Sir John Clerk of Penicuik (1676–1755), 'at that time being dressed up with two battlements covered with lead ... became the best house of the shire of Edin.',[19] a lingering recognition of the symbolic attributes of castellated architecture. On the other hand, Patrick, first earl of Strathmore (1643–95), professed 'that there is no man more against these old fashion of tours and castles then I am', and felt that fortified houses such as Castle Lyon (Castle Huntly, Perthshire) 'are worn quyt out of fashion, as feuds are'.[20] This was one of the blessings which he, as a staunch royalist, attributed to the Restoration of 1660, but he was himself not quite so free from a sense of resistance a short time afterwards upon the accession of Prince William of Orange. And just what are we to make of panels like that at Tullibole Castle (Kinross-shire) which on one side bears the benign inscription 'Peace be within they walles and prosperitie within thy house', and on the other 'The Lord is onlie my defence 2 April 1608', a praiseworthily pious message that is belied by a murderous-looking box-machicolation immediately above?

Although confronted by so many different kinds of ambiguity, no one could pretend that the architectural evidence could support a completely revisionist view of lawlessness and disorder in medieval and post-Reformation Scotland. There is, however, much room for modification to the conventional view of the 'functional' late medieval castle and its 'evolution', chrysalid-like, into the early modern house. Enough has been said to show that one of the principal areas for reassessment is in the relationship between form and function, an issue that enters into the interpretation of virtually every major aspect of the design and detailing of the medieval castle and the fortified house.[21]

This problem applies particularly to the fundamental question of siting. Many castles, the major royal strongholds of Edinburgh and Stirling being obvious examples, occupy a commanding and naturally defensible position on a rocky eminence, a promontory, or an island. Sometimes the site combined convenience of access by sea and/or land with an important strategic purpose such as the guarding of a river-crossing or boat-anchorage. By the later Middle Ages these were long-established principles of fortification with an ancestry going back to early historic and prehistoric times. However, even in these earlier periods, the low-lying and potentially vulnerable positions of some brochs[22] show that other factors may have governed their siting. So far as castles and towers are concerned, it is difficult to know what is the rule and what the exception. Among those that clearly possess a defensive purpose in their setting some, like the elaborate sixteenth-century fortified complex at Craignethan in Clydesdale, were placed where they could be easily overlooked from higher ground near by.[23] Other sites have what might be described as a lurking quality, perhaps tucked into a hollow or behind a hillock as, for example, in the case of Morton Castle in Nithsdale.[24] There, a fourteenth-century forebuilding traverses the lower and somewhat constricted end of a downward sloping promontory, and its original height corresponds with the crest of the hill that fronts it on the main landward approach. Where castles occupy commanding but overlooked sites set into a hillside, or stand on mounds of dubious tactical advantage, it is difficult for us to believe that defence was the exclusive, or even the paramount, concern of their builders. Firm and relatively dry rocky outcrops, natural terraces and sloping ground offered constructional benefits for wall foundations and drainage, as well as providing workable tracts of associated agricultural land.

Some of these inferences appear to be borne out by the local distribution of towers, for example, along the fault-line scarp of the Sidlaws forming the northern rim of the Carse of Gowrie, and by those towers such as Megginch which stand on the low ridges of the Carse itself, occupying what were then the naturally drier and better drained 'island' ('inch') sites in a predominantly flat and boggy landscape.[25] A similar pattern prevailed in the Laich of Moray where the names and settings of, among other establishments, Innes House, Bog of Plewlands (later known as Gordonstoun), and Bog of Gight (*alias* Gordon Castle) testify to the marshy landscape of parts of the then undrained coastal plain;[26] evidently, however, there were patches of land of sufficient quality and extent to support these sizeable residences and their estates. Broken and marshy ground could of course serve as a means of protection, as it almost certainly did at Hermitage Castle in the Borders. A mid-sixteenth-century report refers to it as 'a oulde house not stronng, but ewill to wyn by reasone of the strate grounde about the same',[27] a reference no doubt to its general moorland surroundings, frequently water-logged, as well as to its elaborate system of outworks.

The availability of a reliable water supply was an essential requirement in war and peace. Before the more widespread use of conduits and piped water in modern times, this was an important determining factor in the successful use of a site, but not necessarily in the initial choice. The large and deep draw-wells of the castles of Tantallon in East Lothian (32.3 m.) and Edinburgh (33.5 m.), for example, represent considerable feats of engineering, and show the depths to which an adequate supply of water would be sought on a site that was considered desirable from every other point of view.[28] The water-table was known or found to be easily reached in many castle precincts, and as at Dunnottar Castle in the Mearns cisterns or water-catchments were built or excavated to make thrifty use of the climate.[29] There are, however, a number of sites where the source and nature of the water supply remain unknown, Cardoness Castle in the Stewartry of Kirkcudbright being a good case in point.[30]

Major castles usually commanded the resources of a sizeable estate, and many of them — perhaps the majority — were positioned in close proximity to their more valuable and fertile lands, hence the siting of numerous castles that overlook tracts of land capable of growing cereal crops or of supporting profitable livestock farming, in the hillier upland areas. This direct relationship with the land is often reflected in the nature of the buildings themselves, as well as in their ancillary structures and enclosures.[31]

The nature, size, date and distribution of the medieval buildings in any given area usually provide a rough-and-ready guide to the local pattern and structure of landowning society. As a general rule, the more substantial piles stand at the centres of richly endowed lordships, have the earliest architectural origins within their own provinces, and usually have few, if any, near neighbours. Castles of very different types, such as those associated with the rich little barony of Dirleton in the champaign lands of East Lothian and the one-time thanage of Glamis in fertile Strathmore, share these underlying characteristics.[32] But the pattern is by no means uniform, and on the coastal plain of Buchan the relatively late but sizeable Fraser establishment at Pitullie stands close to the older and even larger centre of Forbes lordship at Pitsligo.[33] Physical neighbourliness to this somewhat uncomfortable degree might also be expected in those areas where small estates and commensurately small lairds' houses were the norm in the sixteenth and seventeenth centuries. This was in fact the case in other parts of the north-east, as well as in Fife and the Borders. There are few parallels, however, to the exceptionally close juxtaposition of Colmslie, Hillslap and Langshaw Towers that stand within a few hundred metres of each other in the valley of the Allan Water, north of Galashiels (plate 7).[34] Colmslie and Hillslap were erected by the Cairncross family in the latter half of the sixteenth century, on lands which they had previously held in tenancy of Melrose abbey; but family history alone does not account for their close proximity. It is not easy to understand the special importance attached to this piece of territory, or to imagine how the lands were shared out in the heyday of the towers.

Even allowing for later social, tenurial and agrarian changes, the settings of many fortified houses remain no more 'defensive' than those of their eighteenth- and nineteenth-century farmstead successors that stand close by or even encapsulate them. This process of continuity is especially noticeable in Fife, at places like Denmylne and Collairnie Castles. A similar process, ranging perhaps from a local sideways shift to complete physical integration, can also be seen at a higher social and architectural level, where later building styles and landscaped surroundings frequently disguise the fundamental continuity of siting. In eastern Scotland, Drum Castle (Aberdeenshire) (plate 8), Guthrie Castle (Angus) and Lennoxlove (East Lothian), among many others, demonstrate how later buildings of different genres have been tacked on to late medieval towers occupying what are eternally desirable and adaptable sites.[35]

There is thus a broad central zone of ambiguity between what might be regarded as a 'defensive' or a 'domestic' site. Whether employing natural advantages or not, the medieval castle appears to have been calculated to overawe by its apparent impregnability or inaccessibility; as in later times, possession was best secured without having to defend it. No band of peasants intent on mischief would parade openly in the landscaped policies of a mansion house any more than they would attempt the same in front of a medieval castle. An obvious point of difference, however, is the castle's provision of inbuilt features that could, if required, provide close-range defence. But the nature and purpose of these defences again pose problems of form and function. What was for show, and what for serious use? How far can thinking of a military nature be read into their designs? What changes were brought about by corresponding changes in weaponry, armaments and methods of siege-warfare?[36]

Man-made defensive features were of three main categories: firstly, outworks and enclosures (i.e., ditches, ramparts, timber stockades and stone curtain-walls) that provided successive deep or tall obstacles in the path of the would-be assailant; secondly, features associated with the upperworks of the curtain-walls and towers, ramparts or high-level platforms from which it was possible to conduct a 'drop on the head' form of defence; and, thirdly, special measures designed to protect the entrances, especially the main gateways, which were vulnerable points in any castle enceinte (plate 9).

The least ambiguous of these elements of defence in military terms, and the most enduring historically, were those involving the construction of earthen or rock-cut ditches and ramparts, techniques that have persisted with modifications into modern times. The island of Inchkeith in the Forth estuary, for example, still retains some of the ditches and trench-systems associated with its late nineteenth- and twentieth-century fortifications.[37] In Scotland, as elsewhere, the earliest castles were substantially of earth-and-timber construction, and survive most characteristically as mottes and baileys, a form of construction that is graphically depicted in the Bayeux Tapestry (plate 10).[38] Many of these, and cognate structures of later date, can reasonably be regarded as products of relatively urgent circumstances, being quicker, cheaper and less demanding to construct than sophisticated buildings of stone and lime. Chronicle sources suggest that the building of the second castle at York in 1069 took approximately eight days to complete.[39] Comparable castle-mounds in the Scottish countryside, even though generally smaller, probably took longer to build, with less manpower and equipment.

A transition from timber to stone and lime in the construction of enclosures and residential quarters became the norm among better-class castles in Scotland from the early thirteenth century onwards; the phenomenon cannot however be regarded as one of purely military origin.[40] It is true that a stone curtain was less easy to breach than a timber stockade. It is also true that in the hands of an intense and well-organised builder like Edward I of England, who brought the resources of a rich kingdom to bear on his military exploits, the circumstances of a stone castle's creation might be similar to those of its earth-and-timber counterparts. But the major Anglo-Welsh castles of the later thirteenth century, just like the grandiose 'first-generation' Norman stone towers of London and Colchester in late eleventh-century England, were in fact more than mere campaign castles: they were clearly intended to put the seal on military conquest. The simple truth was that stone castles were more costly and time-consuming to build. Edward I disbursed about £80,000 on eight castles in north Wales over a period of twenty-five years, and the most efficient single operation was the completion of Conway Castle in five building seasons between 1283 and 1287 at a cost of about £14,000.[41] No private builder could match this scale and pace of operation. The successful prosecution of any campaign of stone castle-building required not only careful preparation, expense and effort, but also physical and legal security of tenure and relatively undisturbed conditions over a number of years. It is not surprising, therefore, to find royal administrative centres such as Kincardine, Kinclaven (Perthshire) and Tarbert in Kintyre among the earliest stone castles in Scotland.[42] Likewise, the major thirteenth-century private castles, such as those of the Vaux family at Dirleton, of the Moravias at Bothwell (Lanarkshire) (plate 11), of the MacSweens at Castle Sween (Argyll), and of the Comyns at Inverlochy (Inverness-shire) (plate 4), arose in unexceptional — and inferentially quiet — circumstances at the hands of rich and powerful landowners.[43] For similar reasons, the early castles grouped around the Firth of Lorn and the Sound of Mull are likely to have been built a decade or even a generation after, rather than during or before, the last military campaign of King Alexander II in that area in 1249.[44] They probably mark the establishment of interdependent royal and baronial authority in a previously Norse-controlled zone of the western seaboard.

Theoretical military requirements undoubtedly governed much of the design of these early stone castles and their successors, but a purely deterministic view of castellar defences and siegecraft leaves much that is unexplained. The reach of scaling-ladders and siege-towers may have helped to determine the minimum heights and positions of castle walls and towers, but many were built far higher, often in places of considerable natural strength and relative inaccessibility. They convey an impression of height for height's sake, a symbolic attribute that doubtless accounts for the enduring popularity of the tower-house. And, whilst perhaps influenced initially by the capabilities of the medieval siege-engineer, the nature and thickness of the castle walls and their associated plinths can more often be related to the height and mass of walling above, or to the ground conditions below, than to the fear of breaching or undermining.[45] Defensive qualities are also traditionally ascribed to other conventional features of building construction such as stone vaulting, newel-stairs and slit-windows. Even the popular argument that military expediency, and in particular the threat of mining, perhaps derived from continental and crusading experiences, dictated the form of the rounded drum towers that became so fashionable in the thirteenth century cannot be convincingly demonstrated. Judging from their design and positioning, some thirteenth-century arrow-slits and sixteenth-century gun-ports could have been used only with great difficulty and very limited effect. By contrast, there is no mistaking the clearly warlike intent of the wide-mouthed cannon-ports associated with artillery fortresses from the sixteenth century onwards.[46]

Traditional accounts suggest a chronological progression from a functional to a decorative or symbolic use, particularly with regard to wall-head defences. But here the only significant development in the medieval period was a tendency towards all-stone in place of timber-and-stone construction for hourds, bretasches and machicolations. Such a long phase of relative stagnation leaves us somewhat uncertain about the balance that their useful and symbolic roles had reached by the later fifteenth century, a half-century or more before open wall-walks and battlemented parapets ceased to be built in Scotland. At the gatehouse there were few discernible 'progressive' refinements in drawbridge design, and portcullises were still being installed in front-rank royal works such as Stirling Castle in the early sixteenth century. The use of sliding wooden draw-bars to secure gates or doors, which continues into modern times, has an even greater antiquity, dating back to prehistory. Possibly the only major defensive innovation in this area originating in the later medieval period was that of the strong, cross-barred wrought-iron gate or 'yett'.[47]

Thus, alongside changes in the forms and emphasis of castle-planning was the underrated element of continuity. The idea of building intermediate and terminal turrets along a stretch of curtain-wall was by no means new in the Middle Ages and clearly derived from Roman practice. Furthermore, throughout the medieval period many lay-outs depended to the greatest extent on the configuration of the site itself. A screen-type forework with centrally-placed gatehouse, terminal towers and, in some cases, interval towers is found, for example, in work of about 1200 at Warkworth Castle in Northumberland; a similar lay-out, probably of mid-fourteenth-century date, occurs at Tantallon and St Andrews, and forms the basis of an early sixteenth-century reconstruction at Stirling Castle. On the western seaboard, developed fifteenth-century towers such as Kisimul, off the island of Barra, and Breachacha, on the island of Coll, differ from late thirteenth-century polygonal 'enclosure-castles' like Mingary and Tioram (Inverness-shire) only in minor matters of emphasis and detail.[48] From the first appearance of the stone-built castle in Scotland in about 1200 through to 1500 and beyond, there is thus a conservative adherence to established principles and techniques of fortification, a conclusion that echoes one reached some years ago in a study of the military architecture of Latin Syria.[49] The need for change in Scottish castle design may well have been less than what has been assumed, for even the advent of gunpowder artillery induced only a small and tardy architectural effect. It was not until about 1520 that fortresses in Scotland began to show a truly novel departure from medieval design, incorporating relatively low and massive curtain-walls with pointed angle-bastions capable of providing cannonfire in virtually all directions. Moreover, given the expense of castle-building and maintenance, a laird's ability to adapt his defences and all his other buildings to suit changing conditions probably always remained fairly limited.[50] The controlling effects of finance are perhaps best summed up in the inscription on Pinkie House (Midlothian) which, translated, reads 'Alexander, Lord Seton, built this house in 1613, not as he would have wished, but according to the measure of his means and estate'.

A similar conservatism can also be observed in domestic planning. The hall and the tower-blocks were the principal residential units of the Scottish medieval castle, and separately or together provided all the required accommodation. Once the fashion for tower-building had taken a firm hold among the nobility in the fourteenth century, it persisted with all grades of landholders for about three centuries, and, within what has been described as a narrow range of general design,[51] considerable variations in shape, size and elaboration were worked on the tower-house theme, giving rise to its famous alphabetical configurations, the so-called L-, T- and Z-plans. Hall-building practices had an even broader timespan. The first-floor hall-block in stone or timber was a feature of Scottish castle-planning

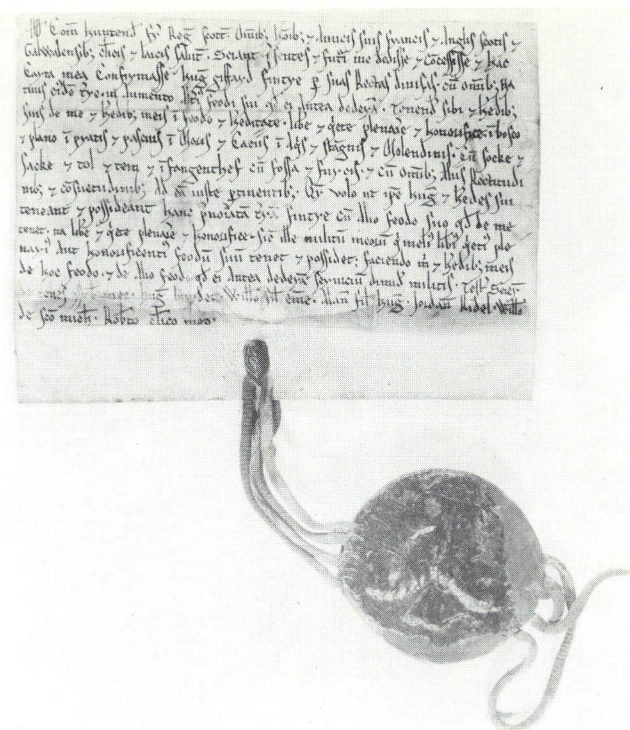

Plate 1. Charter of David, earl of Huntingdon, granting to Hugh Giffard, in feu and heritage, Fintry (Angus), in augmentation of the other feu which the earl had given him, to be held together for the service of half a knight (1173 × 1174; possibly 1185). (Scottish Record Office, GD 28/4 [size reduced]; reproduced by permission of the Keeper of the Records of Scotland.)

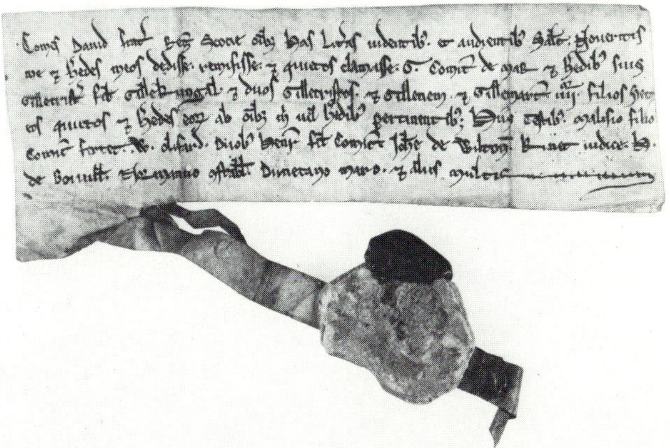

Plate 2. Charter of Earl David, brother of the king of Scotland, quitclaiming to G(illecrist), earl of Mar, Gillecrist son of Gillekungal and the four named sons of Set (1199 × 1207). (British Library, Harl. Chart. 83.C.24 [size reduced]; reproduced by permission of the British Library.)

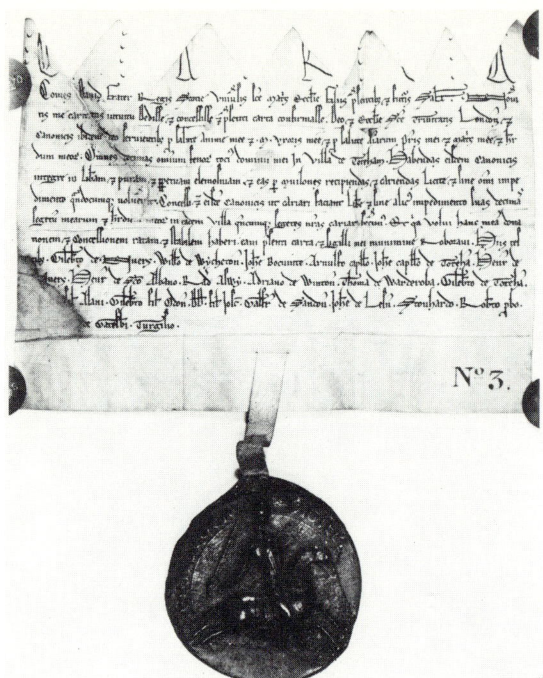

N° 3.

Plate 3. Charter of Earl David, brother of the king of Scotland, granting in alms to the priory of Holy Trinity (Aldgate), London, all the hay-tithes from his whole demesne in Tottenham (Middlesex) (probably *c.* 1209). (British Library, Campbell Chart. xxx, 3 [size reduced]; reproduced by permission of the British Library.)

Plate 4. Inverlochy Castle, Inverness-shire: view by Michel Bouquet, 1849.

Plate 5. Siege-tower: engraving from E. Viollet-le-Duc, *Dictionnaire raisonné de l'architecture française* (Paris, 1858–68), i, p. 365 (also reproduced in *idem, Military Architecture of the Middle Ages,* 2nd edn. [London, 1879], p. 65).

Plate 6. Crichton Castle, Midlothian: arcade detail (Crown Copyright, Royal Commission on the Ancient and Historical Monuments of Scotland).

Plate 7. Colmslie, Hillslap and Langshaw Towers, Roxburghshire: aerial view (Hillslap top centre, Colmslie middle right, and Langshaw bottom, left of centre, in wooded enclosure). (Crown Copyright, Royal Commission on the Ancient and Historical Monuments of Scotland.)

Plate 8. Drum Castle, Aberdeenshire: water-colour by David Bryce, *c.* 1876.

Plate 9. Dalhousie Castle, Midlothian: engraving from F. Grose, *The Antiquities of Scotland* (London, 1789–91), i, facing p. 69.

Plate 10. Motte-building: detail from the Bayeux Tapestry.

Plate 11. Bothwell Castle, Lanarkshire: thirteenth-century donjon (Crown Copyright, Scottish Development Department).

Plate 12. Dalquharran (Old) Castle, Ayrshire: engraving from Grose, *Antiquities of Scotland*, ii, facing p. 198.

Plate 13. Dean Castle, Kilmarnock, Ayrshire (now restored): engraving from Grose, *Antiquities of Scotland,* ii, facing p. 214.

Plate 14. Huntingtower, Perthshire: engraving of former ground-floor hall from Grose, *Antiquities of Scotland,* i, facing p. 245.

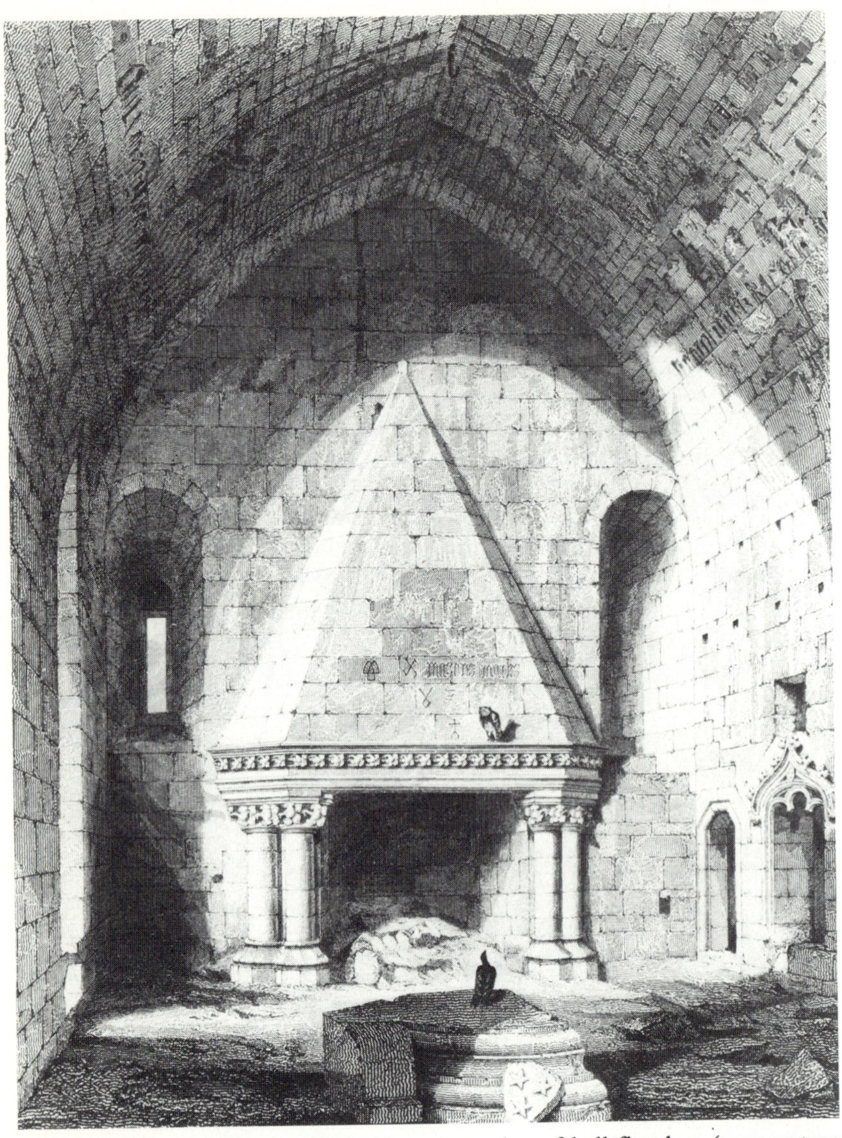

Plate 15. Borthwick Castle, Midlothian: engraving of hall fireplace (now restored) from R.W. Billings, *The Baronial and Ecclesiastical Antiquities of Scotland* (Edinburgh, 1848–52), i, plate 22.

throughout the Middle Ages, and the so-called 'hall-house' or fortified manor-house that stands independently of other major buildings belongs just as much to the later Middle Ages (e.g., plate 12) as it does to the thirteenth century. In any case, the distinction between a hall and a tower is a fine matter of degree, if not wholly imperceptible, in many elongated hall-like towers, particularly in those that date from the later fourteenth and sixteenth centuries. The design of these buildings was based not upon the tower as such, but upon its central feature, the oblong first-floor hall and its attendant chambers.[52]

In major establishments where ceremonial and public affairs justified it, and where wealth and status permitted, a range containing a great hall might be included in the castle establishment. This practice went back to the very beginnings of the feudal castle, but in Scotland became more manifest in the later medieval period when a number of impressive stone-built structures of this kind were erected (e.g., plate 13). The fashion continued into the sixteenth century, often, as at Melgund in Angus or Carnasserie in Argyll, with the difference that tower and hall formed an integral design. Ground-floor halls, a radical departure from tradition in Scottish houses of this rank, first made their appearance in the later sixteenth century, at places like Huntingtower in Perthshire (plate 14).[53] The early appearance of the long gallery and perhaps a slight increase in the amount of space given over to private chambers, as opposed to public rooms, constitute other observable trends;[54] but prior to the seventeenth century there were few other changes in architectural forms to give a clear pointer towards changes in modes of social and domestic life. To assume, for example, that the staffing of large establishments by military or domestic retinues was any the more significant or sinister in one age than another goes beyond what the physical evidence warrants.[55]

Nor do advances in domestic amenity follow a straightforward evolutionary pattern. Original chimneyed fireplaces are absent from major fifteenth-century towers such as Balgonie in Fife and Moy on Mull, places where they might reasonably have been expected, given the constructional skill that was then clearly available throughout the country (plate 15). Great halls such as those at Doune (Perthshire) and Bothwell Castles also seem to reflect a preference for open hearths or braziers for their public functions, with mural fireplaces confined to the private or lesser chambers. *Mutatis mutandis*, the distinction in usage and custom may have been similar to that which later obtained between open hearths in the kitchens and contemporary chimneyed fireplaces in the best or 'ben' rooms of nineteenth-century cottages and croft-houses.[56] Closely integrated kitchens are a marked feature of many late medieval house-plans, but others of later date and comparable quality, such as at Scotstarvit in Fife, had no special provision for cooking or baking actually within the tower.[57] However, by about 1600 the close garderobe or dry earth-closet with its soil-box had probably become the commonest type of toilet among lairds' houses, and the transition from open latrine could be construed as a slight but genuine improvement in sanitary conditions, long before the advent of detached 'little houses' and the even later WCs.

Following the first recorded use of glass for a secular building in Scotland (in the dying King Robert's chamber at Cardross, Dunbartonshire, in 1329),[58] the practice of glazing windows became more widespread during the later Middle Ages. By the seventeenth century the luxury of glazing was not just confined to the upper halves of the more important windows, and the glass might be backed by wooden shutters in the top as well as in the bottom halves of some openings. But there were no fundamental changes in fixed-frame window design and technology until the introduction of the vertical sliding sash-window into Scotland in 1673–4, and more generally after 1700.[59] The general trend, however, would suggest that the cost benefits of increased lighting and reduced draughtiness were considered increasingly worthwhile.

Another area in which there appears to have been some genuine advance was that of stair construction. Although straight flights of stairs were not uncommon in medieval castles, the circular or turnpike stair, often narrow and steep, was the norm until the last quarter of the sixteenth century. Thereafter, the straight flight or scale-and-platt stair, wider and with a much easier going than its predecessors, gradually came into fashion. Even in 1684, however, stairs such as these were still regarded as novel and noteworthy, and Robert Mylne was able to stress their advantages in the sale of his newly built block of mansion-flats in Edinburgh.[60]

A final and apposite comment on these aspects of 'improvement' is provided by an inscription on a panel at Lennoxlove, the East Lothian home of the Maitland family, later earls of Lauderdale: 'Who of the race of Maitland laid the foundation, who raised the tower, envious antiquity has concealed. John Maitland, Earl of Lauder, increased the lights, provided an easier stairway and made it more handsome in the year of the Christian era 1626.' In future assessments of the form, function and 'evolution' of the secular architecture of medieval and early modern Scotland it may be prudent to give 'envious antiquity' some moments' reconsideration, if not the benefit of a few nagging doubts.

NOTES

1. Detailed descriptions of the Scottish buildings and features mentioned here will be found in the standard works of reference: D. MacGibbon and T. Ross, *The Castellated and Domestic Architecture of Scotland* (Edinburgh, 1887–92); RCAHMS, *Inventories* (by county); and the guide books issued by the Scottish Development Department (Ancient Monuments). References cited in this account are in essence supplementary to these sources.

2. For artistic impressions of castles in Scottish and continental landscapes see, e.g., J. Holloway and L. Errington, *The Discovery of Scotland* (National Gallery of Scotland Exhibition Catalogue, 1978), and A.A. Tait, *Robert Adam and Scotland: The Picturesque Drawings* (Scottish Arts Council Exhibition Catalogue, 1972). See also *idem,* 'Robert Adam and the picturesque', in *Lairds and Improvement in the Scotland of the Enlightenment,* ed. T.M. Devine (Dundee, 1978), pp. 31–7.

3. *Origines Parochiales Scotiae* (Bannatyne Club, 1851–5), II, ii, p. 394; NLS MS 1648, Z3/26; *The Jacobite Attempt of 1719,* ed. W.K. Dickson (SHS, 1895), pp. xlv–ix; and for the restoration see the guide book (anon., n.d.).

4. Modern studies have been directed mainly towards the documented relationship between gunpowder weaponry and fortification in the sixteenth century: e.g., I. MacIvor, 'Craignethan Castle, Lanarkshire: an experiment in artillery fortification', in *Ancient Monuments and their Interpretation,* ed. M.R. Apted *et al* (London, 1977), pp. 239–61, and I. MacIvor, 'Artillery and major places of strength in the Lothians and the east Border,

1513–42', in *Scottish Weapons and Fortifications 1100-1800,* ed. D.H. Caldwell (Edinburgh, 1981), pp. 94–152.

5. E. Viollet-le-Duc, *Dictionnaire raisonné de l'architecture française* (Paris, 1858–68), and *idem, Military Architecture of the Middle Ages,* 2nd edn. (London, 1879). In his preface to the latter work, the publisher, J.H. Parker, wrote (at p. iii): 'My reason for republishing it at the present time is because I cannot help seeing how useful it would be for the officers of the English army in Zululand and other parts of South Africa, and in the savage parts of India, wherever the well-disciplined troops of civilised nations come into contact with savages.'

6. E.g., A.H. Thompson, *Military Architecture in England during the Middle Ages* (London, 1912), esp. Ch. 4; but contemporary influences are less noticeable in E.S. Armitage, *The Early Norman Castles of the British Isles* (London, 1912). W.D. Simpson exemplified the mood of a later generation confronted with mobile, efficient armies: see esp. his 'Castles of "livery and maintenance" ', *Journal of the British Archaeol. Assoc.,* iv (1939), pp. 39–54, and ' "Bastard feudalism" and the later castles', *Antiquaries Journal,* xxvi (1946), pp. 145–71.

7. Cf., e.g., S.H. Cruden, *The Scottish Castle,* revised edn. (Edinburgh, 1963), pp. 20–64. For 'hall-houses' as a building-type and their dating, see discussion in *Scottish Weapons,* ed. Caldwell, pp. 23–4, and refs. cited.

8. *Cast. and Dom. Arch.,* a pioneering work of reference, gave full weight to the domestic aspects, as did W.M. Mackenzie, *The Mediaeval Castle in Scotland* (Edinburgh, 1927). Mackenzie took G.T. Clark, and A.H. Thompson, to task for interpreting castle-towers or 'keeps' as mere places of refuge, and not as regular residential quarters: 'G.T. Clark's conclusion, mainly based on Victorian ideas of "comfort", was that "a Norman keep ... was not meant for a residence, save during an actual siege".' *Ibid.,* pp. 230–40, at p. 231, citing G.T. Clark, *Mediaeval Military Architecture in England* (London, 1884), i, p. 136.

9. M.W. Barley, *The House and Home* (London, 1963) and J. Ayres, *The Shell Book of the Home in Britain* (London, 1981) take some account of house design, construction and decoration in Scotland. See also M.R. Apted, *The Painted Ceilings of Scotland, 1550-1650* (Edinburgh, 1966); G. Beard, *Decorative Plasterwork in Great Britain* (London, 1975).

10. What is referred to in *Cast. and Dom. Arch.,* i, p. vi, as 'the gradual progress of Architecture from an early and rude epoch to more modern and refined times, as the growth of our national life and manners'.

11. Above, n. 4; B.H. St J. O'Neil, *Castles and Cannon* (Oxford, 1960).

12. A. Rowan, 'Crichton Castle, Midlothian', *Country Life* (7 January 1971), p. 17. Caerlaverock Castle (Dumfriesshire) exhibits a similar contrast between medieval and Renaissance work, particularly on the eastern side of the courtyard. There is an early scale-and-platt stair, probably of 1586, at Killochan Castle (Ayrshire): Mackenzie, *Mediaeval Castle,* p. 209.

13. Cf. M. Girouard, *Life in the English Country House* (New Haven and London, 1978), pp. 246–56.

14. Mackenzie, *Mediaeval Castle,* pp. 211–12; Cruden, *Scottish Castle,* pp. 151–2; W.D. Simpson, 'The tower houses of Scotland', in *Studies in Building History,* ed. E.M. Jope (London, 1961), pp. 235–6.

15. P.W. Dixon, 'Towerhouses, pelehouses and Border society', *Archaeol. Journal,* cxxxvi (1979), pp. 240–52. Cf. C. Ó Danachair, 'Irish tower houses and their regional distribution', *Bealoideas* (Journal of the Folklore of Ireland Soc.), xlv–vii (1979), pp. 158–63.

16. E.g., Auchterhouse and Murroes House (Angus); Pinkie House (Midlothian); Huntingtower (Perthshire); 'Argyll's Lodging', Stirling; The Binns (West Lothian).

17. Mackenzie, *Mediaeval Castle,* p. 74, and ref. cited.

18. 'By any meanes do not take away the battelment, as some gave me counsale to do, as Dalhoussy your nyghtbour did, for that is the grace of the house, and makes it look lyk a castle, and henc so nobleste, as the other would make it look lyke a peele': *Correspondence of Sir Robert Kerr, First Earl of Ancram and his son, William, Third Earl of Lothian* (Bannatyne Club, 1875), i, p. 64, partly cited (as p. 62) in RCAHMS, *Inventory of Roxburghshire,* ii, p. 485.

19. *Memoirs of Sir John Clerk of Penicuik, Baronet, 1676-1755,* ed. J.M. Gray (SHS, 1892), p. 6.

20. *Glamis Papers: The 'Book of Record',* ed. A.H. Millar (SHS, 1890), p. 33.

21. See also C. Coulson, 'Structural symbolism in medieval castle architecture', *Journal of the British Archaeol. Assoc.,* cxxxii (1979), pp. 73–90.

22. E.g., Dun Telve and Dun Troddan in Glen Beag, Inverness-shire: E.W. MacKie, 'The origin and development of the broch and wheelhouse building cultures of the Scottish Iron Age', *Proc. of the Prehistoric Soc.,* new ser., xxxi (1965), pp. 107–9. I am indebted to Dr J.N.G. Ritchie for this reference.

23. MacIvor, 'Craignethan Castle', p. 240, fig. 1. Craignethan was described in 1570 as 'a strong house ... but situate in a hole, so that it is commanded on every part': *ibid.,* p. 243, citing *Calendar of the State Papers relating to Scotland and Mary, Queen of Scots, 1547-1603* (Edinburgh, 1898–1969), iii, no. 250.

24. *TDGAS,* 3rd ser., xxii (1943), pp. 26–35; *PSAS,* xcii (1958–9), pp. 10–14; Cruden, *Scottish Castle,* pp. 95–6; *TDGAS,* 3rd ser., lvii (1982), p. 73.

25. According to Bishop Pococke in 1760, it was 'all a morassy soil till it was drained some years agoe and is called the Mire of Gaury': *Bishop Pococke's Tours in Scotland, 1747-60,* ed. D.W. Kemp (SHS, 1887), p. 259. Further, J. Donaldson, *General View of the Agriculture of the Carse of Gowrie in the County of Perth* (London, 1794), pp. 11–12, 34–5. The castles in question include Evelick, Fingask, Kinnaird, Megginch and Castle Huntly.

26. A.G. Ogilvie, 'The physiography of the Moray Firth coast', *Trans. of the Royal Soc. of Edinburgh,* liii (1923), pp. 377–404; J.D. Peacock *et al, The Geology of the Elgin District* Memoirs of the Geological Survey, Scotland, 1968), pp. 107–23. For Innes see esp. *RRS,* i, no. 175; C. Innes, *Ane Account of the Familie of Innes by Duncan Forbes of Culloden* (Spalding Club, 1864), pp. 166–72.

27. R.B. Armstrong, *The History of Liddesdale, Eskdale, Ewesdale, Wauchopedale and the Debateable Land* (Edinburgh, 1883), p. cxvi, cited in RCAHMS, *Inventory of Roxburghshire,* i, p. 75.

28. Cf., e.g., the well, rock-cut to a depth of over 200 ft. (60.96 m.), at Henry III's castle at Montgomery on the Welsh March: *Archaeol. Journal,* cxxxviii (1981), p. 18. For the historical background to this castle see *The History of the King's Works,* ed. H.M. Colvin (London, 1963–), ii, pp. 739–42.

29. J. Longmuir, *Dunnottar Castle, its Ruins and Historical Associations,* 10th edn. (Stonehaven, 1894), pp. 90–1. Cf. *Papers from the Collection of Sir William Fraser* (SHS, 1924), p. 49, and *The Register of the Privy Council of Scotland,* ed. J.H. Burton and D. Masson (Edinburgh, 1877–98), vii, pp. 746–7, cited by W.D. Simpson, *Dunnottar Castle* (Aberdeen, 1968), pp. 52–3.

30. For wells and water supply in general see Mackenzie, *Mediaeval Castle,* pp. 129–30.

31. E.g., in the cattle-raiding areas of the Border counties: RCAHMS, *Inventory of Roxburghshire,* i, pp. 43–5; ii, pp. 483–5; *APS,* ii, p. 346. For the development of the policies of landed estates after 1600 see T.R. Slater, 'The mansion and policy', in *The Making of the Scottish Countryside,* ed. M.L. Parry and T.R. Slater (London, 1980), pp. 223–47.

32. For the wealth of the Dirleton estate in the seventeenth century see I.D. Whyte, *Agriculture and Society in Seventeenth-Century Scotland* (Edinburgh, 1979), p. 37. For Dirleton Castle see also W.D. Simpson in *TGAS,* new ser., viii (1927), pp. 1–31, *SHR,* xxvii (1948), pp. 48–56, and *Trans. of the East Lothian Antiquarian and Field Naturalists' Soc.,* iii (1938), pp. 1–18; further, W. Douglas, 'The owners of Dirleton', *History of the Berwickshire Naturalists' Club,* xxvii (1929–31), pp. 75–92. For Glamis, n. 20 above.

33. For Pitsligo see W.D. Simpson, *PSAS,* lxxxviii (1954–6), pp. 125–9.

34. Cf. also the grouping of three towers in Darnick village, near Melrose, of which two survive (RCAHMS, *Inventory of Roxburghshire,* ii, nos. 580–1), and those on the banks of the Kirtle Water in Dumfriesshire: Bonshaw, Robgill and Woodhouse Towers, with Blackwood House not far upstream (RCAHMS, *Inventory of Dumfriesshire,* nos. 1, 107, 368, 460). For Bonshaw see also *TDGAS,* 3rd ser., xx (1935–6), pp. 147–56; *ibid.,* xliv (1967), pp. 224–6.

35. Plans, and copies of plans, relating to later works at Drum and Lennoxlove are deposited in the National Monuments Record of Scotland. For Guthrie see also *Mr David Bryce*, ed. V. Fiddes and A. Rowan (Edinburgh, 1976), p. 122; for Lennoxlove, J.G. Dunbar, 'The building-activities of the duke and duchess of Lauderdale, 1670–82', *Archaeol. Journal*, cxxxii (1975), pp. 217–21.

36. For further discussion of some of the evidence in relation to later medieval castles see the chapters in *Scottish Society in the Fifteenth Century*, ed. J.M. Brown (London, 1977), pp. 153–83, at pp. 159–61, and in *Scottish Weapons*, ed. Caldwell, pp. 21–54, at pp. 30–49.

37. For Inchkeith see, e.g., R.S. Mylne, *The Master Masons to the Crown of Scotland* (Edinburgh, 1893), pp. 53–4; J. Grant, *Old and New Edinburgh*, iii (London, 1882), pp. 290–4; RCAHMS, *Inventory of Fife*, no. 347. For references to early artillery earthworks, *Scottish Weapons*, p. 53, n. 49. The beginnings of modern trench-warfare can probably be dated to the battle of Magersfontein, December 1899: R. Kruger, *Goodbye Dolly Gray* (London, 1983 edn.), pp. 129–30.

38. Above, Ch. 1, and refs. cited at pp. 11–14. Further, E.J. Talbot in *Scottish Weapons*, pp. 1–9.

39. Orderic Vitalis, *Historia Ecclesiastica*, ii, ed. M. Chibnall (Oxford, 1969), ii, p. 222, cited in R.A. Brown, *English Castles*, 3rd edn. (London, 1976), pp. 155–6; Royal Commission on Historical Monuments (England), *Inventory of the City of York*, ii, pp. 59–60, 74. It also took eight days to build an earthwork castle within the fortifications at Dover in October 1066: Brown, *English Castles*, p. 46.

40. Note also the emergence of even greater numbers of Scottish nobles into the stone-building class from the late fourteenth century onwards. Then, as earlier, wealth, political affiliations, the state of the building industry, and tenurial status were important background factors. The extent to which Henry II's codification of possessory assizes and proprietary actions conditioned private castle-building in England from the later twelfth century is a question that has remained unexplored.

41. J.G. Edwards, 'Edward I's castle-building in Wales', *Proc. of the British Academy*, xxxii (1946), pp. 15–81; A.J. Taylor, 'Castle-building in Wales in the later thirteenth century: the prelude to construction', in *Studies in Building Hist.*, ed. Jope, pp. 104–33; A. J. Taylor in *Hist. King's Works*, ed. Colvin, i, pp. 293–408, at pp. 337–54 for Conway Castle and Town.

42. J.G. Dunbar and A.A.M. Duncan, 'Tarbert Castle', *SHR*, l (1971), pp. 1–17.

43. For Dirleton see n. 32 above; for Bothwell, W.D. Simpson in *PSAS*, lix (1924–5), pp. 165–93, *TGAS*, new ser., xi (1947), pp. 97–116, and *Archaeologia Aeliana*, 4th ser., xxxii (1954), pp. 100–15; for Castle Sween, *idem*, *TGAS*, new ser., xv (1960–7), pp. 3–14, and W.D.H. Sellar, 'Family origins in Cowal and Knapdale', *Scottish Studies*, xv (1971), pp. 21–37.

44. Cf. RCAHMS, *Inventory of Argyll*, ii, no. 287; iii, nos. 332–3, 345; W.D. Simpson, *Dunstaffnage Castle and the Stone of Destiny* (Edinburgh, 1958); *idem*, *TGAS*, new ser., xiii (1954), pp. 70–90; H.B. Millar, *ibid.*, xv (1960–7), pp. 53–7.

45. For mining operations at the Norse siege of 'the castle in Bute' (Rothesay) in 1230, see Anderson, *Early Sources*, ii, p. 476; for the few successful mining operations against English castles, Brown, *English Castles*, pp. 190–3. A mine and counter-mine still survive from the siege of 1546/7 at St Andrews Castle: see esp. *Letters and Papers, Foreign and Domestic, of the Reign of Henry VIII* (London, 1862–1932), xxi, II, no. 380.

46. See, e.g., MacIvor, 'Artillery'; J.R. Kenyon, 'Wark Castle and its artillery defences in the reign of Henry VIII', *Post-Medieval Archaeology*, xi (1977), pp. 50–60. For gun-ports, e.g., A.M.T. Maxwell-Irving, 'Early firearms and their influence on the military and domestic architecture of the Borders', *PSAS*, ciii (1970–1), pp. 192–223; D.H. Caldwell, 'Guns in Scotland: the manufacture and use of guns and their influence on warfare from the fourteenth century to *c.*1625' (unpublished Edinburgh University Ph.D. thesis, 1982), ii, pp. 438–528. For bows and arrow-slits, Mackenzie, *Mediaeval Castle*, pp. 103–4; P.N. Jones and D. Renn, 'The military effectiveness of arrow loops: some experiments at White Castle', *Château Gaillard*, ix-x (1982), pp. 445–56.

47. D. Christison, 'On the grated iron doors of Scottish castles', *PSAS,* xvii (1882–3), pp. 98–135; *idem,* 'Additional notices of yetts or grated iron doors', *ibid.,* xxii (1887–8), pp. 286–320.

48. For Kisimul see J.G. Dunbar, *Glasgow Archaeol. Journal,* v (1978), pp. 25–43; for Breachacha, W.D. Simpson, *TGAS,* new ser., x (1941), pp. 26–54, and D.J. Turner and J.G. Dunbar, *PSAS,* cii (1969–70), pp. 155–87; for Mingary and Tioram, W.D. Simpson, *TGAS,* new ser., xiii (1954), pp. 70–90.

49. R.C. Smail, *Crusading Warfare 1097-1193* (Cambridge, 1956), pp. 204–50, esp. pp. 215–17.

50. Apart from a few entries in the fragmentary exchequer records of the thirteenth century, the earliest detailed building accounts in Scotland are those relating to the activities of Edward I described in *Hist. King's Works,* i, pp. 409–22. For the cost and duration of secular building works that can be roughly matched against surviving architecture see, e.g., *ER,* iv, pp. cxxxvi-ix, and refs. cited (Linlithgow Palace); vii, pp. l-iv, (Ravenscraig Castle, Fife); *Accounts of the Masters of Works,* ed. H.M. Paton *et al* (Edinburgh, 1957–), *passim* (royal castles and palaces, mainly Edinburgh, Falkland, Holyrood, Linlithgow, Stirling); Dixon, 'Towerhouses', p. 246, and refs. cited (Branxholme Castle, Roxburghshire, rebuilt March 1571–October 1576 according to inscription on building); *The Diary of Mr James Melvill, 1556-1601,* ed. G.R. Kinloch (Bannatyne Club, 1829), p. 5 (Manse, Anstruther Easter, Fife, June 1590–March 1591). This kind of evidence is more plentiful for the seventeenth century: see, e.g., n. 26 above (Innes House, Moray); *Accounts of the Masters of Works,* ii, *passim*; Mylne, *Master Masons, passim.*

Reasons other than financial may have accounted for the state of some buildings known or said to have been unfinished (e.g., Barnes Castle, East Lothian, MacLellan's Castle, Kirkcudbright, Mars Wark, Stirling, and an unnamed house in Latheron parish, Caithness [Walter Macfarlane, *Geographical Collections relating to Scotland* (SHS, 1906–8), i, pp. 163–4]). The profits as well as the losses of war account for some of the differences in the building abilities of fourteenth-century nobles in Scotland and England: K.B. McFarlane, *The Nobility of Later Medieval England* (Oxford, 1973), pp. 19–40, 92–5, adding G.W.S. Barrow, 'The aftermath of war: Scotland and England in the late thirteenth and early fourteenth centuries', *Trans. of the Royal Historical Soc.,* 5th ser., xxviii (1978), pp. 103–26. Proceeds from plunder seem to have formed the basis of the tower-building activities of some sixteenth-century Scottish lairds, particularly on the West March of the Border: Dixon, 'Towerhouses'; see also D. Hay, 'Booty in Border warfare', *TDGAS,* 3rd ser., xxxi (1952–3), pp. 145–66.

51. J. Summerson, *Architecture in Britain, 1530-1830,* 7th edn. (Harmondsworth, 1983), p. 537. For the earliest group of towers see *Cast. and Dom. Arch.,* i, pp. 143–221; iii, pp. 114–60 (some revision of dating since then); Cruden, *Scottish Castle,* pp. 100–23. Unconvincing claims for the existence of stone tower-houses in Scotland before the fourteenth century were made by W.D. Simpson, *The Book of Dunvegan* (Third Spalding Club, 1938–9), i, pp. xxxix–xl n; see also Cruden, *Scottish Castle, loc. cit*; RCAHMS, *Inventory of Orkney,* ii, no. 619.

52. Mackenzie, *Mediaeval Castle,* p. 208; n. 7 above. Examples of other late medieval 'hall-houses' include Huntly and Drumminor Castles, Aberdeenshire: Mackenzie, *Mediaeval Castle,* pp. 151–2; W.D. Simpson in *PSAS,* lvi (1921–2), pp. 134–63, and *ibid.,* lxvii (1932–3), pp. 137–60; T. Innes of Learney, *ibid.,* lxix (1934–5), pp. 387–97; H.G. Slade, *ibid.,* xcix (1966–7), pp. 148–66. For fortified manor-houses in England see, e.g., D. Williams, *Trans. of the Leicestershire Archaeol. and Historical Soc.,* l (1974–5), pp. 1–16; H.E.J. Le Patourel, *Château Gaillard,* ix–x (1982), pp. 187–98.

53. See n. 16 above; for late medieval great halls, *Scottish Soc. in the Fifteenth Cent.,* ed. Brown, pp. 157–9.

54. Mackenzie, *Mediaeval Castle,* pp. 116, 121–2, 158. For these trends in England, E. Mercer, 'The houses of the gentry', *Past and Present,* v (1954), pp. 11–32; *idem, English Art, 1553-1625* (Oxford, 1962), pp. 12–59.

55. Cf. W.D. Simpson, 'Doune Castle', *PSAS,* lxxii (1937–8), pp. 73–83; *idem,* as in n. 6 above.

56. A. Fenton, *The Hearth in Scotland* (Edinburgh and Dundee, 1981), *passim*; see also the nineteenth-century examples discussed in *Caithness: A Cultural Crossroads,* ed. J.R. Baldwin (Edinburgh, 1982), pp. 88–91.

57. Note also the arrangements at, e.g., the late medieval tower of Kinnaird, Perthshire, where the kitchen is contained in an outbuilding dated 1610.

58. *ER,* i, p. 125; also *Accounts of the Lord High Treasurer of Scotland,* ed. T. Dickson and J.B. Paul (Edinburgh, 1877–1916), i, pp. ccii–iii.

59. Dunbar, 'Building-activities', p. 219, and refs. cited; also H.J. Louw, 'The origin of the sash-window', *Architectural History,* xxvi (1983), pp. 49–72.

60. I.A. Stirling, *The Book of the Old Edinburgh Club,* xiv (1924), pp. 45–8.

10

EXTINCTION OF DIRECT MALE LINES AMONG SCOTTISH NOBLE FAMILIES IN THE FOURTEENTH AND FIFTEENTH CENTURIES

Alexander Grant

The starting-point for this essay comes from two lectures, on the French and English nobilities respectively, by Édouard Perroy and K.B. McFarlane. Perroy's, on 'Social mobility among the French *noblesse* in the later Middle Ages', was delivered to an Anglo-French conference of historians in 1961 and published in *Past and Present* the following year.[1] It was based on his detailed researches into noble families, or *lignages*, within the medieval county of Forez, in south-central France. Among other things, Perroy found that he could identify 215 noble *lignages* in the thirteenth century — taking 'noble' in its widest, continental, sense, and thus including those which in an English context would count as gentry. Of these, 66, or 30 per cent of the total, had already become extinct in the male line by the end of the thirteenth century; between 1300 and 1400, 80 of the surviving 149, or 54 per cent, became extinct; and, between 1400 and 1500, 38 of the surviving 69, or 55 per cent, died out in their turn. Perroy therefore concluded that, roughly speaking, the Forez *noblesse* was losing about half its members in each century, and that the average duration of each noble *lignage* was hardly more than three or four generations. Admittedly Perroy only examined Forez; but, as his title implies, he considered his conclusions could probably be applied to the country as a whole. Certainly the four generations of the greatest French noble house, the Valois dukes of Burgundy (1363–1477), fit the pattern exactly; and — although 'as a subject the French nobility in the later middle ages is hardly an overworked field'[2] — other studies tend to support the general contention.[3]

McFarlane's lecture is 'Extinction and recruitment', part of his Oxford course of 1965 on the English nobility, and included in the published version of his 1953 Ford Lectures, *The Nobility of Later Medieval England*.[4] He looked at the whole of England, but limited himself to the parliamentary peerage, the important men who received individual summonses to attend parliaments, and who eventually, as 'the House of Lords', arrogated the English concept of nobility to themselves. This produced a total of 357 leading families whose genealogical histories are traceable: 136 whose heads had already received individual summonses by 1300, and 221 who did so between then and 1500. McFarlane calculated that by 1500 only 16 of the original 136, or less than 12 per cent, were still surviving in unbroken male descent; and in each 25-year generation but one no fewer than a quarter of the families under examination died out in the male line, with the extinction rate being as high as 35 per cent between 1400 and 1424.[5] This is an even greater turnover than that found by Perroy in Forez. But it must be stressed that McFarlane, unlike Perroy, defined extinction in the male line according to the strict rules of primogeniture. Extinction was reckoned to have taken place when the head of a family died leaving no heirs, or only a female heir or heirs, or a male heir or heirs whose right to the inheritance came through a female. Thus when a noble left daughters but no sons, his family was counted as extinct even if a junior male line continued through brothers and cousins; furthermore, this principle was applied even in the cases of families whose estates were entailed on heirs-male.[6] Such an approach will obviously produce a higher rate of failure in the male line than one which simply measures the survival of lineages. This no doubt explains why McFarlane's researches show more extinctions than Perroy's; once it is allowed for, it may be concluded that survival rates in the male line among the English and French nobilities of the later Middle Ages were probably roughly similar. The main point, of course, is that in both countries, in McFarlane's words, 'the turnover was always rapid, the eminence short-lived, the survivors invariably few'.[7]

Were the English and French experiences also shared by the late medieval Scottish nobility? Did its families, too, suffer from this striking inability to maintain direct male descent for more than a few generations at a time? Before we begin to answer these questions, two preliminary comments are required. First, this essay will follow the practice adopted by McFarlane for defining a family's extinction in the direct male line. Therefore the succession of a collateral male heir by virtue of a tailzie, or entail, will count as the extinction of one line and the creation of another. It might be objected that this approach exaggerates the number of extinctions; but it is necessary in order to make comparisons with the extinction rates calculated for England, and it is also probably the only way of dealing with both entailed and non-entailed inheritances together (something which is necessary because the practice of creating entails only spread slowly and haphazardly among the late medieval nobility). Moreover, since collateral male heirs who inherited through entails were often landowners in their own rights, inheritance through entails could have an important effect on the broad pattern of a country's landownership, just as did inheritances through females. Thus it is the extinction of the *direct* male line, irrespective of whether the inheritance went to a female or to a collateral male branch, which is the significant point.

Secondly, as McFarlane found for England,[8] there is insufficient evidence for a full statistical study including the lesser Scottish nobility (the equivalent of the English gentry[9]), even within a region. This essay will therefore be restricted to the major nobles. But here there is a problem, too. From the mid-fifteenth century the major Scottish nobles, or 'higher nobility', can be equated simply with the parliamentary peerage: the 'lords' (dukes, earls and lords of parliament), who had a hereditary right to individual parliamentary summonses, as opposed to the 'lairds', who did not. Scotland's parliamentary peerage, however, did not emerge in an institutionalised form until the later 1440s;[10] before then, while some nobles were obviously more important than others, the higher nobility as a whole is indefinable. It must have contained dukes, earls and certain barons, but no clear-cut way of distinguishing 'greater barons' from the rest of the baronage exists.[11] As we shall see, the problem is not insurmountable. But because of it, it is best to begin by examining the dukes and earls separately from the rest of the higher nobility, which cannot be identified so easily (at least not before about 1450) and so cannot be analysed with quite the same precision.

The number and rate of extinctions in the direct male line experienced by late medieval Scotland's ducal and comital families are presented in Table 6.[12] It demonstrates clearly that very high extinction rates were suffered in most generations. Few individual families, in fact, survived in the direct male line for any length of time. Thus of the first Scottish dukes, David, duke of Rothesay, died childless in 1402;[13] and although Robert, duke of Albany, had four sons, his line did not survive beyond his grandsons. What happened in most earldoms can be illustrated from the cases of Atholl, Mar and Douglas. The Strathbogie line of earls of Atholl, which suffered forfeiture after 1314 for their English allegiance (albeit briefly reinstated in 1334), became extinct in the direct male line in 1369. John Campbell, to whom Robert I gave the earldom, died childless at Halidon Hill in 1333. Atholl was then held successively by Robert Stewart (eventually King Robert II), his son John, earl of Carrick (eventually Robert III), and his grandson David, duke of Rothesay. After Rothesay's death it was given to Robert II's youngest son, Walter; but his line ended abruptly in 1437 when he and his grandson were executed for their part in James I's assassination. Finally, Atholl was granted to James II's half-brother John Stewart in the early 1450s,[14] and his line held it until 1595. In Mar, the old line of earls had survived more successfully than most, but after Earl Thomas died childless in about 1374, Mar went to his sister's husband, the first earl of Douglas. When the second earl of Douglas died childless at Otterburn in 1388, his sister Isabella inherited Mar, and took it to two husbands, Malcolm Drummond (who died childless in 1402) and Alexander Stewart respectively. Stewart had no legitimate children; and although he arranged with James I for his illegitimate son Thomas to succeed, Thomas in fact predeceased his father, and this comital family died out in 1435. Despite the claims of Lord Erskine, Mar escheated to the crown; it was bestowed in about 1458 on James II's youngest son, who died childless in 1480, and then in 1486 went to James III's youngest son, who also died childless, in 1503. As for the earldom of Douglas, the original direct male line ceased when the second earl was killed at Otterburn. By virtue of a tailzie made in 1342, the main Douglas lands, and with them the title of earl, went to Archibald 'the Grim', illegitimate son of Robert I's companion 'the Good Sir James'. In turn his male line became extinct, strictly speaking, at the notorious 'Black Dinner', when the sixth earl and his brother were put to death, partly at least

Table 6. *Extinctions in the direct male line among Scottish ducal and comital families, 1300–1500 (calculated over 25-year generations)*

	1300–1324	1325–1349	1350–1374	1375–1399	1400–1424	1425–1449	1450–1474	1475–1500
Families at beginning of generation:	13	11	11	9	11	12	11	21
New families during generation:	2	6	6	6	4	6	14	3
TOTAL OF DUCAL AND COMITAL FAMILIES:	15	17	17	15	15	18	25	24
EXTINCTIONS:	4	6	8	4	3	7	4	4
EXTINCTION RATE:	27%	35%	47%	27%	20%	39%	16%	17%

to the benefit of their great-uncle,[15] who under the tailzie became the seventh earl of Douglas. The seventh earl left five sons, but of these, James II killed the eldest, the eighth earl, in 1452, the three younger brothers perished in 1455, and the ninth earl, having forfeited the earldom, eventually died childless in 1491.

As Table 6 indicates, the experiences of these families were echoed in most of the other earldoms. The only exceptions are March (or Dunbar), where the male line seems to have lasted from Cospatric in the eleventh century until 1564[16] (although the earldom itself was forfeited in 1435), Sutherland, where it lasted from the early thirteenth century until 1514, Crawford, where it lasted from the earldom's creation in 1398 until 1542, and several of the new earldoms of the later fifteenth century, whose families (as we shall see) were much more fortunate with respect to survival in the male lines. Otherwise, it is clear that the families of late medieval Scotland's earls and dukes suffered from exactly the same tendency towards extinction in the direct male line as did their counterparts in England and France.

What of the rest of the Scottish higher nobility? As has been stated already, from the mid-fifteenth century this can be identified with the lords of parliament. The 1440s saw 21 lordships of parliament come into existence;[17] in 1452 James II created seven more;[18] and from then until the end of the fifteenth century their number fluctuated between 27 and 33 (new creations were almost exactly balanced by extinctions and promotions to the rank of earl). For the generations after 1450, therefore, extinction rates can be calculated as precisely as with the earls and dukes. But for the fourteenth and earlier fifteenth centuries, our analysis is affected by the fact that the major Scottish barons did not then constitute such an institutionalised and identifiable body.[19] In that period, however, some barons clearly stand out from the mass of the nobility, and so the concept of a higher nobility is not out of place, even although there was no parliamentary peerage. And in fact, by examining contemporary material such as the parliamentary records, it has proved possible to identify in successive generations groups of 30 or more leading barons who can at least roughly be equated with the later fifteenth-century lords of parliament. Analysis of what happened to the families of these barons provides a good, if not absolutely precise, indication of extinction rates among the rest of the Scottish higher nobility during the fourteenth and earlier fifteenth centuries.

We can start, in the early fourteenth century, with the Declaration of Arbroath of 1320, which was ostensibly sent to the pope in the names of eight earls and 31 barons.[20] Being specifically named as a signatory to the Declaration is closely equivalent to receiving a personal summons to parliament, which later was what defined the lords of parliament; and there is a striking coincidence between the number of barons named in the Declaration and the number (27 to 33) of lords of parliament of the later fifteenth century. The following barons are named in the Declaration:

> Walter Stewart, William Soules, James Douglas, Roger Mowbray, David Brechin, David Graham of Montrose, Ingram Umfraville, John Menteith, Alexander Fraser of Touch, Gilbert Hay of Erroll, Robert Keith, Henry Sinclair, John Graham of Abercorn, David Lindsay of Crawford, William Oliphant, Patrick Graham of Lovat, John Fenton, William Abernethy, David Wemyss, William Muschet, Fergus

Ardrossan, Eustace Maxwell, William Ramsay of Dalhousie, William Mowat, Alan Murray of Culbin, Donald Campbell (of Loudon[21]), John Cameron of (?) Baledgarno,[22] Reginald Cheyne, Alexander Seton, Andrew Leslie, Alexander Straiton.

It has, however, been pointed out that the Declaration of Arbroath does not give a complete roll-call of the leading barons of Robert I's regime. Professor Barrow has referred to the omission of 'men such as Andrew Murray of Bothwell, Robert Lauder [of the Bass] and Robert Menzies [of Weem]';[23] the west-coast magnates Angus Macdonald of the Isles, Reginald Macruarie of Garmoran and Colin Campbell of Lochawe are especially conspicuous by their absence;[24] and Robert Boyd, Robert Bruce of Liddesdale (illegitimate son of the king), Malcolm Fleming, Adam Gordon and Walter son of Gilbert (progenitor of the Hamiltons) were also prominent figures in the 1320s.[25] In order to make the analysis as comprehensive as possible, therefore, the families of these 11 barons have been added to those derived from the Declaration, to give a total of 42 in all.[26]

Among these families, the shortest-lived was that of David Brechin, who was executed as an accessory to the Soules conspiracy only four months after the date of the Declaration of Arbroath. The longest-lived, conversely, was easily that of David Graham of Montrose: it has lasted in direct unbroken male descent until the present day. But the fate of the other two families of Graham was rather more typical: John Graham of Abercorn's direct male line had died out by 1350, while Patrick Graham of Lovat's had probably done so by 1367. The complete analysis of the 42 families is as follows.[27]

Extinct in direct male line before 1350: 14 (33%).
(Ardrossan, Brechin, Bruce of Liddesdale, Cheyne, Fraser of Touch, Graham of Abercorn, Keith, Macruarie, Mowbray, Muschet, Seton, Soules, Umfraville, Wemyss.)

Extinct in direct male line before 1400: 7 (17%).
(Cameron of Baledgarno, Douglas, Fleming, Graham of Lovat, Lindsay of Crawford, Menteith, Murray of Bothwell.)

Extinct in direct male line during 15th century: 8 (19%).
(Abernethy, Boyd, Fenton, Gordon, Leslie, Macdonald, Mowat, Murray of Culbin.)

Surviving in direct male line beyond 1500: 13 (31%).
(Campbell of Lochawe, Campbell of Loudon, Graham of Montrose, Hamilton,[28] Hay, Lauder, Maxwell, Menzies, Oliphant, Ramsay, Sinclair, Stewart, Straiton.)

For these families, therefore, the fourteenth century was much worse than the fifteenth, so far as extinction in the direct male line is concerned. Exactly half of them failed to survive the 80 years from 1320 to 1400; but of those which did survive, almost two-thirds also survived beyond 1500 — and well beyond it, in several cases.

Does this pattern of extinction apply to the late medieval Scottish higher nobility below the rank of earl as a whole? For the period from 1350 to 1500, there are unfortunately no individual documents so helpful to the present analysis as the Declaration of Arbroath, but a fairly good idea of the leading barons in each generation can be obtained from the following sources: the arrangements for David II's and James I's hostages negotiated in 1357 and 1423–4 respectively; the records of parliamentary committees and enlarged royal councils in the 1360s and 1390s; an analysis of the possession of baronies in the 1370s and 1420s; the witnesses to royal charters, major recipients of royal patronage, and exchequer auditors throughout the period; and the names of the earliest lords of parliament.[29] In dealing with the families identified in this way, however, it is necessary to allow for promotion to the rank of earl: the extinction of a family after it had risen to comital status (as, most obviously, in the case of the house of Douglas) will have already been counted in the calculations for the earls and dukes. Similarly, if a family clearly lost its prominence in national affairs (as had happened by 1350 with Fenton of Baikie, Murray of Culbin and several of the others named in the Declaration of Arbroath), then it should no longer be included in the calculations of extinction rates, which are here meant to apply only to the higher nobility.[30] Thus for each generation we must ask not only whether a family survived or became extinct in the direct male line, but also whether it gained the rank of earl or lost its earlier prominence. Full details of this exercise are given below, in the Appendix, and the results are summarised in Table 7.

What Table 7 confirms beyond any doubt is that extinction rates among the leading Scottish baronial families — who may reasonably be equated with the higher nobility below the rank of earl — declined steadily and indeed dramatically during the fourteenth and fifteenth centuries. The conclusion can be illustrated by following the descent of certain estates. The barony of Ardrossan, for instance, was created by Robert I for Fergus of Ardrossan, one of the signatories of the Declaration of Arbroath. Fergus left only a daughter, who inherited Ardrossan and

Table 7. *Extinctions in the direct male line among the families of leading Scottish barons and lords of parliament, 1325–1500 (calculated over 25-year generations)*

	1325–1349	1350–1374	1375–1399	1400–1424	1425–1449	1450–1474	1475–1500
Families surviving from previous generation:	—	21	36	35	35	31	32
Additional leading families:	—	34	9	7	3	10	8
TOTAL OF LEADING FAMILIES:	41	55	45	42	38	41	40
EXTINCTIONS:	10	8	5	4	2	3	2
EXTINCTION RATE:	24%	15%	11%	10%	5%	7%	5%
Families which gained earldoms:	1	3	4	1	4*	7*	2
Families which lost national prominence:	9	8	1	2	2	0	0

The figures for 'families surviving from previous generations' have been calculated by subtracting the number of families which became extinct, gained earldoms or lost national prominence from the total number of leading families in each preceding generation.

*This figure includes one family which gained an earldom and then became extinct in the same generation.

brought it to her husband Hugh Eglinton; he in turn was succeeded by a daughter in 1378, and Ardrossan was duly acquired by her husband, John Montgomery — whose descendants in the direct male line possessed it until 1612.[31] Or consider the baronies of Abercorn and Dalkeith, held in 1320 by John Graham. Graham left a son, who died childless soon after 1342, and two daughters. Abercorn went with the elder daughter to William Mure, and then in the 1380s with Mure's daughter and heiress to William Lindsay of Byres — with whose male descendants it remained for over a century, until 1497.[32] Dalkeith, meanwhile, had been acquired by William Douglas of Liddesdale (possibly through marriage with John Graham's younger daughter). When Douglas was killed in 1353 he left only a daughter; in default of sons Dalkeith went through a tailzie to his nephew and heir-male James Douglas — and it stayed with James's male descendants until the direct line died out in 1550.[33] In each example, a sequence of male-line extinctions was followed by a long period of survival in the direct line.

As Table 7 demonstrates, throughout the fourteenth and fifteenth centuries the pattern of male-line extinctions among Scotland's leading barons and lords of parliament contrasts sharply with that found for the earls and dukes — and also with the pattern found for their contemporaries in England and France.[34] Moreover, when the figures in Tables 6 and 7 are combined in order to give an impression of extinctions among the Scottish higher nobility as a whole during the later Middle Ages, the result — presented in Table 8 — still shows significantly low rates of extinction after 1375, especially by comparison with England, despite the high level of failures among the families of Scotland's earls and dukes. Thus in the generations after 1375 the major Scottish families below the rank of earl were so successful at surviving in the direct male line that the general pattern of extinction among late medieval Scotland's higher nobility turns out to be very different from that calculated for other countries.

It is one thing to identify this remarkable Scottish pattern of extinctions, or rather survivals; quite another to explain it. The only concrete point that can be made is

Table 8. *Extinctions in the direct male line among the Scottish and English higher nobilities, 1325–1500*

	1325–1349	1350–1374	1375–1399	1400–1424	1425–1449	1450–1474	1475–1500
Scottish Families							
Dukes and earls:	17	17	15	15	18	25	24
Others*:	40	52	41	41	34	34	38
TOTAL:	57	69	56	56	52	59	62
EXTINCTIONS:	16	16	9	7	8	6	6
EXTINCTION RATE:	28%	24%	16%	13%	15%	10%	10%
English Families							
TOTAL:	192	176	143	113	98	95	81
EXTINCTIONS:	45	50	41	40	25	24	20
EXTINCTION RATE:	23%	28%	29%	35%	25%	25%	25%

*I.e., leading barons and lords of parliament, but excluding those who became earls from the generation in which they were promoted.

that there is a clear connexion with the war with England, which was very intense in the 1330s and '40s, but which slackened off thereafter. During the whole period from 1325 to 1500 there were ten extinctions which can reasonably be attributed to the war; that is, there are ten cases where, had it not been for untimely deaths in battle, there is a fair chance that the family's direct male line would have continued.[35] Eight of these ten extinctions are concentrated into the 1330s and '40s: two occurred at the battle of Dupplin Moor in 1332, two at the battle of Halidon Hill in 1333, three at the battle of Neville's Cross in 1346, and one — the particularly tragic case of Alexander Seton — was due to the fact that at least three of his sons had died in the war during the 1330s, leaving him with just a granddaughter to succeed when he himself died in about 1348. These eight cases account for half the total of extinctions found in the generation 1325–49 — the generation with the highest level of extinctions. If they are discounted, the extinction rate for this generation falls to 16 per cent, which is much closer to the norm for the whole period. Clearly, therefore, the war with England — and particularly the succession of three devastating defeats in 1332, 1333 and 1346 — had a major influence on the pattern of extinctions within the late medieval Scottish higher nobility.

What of the other main causes of untimely death, plague and internal strife? Plague first reached Scotland in 1349, and its attacks were most virulent between then and the end of the fourteenth century. That includes the period from 1350 to 1374,[36] which is the other generation to show a high level of extinctions. But only two magnates are recorded as having died of plague, Thomas Murray of Bothwell in 1361, and Thomas Stewart, earl of Angus, the following year.[37] In both cases their male lines died out with them, but it must be pointed out that they were exposed to the disease in the unusual circumstances of imprisonment (Angus in Dumbarton Castle, at David II's command, Murray in England, where he was a hostage for King David); therefore their deaths, and the resulting extinction of their male lines, cannot be attributed simply to plague.[38] Plague, of course, may well have caused other deaths, and it may also have caused the eventual extinction of direct male lines by killing off nobles' sons (the 1361–2 outbreak of plague was apparently especially dangerous to children). But while that hypothesis would enable us to account for the sharp fall in extinctions after 1375 in terms of the slackening-off of the attacks of plague as well as of the war with England, it is completely unproveable. Moreover, it cannot be argued that the lower level of extinctions in Scotland than in England was because Scotland (as was possibly the case[39]) suffered less severely from plague, for K.B. McFarlane demonstrated that plague seems to have had little effect on the extinctions of nobles' male lines in England.[40]

As for internal strife, this can be shown to have caused nine extinctions: five were due to executions for political crimes, two to deaths in battle during rebellions, and two to killings in private feuds.[41] All but one of these extinctions, however, occurred during the fifteenth century (four in the generation 1425–49); had they not taken place, the overall level of extinctions during that century would have been even lower than it was. Thus they strengthen the point that under normal circumstances fifteenth-century Scottish noble families were exceptionally successful in surviving in the direct male line, but they do not help to explain it at all.

The subject of internal strife, however, is relevant in another way. Contrary to the traditional gloomy view, late medieval Scotland suffered relatively lightly from internal strife, particularly by comparison with England. Between 1350 and 1500 there were far fewer civil wars, rebellions, conflicts and battles in Scotland than in England, and over the century and a half only 30 Scottish magnates died as a result of internal strife, as opposed to no fewer than 70 of their English contemporaries.[42] Scottish political life was thus much less violent or dangerous for the participants than English, and this may help to explain why fewer Scottish families died out in the direct male line. Admittedly K.B. McFarlane argued that the worst bout of English political violence, the Wars of the Roses of the mid-to-late fifteenth century, did not directly cause many extinctions.[43] But, as he also pointed out, the untimely deaths in battle of the heads of families obviously reduced the number of sons that could be fathered,[44] and the civil wars also significantly slimmed the cadet branches of many families. The result would have been to leave families vulnerable to individual cases of ill health or infertility. Thus the greater amount of internal strife in late medieval England may well have contributed, at least indirectly, to the high extinction rates suffered by the English nobility.

Nevertheless the level of internal strife, like the effects of warfare and plague, can at most provide only part of the explanation of why extinction rates were so much lower in late medieval Scotland than elsewhere. In Scotland, as in England, the majority of extinctions — 41 out of 68 between 1325 and 1500 — must simply be attributed to natural causes, namely deaths in childhood, infertility and, most commonly, the birth of daughters only. And the relevant point is, of course, that this total of 41 extinctions due to natural causes is remarkably low; in other words, the late medieval Scottish higher nobility was extremely successful at producing sons, especially after about 1375.

The point is easy to illustrate: for instance, in successive generations during the period 1325–1500 the Campbell lords of Lochawe and earls of Argyll had three, two, five, five and two sons; the Graham lords of Montrose had two, three, five, seven, four and four; the Hamilton lords of Cadzow had two, two, four, three, four and one; and so on. It is a completely different picture from that painted by K.B. McFarlane for late medieval England.[45] But why this was so, and why the families below the rank of earl were so particularly fertile, is still unclear. Presumably magnates and their wives had the same chances of infertility, or of producing nothing but daughters, in Scotland as elsewhere. Also, since Scottish magnates followed the normal practice of marrying within their own social group, the issue of infertility caused by inbreeding cannot be a factor. Some childless marriages, however, may perhaps be explained in terms of nobles' willingness to marry widows past childbearing age in order to gain lands or political advantage. Scottish examples of this include the marriage of Andrew Murray of Bothwell, the Guardian of Scotland in the 1330s, to Robert I's sister Christian Bruce, and the marriage of Alexander Stewart to Isabella Douglas, countess of Mar, which brought him the earldom of Mar in 1404: both ladies were probably in their forties when these marriages took place.[46] But such marriages were probably less common in Scotland than in England,[47] because heiresses themselves were much less common. Only 32 heiresses to magnate estates can be found in Scotland during this period (mostly in the fourteenth century), and several of them did not outlive their first husbands. Now if widowed heiresses were not such a feature of the noble marriage market in Scotland as in England, then the likelihood is that Scottish magnates would generally have married wives of childbearing age — which would help explain their success at producing sons. On the other hand, it must be remembered that this marriage pattern was itself a consequence of the abundance of sons fathered by the Scottish higher nobility. Thus the relative absence of heiresses in the marriage market, like the other points suggested earlier, gives no more than a partial explanation of the high survival rate among late medieval Scotland's magnate families. The general phenomenon, unfortunately, remains something of a mystery.

There is, however, absolutely no mystery about its importance, which may now in conclusion be briefly sketched. Throughout medieval Europe, extinctions in the male line among noble families constituted one of the major influences on the patterns of landownership, wealth and power. When families failed to produce sons, the estates generally went to daughters — normally being partitioned if there were two or more — and thence to their husbands, who would usually have been landowners in their own rights. Or if entails to male heirs were in force (an increasingly common practice in the later Middle Ages), brothers, cousins or more distant collaterals would inherit; again, they would often be landowners already. And sometimes, when there were no heirs at all, estates reverted to the overlord or to the crown. Over several generations, therefore, the varying successes and failures at producing sons experienced by noble families could easily lead to major redistributions of land, with some families' possessions being dispersed due to inheritances by females, and others being enlarged due to the effects of marriages with heiresses and of entails.

In late medieval England, indeed, so many male lines died out that those lucky or fertile enough to survive accumulated territory dramatically;[48] in the 1460s, for instance, the fortunes of inheritance meant that Richard Nevill, 'the Kingmaker', possessed not only most of the Nevill family lands in northern England but also the earldoms of Salisbury and Warwick and many other estates as well.[49] The vast territorial complex amassed by the Valois dukes of Burgundy — before they died out in the male line in 1477 - is another excellent example of what might happen.[50] Fourteenth-century Scotland, too, exhibits several striking cases of the accumulation of territory in this way. The most spectacular is obviously the complicated build-up of the huge territories of the earls of Douglas;[51] the third earl, Archibald 'the Grim', who died in 1400, possessed the 'provincial' lordships of Galloway, Lauderdale and Selkirk, together with no fewer than 24 baronies and many other smaller pieces of land.[52] On a smaller but still major scale, combinations of inheritances through females and through male entails led to the amassing of the great Lindsay estates which became the earldom of Crawford in 1398, and of the great Douglas of Dalkeith estates.[53] Moreover, the dramatic 'Stewartisation' of so many earldoms by Robert II and his sons was made possible by the widespread extinction of comital families' male lines during the mid-to-late fourteenth century.

In the fifteenth century, however — although the acquisition of so much territory by the royal Stewarts and the Douglases had far-reaching repercussions in the reigns of James I and James II — the processes of dispersal and accumulation did not take place to anything like the same extent. There were, for instance, no significant changes in the territories possessed by the Lindsay earls of Crawford or the Douglases of Dalkeith (earls of Morton from 1458) during the century. Extinctions of male lines were becoming increasingly rare, except among the families of earls, and in those cases the crown often took the earldoms into its own possession.[54] Magnates were thus unable to make such spectacular gains through marriage. A few were fortunate, such as the first earl of Argyll, who gained the inheritance of the Stewarts of Lorne, or James II's half-brother the earl of Buchan, who married the heiress to the Ogilvy of Auchterhouse estates, but in general the kind of accumulations that were quite common in the fourteenth century are not to be found in the fifteenth. There are, indeed, only three examples in the entire century of men below the rank of earl gaining magnates' inheritances through their own or their fathers' marriages to heiresses.[55]

The significance of this does not relate simply to the size of magnate estates. When territories were accumulated through marriages to heiresses, they tended to be scattered throughout the country; and when there was a rapid turnover in landownership caused by high rates of extinction in the male line, then local landowning and power structures were bound to be made unstable. Both points appear to be major characteristics of noble society in late medieval England, where bitter legal disputes caused by conflicts over complex inheritances often added to local instability.[56] They are also evident in fourteenth-century Scotland, but they appear to have become much less important features of Scottish society during the fifteenth century, again presumably because inheritance by heiresses or through entails had become so much less common. There was thus — always excepting the cases of the Albany-Stewart and Douglas possessions, seized by James I and James II respectively — a comparatively high degree of continuity, coherence and stability among magnate estates in fifteenth-century Scotland, which no doubt helped to contribute significantly to the generally good political relations discussed by Dr Jenny Wormald in the final chapter of this book.

Furthermore, the fertility of Scottish magnate families meant that they produced not only male heirs but an abundance of younger sons, who often managed to establish lasting cadet branches. The importance of agnatic kinship — that is, male-line relationships — among the late medieval and early modern Scottish nobility is sometimes taken to be a legacy from the Celtic past. Be that as it may, agnatic kinship could hardly be a powerful force if the kindreds themselves were small or non-existent (as seems to have been the case with most magnate families in late medieval England). The sheer demographic vitality of the Scottish higher nobility after about 1375, strikingly apparent from the pages of the *Scots Peerage*, must be a major factor behind the prominence of kinship in fifteenth-century Scottish noble society.

But kinship ties, it has been stressed, were most effective when they operated within a limited geographical area, as was generally the case in fifteenth-century Scotland.[57] Here, again, the pattern of extinction and survival among male lines can be shown to have been a relevant factor. One of the commonest ways of endowing younger sons in the Middle Ages was to give them some of their mothers' lands — provided that their mothers were heiresses. Now that often meant that the cadet's lands were in a different part of the country from the main family patrimony; the endowment of James Douglas of Balvenie, second son of the third earl of Douglas, with his mother's Murray of Bothwell estates in the north of Scotland is a case in point.[58] If the mothers were not heiresses, however, it was much more likely that the cadets would be endowed from the family patrimony.[59] And that, in the circumstances of fifteenth-century Scottish noble society, would have meant that they tended to stay within the family's main geographical sphere of influence, and so be connected to the head of the family by ties of land tenure and geography as well as kinship. The point can be illustrated from many families, for example, by the establishment of Gordon cadets in Aberdeenshire, Kennedy cadets in the south-west, and, perhaps most strikingly, Campbell cadets in Argyll. It provides yet another testimony to the importance that the remarkable fertility of Scotland's late medieval magnate families, especially those below the rank of earl, has for the history of Scottish noble society.

NOTES

1. É. Perroy, 'Social mobility among the French *noblesse* in the later Middle Ages', *Past and Present*, xxi (1962), pp. 25–38.

2. P.S. Lewis, *Later Medieval France* (London, 1968), p. 194.

3. E.g., *ibid.*, pp. 190–5; C.T. Wood, *The French Appanages and the Capetian Monarchy* (Harvard, 1966); M. Jones, 'The Breton nobility and their masters from the civil war of 1341–64 to the late fifteenth century', in *The Crown and Local Communities in England and France in the Fifteenth Century*, ed. J.R.L. Highfield and R.M. Jeffs (Gloucester, 1981), p. 54; J.P. Cooper, 'Patterns of inheritance and settlement by great landowners from the fifteenth to the eighteenth centuries', in *Family and Inheritance: Rural Society in Western Europe, 1200-1800*, ed. J. Goody *et al* (Cambridge, 1976), pp. 252–63.

4. K.B. McFarlane, *The Nobility of Later Medieval England* (Oxford, 1973), pp. 141–70. The tables in the appendix B (pp. 172–6) were added by J. Campbell.

5. *Ibid.*, pp. 144–5, 173–6.

6. *Ibid.*, pp. 172–3.

7. *Ibid.*, p. 143.

8. *Ibid.*, pp. 144, 168.

9. In medieval Scotland the concept of nobility was never restricted to the magnates, or parliamentary peerage, as happened in England during the fourteenth and fifteenth centuries; from the mid-fifteenth century a distinction between 'lords', i.e. peers, and 'lairds', i.e. lesser nobles, was recognised, but the lairds still counted as part of the Scottish nobility.

10. A. Grant, 'The development of the Scottish peerage', *SHR*, lvii (1978), pp. 1-27.

11. See A. Grant, 'The Higher Nobility in Scotland and their Estates, *c.*1371–1424' (unpublished Oxford University D.Phil. thesis, 1975), Ch. 1.

12. This table has been constructed from the list of 'Dukes, Marquesses and Earls (Scotland)' in *Handbook of British Chronology*, ed. F.M. Powicke and E.B. Fryde, 2nd edn. (London, 1961), pp. 466–91, supplemented by the details given in *Scots Pge.* Throughout this essay, specific references will not be given for statements based directly on information contained in these two standard works of reference. The figures in Table 6 differ slightly from those given in A. Grant, 'Earls and earldoms in late medieval Scotland (*c.*1310–1460)',

in *Essays presented to Michael Roberts*, ed. J. Bossy and P. Jupp (Belfast, 1976), p. 26, because in that essay different generational periods were used, and (in order to highlight the low number of earls at any one time) cases of an earl's becoming king without immediately passing on his earldom to one of his children were counted as bringing a comital family to an end, which has not been done here.

13. This has not, however, been counted as an extinction, because Rothesay's male line, that of his father as earl of Carrick, continued through his younger brother James, subsequently James I.

14. Before March 1453, not 'on or before 17 June 1455', as in *Handbook of British Chronology*, p. 469; I am most grateful to Mr Alan Borthwick of Edinburgh University for this information.

15. The complicity of James Douglas, earl of Avandale and subsequently seventh earl of Douglas, in his great-nephews' deaths has sometimes been played down by historians, most recently in Macdougall, *James III*, pp. 9–10. It is therefore worth stressing that in 1440 Earl James was justiciar of Scotland south of the Forth, and therefore had the judicial authority to pass death sentences, which the chancellor, William Crichton (who is generally seen as the main perpetrator of the judicial killings), lacked. For an example of the political use to which Earl James put the office of justiciar see A.I. Dunlop, *The Life and Times of James Kennedy, Bishop of St Andrews* (Edinburgh, 1950), p. 53.

16. There was what seems at first sight a break in 1368, when Patrick, the eighth earl, died without surviving children and was succeeded by his great-nephew George, the ninth earl; but Patrick appears to have had no closer heirs in female lines, and so in this case the direct male line must be counted as continuing.

17. Grant, 'Development of the Scottish peerage', pp. 12–14.

18. *The Asloan Manuscript*, ed. W.A. Craigie (Scottish Text Soc., 1923), i, p. 243.

19. Grant, 'Higher Nobility', Ch. 1. 'Baron' was an institutionalised concept in late medieval Scotland, but it meant a lord who held 'in free barony', and (in contrast to England) never became limited to the peerage; therefore the Scottish baronage cannot be equated with the higher nobility. Cf. the 1428 act stating that 'smal baronnis and fre tenandis' no longer had to come in person to parliament (*APS*, ii, p. 15). See *The Court Book of the Barony of Carnwath*, ed. W.C. Dickinson (SHS, 1937), pp. xix–lv; Grant, 'Higher Nobility', Ch. 3.

20. *APS*, i, pp. 474–5.

21. I.e., the father of Duncan Campbell, the first Campbell of Loudon, who acquired it through marriage in *c.*1318. Donald was the younger brother of Neil Campbell of Lochawe (d. *c.*1316) and uncle of Colin, lord of Lochawe in 1320; he may have been named in the Declaration as a magnate in his own right, or to represent Colin, who is not named in it.

22. Following the identification implied in Barrow, *Bruce*, pp. 427, 474.

23. *Ibid.*, p. 430.

24. For these see, e.g., Barrow, *Kingdom*, pp. 380–2.

25. All received substantial grants of land from Robert I (e.g., *RMS*, i, nos. 46–8, 72, 80, 566, app. i, nos. 48, 53; *HMC, Hamilton*, p. 13), which made them as great landowners as, if not greater than, most of the barons named in the Declaration.

26. That takes the total of 'greater barons' rather above the figure of 30 indicated by the number of later lords of parliament; but in the present analysis it has been thought best to cast the net as widely as possible when trying to identify the baronial component of the higher nobility before about 1450.

27. Details and references are given below, in the Appendix.

28. I.e., the family of Walter son of Gilbert, which adopted the surname Hamilton in the 1370s.

29. References to these sources are given in the Appendix to this chapter.

30. This is a different policy from that of K.B. McFarlane, whose study of extinctions covered the families of everybody who was summoned personally to the English parliament from 1295 on; since the lists of summonses were not standardised until the later fourteenth century, this meant that many families which did not subsequently belong to the peerage

were included (McFarlane, *Nobility*, pp. 144–5, 172). The result is that the total of families examined in each generation is much larger in McFarlane's analysis than in the analysis of Scottish families presented here (cf. Table 8, above); but in fact the numbers summoned personally to English parliaments (eventually the peerage) usually totalled around 50–60 (*ibid.*, p. 268; J.E. Powell and K. Wallis, *The House of Lords in the Middle Ages* [London, 1968], Chs. 13, 18, 21, etc.), which are much the same as the numbers of Scottish higher nobles under discussion here. It should be added that, so far as can be seen from the available material, the same general pattern of extinction and survival is exhibited by those Scottish families which sank out of the higher nobility.

31. *RMS*, i, nos. 51, 616; W. Fraser, *Memorials of the Montgomeries Earls of Eglinton* (Edinburgh, 1859), i, pp. 15–17; *Scots Pge.*, iii, pp. 428–44.

32. *RMS*, i, no. 697, app. i, no. 159, app. ii, no. 815; *Scots Pge.*, vi, pp. 194–7; v, pp. 391–5.

33. *Registrum Honoris de Morton* (Bannatyne Club, 1853), ii, nos. 58, 59, 70, 97; *Scots Pge.*, vi, pp. 194–7, 339–61.

34. The extinction rate for Scotland's leading barons and lords of parliament over the fifteenth century as a whole works out at only 26%, less than half the 55% calculated by Perroy for fifteenth-century Forez; and it must be remembered that Perroy did not define extinction so strictly as has been done here.

35. Murdoch, earl of Menteith, and Robert Bruce of Liddesdale, at Dupplin, 1332; John Campbell, earl of Atholl, and Alexander Bruce, earl of Carrick, at Halidon, 1333; John Randolph, earl of Moray, Maurice Murray, earl of Strathearn, and Robert Keith (along with his grandson and heir), at Neville's Cross, 1346; Alexander Seton, due to his sons' deaths in 1332–3; James, second earl of Douglas, at Otterburn, 1388; and John Stewart, earl of Buchan, at Verneuil, 1424.

36. No magnate family can be shown to have become extinct in 1349, the year when plague first hit Scotland; but one or two of the deaths in the 1325–49 generation which can be dated no more precisely than 'in the 1340s' may perhaps have been caused by the 1349 plague.

37. Androw of Wyntoun, *The Orygynale Cronykil of Scotland*, ed. D. Laing (Edinburgh, 1872–9), ii, p. 505; *Chron. Bower*, ii, p. 365.

38. It is worth commenting that David II, the bishop of St Andrews and 'mony lordis sere' spent Christmas 1362 in Moray, 'Quhill this ded [i.e. plague] wes in South wedand' (Wyntoun, *Orygynale Cronykil*, ii, p. 505); most magnates no doubt avoided the 1362 plague in that way.

39. R. Nicholson, *Scotland: The Later Middle Ages* (Edinburgh, 1974), pp. 148–9; A. Grant, *Independence and Nationhood: Scotland 1306-1469* (London, 1984), pp. 72–5.

40. McFarlane, *Nobility*, pp. 168–70.

41. William Douglas of Liddesdale, killed in feud in 1353; Murdoch, duke of Albany, executed along with two of his sons in 1425 (a third son survived in Ireland, where he died without legitimate issue in 1451, but it is clear that the family's extinction was really due to the executions in 1425); Alan Stewart, earl of Caithness, killed fighting for the crown against the forces of the lordship of the Isles at the battle of Inverlochy, 1431; Walter Stewart, earl of Atholl, executed along with his grandson and heir in 1437; William, sixth earl of Douglas, executed along with his brother and heir in 1440; Archibald Douglas, earl of Moray, killed in rebellion at the battle of Arkinholm, 1455 (he left a son and daughter, of whom nothing is known, but his family's extinction can really be attributed to his rebellion); Hugh Douglas, earl of Ormond, executed after the battle of Arkinholm, 1455 (he left a son, who became a churchman, but his family's extinction can really be attributed to his rebellion); John Stewart, earl of Mar, died in custody (probably executed) in 1479 or 1480.

42. The figures have been culled from *Scots Pge.* and *Comp. Pge.*, while details of the civil wars, etc., can be found in the standard political histories of the two countries. See also Grant, *Independence and Nationhood*, Ch. 7.

43. McFarlane, *Nobility*, pp. 146–9.

44. *Ibid.*, p. 147.

45. *Ibid.*, pp. 143–51.

46. Christian Bruce had borne two children by her first husband, who died before 1305; the dispensation for her marriage to Andrew Murray was dated 1326. Murray did have two sons by an earlier marriage, but they both died childless, and so his line became extinct. Isabella Douglas probably married her first husband, Malcolm Drummond, in the late 1360s. After Isabella's death, Alexander Stewart was briefly married to the heiress of Duffel in Brabant; he had no issue by either marriage, and in 1426 arranged with James I for his illegitimate son Thomas to be made heir to Mar. Thomas, however, predeceased his father, and so his line died out with Alexander in 1435.

47. That such marriages were fairly common in England may be inferred from McFarlane, *Nobility*, pp. 65–7, 153.

48. *Ibid.*, pp. 59–60, 145, 152–6.

49. C. Ross, *Edward IV* (London, 1974), p. 17; R.L. Storey, *The End of the House of Lancaster* (London, 1966), pp. 231–41.

50. R. Vaughan, *Valois Burgundy* (London, 1975), Ch. 2.

51. William, the first earl, inherited the estates of his uncle, 'the Good Sir James' (which formed the entailed core of the Douglas territories), together with the lands acquired by his father; he also held the earldom of Mar through his wife. Then, after the second earl's death in 1388, the entailed estates and title went to Archibald 'the Grim', illegitimate son of 'the Good Sir James'; Archibald already possessed the lordship of Galloway and, through his wife, the Murray of Drumsergart and Murray of Bothwell inheritances. See *Scots Pge.*, iii, pp. 142–63. It is not clear what right Archibald had to the Murray of Bothwell inheritance. His wife, the heiress of the Drumsergart branch of Murrays, was the widow of Thomas Murray of Bothwell; she may also have been Thomas Murray's heiress, or Archibald may simply have been allowed to take over the Bothwell estates by Robert II, in recognition of his political and diplomatic services (as is indicated in *RMS*, i, no. 401).

52. Grant, 'Higher Nobility', pp. 212–14.

53. Ibid., pp. 223–4, 243–5; *Scots Pge.*, iii, pp. 10–17; vi, pp. 338–47.

54. The earldoms of Atholl, Buchan, Caithness, Douglas, Fife, Lennox, Mar, March, Murray, Ormond and Strathearn all came permanently or temporarily into the crown's possession under James I and James II.

55. Alexander Macdonald of the Isles eventually inherited the earldom of Ross from his mother; Alexander Seton married the heiress to the Gordon estates; and William Sinclair of Roslin inherited the possessions of William Douglas of Nithsdale from his mother.

56. See, e.g., McFarlane, *Nobility*, pp. 136–56; G.A. Holmes, *The Estates of the Higher Nobility in Fourteenth-Century England* (Cambridge, 1957), Ch. 1; E.F. Jacob, *The Fifteenth Century* (Oxford, 1961), pp. 318–33 and Map 5; Storey, *End of the House of Lancaster*, *passim*; R.A. Griffiths, *The Reign of King Henry VI* (London, 1981), Ch. 20; N. Saul, *Knights and Esquires: The Gloucestershire Gentry in the Fourteenth Century* (Oxford, 1981), pp. 194–6; M.E. Avery, 'The history of the equitable jurisdiction of Chancery before 1460', *Bulletin of the Institute of Historical Research*, xlii (1969), pp. 135–43.

57. J.M. Brown (now Wormald), 'The exercise of power', in *Scottish Society in the Fifteenth Century*, ed. *idem* (London, 1977), p. 60.

58. *RMS*, ii, no. 43. James Douglas of Balvenie eventually became the seventh earl of Douglas.

59. This could be done in Scotland by subinfeudation, or by a conveyance (made through the common Scottish practice of resignation to the crown for regrant) which reserved the profits of the land to the father during his lifetime. The latter device had much the same purpose and effect as the English use, but was considerably simpler, and did not involve the same risk of litigation. See Grant, 'Higher Nobility', pp. 197–210; cf. McFarlane, *Nobility*, pp. 69–76; Saul, *Knights and Esquires*, pp. 194–6; Avery, 'Equitable jurisdiction', pp. 135–43.

APPENDIX

The purpose of this Appendix is to provide lists of those families below the rank of earl who have been considered for the purposes of this chapter as belonging to the Scottish higher nobility between 1325 and 1500. The families are listed first under each of the generations in which they were prominent and, secondly, alphabetically. Specific references have not been cited for families which are the subjects of individual articles in the *Scots Peerage*.

A. List of families by 25-year generations.
1325–1349

Abernethy, Ardrossan, Cameron of Baledgarno, Campbell of Loudon, Cheyne, Douglas, Fenton, Fraser of Touch, Graham of Abercorn, Graham of Lovat, Graham of Montrose, Hay, Keith, Leslie, Lindsay of Crawford, Maxwell, Menteith, Mowat, Murray of Culbin, Muschet, Oliphant, Ramsay of Dalhousie, Seton, Sinclair, Stewart, Straiton, Wemyss (derived from the Declaration of Arbroath: *APS*, i, pp. 474–5); *plus* Boyd, Bruce of Liddesdale, Campbell, Fleming, Gordon, Hamilton, Lauder, Macdonald, Macruarie, Menzies, Murray of Bothwell (also prominent in the 1320s: see above, at notes 23–5); *plus* Barclay of Brechin, Douglas of Liddesdale, Keith (II) (families prominent in the 1340s).

(The families of Brechin, Mowbray, Soules and Umfraville, all named in the Declaration of Arbroath, have been omitted from the analysis because they did not form part of the Scottish higher nobility in 1325.)

Extinctions: Ardrossan, Bruce of Liddesdale, Cheyne, Fraser of Touch, Graham of Abercorn, Keith, Macruarie, Muschet, Seton, Wemyss.

Promoted to earl: Fleming (Wigtown).

No longer prominent by 1349: Cameron of Baledgarno, Campbell of Loudon, Fenton, Graham of Lovat, Lauder, Menzies, Mowat, Murray of Culbin, Straiton.

1350–1374

Annan, Bisset, Campbell, Cunningham, Dalziel, Danielston, Dishington, Douglas, Douglas of Dalkeith, Douglas of Galloway, Eglinton, Erskine, Fleming of Cumbernauld, Graham of Montrose, Gray, Haliburton, Hamilton, Hay of Yester, Keith (II), Kennedy, Kirkpatrick, Leslie of Ross, Lindsay of Crawford, Lindsay of Glenesk, Livingston, Macdonald, Macdougall, Maxwell, Mortimer, Mure of Abercorn, Murray of Bothwell, Ramsay of Colluthie, Ramsay of Dalhousie, Somerville, Stewart, Stewart of Darnley, Strachan, Vaus, Wallace, Wemyss of Cameron (derived from the list of David II's hostages agreed in 1357 and the membership of parliamentary committees in the 1360s: *RRS*, vi, no. 150; *APS*, i, pp. 495, 497, 501, 506, 508); *plus* Abernethy, Barclay of Brechin, Boyd, Douglas of Liddesdale, Drummond, Gordon, Hay, Leslie, Logie, Menteith, Oliphant, Preston, Seton (II), Sinclair, Stewart of Badenoch (families which may reasonably be considered prominent during part or all of this generation).

(The families of John Barclay and Andrew Valence, who were both listed among David II's hostages, have been omitted because their genealogical details are unclear.)

Extinctions: Barclay of Brechin, Bisset, Douglas of Liddesdale, Macdougall, Menteith, Murray of Bothwell, Vaus, Wallace.

Promoted to earl: Douglas (Douglas), Ramsay of Colluthie (Fife), Stewart (Strathearn).

No longer prominent by 1374: Annan, Dalziel, Dishington, Kirkpatrick, Logie, Preston, Strachan, Wemyss of Cameron.

1375–1399

Abernethy, Campbell, Cockburn of Langton, Cunningham, Douglas of Dalkeith, Douglas of Galloway, Douglas of Nithsdale, Drummond, Erskine, Forrester, Gordon, Graham of Montrose, Hamilton, Hay, Hay of Yester, Keith (II), Kennedy, Leslie, Leslie of Ross, Lindsay of Crawford, Lindsay of Glenesk, Livingston, Lyon, Macdonald, Maxwell, Oliphant, Ramorgny, Seton (II), Stewart of Badenoch, Stewart of Jedworth, Stewart of Lorne (derived from the lists of 'provincial lords' and barons holding three or more baronies given in Grant, 'Higher Nobility', pp. 23–4, 27–9, 37; and from the lists of royal councillors of 1399: *APS*, i, pp. 572, 574); *plus* Boyd, Danielston, Eglinton, Fleming of Cumbernauld, Gray, Haliburton, Montgomery, Mortimer, Mure of Abercorn, Ramsay of Dalhousie, Sinclair, Somerville, Stewart of Brechin, Stewart of Darnley (families which may reasonably be considered prominent during part or all of this generation).

(The families of McDowell of Makerston, Mowat of Fearn and Menzies of Redhall, which each possessed three baronies in the 1370s, have been omitted because they do not appear to have had any national importance at this time.)

Extinctions: Danielston, Eglinton, Lindsay of Crawford, Mortimer, Mure of Abercorn.

Promoted to earl: Douglas of Galloway (Douglas), Leslie of Ross (Ross), Lindsay of Glenesk (Crawford), Stewart of Badenoch (Buchan).

No longer prominent by 1399: Ramsay of Dalhousie.

1400–1424

Abernethy, Boyd, Campbell, Cunningham, Douglas of Balvenie, Douglas of Dalkeith, Douglas of Nithsdale, Drummond, Drummond (II), Dunbar of Cumnock, Dunbar of Frendraught, Erskine, Fleming of Cumbernauld, Gordon, Graham of Montrose, Gray, Haliburton, Hamilton, Hay, Hay of Yester, Keith (II), Kennedy, Leslie, Lindsay of Byres, Lyon, Macdonald, Maxwell, Montgomery, Ogilvy of Auchterhouse, Oliphant, Seton (II), Seton of Gordon, Somerville, Stewart of Lorne (derived from the lists of 'provincial lords', barons with three or more baronies, and hostages for James I assessed at 500 marks or more, in Grant, 'Higher Nobility', pp. 23–4, 27–32, 37; *Rot. Scot.*, ii, p. 242; *CDS*, iv, no. 952); *plus* Cockburn of Langton, Forrester, Livingston, Ramorgny, Sinclair, Stewart of Brechin, Stewart of Darnley, Stewart of Jedworth (families which may reasonably be considered prominent during part or all of this generation).

Extinctions: Douglas of Nithsdale, Drummond, Gordon, Ramorgny.

Promoted to earl: Stewart of Brechin (Atholl).

No longer prominent by 1424: Cockburn of Langton, Stewart of Jedworth.

1425–1449

Abernethy, Boyd, Campbell, Crichton, Cunningham, Douglas of Balvenie, Douglas of Dalkeith, Drummond (II), Dunbar of Cumnock, Dunbar of Frendraught, Erskine, Fleming of Cumbernauld, Forbes, Graham of Montrose, Gray, Haliburton, Hamilton, Hay, Hay of Yester, Keith (II), Kennedy, Leslie, Leslie of Rothes, Lindsay of Byres, Livingston, Lyon, Macdonald, Maxwell, Montgomery, Ogilvy of Auchterhouse, Oliphant, Seton (II), Seton of Gordon, Sinclair, Somerville, Stewart of Lorne (derived from the lists of 'provincial lords', barons with three or more baronies, hostages for James I assessed at 500 marks or more, and early lords of parliament, in Grant, 'Higher Nobility', as above, and *idem*, 'Development of the Scottish peerage', pp. 10–15); *plus* Forrester, Stewart of Darnley (families which may reasonably be considered prominent during part or all of this generation).

Extinctions: Dunbar of Frendraught, Leslie.

Promoted to earl: Douglas of Balvenie (Avandale; Douglas), Dunbar of Frendraught (Moray), Macdonald (Ross), Seton of Gordon (Huntly).

No longer prominent by 1449: Dunbar of Cumnock, Forrester.

1450–1474

Abernethy, Borthwick, Boyd, Campbell, Carlyle, Cathcart, Crichton, Cunningham, Douglas of Dalkeith, Erskine, Fleming of Cumbernauld, Forbes, Fraser of Lovat, Graham of Montrose, Gray, Haliburton, Hamilton, Hay, Hepburn, Hume, Keith (II), Kennedy, Leslie of Rothes, Lindsay of Byres, Livingston, Lyle, Lyon, Maxwell, Montgomery, Monypenny, Oliphant, Seton (II), Sinclair, Somerville, Stewart of Avandale, Stewart of Darnley, Stewart of Innermeath, Stewart of Lorne (families of lords of parliament; see *Scots Pge.*); *plus* Drummond (II), Hay of Yester, Ogilvy of Auchterhouse (families which may reasonably be considered prominent during part or all of this generation).

Extinctions: Keith (II), Ogilvy of Auchterhouse, Stewart of Lorne.

Promoted to earl: Boyd (Arran), Campbell (Argyll), Douglas of Dalkeith (Morton), Hay (Erroll), Keith (II) (Marischal), Leslie of Rothes (Rothes), Stewart of Darnley (Lennox).

1475–1500

Abernethy, Abernethy (II), Borthwick, Carlyle, Cathcart, Crichton, Crichton of Sanquhar, Cunningham, Drummond (II), Erskine, Fleming of Cumbernauld, Forbes, Fraser of Lovat, Graham of Montrose, Gray, Haliburton, Hamilton, Hay of Yester, Hepburn, Herries, Hume, Kennedy, Lindsay of Byres, Lindsay of Byres (II), Livingston, Lyle, Lyon, Maxwell, Montgomery, Monypenny, Oliphant, Ramsay of Bothwell, Ross of Halkhead, Ruthven, Sempill, Seton (II), Sinclair, Somerville, Stewart of Avandale, Stewart of Innermeath (families of lords of parliament; see *Scots Pge.*).

Extinctions: Abernethy, Lindsay of Byres.

Promoted to earl: Cunningham (Glencairn), Hepburn (Bothwell).

B. Alphabetical list of families.

ABERNETHY: prominent from 1320; early lord of parliament.
Extinct 1488; left daughters; lands and title went *via* tailzie.

ABERNETHY (II): lord of parliament from 1488.
Survived past 1500.

ANNAN: prominent 1350–1374.
Survived past 1500. (A. Jervise, *Memorials of Angus and the Mearns*, 2nd, revised, edn. [Edinburgh, 1885], ii, pp. 63–4.)

ARDROSSAN: prominent from 1320.
Extinct by 1349; left daughter. (Fraser, *Montgomeries*, i, p. 15.)

BARCLAY OF BRECHIN: prominent from 1325–49.
Extinct *c.*1369; left daughter. (*Scots Pge.*, ii, pp. 222–4.)

BISSET: prominent from 1350–74.
Extinct *c.*1374. (Last member of family surrendered all claims to father's lands, and so ceased to be a landowner; line no doubt died out shortly afterwards.) (*RMS*, i, nos. 350, 706.)

BORTHWICK: lord of parliament 1452.
Survived past 1500.

BOYD: prominent from 1320; lord of parliament 1452; earl of Arran 1467.
Extinct 1484; left sister.

BRUCE OF LIDDESDALE: prominent from 1320.
Extinct 1332; no heirs. (*Scots Pge.*, i, p. 8.)

CAMERON OF BALEDGARNO: prominent 1320–1349.
Extinct between 1375 and 1399; left (?) daughters. (Barrow, *Bruce*, pp. 427, 474; *Scots Pge.*, iv, p. 333; v, p. 596.)

CAMPBELL: prominent from 1320; early lord of parliament; earl of Argyll *c.*1457.
Survived past 1500.

CAMPBELL OF LOUDON: prominent 1320–1349.
Survived past 1500.

CARLYLE: lord of parliament *c.*1474.
Survived past 1500.

CATHCART: lord of parliament 1452.
Survived past 1500.

CHEYNE: prominent from 1320.
Extinct *c.*1345; left daughters. (W.D. Cheyne-MacPherson, *The Cheynes of Inverugie, Esslemont and Arnage and their Descendants* [Kirkwall, 1943], p. 16.)

COCKBURN OF LANGTON: prominent 1375–1424.
Survived past 1500. (*APS*, i, p. 580; *RMS*, ii, nos. 1156, 1556, 3422.)

CRICHTON: early lord of parliament.
Survived past 1500.

CRICHTON OF SANQUHAR: lord of parliament 1488.
Survived past 1500.

CUNNINGHAM: prominent from 1350–74; lord of parliament 1463; earl of Glencairn 1488.
Survived past 1500.

DALZIEL: prominent 1350–1374.
Extinct (?) shortly after 1379.

DANIELSTON (Dennistoun): prominent from 1350–74.
Extinct 1399; left daughters. (J.W. Dennistoun, *Some account of the Family of Dennistoun and Colgrain* [Glasgow, 1906], pp. 3–6.)

DISHINGTON: prominent 1350–1374.
Survived past 1500. (W. Wood, *The East Neuk of Fife*, 2nd edn. [Edinburgh, 1887], pp. 214–15.)

DOUGLAS: prominent from 1320; earl of Douglas 1358.
Extinct 1388; left sister.

DOUGLAS OF BALVENIE: prominent from 1400–24; earl of Avandale 1437; earl of Douglas 1440.
Extinct *c.*1491; no heirs.

DOUGLAS OF DALKEITH: prominent from 1350–74; early lord of parliament; earl of Morton 1458.
Survived past 1500.

DOUGLAS OF GALLOWAY: prominent from 1350–74; earl of Douglas 1388.
Extinct 1440; left sister; main lands went *via* tailzie.

DOUGLAS OF LIDDESDALE: prominent from 1325–49.
Extinct 1353; left daughter; main lands went *via* tailzie. (*Scots Pge.*, vi, pp. 339–42.)

DOUGLAS OF NITHSDALE: prominent from 1375–99.
Extinct *c.*1419; left sister. (*Scots Pge.*, iii, pp. 163–4.)

DRUMMOND: prominent from 1350–74.
Extinct 1402. (Malcolm Drummond was the first of his house to be prominent nationally; therefore his death without issue in 1402 has been counted as an extinction, although the male line of Drummonds continued through his brother.)

DRUMMOND (II): prominent from 1400–24; lord of parliament 1488.
Survived past 1500.

DUNBAR OF CUMNOCK: prominent 1400–1449.
Extinct between 1475 and 1500; left daughters. (*Scots Pge.*, iii, p. 261.)

DUNBAR OF FRENDRAUGHT: prominent from 1400; earl of Moray *c.*1427.
Extinct *c.*1430; left daughters.

EGLINTON: prominent from 1350–74.
Extinct 1378; left daughter. (Fraser, *Montgomeries*, i, p. 15.)

ERSKINE: prominent from 1350–74; early lord of parliament.
Survived past 1500.

FENTON: prominent 1320–1349.
Extinct *c.*1430; left daughters. (Jervise, *Angus and Mearns*, ii, pp. 44–5; *RMS*, i, no. 942; ii, nos. 30, 220.)

FLEMING: prominent from 1320; earl of Wigtown 1341.
Extinct *c.*1382; left aunts.

FLEMING OF CUMBERNAULD: prominent from 1350–74; lord of parliament 1452.
Survived past 1500.

FORBES: early lord of parliament.
Survived past 1500.

FORRESTER: prominent 1375–1449.
Survived past 1500.

FRASER OF LOVAT: lord of parliament *c.*1460.
Survived past 1500.

FRASER OF TOUCH: prominent from 1320.
Extinct *c.*1340; left daughter. (*Scots Pge.*, vii, pp. 426–9.)

GORDON: prominent from 1320.
Extinct *c.*1408; left sister.

GRAHAM OF ABERCORN: prominent from 1320.
Extinct *c.*1349; left sisters. (*Scots Pge.,* vi, pp. 195–7.)

GRAHAM OF LOVAT: prominent 1320–1349.
Extinct (?) before 1367. *(Scotds Pge.,* vi, pp. 203–4.)

GRAHAM OF MONTROSE: prominent from 1320; early lord of parliament.
Survived past 1500.

GRAY: prominent from 1350–74; early lord of parliament.
Survived past 1500.

HALIBURTON: prominent from 1320–74; early lord of parliament.
Survived past 1500.

HAMILTON (i.e., descendants of Walter son of Gilbert): prominent from 1320; early lord of parliament.
Survived past 1500.

HAY: prominent from 1320; early lord of parliament; earl of Erroll 1452.
Survived past 1500.

HAY OF YESTER: prominent from 1350–74; lord of parliament 1488.
Survived past 1500.

HEPBURN: lord of parliament 1452; earl of Bothwell 1488.
Survived past 1500.

HERRIES: lord of parliament 1489.
Survived past 1500.

HUME: lord of parliament 1473.
Survived past 1500.

KEITH: prominent from 1320.
Extinct 1346; left granddaughter; main lands went *via* tailzie.

KEITH (II): prominent from 1325–49; early lord of parliament; Earl Marischal 1458.
Extinct 1463; left granddaughter; main lands went *via* tailzie.

KENNEDY: prominent from 1350–74; lord of parliament 1458.
Survived past 1500.

KIRKPATRICK: prominent 1350–1374.
Survived past 1500. (*Burke's Peerage and Baronetage,* 105th edn. [London, 1970], pp. 1515–16.)

LAUDER: prominent 1320–1349.
Survived (probably) past 1500. (J.J. Reid, 'Early notices of the Bass Rock and its owners', *PSAS*, xx [1885–6], pp. 54–67.)

LESLIE: prominent from 1320.
Extinct 1439; left daughter; main lands went *via* tailzie.

LESLIE OF ROSS: prominent from 1350–74; earl of Ross *c.*1395.
Extinct 1402; left daughter.

LESLIE OF ROTHES: prominent from 1425–49; early lord of parliament; earl of Rothes 1458.
Survived past 1500.

LINDSAY OF BYRES: prominent from 1400–24; early lord of parliament.
·Extinct 1497; left daughter; lands and title went *via* tailzie.
LINDSAY OF BYRES (II): lord of parliament 1497.
Survived past 1500.
LINDSAY OF CRAWFORD: prominent from 1320.
Extinct 1397; left daughters; main lands went *via* tailzie.
LINDSAY OF GLENESK: prominent from 1350–74; earl of Crawford 1398.
Survived past 1500.
LIVINGSTON: prominent from 1350–74; lord of parliament 1455.
Survived past 1500.
LOGIE: prominent 1350–1374.
Extinct *c.*1480. (W. Fraser, *The Red Book of Grandtully* [Edinburgh, 1868], i, no. 96*.)
LYLE: lord of parliament 1452.
Survived past 1500.
LYON: prominent from 1375–99; early lord of parliament.
Survived past 1500.
MACDONALD: prominent from 1320; earl of Ross 1437.
Extinct 1498; left no legitimate issue.
MACDOUGALL: prominent from 1350–74.
Extinct *c.*1375; left daughters. (*Scots Pge.,* v, pp. 1–2.)
MACRUARIE: prominent from 1320.
Extinct 1346; left daughter. (*Scots Pge.,* v, p. 39; vii, p. 237.)
MAXWELL: prominent from 1320; early lord of parliament.
Survived past 1500.
MENTEITH: prominent from 1320.
Extinct *c.*1360; left sister.
MENZIES: prominent 1320–1349.
Survived past 1500. (*HMC, Reports,* vi, pp. 690–2.)
MONTGOMERY: prominent from 1375–99; early lord of parliament.
Survived past 1500.
MONYPENNY: lord of parliament *c.*1464.
Survived past 1500.
MORTIMER: prominent from 1350–74.
Extinct before 1400. (*Scots Pge.*, iv, p. 272.)
MOWAT: prominent 1320–1349.
Extinct (?) after 1410. (Jervise, *Angus and Mearns*, ii, pp. 106–7; *RMS*, i, no. 929.)
MURE OF ABERCORN: prominent from 1350–74.
Extinct *c.*1382; left daughter. (*Scots Pge.*, v, p. 391; *RMS*, i, no. 697.)
MURRAY OF BOTHWELL: prominent from 1320.
Extinct 1361; no obvious heirs.
MURRAY OF CULBIN: prominent 1320–1349.
Extinct *c.*1440. (*RMS*, ii, nos. 149, 238.)
MUSCHET: prominent from 1320.
Extinct *c.*1345; left daughters. (Jervise, *Angus and Mearns*, ii, p. 109; *Scots Pge.*, vii, p. 36.)
OGILVY OF AUCHTERHOUSE: prominent from 1400–24.
Extinct *c.*1470; left daughter. (*Scots Pge.*, i, pp. 109–10.)
OLIPHANT: prominent from 1320; lord of parliament *c.*1464.
Survived past 1500.
PRESTON: prominent 1350–1374.
Survived past 1500. (*RRS*, vi, no. 41; *RMS*, ii, nos. 26, 87n., 705, 1086, 1228, 3540.)
RAMORGNY: prominent from 1375–99.
Extinct (?) 1403. (*ER*, iii, pp. 571–2.)
RAMSAY OF BOTHWELL: lord of parliament 1485.
Survived past 1500.

RAMSAY OF COLLUTHIE: prominent 1350–1374; temporarily earl of Fife, 1358–60.
Survived (?) past 1500. (*RMS*, i, no. 886; ii, no. 3649.)

RAMSAY OF DALHOUSIE: prominent 1320–1399.
Survived (?) past 1500.

ROSS OF HALKHEAD: lord of parliament *c.*1499.
Survived past 1500.

RUTHVEN: lord of parliament 1488.
Survived past 1500.

SEMPILL: lord of parliament 1488.
Survived past 1500.

SETON: prominent from 1320.
Extinct *c.*1348; left granddaughter.

SETON (II): prominent from 1350–74; early lord of parliament.
Survived past 1500.

SETON OF GORDON: prominent from 1400–24; earl of Huntly 1445.
Survived past 1500.

SINCLAIR: prominent from 1320; early lord of parliament.
Survived past 1500. (From 1375 to 1470 held the Norwegian earldom of Orkney; earl of Caithness, 1455, but earldom went to a junior line in 1476.)

SOMERVILLE: prominent from 1350–74; early lord of parliament.
Survived past 1500.

STEWART: prominent from 1320; earl of Strathearn 1357; king 1371.
Survived past 1500.

STEWART OF AVANDALE: lord of parliament 1456.
Survived past 1500.

STEWART OF BADENOCH: prominent from 1350–74; earl of Buchan 1382.
Extinct *c.*1405; no legitimate issue.

STEWART OF BRECHIN: prominent from 1375–99; earl of Caithness 1401, Atholl 1404.
Extinct 1437; no surviving issue.

STEWART OF DARNLEY: prominent from 1350–74; lord of parliament 1452; earl of Lennox 1473.
Survived past 1500.

STEWART OF INNERMEATH: lord of parliament 1464.
Survived past 1500.

STEWART OF JEDWORTH: prominent 1375–1424.
Survived past 1500. (*Scots Pge.*, iv, pp. 146–52.)

STEWART OF LORNE: prominent from 1375–99; early lord of parliament.
Extinct 1463; left daughters.

STRACHAN: prominent 1350–1374.
Survived (?) past 1500. (Walter MacFarlane, *Genealogical Collections concerning Families in Scotland* [SHS, 1900], ii, pp. 265–71.)

STRAITON: prominent 1320–1349.
Survived (?) past 1500. (C.H. Straton, *The Stratons of Lauriston* [Exmouth, 1939], pp. 2–4, 14–19.)

VAUS: prominent from 1350–74.
Extinct *c.*1358; left daughter. (The William Vaus named in the list of David II's hostages has been taken to be William Vaus of Dirleton, the last head of the senior branch of the family of Vaus; *Scots Pge.*, iv, p. 332.)

WALLACE: prominent from 1350–74.
Extinct *c.*1373; left no issue. (*Scots Pge.*, iii, p. 142.)

WEMYSS: prominent from 1320.
Extinct *c.*1342; left daughters.

WEMYSS OF CAMERON: prominent 1350–1374.
Extinct after 1389. (W. Fraser, *Memorials of the Family of Wemyss of Wemyss* [Edinburgh, 1888], i, pp. 14–17, 45–6.)

11

WILLIAM SINCLAIR, EARL OF ORKNEY, AND HIS FAMILY: A STUDY IN THE POLITICS OF SURVIVAL

Barbara E. Crawford

The Sinclair earls of Orkney have acquired something of a legendary aura about them. As heirs of the most famous earls of the Viking world, remote from the centres of political power in Norway and Scotland, they were almost sovereign in their own territory. The idea that they were semi-regal rulers of a maritime domain has been cultivated by all the family historians, from Father Hay in the eighteenth century to Roland St Clair, a member of a New Zealand branch of the family who compiled a massive amount of information about Sinclairs in all corners of the world at the end of the last century.[1] The loss of the earldom of Orkney in the second half of the fifteenth century has been seen by most writers as a shattering blow to the prestige and position of the Sinclair family, reducing it to the status of any other Scottish baronial house. There is no doubt that the family went through an exceedingly difficult period when the process by which the islands of Orkney and Shetland came to the Scottish crown in the 1460s was underway. How they survived the loss of their northern earldom, how they adapted to the changed circumstances, and how they attempted to cling on to lands and power in the north is a highly instructive story in the survival techniques of an ingenious dynasty. It is not possible in the present survey to do more than sketch in the outline of some of these aspects, for not only are the dynasties of the Roslin and Ravenscraig branches concerned but also the flourishing of a separate comital dynasty in Caithness, the establishing of myriad Sinclair branches in Orkney and Shetland in the wake of the independent earldom, and the growth of a new power structure in the Northern Isles. In all these areas, and particularly in respect of the loss of their northern earldom, the Sinclairs had to survive the grasping clutches of a land-hungry crown, and attempt to manipulate the situation so that they retained the substance of their former power, even if they lost their hereditary title to it.

The family's success, for their survival can probably be regarded as a success story, was due primarily to two men. The first of these was Earl William, last Norwegian earl of Orkney and probably the most powerful and wealthy of all the Sinclairs. Not only was he earl of Orkney from 1434 to 1470, but he also managed in 1455 to get back the earldom of Caithness which had been separated from the Orkney earldom in 1375, when a member of the earldom family had resigned it to the Scottish crown. He thus reunited for a brief period the ancient joint Norse earldoms. He managed to do this probably because of the help he had given James II in crushing the Douglases. At that time (1454–6) he was, moreover, Chancellor of Scotland, although as will be seen his relationship with James became less close in the latter years of the reign. With the king's death in 1460 and the accession of the young minor James III, Earl William was for a while one of the foremost members of the regency. However, the marriage of James III to Margaret of Denmark and the pawning of Orkney and Shetland meant the development of a very difficult situation for the earl, leading eventually to the loss of his Orkney earldom.

It was the second notable member of the family, Earl William's grandson, Lord Henry Sinclair, who restored the family's position in the Northern Isles to something approximating its former status. This remarkable man is better known as one of the most enlightened patrons of the arts in Scotland in the late fifteenth century: 'Fader of bukis, protector to sciens and lair',[2] as he was called by Gavin Douglas, he possessed an extensive library and probably commissioned the Selden Manuscript, which was certainly owned by him. To historians of the Northern Isles he is also remarkable for being the astute businessman who attempted to put the family finances in the north back on a profitable footing when he succeeded in being appointed the crown's tacksman in Orkney and Shetland, and who ensured that the family's remaining estates were maintained intact. He was responsible for the compilation of the earliest rentals in Orkney, which provide such a wealth of information about the economy of the islands not only in the late fifteenth century but far back into the Norse period.

Before looking at the role of these two members of the Sinclair family in detail it is necessary to understand the position of the Sinclair earls in the north and the effects which the pledging of the islands to Scotland in 1468–9 had on their position. As heirs of the Norse earls their powers were extensive and their lands and income valuable. The original foundation of the earldom of Orkney was part of the process of settlement of the Northern Isles by the Norwegian Vikings in the ninth century. Although the way in which the members of the powerful Møre family established themselves in the islands is shrouded in the mists of legendary history, there is no doubt that by the last decades of the ninth century this one family had won control of the islands and held the title of earl by virtue of their family position. Later saga material suggests that they had received their earldom and title by grant from the Norwegian kings; but the main theme running through the history of the earldom of Orkney is of the theoretical claims to control by the kings of Norway and the *de facto* independence which the earls seem normally to have possessed. On occasion their wings were clipped, most notably when Earl Harald Maddadson, who gave tacit support to opponents of King Sverre in the late twelfth century, forfeited Shetland and lost some of his income from Orkney as a result. This event is thought to have been the means by which the kings of Norway managed to acquire most of their royal estates in the islands. As the number of earls in Norway declined, the position of the earl of Orkney became increasingly anomalous, and the kings attempted to regard them as royal officials, holding their title by good pleasure of the crown. But the earldom family never lost the hereditary right to claim the earldom title, even though they always had to get royal approval and undergo some form of installation at a ceremony at the Norwegian court. This was the means by which the crown managed to retain some control over the earls, for the custom remained, up until the late fourteenth century, of *any* male member of the family being able to claim the title and receive a grant of the lands. This right could moreover be passed through a female, as had always been the case from the earliest days of the earldom.[3] This led to a situation of much strife in the islands, particularly on the occasion when the Sinclair family managed to acquire the title. The years after the death of Earl Malise (*c.*1350, leaving five daughters) were full of dispeace in the islands as the earl's grandsons, daughters, and their protectors fought it out for power. Although the eldest grandson was given a grant of royal rights in the islands for five years in 1375, it was not he but Henry Sinclair I, son of Isabella and William Sinclair, who managed to persuade King Magnus Eriksson that he was worthy of the title and grant of lands, and who was installed as earl in August 1379. The document issued in which Henry acknowledged his rights and obligations to the Norwegian crown on this occasion is the first documentary evidence for the earl's constitutional position and his formal relationship with the Norwegian king.[4]

Another important development in the history of the northern earldom took place at this same time, and this was the loss of the Scottish half of the earl's dominion, the earldom of Caithness. Since the tenth century this northernmost part of the Scottish mainland had been held by the Orkney earls also with the title of earl, which they acknowledged to be a dignity granted to them by the Scottish king. Thus they were in the sometimes invidious position of being the vassal of two kings. On the occasions when the two overlords distrusted each other, the earls had to tread very warily; and if there was outright war, as in the mid-thirteenth century, the earl seems to have found it best to avoid his obligations to both kings. During the period of expansion of the Scottish royal government in the north in the late twelfth and the thirteenth centuries, the earls lost a great deal of power, including the whole of the southern part of the Caithness earldom, which was erected into the earldom of Sutherland for the family of Moravia. They also lost half of the remaining earldom lands in Caithness due to divided inheritance.[5] What was left was divided between the five daughters of Earl Malise in the mid-fourteenth century, and the eldest grandson, Alexander of Ard, resigned the title of earl to the Scottish crown in 1375. When Henry Sinclair I acceded to the ancient dignity of the northern earls, therefore, he can only have possessed a fraction of the original lands pertaining to the earls in Caithness, and then without any comital title attached. It was to be his grandson Earl William's achievement that he regained the title of earl of Caithness for the family.

Even before the recovery of the earldom of Caithness the Sinclair earls of Orkney were also powerful vassals of the kings of Scots, for they were the holders of important lowland estates. These were centred in Midlothian, where Roslin became the *caput* at about the time that Henry Sinclair acquired the earldom of Orkney. This branch of the family also had lands at Dysart in Fife and at Newburgh in Aberdeenshire. For the first time, therefore, the earls of Orkney were also the holders of large Scottish estates south of the Dornoch Firth. This was important for two reasons: Norwegian earls now played a significant part in Scottish political life by virtue of their position as landholders in the south, and the fact of their dual allegiance was therefore very much more obvious to the Scottish crown. They continued to be prominent in the events of the Scottish realm: Earl Henry I, for instance, was captured at the battle of Homildon Hill; his son Henry II was admiral of Scotland; and his grandson William's important role has already been mentioned. We do not know precisely what the Stewart kings thought of the Sinclairs' situation. But they can hardly have approved of one of their powerful vassals being subject to another sovereign power — one which possessed islands offshore from the Scottish coast. These islands had been the cause of annoyance to the Scottish kings in the past. Success in acquiring the Western Isles from the king of Norway was no doubt well remembered. The acquisition of the Northern Isles must have been a feature of Scottish foreign policy long before it was achieved. The fact that the Sinclair family held them as an ancient comital honour was central to the whole political situation in the north, and must have been central to the Scottish kings' policy regarding the islands.

That policy is unmistakable. The Stewart kings, James II and James III, were determined to get their hands on Orkney and Shetland. This meant not only the acquisition of sovereignty over them, but also the acquisition of the main source of authority and wealth in the islands, the earldom of Orkney. That this was achieved when the earldom was held by one of the most powerful figures in Scotland in the second half of the fifteenth century is evidence for the determination of James III and his counsellors. It is probable, moreover, that this royal policy had been well known to Earl William long before it was actually put into practice by a series of legal arrangements in 1470–2. The developments during the years 1456–68, when the Scottish crown was negotiating with the Danish King Christian (also king of Norway) in an attempt to resolve their differences, and at the same time striving to get hold of the Northern Isles, were evidently not welcome developments to the earl. Yet on the face of it the problem of attempting to serve two masters could only be fully resolved by the handing of the islands to Scotland. The earl's evident unwillingness to see this situation come about is perhaps to be explained by the realisation that it would mean the ensuing loss of his earldom.

Earl William's unwillingness to participate in or further the Scottish crown's policy in political negotiations with Denmark–Norway is reflected in two extraordinary incidents which took place on the two separate occasions when James II and James III were attempting to start those negotiations with King Christian. The first occurred in the winter of 1456–7 when the governor of Iceland was seized while he was sheltering from a storm in Orkney and imprisoned, along with his wife and household. It appears, from a letter which King Christian wrote to James II (dated April 1457) following the incident, that all the governor's goods and furnishings had been seized, as well as the royal tribute and ecclesiastical rents from Iceland which he was accompanying to Denmark.[6] Although there is no mention of the earl of Orkney's part in this incident, it could not have happened within his earldom without his consent. It is possible that this violation of King Christian's sovereign authority — for the governor of Iceland was a royal official — was deliberately timed. In May 1456 Christian had made a treaty with Charles VII of France in which Charles had promised to bring his good offices to bear to enforce payment of the annual sum of 100 marks which Scotland was obliged to pay to Norway for the cession of the Western Isles.[7] This extraordinary payment, which according to the treaty of Perth was supposed to be paid annually for ever, had lapsed during the fifteenth century, although a treaty renewing the agreement to pay had been made by Scotland and Norway in 1426. There is no evidence that payments were ever renewed thereafter, and Christian made strong representation during the 1450s to get the annual sum once again. The legates of Scotland and Denmark were meant to discuss the problem at a friendly meeting in Paris at Whitsun 1457, but because of the incident against the governor of Iceland, Christian asked that this meeting be delayed. Had this been the whole purpose of the attack on the governor of Iceland, which had thus been engineered by the earl with this precise aim in mind? Although there is no means of knowing exactly what James II's policies were about the Northern Isles at this date, it was going to be very clear in 1460 that he was determined to try and get hold of them through the negotiating processes with Denmark–Norway. Although yet young, James II had already shown himself aggressive in his foreign relations, conducting a campaign against England in 1456, and (more pertinently) investing his son with the lordship of Man in November 1455 and sending an expedition to the island, an act of 'blatant aggression'.[8]

Certainly there is evidence of a significant change in Earl William's relationship with King James in the winter of 1456–7. From being one of his foremost supporters in the crisis with the Douglases, and holding the highest position in the royal administration — that of chancellor in 1454–6 — the earl completely fades out of the central records for the next few years, and must have been permanently absent from court. The favour in which he had been held is very evident from his success in regaining the ancient earldom of Caithness for himself and his heirs in 1455. This grant was in marked contrast to James's general policy of retaining lands in the hands of the crown wherever possible. It was made in compensation for claims to the lordship of Nithsdale, which the earl had through his mother; but there is a possibility that the grant may have been made as part of a bargain which was being driven at this time between the king and the earl over the future of his Orkney earldom.[9] Scottish policy was probably being formulated in response to the renewed Danish demands for the 'annual'. Yet the good relations between the king and the earl suddenly soured and William ceased to be chancellor in the winter of 1456 (his last known act as chancellor was on 20 October 1456). It was at this juncture that the attack on the governor of Iceland was carried out. There is no obvious reason why the earl should have ceased to be chancellor, but a possible explanation is that his continued possession of the office became incompatible with the hardening of James II's attitude regarding the Northern Isles and the Orkney earldom. Whether he was removed from the chancellorship *before* or *after* the attack on the governor of Iceland cannot be determined. But the coincidence of the two events suggests that they must in some way be linked. James's plans for the acquisition of the Northern Isles were made very plain in the negotiations which finally took place between the Scots and the Danes before the French king at Bourges in 1460. (Several planned meetings had been cancelled or postponed in the intervening years.)[10] Although the Scots were the defaulters on the annual payment, they demanded, as well as its remittance, that Orkney and Shetland be handed over to the Scottish crown as part of a marriage alliance between the two countries. It was hardly surprising that the Danish negotiators refused to come to any arrangement over the Northern Isles, for the Scottish demands were audacious.

However, James II's death intervened to disrupt the negotiations which were taking place between the Scots and the Danes, and the plans of that aggressive monarch collapsed. Earl William was, for a while, released from the problem of reconciling the interests of his personal position and the political plans of his Scottish monarch. There is even evidence to show that he attempted to come to a more amicable arrangement with King Christian, whom he appears to have ignored up to this time.[11] He was also busy once more at the helm of the Scottish state, for he was a regent during the first years of the minority of James III. Any importance he had regained in government probably ceased, however, with the death of Bishop Kennedy (1465) and the rise of the Boyds. There is no evidence that the earl had any connexion with the Boyds, and an eighteenth-century family history of the Sinclair earls (in private possession) is probably right when it says that Earl William and the Boyds were opposed. Indeed, it suggests that the Boyds deliberately sought to reduce the power of the earl by reviving the Danish marriage question; and certainly it is noticeable that the Danish question was revived at just the same time as the Boyds acquired control of the king. They abducted him from Linlithgow in July 1466, and in October the matter of the 'annuale of Norway' was raised in the parliament as well as the question of the young king's marriage. The family history referred to above mentions also a secret correspondence between the Boyds and Christian for the purpose of plotting the overthrow of Earl William, although as with other theories of 'collusion' nothing very substantial seems to lie behind this theory.[12] But, strikingly, at this point occurs the second of the two incidents which the raising of the Danish question seems to have aroused, ten years on from the previous one. It is remarkably similar to the capture of the governor of Iceland in Orkney in 1456–7: in 1466–7 the bishop of Orkney was captured by the son of the earl, within a few months of the discussion about the young king's marriage in the parliament of October 1466. Bishop William Tulloch was thrown into prison, bound in chains, and constrained to take oaths, about which Christian wrote two letters complaining to the Scottish council and James III on 31 May 1467.[13] The victim of the second attack was also a Danish royal official, for the bishop had shown himself willing to act on King Christian's behalf in the islands and to represent his interests. In 1462 he had promised his loyalty and service to King Christian as a Norwegian councillor of state. The outrage perpetrated against him in 1466–7 was stated to have been carried out by the earl's eldest son who, as will be seen (below, p. 245), was later to be deprived of his main inheritance by his father, and who was probably in some respects irrational in his actions. His intention on this occasion would, however, appear to have been logical enough — to disrupt negotiations which he did not consider to be in the family's long-term interests.[14]

The effect of this incident was not long lasting. Bishop William was free in Shetland in June 1467 to present a candidate to a living, and in January of the next year arrangements were made in the Scottish parliament to send an embassy to Denmark before March or April to choose a bride for James; instructions on 'the matter of Norway' were also to be given to the embassy. In July the members of the embassy were named, and the visit to Denmark must have taken place over the summer, for the marriage treaty of Christian's daughter Margaret and James III of Scotland was ratified by Christian on 8 September 1468. Thomas Boyd, recently created earl of Arran, was a member of the Scottish embassy, as also was Bishop William Tulloch, rather surprisingly. He seems to have been notably successful in keeping in with both Christian of Denmark and the Scottish king. As the earl's star in the north was eclipsed, the bishop's shone even brighter.

Earl William's worst fears were confirmed. The marriage treaty with Denmark resulted in the handing of the islands of Orkney and Shetland to Scotland as a pledge for the payment of the princess's dowry of 60,000 florins of the Rhine. The aims of the Scots had been made plain in the earlier negotiations which had taken place under the auspices of Charles VII in 1460, when the demand had been made that Orkney and Shetland be handed over to Scotland. The Scots did not succeed in getting all their demands in 1468, which suggests that Christian resisted them as far as he could. But he was keen to make a weighty marriage alliance, he was heavily involved in war with Sweden, and he was deeply in debt. These three factors resulted in the agreement to the pledging of 'all and sundry of our lands of the islands of the Orkneys with all and sundry rights, services and their rightful pertinents, pertaining or that in whatsoever manner may pertain to us and our predecessors, kings of Norway, by royal right', for 50,000 florins.[15] In the following year, Shetland was pledged in the same terms for 8,000 florins, and Christian must have raised the remaining 2,000 florins. There is no evidence that Christian intended this to be anything but a temporary measure. The Scots, on the other hand, were determined that it was the beginning of a permanent situation. By stepping into the king of Denmark's shoes they did not, however, achieve permanent possession, for the situation could be legally reversed whenever Christian might manage to raise the dowry money and thus regain the Northern Isles. It is not exactly clear what King James actually acquired in the way of lands or income by receiving the islands in pledge in 1468–9. It has been argued that it may have been only temporary occupation of the royal estates in the Northern Isles, although it seems that a great deal more was actually transferred by the transaction – including the right to annual skat (tax) from the 'odal' landholders in the islands.[16] What is clear is that the tenurial situation in the Northern Isles was deeply complicated, and was very different from the landholding situation in any feudalised part of Scotland. Moreover, the most powerful force in the islands was the earl — not only from his landed possessions, but also from the ancient and deep-rooted rights which he had as ruler of the islands, as controller of the revenues, and as all-powerful judicial and legal authority. Whatever rights and incomes the Norwegian kings might have obtained over the centuries, they were only realised with the goodwill of the earl. The difficulties which King Christian had experienced in the 1450s and '60s of getting in what was his just income are very clear from the Danish sources. King James determined that he would resolve both these problems by acquiring the earldom rights himself. Thus he would obtain a permanent position in the islands, whatever the future attempts to repossess sovereignty over them by the Danes; and he would be in possession of all the rights and privileges whether royal or comital, the distinction between the two not being easy to maintain. There seems little doubt that this was Stewart policy, may have been so for some time, and was well known to the Sinclairs. James was soon to show himself capable of very decisive action, for immediately following the royal marriage the Boyds were removed from their powerful position, and the king himself was the instigator of the charges against them.[17] He must also have been the driving force behind the acquisition of the earldom rights, which took place in September 1470.

This 'excambion', which has been subjected to differing interpretations, is considered by some Orkney historians to have been a shameful transaction because it apparently gave Earl William only a castle in Fife in exchange for all his earldom powers and lands. Now the earl is specifically said to have resigned the castle of Kirkwall and all his right in, or claim to, the earldom of Orkney. But by the process of the transfer of sovereignty in 1468 he had been put in a very difficult position regarding the earldom lands, for with every change of overlord he was supposed to get a renewed grant of the earldom lands and of the royal lands which the earls held on behalf of the Norwegian king. It is clear, however, that after Christian's accession to the throne of Denmark–Norway Earl William had never got such a reaffirmation of his grant, for the Danish king threatened reprisals against him for this failure on several occasions in the early 1460s. The earldom estates were official estates which were held by the earl in respect of the title which he was given by the king and which he did not simply acquire by inheritance. Therefore the king of Scotland could justifiably assume control of them when he replaced King Christian as the earl's sovereign. In consequence, what Earl William resigned in 1470 was *only* the castle of Kirkwall along with his family's theoretical right to claim the earldom (*totum ius eius comitatus Orchadie*) and *not* all the earldom lands and powers. What he was given in return was Ravenscraig Castle, an annual pension of 50 marks (increased dramatically to 400 marks the next year), licence to reside in whatever place he chose within Scotland or without, the right to have his rents and farms taken to his place of residence without impediment for the rest of his life, exemption from all parliaments, embassies and all other public duties unless he wished to participate, confirmation of all previous grants of his offices in Caithness (his title to which was quite unaffected by the excambion), and quittance of all debts or sums of money or claims of any kind which might be made upon him by the king of Denmark. King James also made a final promise regarding the earl's lands and rents, which will be discussed later.[18]

The impression given by this series of privileges is not that Earl William had entirely lost face in the transaction. These grants in favour of the earl suggest that to some extent he must have dictated the terms of the excambion, particularly as regards the cession of the up-to-date royal castle of Ravenscraig, which made a very fine *caput* for his Fife estates at Dysart. There is also evidence that Earl William had a very constructive policy for the retention of Sinclair power and influence in the Northern Isles.

This policy concerns certain lands which appear in the Orkney rentals, compiled by Earl William's grandson, Lord Henry Sinclair, in 1492 and 1502. These are a category of land called 'conquest', different from both the earldom or royal estate, and their existence has been long known to Orkney historians. J.S. Clouston studied their extent, and using his figures in *The Orkney Parishes* there appear to have been 412 pennylands of conquest land throughout those parts of Orkney covered by the rentals, compared with 336 pennylands of earldom land and 673 pennylands of royal land. (A pennyland was a division of land evidently worth one penny when first used, and a division of a much larger unit, the ounceland, although by the fifteenth century pennylands had come to vary very much in size.) Roughly one-third of the lands of all the independent 'odal' farmers of Orkney appears to have been converted into conquest lands by the time of the compilation of the rentals.[19] Who had secured these 'conquests' (= acquired lands as opposed to inherited lands)? Primarily, Earl William Sinclair. The 1502 rental states in a memorandum on the island of Walls that the land paying rent 'is all bocht and conqueist be erle William as this rentale beris quhat wes conquest and quhat wes uther menis'.[20] The main purpose of the compilation of the 1502 rental was evidently to establish the extent of the conquest lands and get in rent from them. This shows that Earl William had acquired by purchase and other means a huge personal estate in Orkney, as also in Shetland, although the evidence from the latter is only fragmentary. The purpose behind this policy can only have been to ensure that the earl and his family retained a landed presence in the islands, even though they might be deprived of their earldom and their political power as the king's representatives. As has been suggested, Earl William was probably aware of the royal policy concerning the islands from the mid-1450s. That his fears were not ill-founded is borne out by what actually happened. By 1470 he had been deprived of the ancient comital estate throughout Orkney, which had included much of the best land in the islands, and he had been deprived of the political authority which had given him the control of the royal estates and of the collection of the skats of butter and malt from all the 'odal' farmers. This is not to mention the judicial and other ancient rights and privileges which as earls he and his ancestors had enjoyed for generations. It must have meant a steep drop in the annual income which Earl William had been accustomed to enjoy, and which was only partly offset by the pension which he was granted for life by James III as part of the excambion arrangement.

When facing this prospect, which the earl must have had to do in 1460 if not before, it cannot have escaped him that the loss of his earldom would mean the loss of all his family estates in the islands. There appear to have been different kinds of land pertaining to the earldom in Orkney, for two distinct names are applied to earldom land in the rentals: 'auld earldom' and 'bordland' — the latter being a term for mensal estates which had probably been imported from Scotland. Both quite clearly pertained to the dignity of earl and would have to be resigned with the title. However, personal estate which the earl himself had purchased was in quite a different legal category, and could in no way be regarded as an adjunct of his office. There was a complete distinction in feudal law between inherited land and acquired land, and the latter could be acquired by purchase, donation, or even excambion.[21]

It is for this reason that these purchased estates are always referred to in the rentals as 'conquest' — to distinguish them from lands which had pertained to the earl by reason of his office. He might, as is said in one case, have made 'rady payment in louse guid 't rady money',[22] but in some instances the lands were acquired in exchange for relief from skat burdens, which did not cost the earl anything but apparently gave him possession of the land exchanged. The piecemeal nature of many of the purchases is quite apparent from the entry concerning land acquired in Stennes, bought in three different lots from different people at different dates. In general the conquest lands were outlying portions of 'odal' estates, although there are three examples of whole large estates being acquired.[23] Clouston suggested that most of this purchasing had been done not long before the earldom came into the hands of the crown in 1470. One important land transaction — an excambion, not a straight purchase — took place no later than 1460–1, however, as it was agreed with Bishop Thomas of Orkney who resigned the see at that time. It is quite clear that a great deal of land was coming into Earl William's hands in the latter part of his period as earl, and the impetus behind this development is readily explained by the impending political change. Clouston thought that the odallers themselves may have taken the initiative in getting rid of some of their lands because of the political uncertainty, although it is not clear what the advantages were in so doing. A more recent suggestion has been that the sale of lands relates to the state of economic depression which is apparent in some parts of Orkney from the 1492 rental.[24] This may certainly help to explain why so many 'odal' families were willing to part with some of their lands. Yet such a massive programme of land acquisition on the part of the earl is most unlikely to have been dictated entirely by the needs of his subjects, although he may have benefited from a difficult economic situation by being able to acquire land fairly cheaply. We know that in the mid-1450s Earl William was in debt to his father-in-law, to whom he pledged some of his Caithness estates;[25] this was perhaps partly caused by his purchase of 'odal' land in Orkney. He was clearly in need of money in the north, and not likely to have embarked on a land-purchasing programme which did not suit his own particular estate policies.

New evidence shows that the policy of acquisition of the conquest lands was vindicated, for the crown was unable to get hold of them at the excambion with the earl in 1470. The document transcribed below in the Appendix shows just how important the lands acquired by Earl William in Orkney and Shetland were to the Sinclair family. It summarises the struggle which dominated most of the sixteenth century between the main (Ravenscraig) line of Sinclairs and the cadet branches descended from Earl William which had settled in the north. This struggle was over the earl's conquest lands, as well as some acquired later by his grandson Lord Henry Sinclair and by his illegitimate son Sir David Sinclair (below, p. 248). The document relates how conquest lands had been acquired by William, earl of Caithness and Lord Sinclair, in Orkney and Shetland, and that King James had declared 'he had na rycht therto'. This appears to be an admission by the crown that these lands did not form part of the earldom estate, suggesting that there may have been some dispute over the legal status of the conquest lands — which is not at all unlikely. Earl William would have been able to show that these lands were private acquisitions which according to feudal law the crown could not treat as earldom estate. The document goes on to say that King James issued the earl with a letter under the privy seal assuring him and his descendants of the future possession of these lands without any impediment. The date of this letter is given as 3 February 1471/2, before the regular recording of privy seal business, so that there is no central record of this letter.

There may, however, be a surviving charter in the central records which relates directly to the conquest lands, for one of the charters granted to Earl William under the great seal in September 1470 as part of the excambion can be interpreted as bearing directly on the retention of lands in the north. In this, the king promised that he would receive the resignation of the earl's lands and rents and possessions whensoever he wished to resign them, and that he would regrant them by charter and sasine, to be held as freely as they were held before the resignation without anything at all having to be done or paid to the king.[26] It would appear that this refers to the earl's northern estates, for it certainly concerns lands which he held already, but which there is no mention he held by any grant or charter. He was perhaps preparing himself for the process of acquiring a feudal charter and guarantee for his conquest lands; being 'odal', they were not held of any superior. Nor were they liable to any feudal dues (although the odaller paid land taxes or skat to the crown), and Earl William seems concerned to continue to hold them as freely as he does already, evidently wishing to avoid any new impositions. The letter later granted to him under the privy seal, declaring that he and his successors and factors should 'be anserit' of the conquest lands without any impediment, suggests that the new royal officials in the islands may have been regarding the conquest estates as part of the former earldom estate and failing to recognise the former earl's continued rights to them. The political situation in the islands since the pledging and excambion was so changed that constant vigilance must have been required for the Sinclairs to be able to maintain their hold on the conquest lands, even though they had legal assurances from the crown of their right to them.

As in the latter days of Norwegian control, it was the bishops to whom the king looked to administer his lands and rights in the islands. The lease of the lordships of Orkney and Shetland was held by Bishops William Tulloch and Andrew Painter, from 1474 to 1488. There was an apparent reluctance on the part of the crown to allow the Sinclairs to maintain their hereditary control in the islands by getting their hands on the substance of power, although in the long run the bishops were unable to withstand 'the determination of the Sinclair family to maintain their influence in the lands that had been taken from them by James III'.[27] Earl William's grandsons Lord Henry Sinclair and Sir William of Warsetter, who presumably shared the inheritance of the conquest lands, managed to establish themselves in positions of power in the islands. Henry Sinclair first appears in the exchequer accounts as 'farmer' of the lordships under the bishop in 1484, but the 1502 rental suggests that he may in fact have had some control over the accounts since 1480, for there are references to a period of twenty-two years 'that I gat never the scats thereof' and to twenty-two years 'bigan in my tyme'.[28] This points to the year 1480 as marking the occasion when he had acquired rights over the skats of Orkney. This was close to the date of Earl William's death, which took place between Martinmas 1479 and Whitsunday 1480, suggesting that Henry took over some control of the family's conquest lands in Orkney on his grandfather's death. He certainly had control over the tacks of the Northern Isles before his name appears in any official capacity in the exchequer records, and well before he received an official grant of the tack in 1489.[29] But even in the brief period of time between Earl William's resigning his right in the earldom to the crown and the acquisition by his grandson, Henry, of administrative authority in the islands, the bishop had been able nevertheless to divert some of the income due to the crown in the form of skat to his own benefit. The rentals which Henry compiled in 1492 and 1502 were an attempt to restore the situation to what it had been before the pledging of the islands and to present a 'picture of his whole family lands as they had existed in the days of Earl William'.[30] That Henry did indeed restore the situation to his own satisfaction, and had full control of the conquest lands, is clearly stated in the family document (see Appendix). The real problems started on his death at Flodden, when he left a minor, and royal officers were put into the islands who 'intromitted' with the conquest lands and those of Sir David Sinclair (below, p. 248). Thereafter the Ravenscraig Sinclairs appear to have lost control of the conquest lands and never succeeded in getting their hands back on them. An internal power struggle developed in the north culminating in the battle of Summerdale in 1529. This was very much a civil war of Sinclair against Sinclair, and the struggle was particularly over possession of conquest lands — probably Lord Henry's and Sir David's — between Lord Henry's son and heir, William, and the family of Sir William of Warsetter who had got control of the island administration.[31] William, Lord Sinclair, succeeded in having commissions granted for the holding of an enquiry into the family lands in the north, but through 'occasion and trubill' and 'civil werres' these failed to achieve a just settlement. His son, another Henry (fifth Lord Sinclair), was responsible for the final attempt to get some support for their claim, and the 1581 document transcribed in the Appendix was drawn up by him. Its drafting may relate to the elevation of Earl Robert Stewart to the earldom of Orkney and lordship of Shetland in August of that year. We do not know the result of this petition; it was remitted by the Lords of Articles to the Lords of Session, but we can guess that the fifth Lord Sinclair failed to get any action taken on his behalf as his father had failed before him. Their persistence in the face of solid opposition in the islands is testimony to the value of those family lands in both Orkney and Shetland which were the remainder of the great Sinclair empire in the north.

It is to be hoped that Earl William never divined the family troubles and wars which were going to ensue over possession of those conquest lands which he had expended so much money and effort acquiring in the years prior to the impignoration of the islands of Orkney and Shetland to Scotland. He may well, however, have had fears about the outcome of his other estate policies by which he divided up his southern lands among his sons in the years before his death. Two of these sons have been referred to already: William 'the Waster', son of his first marriage, and Sir David Sinclair, his only known illegitimate son. From what can be gathered together about

Table 9. *Earl William Sinclair's descendants*

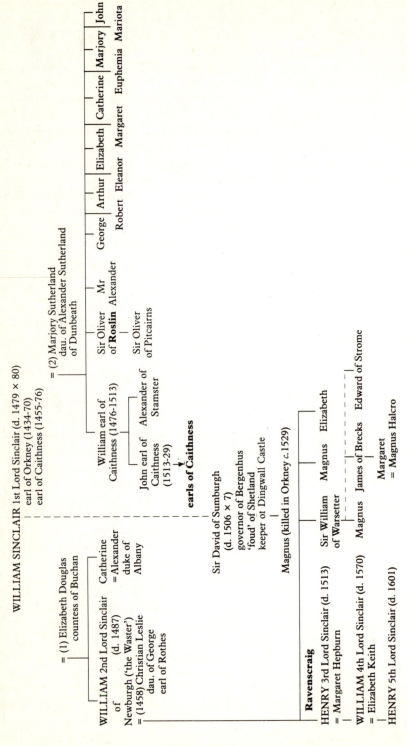

WILLIAM SINCLAIR 1st Lord Sinclair (d. 1479 × 80)
earl of Orkney (1434-70)
earl of Caithness (1455-76)

= (1) Elizabeth Douglas
countess of Buchan

- WILLIAM 2nd Lord Sinclair of Newburgh ('the Waster') (d. 1487)
= (1458) Christian Leslie
dau. of George
earl of Rothes
- Catherine
= Alexander
duke of
Albany

= (2) Marjory Sutherland
dau. of Alexander Sutherland
of Dunbeath

- William earl of Caithness (1476-1513)
  - John earl of Caithness (1513-29) → **earls of Caithness**
  - Alexander of Stamster
- Sir Oliver of **Roslin**
  - Sir Oliver of Pitcairns
- Mr Alexander
- George
- Robert
- **Arthur**
- Eleanor
- **Elizabeth**
- Margaret
- **Catherine**
- Euphemia
- **Marjory**
- Mariota
- **John**

(illegitimate, dashed line:)
Sir David of Sumburgh
(d. 1506 × 7)
governor of Bergenhus
'foud' of Shetland
keeper of Dingwall Castle
- Magnus (killed in Orkney *c.*1529)

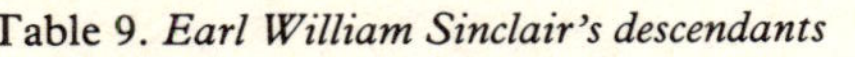

(descendants of WILLIAM 2nd Lord Sinclair:)

Ravenscraig
HENRY 3rd Lord Sinclair (d. 1513)
= Margaret Hepburn
WILLIAM 4th Lord Sinclair (d. 1570)
= Elizabeth Keith
HENRY 5th Lord Sinclair (d. 1601)

- Sir William of Warsetter
  - Magnus
  - James of Brecks
    - Margaret
    = Magnus Halcro
  - Edward of Strome
- Magnus
- Elizabeth

these two scions of the last earl of Orkney, they appear to have pursued rather different policies as regards the possession of land, and they make a fascinating comparison. William, the earl's eldest son, was born with all the advantages of his station, yet he appears to have failed to live up to the ideal of what was expected of an eldest son in a feudal society. David, the earl's illegitimate son, although born with the disadvantages of his birth, succeeded however in making a career for himself and becoming a very powerful and respected individual in the service of both the king of Norway and the king of Scotland. He ended his life with a knighthood granted to him by both these kings.[32] His half-brother, the elder William, never appears to have held the dignity of earl which should automatically have been his by right as the eldest son of the earl of Caithness. The reason for this seems to have been that he was deliberately excluded from the inheritance of the earldom of Caithness by his father. It is quite clear that he was left out of a settlement of the main estates made by the old earl in 1476,[33] but he was not entirely disinherited, for he continued to hold the estate of Newburgh in Aberdeenshire and he took the title of Lord Sinclair after his father's death. He was in possession of the lands of Newburgh and of Carden in Stirlingshire by 1459, perhaps having received them on the occasion of his marriage to Christian Lesley in 1458. He also used the title 'master of Caithness', and evidently attempted to pursue his claim to the earldom, but he never succeeded in getting possession. In 1476 the earldom of Caithness was handed over to Earl William's son by his second marriage, also called William, and the estate of Roslin and the lands of Herbertshire (Stirlingshire), with adjoining interests, were made over to the earl's son Oliver, also by his second wife.[34] It is clear from later evidence that the Fife estates were likewise given to Oliver by his father before his death.

Why was there this evident prejudice against the elder William? It was perhaps because his mother had been a Douglas; and the fact that the eldest son of the second marriage was also called William suggests that there may have been an intention from the start to treat the children of the second marriage as the earl's main heirs. There is also clear evidence that the elder William may not have been considered competent enough to be his father's main heir. He has acquired the nickname 'the Waster', and this stems from a verdict of idiotry of 17 April 1482, when he was declared *incompos mentis et fatuus* and 'a waster of his lands and goods', and was said to have been in that condition for sixteen years.[35] The reason why the verdict was procured at this particular date may have had something to do with the elder William's relations with his half-brothers, for after his father's death in 1479 or 1480 he was undeniably active in getting possession of what he considered his rightful inheritance. His half-brother Oliver must have expected trouble, for not long after his father's death, in July 1480, he made a bond with George, Lord Seton, in which the latter promised to help 'in the peacable brookeing and joiseing of the lands of Roslin, Pentland and Pentlandmoor ... Dysart and Ravenscraig after the tenor of his [Oliver's] enfeoffments made till him thereupon'.[36] Oliver was unable to resist outright his elder brother's claims, however, and in February 1481 an agreement was drawn up between the two half-brothers, in which Oliver renounced the lands of Cousland (Midlothian), Dysart and Ravenscraig, while William and his son renounced 'all Right, Claim and Title of right' which they may have had to the lands of Roslin, Pentland, Morton (Midlothian) and Herbertshire. Both parties agreed in all time to come 'to stand in a firm and true friendship and kindness as Carnell brethren should doe and aither of them to Help further and supply other in all their actions, causes and quarrels moved and to be moved'. Sir Oliver further agreed to do worship and honour to the said William 'as effeiris and accords him doe to his eldest brother', and, significantly, if there should happen 'any plea or debaitt to be betueist the said William and William his younger brother for the earldom of Caithness Oliver was to stand evenly between them as he should do between his brothers and tak no partiall part in either of them'.[37] This makes it quite clear that the new Lord Sinclair also intended to lay claim to the earldom of Caithness.

What one suspects is that Lord Sinclair's son, Henry, was the moving spirit behind this burst of activity. As we have already seen, Henry Sinclair was active in Orkney in 1480, the probable year of his grandfather's death. He was also named in February 1481 as acting with his father in the agreement with his uncle Oliver. In later documents Henry described himself as son and heir to William Sinclair 'and also aire to umquile William Earl of Caithness and Lord Sinclair his grandfather'. In 1487 he called himself 'master of Caithness' as his father had done, and in 1489 he was declared in parliament to be 'heretar' to his father and grandfather 'Lordes Sinclar for the tyme', and therefore 'cheiff of that blude'.[38] Those members of Earl William's family who thought that they had got their inheritance all nicely sewn up at the expense of the unfavoured elder brother must have got a nasty shock when they found their nephew pursuing his rights with vigour and claiming to be his grandfather's heir. The family agreement of February 1481 had certainly not established harmonious relations for very long, for just one year later, on 17 April 1482, the verdict of idiotry was brought against William, Lord Sinclair — presumably by members of the family who had lost out in the agreement. An idiot was placed in the care of his nearest agnate,[39] and by a recent act (1475) it had to be stated how long an idiot had been in that condition and any deeds made by him since that date could be 'reduced' (annulled). In 1483 William was pursuing a cause against Sir Oliver 'for withholding from William the charters and fiefings of the said lands contrary to his band of obligation', which may have been because of the verdict of idiotry. In the next year William was 'comperand for his interests' before the Lords Auditor, so the verdict cannot have been taken too seriously.[40]

There must, however, have been some justification for the bringing of a brieve of idiotry; is there any evidence that the eldest son of the old earl was really incapable of looking after his affairs, and a waster of his lands and goods? The year in which he is supposed to have succumbed to that condition, 1466 — sixteen years before the bringing of the brieve — was in fact the year in which the bishop of Orkney had been imprisoned by the eldest son of the earl of Orkney, although, as has been discussed, that event may have had more behind it than merely the impetuous action of an imbecile young man. The retour of inquest concerning his insanity says that he had alienated his land and other goods and laid them waste *absque aliqua rationabili causa* (original retour in private possession). As early as 1465 he had granted out certain lands to one Malcolm MacLery.[41] There are several records of the alienation of lands and fishing rights on his Newburgh estates, and some of these were pledged for loans of money, as for instance in 1477, when the fishings on the Ythan were alienated heritably by him, with the consent and assent of Christian Lesley, his wife, to James Ogilvy of Deskford until 645 marks had been paid in the cathedral church of Aberdeen.[42] Towards the end of his life he sold Archadlie, in the barony of Newburgh, to Patrick Gordon, again with consent of his wife, *pro debitis suis acquitandis ac sustentatione vite sue.*[43] A letter of assignation to the earl of Erroll about the same time authorised the earl to redeem William's wadset lands in Newburgh and hold them himself.[44] Even some of the Ravenscraig estates would appear to have been alienated after he had acquired them from his brother Oliver in 1481, for the lands of Wilston and Carberry which usually went along with Ravenscraig were granted out to Nicholas Ramsay in 1486.[45] There is therefore clear evidence that William 'the Waster' was in need of money, the reason for which is not known, although it could possibly have been to pay off his father's debts. However, the verdict of idiotry considered that he had wasted his lands and goods 'without any reasonable cause'. Any damage done to the family estates would have been put right by his son. We have seen that Lord Henry was an exceedingly efficient administrator of his lands and goods, with a shrewd approach to the restoration of his father's estates. A decree arbitral of 1498 shows him acquiring from his mother quitfeftments and terces from his father's estate, in which she made her son 'Hir full assignar and cessionar In and to all and hale hir landis annuell rentis ... belanging and pertenyit to hir' (MS in private possession). It is evidently endorsed in Lord Henry's own hand: 'The decreit gevin betuix my moder and me'. The Orkney rentals show the same personal control and direction of his economic affairs. Whatever defects of intellect his father may have had were certainly not passed on to the eldest son, who was in all ways the true heir to his grandfather.

If the old Earl William was disappointed in his eldest son, he had reason to be proud of the achievements of his one known illegitimate son, Sir David. It seems likely that David was the offspring of a union in the Northern Isles for he spent most of his life in the north, and was particularly closely attached to Shetland, where Sumburgh became his main seat — his usual title being Sir David Sinclair of Sumburgh, knight. There is much evidence to show that David Sinclair was as active in acquiring land in Shetland (and Orkney) as his father had been. He also inherited land from his father and was probably on the same footing as his half-brothers and sisters in this respect, for illegitimacy was no bar to inheritance under Norwegian law. In his will Sir David left 'all the landis that I possessit eftir my Fader died in Zetland' to his nephew Lord Henry.[46] But he also succeeded in gaining possession of his brothers' and sisters' shares of the family inheritance in Shetland. In a charter of 1498 thirteen of Earl William's children are named as granting their 'odal' portions in Sumburgh and throughout Shetland to Sir David.[47] William 'the Waster' was himself dead by this date, so if he had been included in the division of conquest lands which this charter shows had taken place in Shetland, we have no evidence of it. (His son Henry in any case probably preferred to hold on to his Shetland inheritance because of his involvement in the north.) As mentioned,

Sir David left his 'odal' lands in Shetland to Lord Henry, and he left objects of value to Henry's wife and son. This tells us that Sir David and Lord Henry were on good terms, which other evidence also suggests. When Lord Henry acquired the tacks of the lordships of Orkney and Shetland, Sir David shared the administration with him by acting as 'foud' of Shetland. In the family quarrel which broke out in Orkney in 1529, Sir David Sinclair's son Magnus joined in on the side of Lord Sinclair against the sons of Sir William of Warsetter — and was slain by them.[48] Sir David's political career was very successful (above, p. 245) and was the probable source of his great wealth, with which he was able to build up such a large estate in both Orkney and Shetland. Several of the documents concerning his purchases in the north are extant, and their extent is also known from an inventory drawn up some years after his death.[49] It seems very likely that the first Shetland rental (early sixteenth century) was compiled by Sir David and organised in some way to keep a record of his and Lord Henry's purchases, but the reference to the compiler of the rental as 'my Lord' is completely non-specific. Nor is it clear exactly how the record of the skats and rents of different kinds of lands is organised (information from Brian Smith, Shetland Archivist).

The Scottish crown was able to acquire Sir David's inherited estates in the north by reason of escheat for bastardy. The first evidence for this is a grant of Sir David's goods to Lady Sinclair (Lord Henry's widow) in 1524.[50] But the 1581 document (see Appendix) shows that the Ravenscraig Sinclairs considered themselves to be the heirs to Sir David's lands. In that document the first reference to these lands is when the fifth Lord Sinclair complained that the conquest lands originally acquired by Earl William and the lands of Sir David 'to quhom I succeid as narrest and lauchfull air' had been administered by royal officials during his father's minority. This lasted for the period 1514–26, during the latter part of which Lady Sinclair was given a grant of the escheated lands as mentioned. The 1581 document says clearly that thereafter it was the conquest lands of Lord Henry and of Sir David over which trouble was generated and to which Henry's son and grandson were laying claim. The original conquest lands of Earl William appear to have been written off by them, and indeed were added to the royal estates as can be seen from later rentals. From other evidence it is known that the royal lands in the Northern Isles were given to James V's queens as dowry,[51] which caused trouble with Sir Oliver Sinclair of Pitcairns and William, fourth Lord Sinclair. These two clashed over possessions in Shetland which were perhaps the conquest lands of Sir David,[52] and Lord William Sinclair was struggling in 1548 to maintain his rights to his father's lands in Orkney and Shetland against both the queen-mother's advocates and the 'folds and bailies' of Orkney and Shetland, who had refused to execute royal letters of cognition.[53]

The determination of all parties concerned to secure as much as they could of the conquest lands of Earl William, and those of his son and grandson, is an indication of what their value must have been. The 'occasion and trubill in thai partis' referred to in 1581 is well known from other sources, and it had culminated in the clash at Summerdale in 1529 between William, Lord Sinclair, and his cousins the sons of Sir William of Warsetter, with many other Sinclairs from both Orkney and Shetland participating. As has recently been made clear, the crown made little effort to ensure that Lord Sinclair's attempts to get redress against his violent cousins were given any legal support, and his son William died in the hands of his cousin (as did the son of Sir David Sinclair).[54] Several commissions were issued to the sheriffs and 'fouds' to take cognition by inquest of the situation regarding the family lands, but the Lords Sinclair failed to get possession of what they felt so passionately was their just inheritance in the north.

What appears to have happened is that after Lord Henry's and Sir David's deaths the cadet branches, and particularly Sir William of Warsetter's family, who had settled in the north, got their hands on all that remained of the northern Sinclair empire. It did not prove possible for the head of the clan to attempt to rule the family estates in both southern Scotland and the islands, particularly when the fourth Lord Sinclair had a disastrously long minority. The demise of the earldom of Orkney meant that the strong control exercised by that member of the earldom family appointed to the position of earl had vanished. Instead there was a proliferation of cadet family branches, which the custom of 'odal' inheritance and equal division of lands among all sons and daughters (legitimate or illegitimate) allowed to flourish. From the salvage of the great Sinclair earldom therefore arose the numerous Sinclair landed families who established themselves on the best available *heid-bol* (chief farm) of former 'odal' estates. Thus the historian is confronted with the confusion of Sinclair families who appear in Orkney and Shetland in the sixteenth century, including the Sinclairs of Warsetter, of Brecks, Strome, Brough, Ness, Evie, Havera, Houss, Quendale, Aith, St Ninian's Isle, Hunto, Sumburgh, Eday, Stromness, Tuquoy, Campston, Essinquoy, Isbister, Ustaness and Voster, to mention just some of them. One or two of these Sinclairs, like Sir James Sinclair of Brecks,[55] managed to win the confidence of the Scottish crown and to be raised in status, or, occasionally, to be given the tack of the royal lands and lordships, like Sir Oliver Sinclair of Pitcairns was in 1541. But none of them ever really regained political control in the islands of the kind that Lord Henry had exercised. The lordships of Orkney and Shetland, and eventually the revived earldom title, came to be recognised as the perquisite of members of the royal family — which an act of parliament of 1472 had ordained should be the case.[56] Across the Pentland Firth in Caithness, a similar proliferation of landed Sinclair families is apparent, branches of the earldom family and descendants of Earl William's son of his second marriage. This remarkable old earl had certainly ensured that the name of Sinclair would continue to be a permanent feature of the north. He achieved this through his estate policies — the reacquisition of the earldom of Caithness and the purchase of a private estate in the islands. Without embarking on these, the name of Sinclair might have vanished from the roll of northern landowning families during the drastic political changes that occurred in the years 1468–72.

NOTES

1. *Genealogie of the Sainteclaires of Rosslyn,* ed. R.A. Hay (Edinburgh, 1835); R. St Clair, *The Saint-Clairs of the Isles* (Auckland, 1898).
2. *The Aeneid of Virgil,* trans. G. Douglas (Bannatyne Club, 1839), i, p. 6.

3. B.E. Crawford, 'The earls of Orkney-Caithness and their relations with Norway and Scotland' (unpublished St Andrews University Ph.D. thesis, 1971), p. 40.

4. *Records of the Earldom of Orkney* (SHS, 1914), no. 11.

5. Above, pp. 32–4.

6. B.E. Crawford, 'The pawning of Orkney and Shetland: a reconsideration of the events of 1468–9', *SHR,* xlviii (1969), p. 39; *Norges Gamle Love,* 2 Raekke (Christiania, 1912–18), ii, p. 129.

7. *Diplomatarium Christierni Primi,* ed. C.F. Wegener (Copenhagen, 1856), no. 55.

8. Macdougall, *James III,* p. 42.

9. This seems more likely than the explanation (cf. *ibid.,* p. 39) that it was to appease the earl over claims he may have had to the earldoms of Mar and Garioch through his deceased wife: see my arguments in Crawford, 'Earls of Orkney-Caithness', pp. 297–8.

10. Ibid., pp. 303–4.

11. Ibid., p. 310.

12. Crawford, 'Pawning', p. 36.

13. *Idem,* 'Earls of Orkney-Caithness', p. 324.

14. The young William Sinclair called himself 'master of Orkney and Caithness' at this time (*RMS,* ii, no. 844). He also acted high-handedly to retrieve a debt owed from his deceased mother's estate in 1456: *Scots Pge.,* vii, p. 570.

15. *Charters and other Records of the City and Royal Burgh of Kirkwall,* ed. J. Mooney (Third Spalding Club, 1952), p. 107.

16. B.E. Crawford, 'The earldom of Orkney and lordship of Shetland: a reinterpretation of their pledging to Scotland in 1468–70', *Saga Book of the Viking Soc.,* xvii (1967–8), p. 168.

17. R. Nicholson, *Scotland: The Later Middle Ages* (Edinburgh, 1974), p. 419.

18. *RMS,* ii, nos. 996–1002.

19. J.S. Clouston, *A History of Orkney* (Kirkwall, 1932), p. 256.

20. A. Peterkin, *Rentals of the Ancient Earldom and Bishoprick of Orkney* (Edinburgh, 1820), p. 26.

21. Sir William Craigie and A.J. Aitken, *Dictionary of the Older Scottish Tongue* (London, 1931–), under 'conquest'.

22. Peterkin, *Rentals,* p. 52.

23. J.S. Clouston, 'The Orkney lands', *Proc. of the Orkney Antiquarian Soc.,* ii (1923–4), p. 65.

24. W.P. Thomson, 'Fifteenth-century depression in Orkney: the evidence of Lord Henry Sinclair's rentals', in *Essays in Shetland History,* ed. B.E. Crawford (Lerwick, 1984), Ch. 7.

25. *Idem,* 'Earls of Orkney-Caithness', p. 291.

26. *Idem,* 'Earldom of Orkney and lordship of Shetland', p. 171.

27. P. Anderson, *Robert Stewart, Earl of Orkney, Lord of Shetland, 1533-93* (Edinburgh, 1982), p. 21.

28. Peterkin, *Rentals,* pp. 48, 91.

29. *RMS,* ii, no. 1842.

30. Anderson, *Robert Stewart,* p. 21.

31. Clouston, *Hist. of Orkney,* p. 284; Anderson, *Robert Stewart,* p. 22.

32. B.E. Crawford, 'Sir David Sinclair of Sumburgh, "foud" of Shetland and governor of Bergen Castle', in *Scandinavian Shetland,* ed. J. Baldwin (Edinburgh, 1978), pp. 1–11.

33. *Scots Pge.,* ii, pp. 332ff.

34. *RMS,* ii, nos. 1267, 1270–1.

35. *Scots Pge.,* vii, p. 570.

36. *Genealogie of the Sainteclaires,* ed. Hay, p. 110.

37. SRO GD 164/18/4; *Genealogie,* p. 82.

38. *APS,* ii, p. 213.

39. J. Erskine, *An Institute of the Law of Scotland,* ed. J. Rankine (Edinburgh, 1902), p. 88.

40. *The Acts of the Lords Auditors of Causes and Complaints,* ed. T. Thomson (Edinburgh, 1839), pp. cxxxiii, 114.

41. *RMS,* ii, no. 844.
42. *Scots Pge.,* vii, p. 570; SRO GD 164/50/404 (1); MS list of charters concerning alienation of fishings on the Ythan (in private possession).
43. *RMS,* ii, no. 1678.
44. *Illustrations of the Topography and Antiquities of the Shires of Aberdeen and Banff* (Spalding Club, 1847–69), iii, pp. 102–3.
45. *RMS,* ii, no. 1657.
46. *The Bannatyne Miscellany* (Bannatyne Club, 1827–55), iii, p. 107.
47. A. Peterkin, *Notes on Orkney and Zetland* (Edinburgh, 1822), app., no. 1.
48. Anderson, *Robert Stewart,* p. 24.
49. *Records of ... Orkney,* pp. 420–5.
50. *Scots Pge.,* ii, p. 336.
51. Anderson, *Robert Stewart,* p. 27.
52. *The Scottish Correspondence of Mary of Lorraine, 1543-60,* ed. A.I. Cameron (SHS, 1927), pp. 85–6.
53. SRO GD 164/50/3. I am grateful to Dr Peter Anderson for help with elucidation of this aspect of the struggle over the conquest lands.
54. Anderson, *Robert Stewart,* pp. 24–5.
55. J.S. Clouston, 'James Sinclair of Brecks', *Proc. of the Orkney Antiq. Soc.,* xv (1939), pp. 61–8.
56. *APS,* ii, p. 102.

APPENDIX*

PETITION OF HENRY, LORD SINCLAIR, TO THE KING IN PARLIAMENT CONCERNING HIS CLAIM TO FAMILY LANDS IN ORKNEY AND SHETLAND. 18 NOVEMBER 1581.

Unto your Maiestie and lordis of parliament humlie menis and schawis Henry now Lord Sinclair successour to umquhile Williame, erle of Cathnes, Lord Sinclair Quha co[n]queist certaine landis heretabillie within the boundis of the lordschippis of Orknay and Zeitland Quhilk your grace's predicessoris King James the therd of maist worthie memorie declarit he had na rycht therto And be his letter under the privie seill willit that my said predicessour his successoris and thair factoris suld be anserit of the samin without impediment As the said letter of the dait the thrid day of Februar the yeir of god Im iiiic lxxi yeiris proportis Be wertew of the quhilk the said umquhile Williame, Erle Cathnes and Henry, Lord Sinclair my guidsir bruikit the saidis landis to his deceis quhilk wes in the feild of Flowdoun And be the minoritie of umquhile Williame, Lord Sinclair my fader the saidis landis and als the landis of umquhile Sir David Sinclair his eme to quhom I succeid As narrest and lauchfull air wer Intromettit with be the officiaris Impute be your hienes dairrest guidsir king James the fyft of guid memorie Quha upoun the sute of my said said[1] umquhile fader directit his grace's commission to umquhile Oliver Sinclair gevand him power to tak cognition Quhat possessiouns landis and rowmes the saidis umquhile Henry, Lord Sinclair my guidsir umquhile Sir David Sinclair and utheris our freindis (to quhom I succeid air) had within the saidis lordschippis of Orknay and Zeitland And gif my said umquhile fader had rycht therto To caus him be anserit therof thankfullie and bruik the samin siclyk as his predecessoris did of befoir As the said Commissioun subscryvit with his hand and under his hienes signet Off the dait the xxi day of Marche and of his hienes Regnne the xxviii yeiris beiris/ Lyk as my said umquhile fader and I than his appeirand air continewing in our persute of our rychtis of the saidis landis presentit supplicatioun to your hienes darrest moder Berand that the said umquhile Henry Lord Sinclair my guidsir and umquhile Sir David Sinclair knycht To quhom I aught and suld be air conqueist certaine particular landis and rowmes within the Iles and boundis of Orknay and Zeitland respective fra the quhilkis my said umquhile fader wes stoppit and debarrit throwe occasioun and trubill in thai partis Upoun the quhilk hir grace willing and being of mynd that my said umquhile fader and I sould nawyss be hurt of ony our landis or rowmes within the Iles and boundis foirsaidis quhairunto I haif rycht and titill be my said umquhile guidsir and Sir David Sinclair Directit hir hienes Commissioun under hir handwrit and signet To the shereff of Orknay and failzeing of him be absens or refuiss To his Lovittis makand thame shereffis of Orknay and

* I would like to acknowledge the help of Mr R. Smart, Keeper of Muniments, St Andrews University, in transcribing this document.

fowdis of Zeitland in that part chargeing thame to tak cognitioun be Inqueist of the cuntrie According to the auld ordour observit in thai partis Quhat landis and rowmes within the Iles and boundis of Orknay and Zeitland pertenit to the said umquhile Henry Lord Sinclair my guidsir and umquhile David Sinclair his eme and to retour the samin and put thame in writ befoir attentik connotaris Swa that efter the sycht thairof hir grace mycht gif Infeftmentis of the saidis landis and rowmes to my said umquhile fader and me than his appeirand air foirsaid Conforme to our Rychtis and titill foirsaid As hir said Commissioun of the dait the xxviii day of marche and hir grace's Regnne the xxv yeir in lyk beris Quhilk cognition be occasion of civill werris tuik not effect Quhairthrowe I haif beine and wilbe frustrat of my rycht of my saidis landis and rowmes Nochtwithstanding the ressonabill sutt of my predicessoris and my selff fra tyme to tyme as said is without your grace's previe remeid Maist humlie heirfoir I beseik your Maiestie and lordschips To haif consideratioun of the premisses And that your lordschips will grant Comission To [ ] Makand thame and Ilk ane of thame Coniunctlie and severalie shereffis of Orknay and fowdis of Zeitland in that part To tak cognitioun be Inqueist of the cuntrie According to the auld ordour observit in thai partis quhat landis and rowmes within the boundis foirsaid respective pertenit to my said umquhile guidsir and umquhile Sir David Sinclair And to retour the samin and put thame in writt befoir attentik notaris to your Maiestie Swa that thaireftir your grace may gif me Infeftmentis of the saidis landis and rowmes Conforme to my said rycht and titill and commissioun grantit grantit[1] be your hienes darrest moder to me therupon of befoir And your hienes and lordschips gratiouss anser I humlie beseik.

Endorsed: Apud Halyrudhous xviii Novembris lxxxi
The lordis of articlis remittis this complaint to begein in to the lordis of sessioun quhome befoir the samyn will get ane ressonabil anser.

Source: Document in private possession.

Note: [1]Sic.

12

CROWN *VERSUS* NOBILITY: THE STRUGGLE FOR THE PRIORY OF COLDINGHAM, 1472–88

Norman Macdougall

In a recent masterly analysis of the politics of fifteenth-century Scotland, Dr Jenny Wormald destroyed the traditional view of the period as one of almost continual conflict between overmighty and irresponsible magnates and a harassed monarchy struggling for survival.[1] She emphasised instead the political norm — co-operation between crown and nobility, a co-operation which worked because each side had something to offer the other. On the one hand, crown patronage was extensive, and included grants of royal land on very favourable terms, offices at court or in the localities, and remission from customs dues or feudal casualties. On the other, the loyalty of the magnates, greater and lesser, was essential to the efficient running of a decentralised state, in which the king could not afford a contract army or salaried justices and therefore relied heavily on delegating authority to members of the nobility in their own localities, above all in the highland west, the north-east and the Borders.[2]

However, Dr Wormald also noted exceptions to her general rule of crown-magnate co-operation, exceptions which she explained in terms of irresponsible acts by individual kings rather than by the magnate class. Quite the most remarkable of these was the protracted struggle between James III and the Border family of Hume over the revenues of the priory of Coldingham, an intermittent conflict which was resolved only by the rebellion of 1488 which cost the king his life. This was a unique event in late medieval Scottish politics; a Stewart king was not only successfully defied for sixteen years by a single Border family, but his belated efforts to coerce that family produced a major revolt in which members of the rebel faction were actively seeking his deposition, while those who could generally be relied upon to assist the crown remained aloof from the struggle and allowed their sovereign to perish. For once, the intensely conservative Scottish political community, which normally countenanced or even supported royal Stewart assaults on rebellious or recalcitrant magnates, failed to obey the rules, a remarkable fact which calls for some explanation.

The Benedictine priory of Coldingham, lying some ten miles north of Berwick upon Tweed, was a dependent cell of the cathedral priory of Durham which had flourished until the wars of independence made the existence of an English house on Scottish soil, populated by monks with divided political and ecclesiastical loyalties, much less acceptable to the Scots; and from a peak of some thirty monks at the end of the thirteenth century, the priory's population had declined sharply until the final expulsion of English monks in 1462.[3] The instruments of that expulsion, and of the complex litigation which followed, were two Humes, Patrick and John, themselves rivals for the Coldingham spoils. Patrick Hume, a graduate of St Andrews and archdeacon of Teviotdale[4] but not a member of the main branch of the Hume family, had had a claim to the priory in commend since 6 August 1461; John Hume, the second son of Sir Alexander, first Lord Hume, was probably already dean of the chapel royal at St Andrews,[5] and was supported by his powerful father against Patrick Hume in his efforts to acquire the commend of Coldingham for himself. Neither Hume was in the least deterred in his ambitions by the sentence of excommunication belatedly imposed on both in 1467 following repeated and frustrating appeals to the Roman Curia by Prior Richard Bell of Durham; and in fact all that was left to the unfortunate prior was to appeal to James III to allow the re-population of Coldingham by Durham monks. In a letter to the Scottish monarch written at the end of 1471, Prior Bell reminded King James that both Patrick and John Hume were excommunicate, and begged the king to display the respect for, and obligations towards, St Cuthbert which had been shown by all previous Scottish rulers.[6]

James III's swift response revealed his contempt for St Cuthbert, Prior Bell, and Paul II's excommunication of the Humes. On 6 April 1472 the king secured the approval of the new pope, Sixtus IV, for the suppression of the priory of Coldingham and the allocation of all its revenues to his chapel royal of St Mary of the Rock at St Andrews.[7] Clearly King James now discounted Durham's feeble claims to Coldingham, recognising that a decade had passed since the priory's seizure and that successive priors of Durham, Burnby and Bell, had failed to win effective support, either in Rome or elsewhere, for the restoration of Coldingham to its mother-house. James III's cynical intervention underlined his view that the disposal of Coldingham and its revenues was purely a matter of Scottish politics, and that accordingly his only rivals were the Humes. In the three years since his effective assumption of power in 1469, King James had emerged as an ambitious, aggressive and over-confident personality with a dangerously exalted view of Stewart kingship, and his efforts to suppress the priory of Coldingham were paralleled by other forceful schemes, including the annexation to the crown of the earldom of Orkney and the lordship of Shetland, and the projected invasion of Brittany with an army of six thousand men.[8] To finance the latter, the king had imposed a tax on the estates of some £5,000, an action which caused the Scottish clergy in the parliament of February 1472 to protest, vigorously and successfully, that King James ought not to leave his realm open to English attack by going abroad; that in the event of his death, he had as yet no issue to succeed him; and that in any case he should avoid levying extraordinary taxation.[9] This was a mild warning to a wilful and irresponsible ruler;[10] and it may have moved the king towards a more cautious approach to the problem of Coldingham.

Thus on 3 April 1473, almost a year after his formal suppression of the priory, King James successfully petitioned Sixtus IV to accept a new scheme for the allocation of its revenues. Patrick Hume would resign his right to Coldingham and thereupon it would be finally suppressed. Part of its revenues would be transferred to the chapel royal at St Andrews; the other part would then be applied to the erection of a royal chapel at Coldingham, a collegiate church with dean and prebendaries, and with Patrick Hume as the first dean.[11] On the face of it, this appears a reasonable compromise solution, for all the Scots in the case — the king, Patrick Hume and John Hume — were determined that Coldingham should remain in Scottish hands; and James III may indeed have seen the priory's importance as primarily geographical, lying as it did just north of Berwick, a burgh only recently surrendered by the English. Thus he may have been attempting to find a formula which would to some extent satisfy both Hume rivals, the king maintaining royal authority but somewhat moderating his severity of the previous year. Patrick Hume would retain royal favour and secure preferment by being accepted as dean in the new collegiate church of Coldingham; and John Hume, who was already dean of the chapel royal at St Andrews,[12] would have to satisfy himself with the reallocation of only part of the Coldingham revenues to enrich St Mary of the Rock. From the king's point of view, however, the main attraction of the new proposals, unlike those of 1472, was that he would not now have to wait for the death of Patrick Hume, the commendator of Coldingham, before suppressing the priory.

This revised scheme was, however, doomed to failure from the start simply because it rejected John Hume's claim to the priory of Coldingham. He and his kin had no intention of settling for half the revenues and unwelcome royal interference in the south-east, and he had the backing of the entire main Hume family — his younger brothers George Hume of Ayton and Patrick Hume of Fastcastle, and his nephew Alexander, master of Hume and later second Lord Hume. Above all, in the early stages of the dispute the most formidable of the Humes was Alexander, the first Lord. Bailie of Coldingham from 1442, confirmed in this office for life in November 1472, a lord of parliament from August 1473, and a warden of the Marches by 1476, Alexander, Lord Hume, steadily increased his own and his family's power in south-east Scotland; and until his grandson and successor became politically active in the 1480s, the first Lord's ambitions for extending his local prestige and authority seem to have centred on the retention by his second son, John, of Coldingham priory and its revenues. Territorially as well as financially, possession of the priory was important to the Humes, for Coldingham lay at the heart of the growing Hume empire in south-east Scotland, the barony created by James II and including Dunglass, Birgham and Chirnside in the Each March, close to Berwick, and containing the lion's share of the forfeited earldom of March.[13]

Thus James III, in lending his support to Patrick Hume as dean of a new collegiate church at Coldingham, took a false step and alienated the main branch of one of the major Border families. John Hume's response was to appeal to Rome; and in August 1473 he managed to secure papal approval of Patrick Hume's resignation of his right to the priory and a new provision for himself as prior.[14] Presumably, however, the king did not recognise John Hume's new status, for on 11 October 1473 Patrick Hume is described as 'dean of the chapel of the king of Scots'.[15] Stalemate had now been reached: Patrick Hume was dean of Coldingham, and supported by the king, who claimed that a new collegiate church had been erected there; but John Hume, thanks not only to his papal provision as prior but also to the support of his kin in the south-east, was in actual possession of the fruits, and so actively obstructed the king's new foundation.[16] Negotiation between king and pope followed to produce yet another agreement which left John Hume in possession of Coldingham — a change which may well reflect Lord Hume's strength in the locality — but only if he consented to give Patrick Hume part of the fruits of the monastery each year and accepted the royal suppression of the priory and erection of a collegiate church, 'in which royal ordinance', John Hume later protested, 'he acquiesced out of fear'.[17] This unsatisfactory compromise seems to have remained in force till it was rendered obsolete by Patrick Hume's death, some time before 17 October 1478.[18]

The toruous Coldingham manoeuvres of the 1470s, complicated by the existence of four contenders whose motives and actions are frequently difficult to comprehend, did not end in 1478 with the demise of Patrick Hume; but the struggle becomes much simpler to understand. The claims of Patrick Hume were removed by death, those of the priory of Durham by the ambition and intransigence of the Scottish king.[19] After 1478 there were two conflicting parties only, James III and the main branch of the Hume family; and two schemes for the future of Coldingham, the royal one for the erection of a collegiate church and the allocation of part of the former priory's revenues to the chapel royal, and that of John Hume, strongly supported by his father, brothers and nephew, for the restoration of the priory with himself as prior. A further stalemate ensued. The king, preoccupied with growing opposition at home and the outbreak of war with England in April 1480, seems to have made no effort to press his scheme to erect a collegiate church at Coldingham; and John Hume, understandably enough, had no intention of furthering James III's plans, but waited his chance to have the priory restored by the pope.[20]

The Humes must however have realised that papal acceptance of their right to Coldingham and its revenues was not the only, or indeed the main, prerequisite. The dispute was essentially a domestic one in which only a change of heart by the king could really benefit them; and there must have been a strong temptation for the entire Hume faction to join the disaffected during the major political crisis of 1482–3, to win from James III by coercion what they had failed to achieve by negotiation. In what amounted to a palace revolution, James III was seized by the earls of Buchan and Angus at Lauder Bridge in July 1482, and imprisoned in Edinburgh Castle, while an enormous English army entered Edinburgh unopposed to support the claims of King James's brother Alexander, duke of Albany, to the Scottish throne. In the event, the shifty Albany was quite unacceptable as king, but for a time he enjoyed some support,[21] and until the recovery of power by James III the following January it was natural for those who had fared badly under the king during the 1470s to consider throwing in their lot with the Albany faction. The Humes probably began by reckoning that Albany, as the victor in the struggles of summer and autumn 1482, should be supported as a potential head of government and dispenser of royal patronage; but in spite of their rivalry with James III over Coldingham, their support for Albany is likely to have been lukewarm at best. He had done them no favours in the summer of 1482 by leading an English army of twenty thousand through their lands in the south-east; and the only tangible result of the campaign had been the English recovery of Berwick in August 1482, an achievement which might well put Hume control of Coldingham in jeopardy, and which certainly raised the spectre of a renewal of Durham's claims to the priory. It is therefore not surprising to find a certain amount of evidence to suggest that, in the winter of 1482–3, when Albany found his political position in Scotland gradually weakening and considered reverting to his English treasons, the Humes abandoned him and threw their support behind James III, probably in the hope that their grateful monarch would duly reward them with full control of the Coldingham revenues once he had recovered power.

Hume intervention, when it came, was dramatic and effective. On 30 December 1482 Albany, who had left the court in Edinburgh shortly after Christmas and retired to his castle at Dunbar, granted to Alexander Hume (the future second Lord), for faithful service done and to be done, twenty husbandlands in the town and territory of Leitholm, in the earldom of March and sheriffdom of Berwick. The witnesses to this charter included the earls of Buchan and Angus, both of them men with bad records in the early stages of the crisis; and it is likely that Hume was also present at Dunbar.[22] This charter is of considerable political significance, because a fortnight after it had been granted, Albany appointed two of the witnesses — his steward, Sir James Liddale, and the earl of Angus — to act as his commissioners in travelling to England and negotiating with Edward IV; and these negotiations led in turn to a renewal of Albany's treasonable schemes to replace James III as king with English assistance.[23] Thus it is clear that by the end of December 1482 Albany had reverted to his original plan of calling once more upon English aid; and the charter of 30 December, with its reference to services still to be performed by Hume, probably represents an attempt on Albany's part to secure local support.

It failed disastrously. Only four days later, on 3 January 1483, James III had somehow become aware of the plot; for in a letter written from Edinburgh to Sir Robert Arbuthnott of that Ilk, the king remarked that 'we are sikkerly informit that certan persons, to grete nowmer, were gadderit tresonably to haf invadit our person this last Thursday'. In 1483, 3 January was a Friday, so King James was presumably referring to Thursday 2 January. He asked Arbuthnott to come to his assistance 'as ye luf the welfar of owr persone, succession, realme, and liegis, and ye sal haue special thank and reward of ws according to your merit'.[24] As Arbuthnott was only a knight whose lands lay in the Mearns rather than close to Edinburgh, it is inconceivable that he was alone in receiving royal letters asking for assistance; presumably such letters were sent to a large number of King James's supporters. In view of the fact that the Arbuthnott letter mentions a projected seizure of the king within a few days of Albany's gathering of adherents at Dunbar, it seems likely that the Albany faction was the treasonable gathering to which the letter refers.

But how had King James uncovered the Dunbar plot so swiftly? The most likely explanation is that his information came direct from Alexander Hume. What had probably happened was that on 30 December, when making the grant of the Leitholm lands to Hume, Albany had revealed to him his intention of imprisoning James III once more, and indicated that the earls of Buchan and Angus were prepared to support him in another Lauder Bridge. Hume, shrewdly calculating that the king was likely to be the ultimate winner of the 1482–3 struggle, either sent a messenger to Edinburgh or went there himself to inform on Albany and his associates. What happened subsequently is obscure; but it is clear that the Dunbar plot was thwarted simply by its contents being made known to King James in good time, and that at some point between 30 December 1482 and 19 March 1483, Albany arrested Alexander Hume, and some of his friends and kinsmen, because he had received information that the king had ordered them to kill him.[25]

The Humes had chosen wisely. By March, Albany was struggling to reach an accommodation with James III, who had recovered power to the extent that he was able to summon to Edinburgh a parliament largely composed of royalists; in April Albany's main prop in his English treasons, Edward IV, died; and in July the duke, having prudently fled from Dunbar to England, was at last forfeited in parliament at Edinburgh.[26] Amongst those rewarded for changing sides at the right time were the Humes. On 2 July 1483 James III confirmed Albany's grant of the Leitholm lands, made on 30 December 1482 to Alexander Hume;[27] and on 11 January 1484 the king followed this up by making a further grant to Hume, for unspecified faithful service, of the lands of Chirnside in Berwickshire, which had fallen to the crown as a result of the forfeiture of Alexander, formerly duke of Albany, earl of March, Mar and Garioch.[28] The day before, the king had made a similar grant to his 'familiar household squire', John Hume (son and heir of George Hume of Ayton, and therefore Alexander Hume's cousin), of £12 worth of the lands of Duns in Berwickshire, forfeited by Albany the previous June.[29] These grants of land formerly held by Albany make it clear that James III had reason to be grateful to two of the Humes; and it seems probable that John Hume was one of the 'friends and kinsmen' of Alexander Hume said to have been employed in an attempt to kill Albany early in 1483.

Thus the main branch of the Hume family were clearly in favour following the royal recovery of power in 1483. Yet the problem of Coldingham remained unresolved, possibly because the king, as in so many other instances, had failed to distribute adequate rewards to his supporters. John Hume's £12 worth of lands in Berwickshire was after all small beer compared with his uncle and namesake's claim to Coldingham priory, which in spite of its decline during the century remained, as Professor Dobson reminds us, 'one of the richest of border prizes'.[30] From a political standpoint, the months following the crisis of 1482–3 would have been an ideal time for the king to display generosity in the south-east by abandoning his schemes of the previous decade and confirming Hume possession of Coldingham priory; for he badly needed assured loyalty in the Borders, and it would have to be bought. But King James not only failed to pay the price, but seems not to have realised that it was necessary to make any payment at all. Worse still from the point of view of the crown, the Humes now enjoyed King James's trust.

The opening of the final stage of the conflict involved duplicity and defiance of the crown on the part of the Humes. Early in the pontificate of Innocent VIII — that is, after 12 September 1484 — John Hume, Lord Alexander's second son, promised the king that he would go to Rome to procure the division of the remainder of the Coldingham fruits into prebends; and on this understanding he was issued with royal letters of recommendation to the new pope. However, on arriving in Rome, Hume misused his letters to extort from the pope a revocation of King James's plans for suppression of the priory and its erection as a collegiate church, while Innocent VIII confirmed Hume's rights as prior of Coldingham, and ordered the abandonment of the short-lived and partly erected collegiate church there.[31]

At a stroke, the Humes had recovered their right to the entire wealth of Coldingham; but as the move involved open defiance of the king, we must ask why John Hume thought that he could get away with it. He was probably encouraged by a precedent involving the see of Dunkeld the previous year. On 28 August 1483, Bishop Livingston of Dunkeld, the chancellor, had died;[32] and within a month of his death, Alexander Inglis, dean of Dunkeld, archdeacon of St Andrews, clerk register and clerk of the king's council, had been elected bishop by the Dunkeld chapter on the nomination of James III.[33] But the following month, on 22 October, Pope Sixtus IV had provided George Brown to the see.[34] Brown, while acting as *orator regis* for King James at the papal Curia, had taken advantage of his friendship with Cardinal Rodrigo Borgia, the papal vice-chancellor, to persuade Sixtus IV to quash the election of Inglis to Dunkeld and have himself appointed to the vacant see.[35] Despite James III's initial refusal to accept Brown in place of Inglis, his own nominee, and his protests in the parliament of May 1485 about the pope's action, by August of the same year a compromise had been reached and Brown was thereafter regularly styled bishop of Dunkeld.[36] Brown's misuse to his own advantage of his position as royal orator at the papal Curia in 1483 must have suggested to John Hume the method by which he was to recover the priory of Coldingham with some show of legitimacy in the following year; and James III's failure to quash Brown's election to Dunkeld must have encouraged Hume, supported as he was by his father, younger brothers and nephew, to continue to defy the king.

The papal letters restoring the priory would have reached Scotland before the parliament of May 1485 assembled; and the king, who must have been furious at Hume's abuse of his letters, ordered his ambassadors to Rome to exhort the pope to grant 'ane ereccioun of coldingaham to our souueran lordis chapell in the best forme outhir be commissioun or vthir wais as thai think maist expedient and may best gett with decrete of diuisioun of the samyn priory in to prebendis be extinccioun of Religioun and the ereccioun maid of befor be oure haly faderis predecessoris'.[37] This was, in short, a complete reversal of the revocation granted to John Hume and a return to the king's original scheme of 1472 for suppression of the priory. Although the Scottish embassy to Rome, led by Archbishop Scheves and Bishop Blacader, was delayed until the end of 1486,[38] the king's request was ultimately successful. On 28 April 1487, Innocent VIII reversed his decision in favour of Hume and ordered a return to the arrangement of 3 April 1473, that is, to Sixtus IV's acceptance of the suppression of Coldingham and the reallocation of its revenues, in part to the chapel royal, and in part to the erection of a collegiate church at Coldingham itself. Pope Innocent also gave instructions to 'inhibit the executors and subexecutors of the pope's letters granted to the said John Hom to proceed to any further execution of them, to decree null and void whatever has been hitherto or in future may be attempted in this behalf by them and others', and to make prebends at Coldingham 'in all respects as if the letters aforesaid had been directed to them from the beginning by the said Pope Sixtus and during his lifetime [a reference to the papal letters of 3 April 1473], and as if in virtue thereof they had begun to proceed to their execution'[39] — a clear indication that John Hume had done little or nothing towards the erection of prebends at Coldingham.

Ultimately, therefore, the pope took the side of James III in the Coldingham dispute; but the suppression of the priory and its removal from Hume influence had still to be achieved. King James was determined to take active steps to enforce the papal decision in his favour; and as John Hume had blatantly misused the royal letters granted to him in 1484, the maintenance of royal authority in Scotland was also at stake. Fulsome support for the king had recently poured in from Rome. In 1486 Innocent VIII sent James III the Golden Rose, a signal mark of papal favour;[40] and in the same year a papal legate, James Pasarella, bishop of Imola, was sent to Scotland to order clerks and laymen of every rank to obey the king.[41] Most important of all, as a belated response to the king's request in May 1485 that only persons 'as is thankfull to his hienes' should be promoted to important benefices,[42] on 20 April 1487 Innocent VIII reinforced James III's authority in ecclesiastical affairs by granting an indult which went a long way towards settling the problem of nominations to the most valuable vacant benefices. This was the main problem raised by the Dunkeld and Coldingham disputes; and the pope now conceded that when vacancies occurred in any cathedral church or monastery exceeding in annual value 200 florins gold of the Camera, he would refrain for at least eight months from making provisions to them, and meanwhile would wait for letters from the king (or his successors) petitioning on behalf of candidates of his choice.[43] Eight days later, on 28 April 1487, Pope Innocent gave James III the chance to exercise his authority in matters of ecclesiastical patronage by accepting his scheme for the suppression of Coldingham.

Armed with the papal blessing, King James summoned parliament to meet in Edinburgh in October 1487. There was a large attendance — about eighty in all — but none of the Humes was present.[44] They may have been aware in advance of the legislation regarding Coldingham which the king intended to introduce. A statute ordered 'that inhibicioun be gevin to all [the king's] liegis spirituale and temporale that none of thame take apoun hand to do or attempt ocht to be done contrare the vnion and ereccioun made of the priory of Coldingham to his chapell Riale or to mak ony impetracioun thirof at the Court of Rome or to public or vse outhir bullis or processis purchest or to be purchest contrare the said vnion and ereccioun vnder the payne of tressoune tinsale and forfature of life lande and gude'.[45] Taken together with the gap of six months between the publishing of Innocent VIII's bulls supporting the king and King James's first moves to enforce them by act of parliament, the strong language of this statute suggests that James III had encountered stiff resistance to his plans. Certainly John Hume, who continued to regard himself as prior of Coldingham, had ignored the new bulls; he had, after all, another set of bulls granted as recently as 1484–5 by the same pope, and presumably had no intention of obeying the new ones unless he were coerced. The reference in the statute of October 1487 to lieges spiritual *and* temporal indicates that John

Hume had obtained widespread support for resistance to the king, support which as events were to show was not confined to his Hume kinsmen.

As the struggle entered what proved to be its final phase, the outcome turned on the ability of James III to coerce the Humes into acceptance of his suppression of Coldingham priory. To some extent we may sympathise with King James. Freed at last of the men who had defied and constrained him during the crisis of 1482–3, having recovered Dunbar Castle from the English in 1486,[46] moving towards an alliance with Henry VII,[47] and assured of full papal support, the king may have felt that he was in a strong enough position to act decisively against the Humes. The contempt for royal authority shown by John Hume in his misuse of the king's letters in Rome in 1484–5 came especially badly from a man who held the position of dean of the chapel royal at St Andrews, who had been allowed the office of dean of Coldingham by King James, and whose relatives had been the recipients of royal patronage since the early 1470s.

Yet royal authority may not have been the only issue at stake. There exists some evidence to suggest that James III's parliamentary assault on the Humes was initiated partly because the king had decided to transfer his chapel royal from St Andrews to Restalrig near Edinburgh, and that this was a project in which he took great pride. King James's original intention in suppressing the priory of Coldingham in 1472–3, as we have seen, was to reallocate its revenues to his chapel royal of St Mary of the Rock at St Andrews;[48] but in subsequent correspondence on the subject St Andrews is not specifically mentioned. By contrast, Restalrig was the king's own foundation late in the reign. On 13 November 1487 papal bulls were published confirming the foundation by James III of a collegiate church close by the parish church of Restalrig. The royal supplication for its erection had been registered at Rome as early as 7 May 1487,[49] and it arose out of a dispute between Archbishop Scheves, the king's discarded familiar, and John Frissel over the parish church of Lasswade, out of which a canonry and prebend had been erected in the church of St Salvator, St Andrews. Scheves claimed that Lasswade had formerly been united and appropriated by papal authority to the archiepiscopal *mensa* of St Andrews in perpetuity, while Frissel quoted the same authority for his own provision to Lasswade. Clearly Frissel had the backing of the king, and at length Scheves gave way; the royal supplication proposed Frissel as the dean of a collegiate church at Restalrig, and the pope, in the bulls of 13 November 1487, duly acceded to the royal request, suppressed the prebend, and annexed Lasswade to Restalrig.[50]

Long before formal papal approval of the project was secured, however, the construction of the new collegiate church was underway. In the exchequer year July 1486–July 1487, a payment of £10. 16s. had been made for slates *ad capellam domini regis contiguam ecclesie parrochali de Lestalrig*;[51] and if Boece is to be believed, the king had taken the papal legate, the bishop of Imola, to see the chapel, presumably while it was still under construction, in the spring or summer of 1486.[52] The bulls of erection of Restalrig make clear the king's great enthusiasm for his new foundation: this was the chapel 'which James, king of Scots, has caused to be sumptuously built at his own expense, and which he has endowed with estates and possessions'.[53] With regard to the expense of constructing the chapel, the wording of the bulls of erection is naturally the same as the king had used in his supplication of 7 May 1487, and is indicative of his need for ready cash. If Restalrig had taken the place of St Mary, St Andrews, as the chapel royal, a strong reason for James III's determination to suppress the priory of Coldingham and annex half its revenues 'to the Kingis chapell' would be provided. Ten years later, in 1497, John Frissel is described as *decanus capelle regie de Lestalrig*;[54] and it may have been King James's intention to make Restalrig his chapel royal from the outset of the pontificate of Innocent VIII, taking advantage of his improved relations with the papacy to do so. The last known references to St Mary, St Andrews, as the chapel royal occur in the early 1470s when, as we have seen, the king's original schemes of appropriating all or part of the Coldingham revenues had been given papal approval.[55] The chapel royal at Stirling, which Pitscottie mistakenly attributes to James III's last years,[56] was in fact erected by papal bull on 2 May 1501, on the petition of James IV; and at that time the provostry of St Mary of the Rock, St Andrews, was to be erected into the deanery of Stirling.[57] Clearly, therefore, there was no longer a chapel royal at St Andrews in 1501; and it is possible that the length of time required for the transition from St Andrews to Stirling — from 1484 to the late 1490s — may be explained by a scheme by James III to transfer his chapel royal from St Andrews to his own creation of Restalrig, a scheme which was cut short by the king's death in 1488 and his successor's preference for Stirling.[58]

It may be added that Restalrig would have been a most appropriate site for James III's chapel royal. Much more than his predecessors or his immediate successors, King James chose Edinburgh as his normal place of residence; and Restalrig, only two miles from Holyrood Palace, had the obvious advantage of geographical convenience. St Andrews, on the other hand, does not figure to any great extent in what is known of James's itinerary; the records show him to have been there only twice, in November 1464 and from March until June 1465.[59] He may have visited St Andrews during subsequent progresses to Perth and Falkland; but the burgh does not seem to have seen much of him, and he may have considered that his chapel royal should be found much closer to Edinburgh, where he spent most of his time. Hence the construction of an elaborate chapel at Restalrig, and hence also the king's persistence in his efforts to acquire the Coldingham revenues. Everything now depended on whether James III would proceed beyond parliamentary threats.

The issue was not long in doubt. On 29 January 1488, the three estates meeting in parliament at Edinburgh recalled the statute made three months before, threatening with forfeiture anyone who attempted to resist the suppression of the priory of Coldingham. Since that time, certain unspecified temporal persons had defied the statute, and they were to be summoned to answer for their crimes on 5 May. This is clearly a reference to John Hume's relatives, and to their friends and neighbours in the south-east, the Hepburns, all of whom were absent from the parliament, and all of whom were to be substantially rewarded after James III's death at the battle of Sauchieburn. In order to make royal coercion effective, parliament ordered that a number of representatives should be chosen from each estate to sit in judgement on the offenders, and this committee was also to have 'the hale power of the body of the parliament ... to avise common and conclude apone sic vthir materis as sal occur in the mene tyme'.[60] Precedents for such committees were numerous — there had already been five during the period of James III's active rule[61] — but the 1488 committee was much the largest, numbering fifty and reading like a full assembly of the estates in parliament. Side by side with committed royalists — Archbishop Scheves (out of favour but still a king's man), Bishop Elphinstone, the earls of Crawford and Atholl, Lords Bothwell and Avandale — were to be found the king's future enemies: the bishops of Glasgow and Dunkeld, the earls of Argyll and Angus, and Lords Drummond and Lyle. The creation of this cumbrous and unsatisfactory body, wholly unfitted to take action against the breakers of the Coldingham statute both because of its size and because it contained some — perhaps many — who sympathised with the Humes, reveals a remarkable insensitivity to political realities on the part of James III. Totally preoccupied with pursuit of the Humes and the Coldingham revenues, the king appears to have been unaware of plans for a greater and much more serious defiance of his authority in which the leading spirits were his chancellor, Colin Campbell, earl of Argyll, and King James's eldest son, the duke of Rothesay.

For the truth is that the Coldingham dispute was the occasion, but not the cause, of James III's downfall. On their own, or even with the support of their neighbours, it is unlikely that the Humes could successfully have withstood a royal military expedition; but in 1488 a far bigger issue was involved than the fate of the priory and its revenues, namely, the future of the king himself. For over eighteen years James III had pursued arbitrary, overbearing and — on occasions — illegal policies in his dealings with prominent Scottish nobles and ecclesiastics. His dangerously exalted concept of his office led him to sit in Edinburgh and delegate responsibilities in crises to magnates who were expected to perform difficult or dangerous tasks without receiving adequate, or any, reward.[62] His failure to do his job properly in the field of criminal justice, by riding out regularly on justice-ayres, was much criticised, as was his undermining of justice by selling remissions.[63] His efforts to levy taxation in successive parliaments were strenuously resisted;[64] and in the early 1470s parliament was already reproaching him for his secretiveness in conducting foreign diplomacy without even consulting his council.[65] James's relationships with his kin were appalling, one brother, the duke of Albany, being driven to exile, treason and eventual forfeiture, the other, the earl of Mar, dying in mysterious circumstances when under arrest, while the king's sisters bore children to his forfeited enemies, Boyd and Crichton.[66] Even in such circumstances rebellion against a Stewart king was undertaken only with reluctance, and the palace revolution of 1482–3 should have served as a warning to James; he still had friends, but he must guarantee their loyalty through an even-handed distribution of rewards.

The warning was ignored in the 1480s as it had been in the '70s; and King James's attitude became even less acceptable because while he continued to add to the number of his potential enemies — the bishops of Dunkeld and Glasgow, William, Lord Crichton, the Humes, the earl of Angus — and at the same time failed to acquire new friends, he was also burdened with unpopular supporters who had proved broken reeds in the crisis of 1482 but whom he could not abandon completely, above all Archbishop Scheves and former Chancellor Avandale.[67] Even the king's strengths — in foreign diplomacy and in his relations with the papacy — were of little value to him if he could not control his own subjects. King Henry VII, a usurper of uncertain standing in England, was unlikely to be able to provide James with armed assistance against rebels even if he had wanted to. Likewise, Pope Innocent VIII was happy to send James the Golden Rose, the indult, and a legate to threaten the king's rebellious subjects with excommunication; but when the rebellion was over and the king was dead, the pope was equally happy to take the rebels' money to grant them absolution, and to send the Golden Rose to the nominal leader of the 1488 revolt, James IV.[68]

It is therefore against this background of fear and mistrust of James III by a growing number of the Scottish political community that the final stage of the Coldingham dispute must be viewed. In seeking support for coercion of the Humes, the king was in fact threatening many magnates; and the statute of October 1487 was so general that it could include all those whose view of the future of Coldingham over sixteen years had differed from that of the king. In any case, the Humes were only the tip of the iceberg; linked by marriage to the keeper of Stirling Castle, James Shaw of Sauchie,[69] who had possession of the heir to the throne, they were also supported by their neighbour Patrick Hepburn, Lord Hailes, and by the formidable Archibald, fifth earl of Angus, a man who had been neither pardoned nor punished for his part in the seizure of the king in 1482, but who certainly shared Hume and Hepburn mistrust of James III's interference in the south-east.[70]

As we have emphasised, however, the last stage of the protracted dispute over Coldingham was the occasion rather than the cause of the rebellion of 1488; of more concern to many of the Scottish political community, including some royal councillors, was King James's creation, in the parliament of January 1488, of his second son James as duke of Ross and earl of Edirdale.[71] This act, adding to other favours already lavished on his second son,[72] may have led King James's heir James, duke of Rothesay, to believe that his father intended to cut him out of the succession. For the king's loyal chancellor Colin Campbell, earl of Argyll, this creation probably seemed the prelude to increased royal interference in the north-west Highlands, an area which since the forfeiture of John Macdonald, earl of Ross, in 1475 Argyll had come to regard more and more as his own. His defection from the royal side seems to have occurred sometime in February, as by the 21st of that month James III had replaced him as chancellor with Bishop Elphinstone.[73] The loss of Argyll was a serious blow for King James, as the earl's loyal service to the crown stretched back two decades — as master of the household, chancellor, councillor, and royal lieutenant in Argyll. When he defected he took with him two royal councillors, Lords Drummond and Oliphant, whose families were related to his through marriage; and he may well have been the 'brains' behind the rebellion, recognising that only the possession of the heir to the throne gave the disaffected, deep and justified though their grievances were, a chance of success.[74]

Thus when James III used the three estates to threaten with forfeiture 'certain unspecified temporal persons' who had acted in defiance of his statute of October 1487 suppressing the priory of Coldingham, he was in fact declaring war on a substantial portion of the Scottish political community; certainly many magnates would not feel safe so long as he continued to rule. The sequel was civil war, a dreary and protracted business in which James III managed to excel himself in public deceit, promising in Aberdeen to negotiate a settlement with the rebels and his son, involving his loyal northern lords in the initial proposals, then immediately repudiating an agreement which he had signed, and launching a fresh attack in the south.[75] The Humes certainly rejoiced over James III's death at Sauchieburn on 11 June 1488; but there must also have been many royalists who allowed themselves a private sigh of relief at the news.

Unquestionably, however, the principal beneficiaries of successful rebellion were the Humes. Alexander Hume, who succeeded his grandfather and namesake as Lord Hume about 1492, fared best; he became chamberlain for life, keeper of Stirling Castle, and guardian of James IV's younger brother John, with the revenues of the earldom of Mar and Garioch assigned to him from 1490, and the office of warden of the East Marches for seven years from 1489.[76] His three uncles also received rewards. George Hume of Ayton acquired the lands of Easter Rossie (in Collessie), Fife, in July 1488;[77] and in February 1490 the town and lands of Duns in Berwickshire, which he held by charter from James III, were erected by James IV into a free burgh of barony.[78] Patrick Hume of Fastcastle was granted the Ayrshire lands of the forfeited John Ross of Montgreenan, one of James III's principal supporters at Sauchieburn;[79] and, most important of all, John Hume was confirmed by the new regime as prior — not dean — of Coldingham.[80]

Thus the long struggle between James III and the Humes for control of the revenues of the priory of Coldingham was finally settled, not by further appeals to the Roman Curia by both sides, but by the king's death in battle against his own subjects in June 1488. His failure lay not in his aggression — his two predecessors had stepped beyond the law often enough in their assaults on powerful families — but in his inability to realise that if he assailed a magnate family, he must have support from others, especially in the locality involved. In the south-east of Scotland, James III had virtually no support, but many potential or real enemies; yet he persisted in forcing a conflict while at the same time threatening other powerful magnates without whose assistance he had no chance of winning. The struggle for Coldingham came to an end with his death; but the events of 1488 cast a long shadow over the ensuing reign. Not for almost a decade would the reluctant victor of Sauchieburn, James IV, succeed in freeing himself from the counsel of the rebel nobility who had made his victory possible. His subsequent popularity with the great majority of the Scottish magnates reflects his desire to please, to conciliate, to avoid confrontation; it also illustrates that he saw 1488 as a warning, and that he accepted — as his father had never done — the severely limited extent of royal Stewart power.

NOTES

1. See below, Ch. 13, and also 'The exercise of power', in *Scottish Society in the Fifteenth Century,* ed. J.M. Brown (London, 1977), pp. 33–65.

2. See further J.M. Wormald, *Court, Kirk and Community: Scotland 1470–1625* (London, 1981), pp. 3–26, for a recent summary of Dr Wormald's views on late medieval/early modern Scottish kingship.

3. For the history of Coldingham in general see A.L. Brown, 'The priory of Coldingham in the late fourteenth century', *The Innes Review*, xxiii (1972), pp. 91–101, and R.B. Dobson, 'The last English monks on Scottish soil', *SHR*, xlvi (1967), pp. 1–25.

4. *Acta Facultatis Artium Universitatis S. Andree, 1413-1588*, ed. A.I. Dunlop (SHS, 1964), pp. 36–45; *idem, The Life and Times of James Kennedy, Bishop of St Andrews* (Edinburgh, 1950), pp. 47, 52–3. The origins of Patrick Hume's struggle with his kinsmen for control of Coldingham are obscure, though Dobson, 'English monks', pp. 13–14, supplies part of the answer.

5. W. Fraser, *The Lennox* (Edinburgh, 1874), ii, p. 93.

6. For details see Dobson, 'English monks', esp. pp. 10–18, 20–1.

7. *CPL*, xiii, p. 14. It should be noted that the suppression of the priory was intended by the pope to take effect only 'on the death or resignation of the present prior, titular or commendatory'. The idea of expelling Durham monks from Coldingham was no mid-fifteenth-century innovation. Robert II had initiated the struggle in July 1378, when he proposed to replace Durham monks with other Benedictines from Dunfermline: Dobson, 'English monks', p. 3 with n. 4.

8. *APS*, ii, p. 102.

9. *Ibid.*

10. For details of James III's arbitrary behaviour between 1469 and 1474 see Macdougall, *James III*, pp. 90–8, 102–3, 108–9.

11. *CPL*, xiii, p. 19.

12. Fraser, *Lennox*, ii, p. 93.

13. *RMS*, ii, no. 1093; *APS*, ii, p. 103; *CDS*, iv, no. 1438. James III's confirmation of Alexander Hume as bailie of Coldingham for life in November 1472, only seven months after his attempted suppression of the priory, is puzzling and inconsistent. It may perhaps be explained as part of the later compromise solution of 1473. For the Hume territorial power base see *Scots Pge.*, iv, pp. 448–9.

14. Rome, Vatican Archives, Registers of Supplications, 694, fo. 129v.

15. Ibid.

16. *CPL*, xiv, pp. 45–6.

17. *Ibid.*

18. Vatican Archives, Reg. Supp. 774, fo. 131r.

19. For the fruitless efforts of the priors of Durham to recover Coldingham through litigation at the papal Curia, see Dobson, 'English monks', pp. 20–4.

20. John Hume is described as 'dean of the chapel of the king of Scots' on 21 February 1484: *CPL*, xiii, pp. 192–3. This title may of course refer to the chapel royal at St Andrews; but if Coldingham is intended, Hume's title of dean may be explained by the fact that in 1484 he deceived James III into thinking that he was going to fall in with his wishes regarding the erection of a collegiate church at Coldingham, and he was furnished with royal letters later that year to allow him to travel to the papal Curia to achieve this end.

21. For details of the crisis of 1482–3 see Macdougall, *James III*, pp. 158–83. It should be noted that, in spite of James III's undoubted unpopularity, Albany was not acceptable to the three estates even as lieutenant-general, far less as king: *APS*, ii, p. 143; *RMS*, ii, no. 1533 (SRO MS Register of the Great Seal, xi, fo. 31).

22. *HMC, Athole and Home*, p. 155.

23. *Foedera*, xii, p. 172.

24. A. Nisbet, *A System of Heraldry* (Edinburgh, 1816), ii, app., p. 83.

25. SRO State Papers, No. 19.

26. For details of the political collapse and flight of Albany during the spring and early summer of 1483, see Macdougall, *James III*, pp. 185–9.

27. *HMC, Athole and Home*, pp. 155–6.

28. *RMS*, ii, no. 1572.

29. *Ibid.*, no. 1571.

30. Dobson, 'English monks', p. 3.

31. *CPL*, xiv, p. 47.

32. A. Myln, *Vitae Dunkeldensis Ecclesiae Episcoporum* (Bannatyne Club, 1831), p. 26.

33. *Calendar of the Laing Charters 854-1837*, ed. J. Anderson (Edinburgh, 1899), p. 191; Myln, *Vitae*, p. 26.

34. C. Eubel, *Hierarchia Catholica Medii Aevi* (Münster, 1898–1910), ii, p. 163.

35. Myln, *Vitae*, p. 26.

36. *APS*, ii, p. 171. For a full discussion of the disputed election at Dunkeld see J.A.F. Thomson, 'Innocent VIII and the Scottish Church', *The Innes Review*, xix (1968), pp. 23–5, and Macdougall, *James III*, pp. 223–5.

37. *APS*, ii, p. 171.

38. This embassy is discussed at length in Thomson, 'Innocent VIII', pp. 26–7.

39. *CPL*, xiv, pp. 47–8.

40. *Calendar of State Papers and MSS existing in the Archives and Collections of Milan*, i, ed. A.B. Hinds (London, 1912), p. 247; C. Burns, *Papal Gifts to Scottish Monarchs: Golden Rose and Blessed Sword* (Glasgow, 1970), pp. 19–22.

41. Theiner, *Monumenta*, pp. 496–9; *CPL*, xiv, p. 51.

42. *APS*, ii, p. 171.

43. *CPL*, xiv, p. 4.

44. *APS*, ii, p. 176.

45. *Ibid.*, p. 179.

46. *ER*, ix, p. 523.

47. *Rot. Scot.*, ii, p. 481.

48. *CPL*, xiii, p. 14.

49. Vatican Archives, Reg. Supp. 870, fos. 264–5.

50. *CPL*, xiv, pp. 211–13; J. Herkless and R.K. Hannay, *The Archbishops of St Andrews* (Edinburgh, 1907–17), i, p. 132.

51. *ER*, ix, p. 540.

52. *Hectoris Boetii Murthlacensium et Aberdonensium Episcoporum Vitae* (Bannatyne Club, 1825), pp. 76–7.

53. *CPL*, xiv, p. 212. For the curious architectural features of Restalrig see I. MacIvor, 'The king's chapel at Restalrig and St Triduana's aisle: a hexagonal two-storied chapel of the fifteenth century', *PSAS*, xcvi (1962–3), pp. 247–63.

54. *ER*, xi, p. 2.

55. *CPL*, xiii, p. 14.

56. Robert Lindsay of Pitscottie, *The Historie and Cronicles of Scotland* (Scottish Text Soc., 1899–1911), i, p. 200.

57. Watt, *Fasti*, pp. 334–5.

58. The only objection to Restalrig as the chapel royal in succession to St Andrews is a single reference to James Oliphant, on 11 April 1495, as dean of the chapel royal: *Protocol Book of James Young 1485-1515*, ed. G. Donaldson (Scottish Rec. Soc., 1952), p. 790. This cannot be Restalrig, for Frissel was still dean there; and Stirling was not erected until 1501. It is possible, however, that while the actual construction of Stirling was under way in the 1490s, a caretaker dean was appointed by James IV; and this role would fit Oliphant very well, as he was the first dean of Stirling when it was eventually erected in May 1501: *History of the Chapel Royal of Scotland* (Grampian Club, 1882), p. 2.

59. *RMS*, ii, nos. 821, 828–33.

60. *APS*, ii, p. 182.

61. *Ibid.*, pp. 97, 101, 108, 114, 119.

62. For example, George, earl of Huntly, who had recovered much of Lochaber — and Dingwall Castle — for the king in the Ross rebellion of 1476, was fobbed off with a gift of 100 marks, while the keepership of Dingwall went to John Stewart, Lord Darnley, whom the king was attempting to pacify for having deprived him of the title of earl of Lennox: *Miscellany of the Spalding Club* (1841–52), iv, p. 134; Fraser, *Lennox*, ii, p. 115.

63. For complaints about justice-ayres see *APS*, ii, pp. 104, 122, 139; for remissions, *ibid.*, pp. 104, 118.

64. Macdougall, *James III*, p. 301.

65. *APS*, ii, p. 103.

66. For a recent assessment of the fates of Albany and Mar see Macdougall, *James III*, pp. 128–33; for James's sister Mary, *ibid.*, pp. 88–9, 171–2, 189; and for his sister Margaret, *ibid.*, pp. 140–3, 198–9. For a short summary of the relationships between James III and his kin see W.C. Dickinson, *Scotland from the Earliest Times to 1603*, 3rd edn., revised A.A.M. Duncan (Oxford, 1977), pp. 247–8.

67. Macdougall, *James III*, Chs. 9, 10, *passim*.

68. Vatican Archives, Reg. Supp. 918, fo. 17v; 947, fo. 95r–v; Burns, *Papal Gifts*, p. 22.

69. *ER*, x, pp. 2–3; *Scots Pge.*, iv, p. 336.

70. Macdougall, *James III*, pp. 200, 242, 245; *APS*, ii, p. 210.

71. *Ibid.*, p. 181.

72. Macdougall, *James III*, pp. 219–20. James III's second son James was already marquis of Ormond, earl of Ross, and lord of Brechin.

73. *RMS*, ii, no. 1707.

74. For a brilliant short summary of Argyll's career and attitudes see A.L. Brown, 'The Scottish "Establishment" in the later fifteenth century', *Juridical Review*, xxiii (1978), pp. 89–105, esp. pp. 96, 101–2.

75. For the civil war see Macdougall, *James III*, pp. 245–58.

76. *RMS*, ii, nos. 1781, 1919, 1893.

77. *Ibid.*, no. 1757.

78. *Ibid.*, no. 1937.

79. *Ibid.*, no. 1785.

80. *APS*, ii, p. 215; *The Acts of the Lords Auditors of Causes and Complaints*, ed. T. Thomson (Edinburgh, 1839), p. 143.

13
TAMING THE MAGNATES?

Jenny Wormald

The fifteenth century has been the neglected century of Scottish history. Traditionally it was written off as one of the most lawless periods of the Middle Ages, and for that reason one of the least interesting. Only a few incidents stand out as familiar and these are, without exception, cases of conflict between king and magnates: the murder of James I, the struggle between James II and the Black Douglases, the crises at Lauder, where James III's favourites were hanged by a dissident nobility, and Sauchieburn, where James himself was killed. The traditional interpretation was that this was a period which saw a power struggle in which one or other side sometimes gained the upper hand, but which neither side actually won. The puzzle is why this should have been so. Why should the magnates of the fifteenth century, unlike their predecessors of, say, the twelfth and thirteenth centuries, have apparently moved into direct and open opposition to the monarchy? A possible explanation — one which has been put forward for the whole of northern Europe — is that this century saw the final decline of 'medieval' ideas in both church and state, that the European society of this period was in its last decadent stages, about to be transformed by the new ideas of the modern world. Applied to Scotland, this would explain the curious belief that the overmighty nobility who fought and killed James III in 1488 became the rather more civilised and co-operative magnates under the Renaissance king, James IV. Another possibility, however, is that there is no good answer to the question why there was general conflict between crown and nobility because there was in fact no such conflict. Rather, there were two ruthless, tough and unscrupulous kings who were very powerful indeed, and who hounded out the two greatest magnate families of the early fifteenth century; and a third king who, after twenty years of arbitrary and ill-judged rule, provoked an unexpected and short-lived rebellion which, remarkably, succeeded.

One major problem about the fifteenth century is the serious lack of reliable contemporary sources, both record and chronicle. Historians turn with relief to the reign of James IV simply because so much more information is available; the daily life of the king, for example, can be described in a way which is not possible for earlier monarchs because the treasurer's accounts, which give a wealth of detail, have survived continuously after 1488, but for only one year before that date. Much of our information about the fifteenth century, and in particular its crises, has therefore been drawn from the writings of sixteenth-century chroniclers, the best known of which is the racy, entertaining and almost wholly unreliable history by Robert Lindsay of Pitscottie, produced in 1579. Recent research has shown that the traditional and previously accepted account of James III as the king who antagonised his nobility because of his dependence on low-born favourites, the mason, the tailor, the musician, is a legend developed by sixteenth-century writers without any contemporary justification. Likewise the Black Douglases, who dominated the early years of James II's personal rule, emerge as opponents of royal authority on the grand scale in Pitscottie's story; but one of his main examples of their overweening defiance is as much invention as his account of James III, for it turns on their illegal execution of one Thomas Maclellan, tutor of Bombie, a man for whose existence there is no evidence at all.

If the details which have gone into the building up of the idea of the overmighty nobility are suspect, the idea itself contains inexplicable paradoxes. While two of the kings of this period died violent deaths at the hands of their subjects, there remains the impressive fact that the ruling house survived unchallenged in spite of its problems and misfortunes. This in itself may seem a weak enough statement. But it is put into context when the Scottish situation is compared with that in England, where between 1399 and 1485 the crown was six times shuttled violently between the rival houses of Lancaster and York. In Scotland, the possibility that the legitimacy of the descendants of the first marriage of Robert II might be disputed has been used as the basis of the idea that the descendants of the second marriage entertained dynastic ambitions; it has been suggested that these ambitions lay behind the murder of James I, and had their part in the Douglases' opposition to James II. This attempt to find a Scottish parallel to the York-Lancaster rivalry seems highly dubious. First, it rests on the assumption that the descendants of the second marriage let their claim lie between 1406 and 1424, when the king was an English prisoner and the government therefore at its most vulnerable, and chose to press it in 1437 against a strong and effective ruler, having failed to take the elementary step of securing the person of the heir to the throne; and second, the actions of the Douglases after the murder of the eighth earl in 1452, while provocative enough, suggest revenge rather than genuine dynastic considerations. In fact, there was only one undoubted usurpation attempt in fifteenth-century Scotland, that of James III's ambitious and totally irresponsible brother Alexander, duke of Albany; and the most significant feature of that episode was that Alexander found virtually no support in Scotland, in spite of the very obvious deficiencies of the king. This contrasts sharply with England, where men were amazingly willing to support rebellions, however slight their chances of success. The appeal of such a gamble was of course, as English experience showed, the appreciable reward if the rebellion was successful. Here was an opportunity for self-interested advancement for the 'overmighty' Scottish magnates. Yet they made no use of it.

There were also the opportunities offered by the appalling problem of recurrent royal minorities, a problem which, while bad enough in the intermittent form in which it appeared in other countries, amounted to staggering proportions in Scotland where in the period 1406–88 there was no adult ruler for thirty-eight years. Yet with a few exceptions, these opportunities were not exploited; only four families — the Douglases, Livingstons and Crichtons in the 1440s, the Boyds of Kilmarnock in the 1460s — turned the situation to their advantage. In this century, the nobility had an unparalleled chance of self-aggrandisement at the expense of the crown. That they let it go is strong evidence of the position of prestige and respect which the fifteenth-century monarchy enjoyed, a position which is completely at odds with the idea of the 'overmighty' nobility. Indeed, so self-confident were these kings that they felt it unnecessary to resort to the usual pursuit of monarchs of surrounding themselves with a mystique based on a mythical line of ancestors, bolstered up by signs of unusual saintly or divine favour; the use of the name *Jacobus Seneschallus* — James the Steward — shows how unconcerned they were to obscure the fact that their origins were neither mythical nor divine.

In terms of the traditional concept, it is curious that 'the nobility' did not challenge the crown in such apparently favourable circumstances. But there is obviously a problem of terminology here. It is all too convenient to refer to 'the nobility' rather than to 'a few of ...' or 'some of the nobility'. But it is seriously misleading to do so. 'The nobility' suggests a static group, regarded by the crown as a consistent single threat. This obscures the fact that there was a major change in both personnel and titles by the mid-fifteenth century; the paradox here is that the crown, supposedly fearful of 'the nobility', managed to rid itself, partly by its own efforts, of many of them, and then proceeded to recreate the threat by replenishing the ranks.

The factors which produced the mid-fifteenth-century change show the idea of 'taming the magnates' to be an oversimplification. Indeed, it is both a gross understatement and exaggeration when applied to the policy of James I. Annihilating might at first sight seem to be a better word. In 1424 there were fifteen earldoms (excluding the earldom of Orkney) and one dukedom. In 1437, when James died, the dukedom had gone, and the earldoms had been reduced to eight. The revenue of one of these was in the hands of the crown; one was held by a woman, the daughter of James I; two earls were in England as hostages; and only four earldoms remained with the families who had held them in 1424. The other seven had all fallen to the crown, either because of forfeiture or because of the failure of direct heirs, that situation so dangerous for any medieval landowning family, and certainly disastrous with a king as acquisitive and unscrupulous as James I.

James had returned from England in 1424. He was a complex personality, an accomplished poet and good family man, vigorous, extremely efficient, and vindictive. The vigour and efficiency at once showed themselves in the flood of legislation poured out by his first three parliaments, the first of which was held in the minimum possible time after his return; in his attempts to reform parliament on English lines, which were unsuccessful; and in his rather more successful attempts to make administration more effective. His vindictiveness, which was understandable enough after eighteen years' enforced absence in England, but at the same time repellent in its cold and calculating quality, was less immediately apparent. James waited for a year, during which he seems to have been on good enough terms with the former governor Murdoch, duke of Albany, who had negotiated James's return and created no problems for the king when relinquishing his office. Then, entirely unexpectedly, James turned with great savagery on Murdoch, the two sons of Murdoch on whom he could get his hands, and, worst of all, Duncan, earl of Lennox, an old man of about eighty whose only crime, apparently, was that of being Murdoch's father-in-law: in May 1425, they were all tried and executed at Stirling. James's delay of a year may be explained on the grounds that he was consolidating his position before taking such drastic action; the action itself is much more difficult to explain in any terms other than those of personal and unrelenting animosity reinforced by greed — because the windfall from the wholesale destruction of the Albany family, the earldoms of Fife and Menteith and the revenues of Lennox, was of course considerable.

The same personal vindictiveness showed itself again in the treatment of Malise Graham, earl of Strathearn. Graham, a descendant of Robert II's second marriage, not only lost his earldom but was sent to England in 1427 as a hostage, and remained there until 1453, with only the less valuable earldom of Menteith as compensation. The sending of hostages to England, as security for his unpaid ransom, was used by James on other occasions as a convenient device. Most hostages remained in England for short periods, of one, three or five years. Graham was a notable exception; David, master of Atholl, son of the last surviving son of Robert II, was sent south in 1424 and died there in 1434; and John, earl of Sutherland, was in England from 1427 until 1444, or possibly 1448. And acquisitiveness lay behind the king's contention that the earldom of Ross had lapsed to the crown after the death of John Stewart, earl of Buchan and Ross, in 1424; acquisitiveness likewise determined the exclusion of the Erskine claimant to the earldom of Mar after the death of Alexander Stewart, earl of Mar, in 1435.

The greed and vindictiveness of James I can be amply demonstrated. The question remains whether his treatment of these magnates can be explained simply in these terms, or whether — as with his reorganisation of financial administration — greed and a genuine desire for more effective royal government intermingled to produce a consistent policy. Did James, in other words, regard it as essential, not only to 'tame' individual magnates or magnate families, but to reduce magnate power as such? It has been suggested that such an intention was the motive behind the act of 1428 which attempted to bring the lairds as shire representatives to parliament, thus introducing an equivalent to the English House of Commons. Here is a clear example of the influence of his English experience. Yes — but one cannot be selective about the English influence, and argue that James saw the introduction of a lower house as a means of counteracting magnate power when his English experience must have shown him that the Commons in England were by no means consistent supporters of the monarchy against the lords, and indeed sometimes acted in the reverse role. In Scotland, the lairds were allied to and depended on the magnates; a wedge could not have been driven between them, and in any case that alliance was not necessarily an anti-social force, but one which medieval kings used to their advantage. What James actually wanted in his attempted reforms can be seen in his legislation of 1426, which demanded that acts of parliament should be registered and circulated throughout the country that all might know his laws; in that year, he himself complained about and tried to legislate against absenteeism on the part of the magnates. The legislation of 1428 was an extension of his desire that his Scottish parliament should be more like the parliament he had seen in England, in being more representative and having its legislation more widely known; hence the lairds should be brought in, both to take part in the work of parliament, and to transmit it back to the localities.

The legislation of James's first three parliaments has similarly been seen as a reaction to the situation before 1424 in which, so it is argued, the irresponsible and overmighty magnates, freed from control by the king, had increased the extent of lawlessness in Scotland. To a limited degree this was true, but only in respect of certain individual nobles, and for the period before 1400 rather than after. The great theme of the first years of James's reign, justice for rich and poor alike, is not peculiar to this period. 'The pur comownis' appear time and again in parliamentary legislation of the fifteenth and sixteenth centuries. Concern for the lower strata of society had no doubt a certain propaganda value; but it was a genuine enough reflection of a fundamental social tenet of medieval society, the protection by the great of the lesser men who depended on them. James's legislation, therefore, did not consist of exceptional measures for an exceptional situation.

What was exceptional was the nature of the nobility; and it is this, along with his own unpleasant characteristics, which explains James's actions. In the period 1371–1424, the extensive family of Robert II had so successfully cornered the market that in 1424 eight of the fifteen earldoms were held by Stewarts. What James quite clearly embarked on was a family vendetta. Thus the Albany family were exterminated; Malise Graham lost his earldom and his freedom. But the Lord of the Isles, a greater troublemaker than any Stewart in this reign, was merely temporarily imprisoned. And the most notable example of all was the earl of Douglas. The greatest heights of Douglas power were not reached until the minority of James II. But the earl of Douglas under James I was nonetheless a man of great power and influence; and if James indeed had a policy of 'taming the magnates' as a class, then his inaction against Douglas, apart from imprisoning him briefly in 1431, apparently because of suspected dealings with England, was an aberration totally unbelievable in a man of James's ruthless intelligence and efficiency. There are exceptions to this general view: to one Stewart, Walter, earl of Atholl, James showed no animosity, though in 1437 this did not pay off. But on the whole, the most consistent explanation of James's attitude is that he was determined to 'tame' not the nobility but the Stewart nobility; and so successfully did he do so that in the minority of James II the only Stewart earl left was Malise Graham, in England.

It has already been said that there is no evidence that any of the Stewart nobility had dynastic ambitions. But James clearly felt hemmed in by too many magnates close in blood to the crown, and regarded attack as the best form of defence. Why should he have felt this? In general, such a concentration of power in the state was a potential danger. And possibly James's English experience, which influenced his ideas on government and his ideas on the burning of heretics, also influenced him here and heightened his concern: he had seen that English rebels readily found support, and he may not have felt inclined to wait for the situation to arise in Scotland. In the event, the family vendetta which he had begun was taken up by the other side, not to overthrow his line, but to remove a tyrant. When the final crisis came, even Atholl, the one Stewart who had not suffered under James, joined those who had; and James was murdered by a small and unrepresentative group of people, engaged not in a power struggle between crown and nobility, but in a family feud.

The depletion of the magnate class by 1437 cleared the way for the spectacular rise to power in the minority of James II of the lesser families of Livingston and Crichton. It also threw into sharp relief the growing power of the Douglases. By 1449 there were eight earls in Scotland; three of them — Douglas, Ormond and Moray — were Douglas brothers, whose lands gave them powerful areas of influence both in the south-west, centred round their massive stronghold of Threave near Castle Douglas, and in the north. Again there was a concentration of power which the crown might well view with alarm. Beyond that it is impossible to show any real threat by the Douglases. Only in the rationalisation of events found in later accounts is there any real suggestion that they were abusing the power they had. And the idea that James II brought them down because of their treasonable dealings with England can be demonstrated only after James's murder of Earl William in 1452. It cannot be substantiated before then, for the evidence is simply not available; indeed, apart from the episode in the reign of James I, the Douglases had a long tradition of friendship with France, to the extent that the fourth and fifth earls had held French titles, the fourth being killed at Verneuil in 1424 while fighting for the French against the English. Open provocation first came not from the Douglases but from the king. In 1450–1, while the earl was abroad, James took over his lands of the earldom of Wigtown, and built up as a rival family in the south-west the Kennedies of Dunure. What the Douglases apparently wanted was to be left to enjoy their vast possessions. The crown's inroads into these possessions sparked off the chain of events and worsening relations which led to the famous murder in February 1452. This murder left James in a highly vulnerable position; and he survived only because most of the magnates, once again failing to take advantage of an opportunity to fulfil the role ascribed to them of opposing the crown, supported the king against the Douglases so completely that when the final conflict came in 1455, the Douglases were left entirely without allies and easily defeated. It was a curious, dangerous affair. It is impossible to prove that the king's actions were justified, to be sure that the Douglases were an actual rather than a potential threat. But the parallel between James II and his father, the ruthlessness with which they reacted, seems fairly close. And not only the ruthlessness. The acquisitiveness of James I is seen again in James II's unscrupulous annexation of the earldom of Moray when direct male heirs had failed, and his exclusion of the Erskine claimant to the earldom of Mar; and it may well have been a large part of his attitude to the Douglases.

The crisis which resulted in the crushing of the Black Douglases has overshadowed by its drama the other events of the reign. The other side of the story of James II's relations with his nobles is much more prosaic, but also much more important. In 1444–5, during his minority, the earldom of Huntly had been created. After the Douglas murder, in 1452, the crown used its patronage to attract or reward support, and created three further earls and a number of lords of parliament; two of the earldoms were short-lived, but the third, the earldom of

Erroll, was another creation of major significance. Finally in 1457–8 came four more: the earldoms of Argyll, Morton, Rothes and Marischal. The reign of James II in fact saw the first of two groups of creations which brought to the top families who were to dominate Scottish politics in the sixteenth century; the second group came with James IV. What had happened was that the peerage had been changed beyond recognition: the old dominance first of the Stewarts and then of the Douglases had gone, and the crown now gave influence and high position to families who had served it well, and who were to continue to do so with a remarkable degree of consistency. The Gordons, earls of Huntly, and the Campbells, earls of Argyll, for example, both had a record of crown service which was interrupted in the first case only in the late sixteenth century, and in the second not until the seventeenth, apart from a temporary break in the pattern during the political turmoil of the last few months of James III's life. Their position as the representatives of royal authority in the north and west is better known in the sixteenth century, but both James II and James III used them in this role; and if it was a gamble to give men power in fifteenth-century Scotland, then the gamble paid off handsomely, for these magnates, while naturally intent on building up their own prestige and dominance, at the same time served the crown both in the central government and in the localities. A striking example of this is seen in the reign of James IV, when the king first instructed the earl of Huntly to take bonds of allegiance from all landowners north of the Mounth as a means of giving the earl formal control, then got his obligation to build a tower at Inverlochy as a focal point for Huntly's exercise of royal authority, and finally forgave him for failing to complete it, because his presence had been required at court. This was the busy — and typical — life of a leading Scottish magnate.

The magnate problem of the early fifteenth century was one of two families, Stewart and Douglas, who had built up too great a concentration of power and wealth. Greed and fear of this power on the part of two strong and ruthless kings had brought them down. After 1455, the issue changes completely. The last years of James II's reign were years of good relations between the crown and its magnates, years when the power of the crown was seen at its height, when the king, far from feeling that he was the insecure head of a state which was backward by European standards and wracked by an internal power struggle, pursued active and effective policies both abroad and at home. His foreign policy was aggressive and high-handed to the point of making the amazingly arrogant offer of arbitrating in a dispute between the French king and the dauphin. At home, he showed the same interest in justice as had his father, and so successful was he that in 1458 the parliament which, as it happened, was his last, paid him a fitting and impressive tribute:

> God of his grace has send our soverane lorde sik progress and prosperite that all his rebellys and brekaris of his justice ar removit out of his realme, and na maisterfull party remanande that may caus ony breking in his realme (*APS*, ii, p. 52)

— a comment which incidentally suggests that the king, and his most powerful subjects, were at one in disliking the potential threat of one family who had too much power and who therefore 'may caus ony breking'.

This period anticipates the reign of James IV, which has always been regarded as one in which the power struggle had abated. These years were interrupted by James II's death in 1460, and the problem of another minority, in which the Boyds of Kilmarnock seized temporary control. More serious, however — for the new king had no difficulty in taking over government and bringing down this family in 1468–9 — was the personality of James III himself. In this reign, the problem was not that of the crown taming the magnates; it was the magnates who were trying to tame the crown. The traditional account of James III's downfall, that it was brought about by the widespread resentment by the nobles of the king's reliance on low-born favourites, is legend. Like many other kings, James did have favourites, but they were neither numerous nor low-born; and the explanation of his failure lies elsewhere. James was a man of grandiose and exalted ideas of kingship, and at the same time a man who was lazy in the business of government and who acted on arbitrary whim. He indulged in wild schemes of continental expansionist campaigns, to the extent of giving the impression that all he wanted was to get out of Scotland. He completely failed to understand how to use and gain the trust of his most powerful servants, failing to reward Huntly, for example, for his service against the Lord of the Isles in 1476, and giving and taking away lands and offices without reason or justification, thus producing a state of tension and uncertainty among the nobles which prevented any hope of co-operation and good relations. He tried to centralise government in Edinburgh, rarely moving from the capital except on hunting holidays to Falkland. This was an age when Scottish kings were expected to travel throughout their kingdom, being seen by their subjects and taking a personal part in the exercise of justice and the control of the troubled areas of the country, and James's failure to do this increased the idea that this king was remote, uninterested and ineffective. Time and again parliament begged him to do his job properly, pointing out, for example, in 1473 that the business of a king was to govern his country and not to rush off on foreign expeditions. Here it would appear that the magnates were more politically responsible than the crown.

Yet despite all this, until the last few months of the reign respect for the monarchy outweighed the fact that James III was personally disastrous, for the great majority of the magnates. By February 1488, a few men were moving towards rebellion: the earl of Angus, a chronic and individualistic troublemaker, and Argyll, whose long-term loyalty to the king was undermined, between October 1487 and February 1488, by a series of adverse actions, ending with his arbitrary dismissal from the chancellorship which he had held since 1483; and a small number of lords who had suffered from James's high-handed and whimsical dealings. The very different situation, in June 1488, when the rebel army was stronger than the king's, was the result not of a general willingness to join the bandwagon of revolt, but of James's own utter folly in breaking the agreements made with his opponents at Aberdeen and Blackness in April and May. Some of the nobility, who had supported him up to that point, failed to turn up to fight for him at Sauchieburn; after this doubledealing, they perhaps preferred to solve the problem of the conflict between loyalty to the crown and the feeling that James had finally shown himself impossible to serve by remaining neutral.

The rebels of 1488 — surprisingly — won everything because James was killed, though it is by no means certain that they had wanted so extreme a solution. Whatever their aims, however, the nobles who in the reign of James III apparently fitted into the concept of 'overmighty' magnates now became, after 1488, the co-operative nobility of James IV; the same people, not a new and better generation. Angus continued to cause trouble; Huntly, Argyll and others like them to serve the crown. The fifteenth century had been a time of intermittent conflict: James I and the Stewarts, James II and the Douglases, a group of the harassed nobility against James III. None of this adds up to a power struggle between 'crown and nobility', with an underlying ideology which caused the crown to regard the magnates as a social and political class as a threat. The reality was very different. Kings and nobles were recognised, and regarded themselves, as the highest ranks in a hierarchical society, a society in which the king, the motivating force in government, relied primarily on the greatest men in his kingdom for counsel and advice and for co-operation in the practical business of running his country. These were the men close to the king; many were his friends, the men who shared his interests and pursuits. In parliament and on the council, while few of them were interested in the minutiae of government, who better to fulfil the traditional role of the king's principal councillors than the magnates, those nearest to him in rank and outlook? And in the localities, who better — indeed, who other — to maintain royal authority than the nobles with their pre-eminent position based on their widespread alliances with their kindreds, the lairds and their tenants and servants, alliances based on protection by the magnates in return for the service and loyalty of their dependants. Fifteenth-century Scotland was a unified nation. It was also a network of local societies — and for many, the locality was still more meaningful than the country — in which chances of survival, of safety of life, land and goods, depended on the fulfilling of the contract by which lesser men gave service to the great in return for the very real benefit of their protection and maintenance.

In any case, life for the magnates of fifteenth-century Scotland was not always a matter of high politics and feuding. Their interests lay not in opposition to the crown, but in enriching themselves by extending their lands, and the best way to do this was through crown service or by advantageous marriage. They were intensely conscious not simply of their position in the political state, but also of their place in society. To some extent they may have been threatened, as were the nobility in other European countries, by economic pressures; the great were no longer so distinguished by wealth from lesser men as they had formerly been. And the very fact that many of them had been raised from laird to earl or lord also produced pressure to ensure recognition of rank from those who had formerly been their social equals. Thus, for example, the written bond of manrent and service, given by lairds to earls and lords, became a commonplace document in Scotland from the mid-fifteenth century. Here was a means of securing formal recognition. And in this century and the next, the government gave its blessing to the increased awareness of social status and desire to define that status in repeated legislation on the dress, the food, the size of retinue which only the great could enjoy. The lesser one's rank, the less elaborate one's style of life. Their self-consciousness in this, their desire to make a splash, is exemplified by the magnificence of the retinue of William, earl of Douglas, on his visit to Rome in 1450; the impression this made on the pope was not apparently tinged by any cynicism about the provincial come to town. And if they could not emulate the crown in its acquisition of artillery, that most expensive and supreme status symbol whatever its defects as an effective weapon, they could and did emulate it on a smaller scale in both secular and ecclesiastical building, of which William Sinclair's collegiate church at Roslin is the most striking example. And both Sinclair and Archibald Douglas, earl of Moray, were literary patrons. Some of them sought fortune abroad. This was an obvious outlet for younger sons, many of whom found a profitable career fighting in France, where their value can be seen in the formation by the French monarchy of a Scots Guard in 1445, and where at least one 'soldier of fortune', Bernard Stewart, Lord d'Aubigny, gained an international reputation. But it was not only younger sons; the earls of Douglas and Buchan both fought in France, and were rewarded with French titles before being killed at Verneuil.

The fifteenth century was a time of political upheaval, of redistribution of power and wealth from the hands of two families to a wider, non-royal group. But it was not a time when existing concepts of society, of the place of the crown and the place of the magnates and their close and co-operative relationship with one another, were in any serious way challenged. The early sixteenth-century *Porteous of Noblenes*, a work which described the twelve virtues of a nobleman, put second on the list loyalty; the nobles

> ar nocht sa hie set nor ordanit for to reif or tak be force in ony way bot thai ar haldin in werray richt and resoun for to serf thair king and defend there subiectis (*The Asloan Manuscript*, ed. W.A. Craigie [Scottish Text Soc., 1923], i, p. 174).

This was not mere literary piety. Many nobles of the fifteenth century did indeed 'serf thair king and defend there subiectis'. At no time did they regard themselves as involved in a power struggle with the monarchy; nor did the crown, which smashed them when they became too powerful, as two families did, but built them up and rewarded them when they served their king. Two magnate families and one king threatened the ideal. For the rest, they saw themselves on the whole as allies.

BIBLIOGRAPHICAL NOTE

Originally published in 1972, this essay is included in the present book because it was the first attempt in print to question the long-held assumption that late medieval Scotland was lawless and violent, and that those responsible for its lamentable state were the 'overmighty' aristocracy. This assumption can be traced back to the critical views of late sixteenth-century English observers: see, for example, BL MSS Add. 19,797 and 35,844. In Scotland, the theme was taken up from the seventeenth century onwards by historians and lawyers such as William Drummond of Hawthornden in his *History of the Lives and Reigns of the Five James's, Kings of Scotland* (Edinburgh, 1711), Andrew McDouall, Lord Bankton, *An Institute of the Laws of Scotland* (Edinburgh, 1751), William Robertson, *The History of Scotland* (London, 1759), and P.F. Tytler, *History of Scotland* (Edinburgh, 1841–3). In the twentieth century, it was reiterated by E.W.M. Balfour-Melville, *James I* (London, 1936), and A.I. Dunlop, *The Life and Times of James Kennedy, Bishop of St Andrews* (Edinburgh, 1950) — the only substantial writings on the fifteenth century — and it continued to inform general histories of a more of less serious nature, and work on the sixteenth century as well. The problem of aristocracies is not, of course, either peculiarly Scottish or late medieval. Bibliographical illustration of this point would be a book in itself; but at least three recent outstanding publications may be mentioned here: K. Leyser's *Rule and Conflict in an Early Medieval Society: Ottonian Saxony* (London, 1979) and *Medieval Germany and its Neighbours, 900-1250* (London, 1982), and the collection of essays *The Medieval Nobility*, ed. and trans. T. Reuter (Amsterdam, 1978). But inasmuch as the fifteenth- and sixteenth-century Scottish aristocracy was singled out for particular opprobrium, it was part of a late medieval historiographical tradition; all over Europe, crown and nobility were believed to have been locked in combat throughout the fifteenth century, that century of medieval doldrums, decline, decay. This characterisation was exemplified most brilliantly and movingly in J. Huizinga's *The Waning of the Middle Ages* (London, 1924). Otherwise, the fifteenth century was the neglected century. To say that it is no longer so, and that historical perceptions of it have radically changed, is to say that modern historians, of England, Scotland and elsewhere, have followed the lead of one man, K.B. McFarlane, whose writings, beginning with 'England: the Lancastrian kings' in *Cambridge Medieval History*, viii (Cambridge, 1936), and otherwise conveniently collected in posthumous publications, *Lancastrian Kings and Lollard Knights* (Oxford, 1972), *The Nobility of Later Medieval England* (Oxford, 1973), and *England in the Fifteenth Century* (London, 1981), though now challenged in some of their details, have laid down unchallengeable guidelines. In Scotland, the work which has appeared in the last decade has brought the fifteenth century out of its dark period of neglect in a way which fits well into the insights of historians of other societies, even if the volume of publication is inevitably smaller. The sixteenth-century legends — the equivalent of the Tudor myth of fifteenth-century England, so effectively exploded by C.J. Kingsford, *Prejudice and Promise in Fifteenth-Century England* (London, 1925) — were shown up in all their glaring unreality by Norman Macdougall, 'The sources: a reappraisal of the legend', in *Scottish Society in the Fifteenth Century*, ed. Jennifer M. Brown (London, 1977). The aristocracy itself is the subject of the articles by A. Grant, 'Earls and earldoms in late medieval Scotland, *c.*1310–1460', in *Essays presented to Michael Roberts*, ed. J. Bossy and P. Jupp (Belfast, 1976), and 'The development of the Scottish peerage', *SHR*, lvii (1978), and his thesis 'The Higher Nobility in Scotland and their Estates, *c.*1371–1424' (Oxford University D.Phil. thesis, 1975); my article Jennifer M. Brown, 'The exercise of power', in *Scottish Society*, ed. Brown, and my thesis Brown, 'Bonds of Manrent in Scotland before 1603' (Glasgow University Ph.D. thesis, 1974). On feuding see J. Wormald, 'Bloodfeud, kindred and government in early modern Scotland', *Past and Present*, lxxxvii (1980). 'Revisionism' from a different angle is convincingly put forward by G. Stell, 'Architecture: the changing needs of society', in *Scottish Society*, ed. Brown, and 'Late medieval defences in Scotland', in *Scottish Weapons and Fortifications 1100-1800*, ed. D.H. Caldwell (Edinburgh, 1981). In more general works, R. Nicholson's magisterial *Scotland: The Later Middle Ages* (Edinburgh, 1974) takes up the theme of crown-magnate conflict, and argues for the victory of the crown; J. Wormald, *Court, Kirk and Community: Scotland 1470-1625* (London, 1981) takes the different view that there was no long-term general conflict in the fifteenth century. The three fifteenth-century kings have all received attention, in A.A.M. Duncan's lively pamphlet *James I, 1424-1437* (Scottish History Department Occasional Papers, 1, Glasgow, 1976); A. Grant's brief but thought-provoking note on the crisis of James II's reign, 'The revolt of the Lords of the Isles and the death of the earl of Douglas, 1451-1452', *SHR*, lx (1981); and, finally, the full-length book which, along with Barrow, *Bruce*, brings the total of near-definitive studies of Scottish monarchs to two, Macdougall, *James III*. All this work, firmly grounded on local, family and central archives, takes the subject into the realms of new ideas and positive academic debate. It is a world away from the old approach.

INDEX

This index is selective rather than exhaustive. In particular, no attempt has been made to incorporate items from the list of mottes printed at pp. 13–21, or from the lists of families printed at pp. 225–31. Places in Great Britain, save for county towns and other well-known centres, are located by pre-1975 county. As far as seems necessary, the name of the parish has been added for places of less than parochial status.